SHATTERED AIR

SHATTERED AIR

A True Account of Catastrophe and Courage on Yosemite's Half Dome

BOB MADGIC
with Adrian Esteban

ILLUSTRATIONS BY WILLIAM L. CRARY

 BURFORD BOOKS

Printed in the United States of America.

10 9 8 7 6 5 4 3 2 1

Library of Congress Cataloging-in-Publication Data

Madgic, Bob.
  Shattered air : a true account of catastrophe and courage on Yosemite's Half Dome / by Bob Madgic with Adrian Esteban ; illustrations by William L. Crary.
    p. cm.
  ISBN 1-58080-130-7 (hardcover)
  1. Rock climbing accidents—California—Half Dome. 2. Search and rescue operations—California—Half Dome. I. Esteban, Adrian. II. Title.

  GV199.42.C2M34 2005
  796.522'3'028'9--dc22

                                    2005001763

This book is dedicated to Robert Frith and Brian Jordan.

CONTENTS

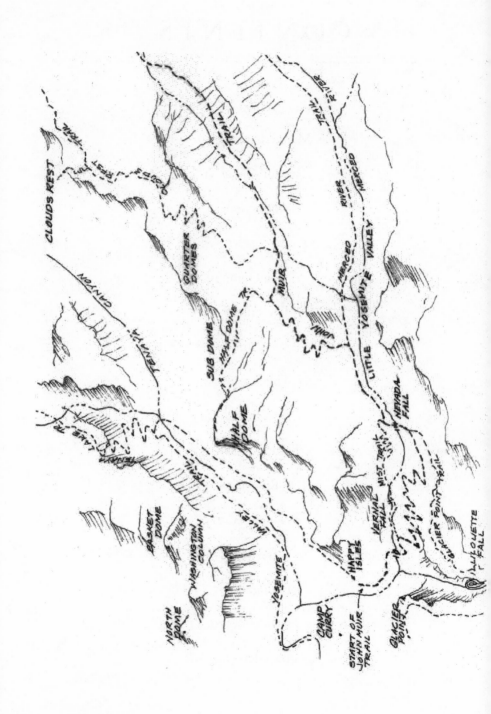

MAIN CHARACTERS

◄○►

ESTEBAN AND RICE'S PARTY
Adrian Esteban
Tom Rice
Bob Frith
Bruce Weiner
Bill Pippey
Brian Jordan
Bruce Jordan
Karl Buchner
Steve Ellner

MIKE HOOG'S PARTY
Mike Hoog
Linda Crozier
Rick Pedroncelli
Dan Crozier
Jennie Hayes

BRIAN CAGE'S PARTY
Brian Cage
Zip Cotter
Clu Cotter
Paul Kolbenschlag
Monroe Bridges
Steve White

OTHER HELPERS
Renee Miller
Brutus

THE ROCK CLIMBERS
Ken Bokelund
Rob Foster

YOSEMITE PERSONNEL

Colin Campbell
(first ranger to arrive on the summit of Half Dome)

Steve Jackson
(trail maintenance individual who accompanied Campbell)

John Dill
*(search and rescue technician who used a bullhorn
to communicate with the helpers on the summit)*

James Reilly
(supervising ranger throughout the episode)

Gary Colliver
(ranger who accompanied Medi-Flight to the summit)

Dan Horner, Mike Mayer, Paul Ducasse
*(park medics who left the Valley on horses
en route to Little Yosemite Valley)*

Ron Mackie, Scott Emmerich
(rangers who carried out the rescue in Tenaya Canyon)

Evan Smith, Dan Dellinges, J. R. Tomasovic, Jim Tucker
(rangers who prepared the bodies for removal on Sunday morning)

MEDI-FLIGHT AIR AMBULANCE SERVICE
Al Major, pilot
Bill Bryant, paramedic
Maggie Newman, nurse

AUTHOR'S NOTE

THE EPISODE ON HALF DOME in 1985 was extraordinary. But lightning itself can impact anyone, anywhere in the world. This universality distinguishes it from more regional natural forces such as cyclones, hurricanes, and earthquakes. As a result of my own unforgettable experience, its dangers have been long imprinted on my mind. It went like this. In the late 1970s, I planned a one-day, fifteen-mile round-trip hike to the Mokelumne Wilderness canyon in the Sierra Nevada. Joining me were my wife, Diane, and our three children: Jennifer, sixteen; Kirk, fourteen; and Doug, twelve. The trek first involved a three-and-a-half-mile ascent up to the bare summit of Mount Reba at 8,750 feet in elevation. From there it was a four-mile drop down to the canyon floor and the Mokelumne River.

It was the return hike that proved most memorable.

After a picnic lunch and fishing the river, we headed back up the steep trail. As we approached Mount Reba in late afternoon, what had been a sparkling blue sky with a few billowy cumulus clouds was now covered by dark thunderheads. At the summit we were greeted by rain, while vicious streaks of lightning and sharp thunderclaps rocked the heavens to the east. We should have retreated down to tree level and waited for the storm to end. We didn't, mainly because I foolishly thought that as long as the lightning stayed to the east of us, two to three miles away at most, we'd be okay.

As the storm grew in intensity, with jagged spears of lightning striking nearby treetops and ground, accompanied by earsplitting thunder, my wife, who is rightly terrified of lightning, started running down the bare mountain slope, quickly joined by our three children. I, too, broke out into a run when a bolt struck to the west, placing us in the middle of the inferno. Fear drove us, our exhausted, wobbly legs gaining strength where none existed moments earlier. Up ahead Diane shrieked and fell down. Kirk, running alongside her, thought she was struck by lightning. Fortunately she only stumbled on loose rocks, but it was a hard fall. With scraped hands and knees, she got up and continued running.

Panic-stricken, we raced down the open terrain, frantically trying to outrun the next lightning bolt. The rain turned torrential, drenching us as we half ran, half stumbled, desperate to reach tree line a mile down from the ridge. Once there, we pushed our way through dense woods until we arrived at the meadow where our small yellow Honda was parked. Bomb blasts of lightning continued to rock heaven and earth. Likening this to a World War I battlefield, I sprinted across the naked field and threw myself into the car.

Never before or since have I experienced such raw, fearsome power. Never have I felt so vulnerable. What's so terrorizing is lightning's randomness—that at any moment a killing bolt can come from anywhere and strike you.

We were extremely fortunate that day. My judgment and actions were irresponsible to the extreme. If anyone had been struck, perhaps killed, I would have had to live with the tragedy for the remainder of my life, if indeed I survived. Yet it wasn't until I started writing this book and dissecting the Half Dome disaster that I fully internalized the reckless and uninformed leadership I carried out and which placed my family in that enormously high-risk situation. My daughter pointed this out to me when I was discussing with her the actions of the Half Dome leaders. It was a sobering realization.

Another reason why the 1985 Half Dome incident stayed etched in my mind was that I indirectly knew one of the participants—the son of a woman who worked in my office. He was one of four hikers (out of nine) who blessedly did not reach the summit that day. I have told this story often, how with different circumstances, he would have been there at the top when lightning struck and possibly killed. When I ended my career in education and looked to writing to keep me engaged, I quickly concluded that a broad audience might exist for the Half Dome story, which at the time received wide media attention. I placed a phone call to my co-worker's son, and now seven years later, the book is published.

I had great luck in tracking down almost all of the people who contributed one way or another to that 1985 episode. Out of over forty participants, I failed to locate only one key person. (That's Renee Miller, one of the main helpers that night. Perhaps she'll contact me if she sees this book.) College alumni offices proved key in two critical cases. So, too, was the Internet for a few others. Once I contacted a person, he or she usually was able to provide information on someone else. One connection was extremely fortuitous. There were only two rock climbers on the face of Half Dome at that time, and one just happened to be the son of my college classmate. He read about this project in the *Amherst Alumni Journal* and thought it sounded like the very time his son was there. Amazingly, it was.

Yosemite National Park was exceptionally responsive to my requests, as indeed were all national park personnel whom I contacted. Without park reports I would not have been able to complete this project. The National Park Service heroically carries out its multifaceted responsibilities, albeit with insufficient resources. Our parks deserve more from our nation.

Medi-Flight Air Ambulance service personnel were also all fully cooperative and helpful.

Nothing takes the place of on-site research. I hiked to Half Dome's summit twice since I began this project (I had been up there years earlier as well). Adrian Esteban and Bill Pippey—two primary players in the 1985 event—joined me on one of the excursions. I also went to Kings Canyon National Park and retraced the steps of the individual who was killed by lightning the same day as the Half Dome incident. It took a little doing, but my wife and I found the rock enclosure in which he took cover and where his body was discovered. I also hiked to Paradise, located on a small tributary off the Merced River. I didn't jump from the ledge into the pool. (The reader will understand this reference shortly into the story.)

Not everyone involved one way or another in the story supported its telling, including one central participant. The text will identify who he is. Fortunately, a wide range of participants enthusiastically embraced the project, including most of the main characters. Adrian Esteban's recollections, insights, and voice are central to the book throughout.

To present as accurate rendition of the story as possible, I used quotation marks in the text only for a direct statement from an individual, either as presented to me or as quoted in a newspaper account or other formal documents. When individuals I interviewed recalled statements and conversation, they appear without quotation marks if I included them.

Lastly, a word about lightning injuries and treatments. After becoming acquainted with this complex field, I've learned that much of the terminology and reports on the medical aspects of lightning as presented in 1985 do not accurately convey what is known today. New findings are being uncovered each year. For the most part I retained the 1985 language, for example with coroner and medical reports, even though it may be inaccurate according to current information. On a very limited basis I attempted to bring the field up to date in chapter 10—Aftermath.

Bob Madgic
Anderson, California
June 2005

INTRODUCTION

The great Tis-se-yak, or Half Dome, rising at the upper end of the valley to a height of nearly a mile, is nobly proportioned and lifelike, the most impressive of all the rocks, holding the eye in devout admiration, calling it back again and again from falls or meadows, or even the mountains beyond. . . .—John Muir

I N THE FALL OF 1849, two men tracked a grizzly bear deep into the central Sierra Nevada in the hope of shooting it. They got lost. Trying to find their way back to camp, the men followed an Indian trail that led instead to "a valley enclosed by stupendous cliffs." Not far off, a waterfall dropped from a cliff below three jagged peaks into the valley. The hunters also noted "a rounded mountain . . . which looked as though it had been sliced with a knife as one would slice a loaf of bread." They called it the Rock of Ages.

This is the first recorded description of Yosemite Valley and Half Dome.

Native Americans probably visited Yosemite Valley, which is only one-half to one mile wide and less than seven miles long, as far back as ten thousand years. People of Miwok lineage most likely took up residence in the valley about a thousand years ago, living peacefully among its natural riches and beauty, and drawing water from a river that Spanish explorers named the Merced, in honor of the Virgin Mary.

-◄o►-

ONE EXPLANATION OF THE NAME *Yosemite* holds that it was a corruption of *uzumati* or *uhumati,* Native terms for "grizzly bear." Apparently the Miwok had divided themselves into two clan-like social groupings, and one of them was generally identified with the grizzly bear. A second interpretation draws from the linguistic roots of the Miwok language: *Yo'hem-iteh* means "they are killers."

In time other Indians in the region began calling these valley dwellers "Yosemites." Grizzly bears were dangerous, and people beyond the hidden valley came to regard the Natives who lived there as equally ferocious. Outsiders may have referred to them as both grizzlies and killers.

Regardless of its origin, the name doesn't honor the now extinct California grizzly, *Ursus arctos californicus.* Rather, it venerates the Natives who once inhabited the lush green valley known as Ahwahnee—"the big mouth" or "place of the big mouth." They referred to themselves as Ahwahneechees. The Ahwahneechees called the strange mountain with the cutoff side *Tis-se-yak.* According to legend, a woman by that name entered the valley with a great conical gathering basket and slaked her thirst by drinking all of the water in the valley's only lake before her equally thirsty husband, Nangas, arrived. Upon seeing what Tis-se-yak had done, an angry Nangas beat her. She retaliated by throwing her basket at him. For their wickedness, both were turned into stone: She became what is now known as Half Dome, her husband became the Washington Column, and her basket became Basket Dome. The dark streaks on Half Dome's face are the tears that Tis-se-yak shed as she ran from Nangas, and the human profile seen from some vantage points is that of her in mourning.

—◦—

IN THE LATTER HALF of the eighteenth century, disease spread among the Ahwahneechees, forcing the survivors to leave the valley. Many trekked to the eastern side of the Sierra Nevada to the Mono and Kuzedika Paiute villages. There were no inhabitants in Ahwahnee for several decades. Living among the Monos was Teneiya, son of an Ahwahneechee chief and a Mono mother. The chief told Teneiya about the remote river valley where his people had lived. After his father died, Teneiya traveled there on foot. When he arrived in the valley, he knew at once it would be his home. Teneiya returned to the Mono village to gather followers—family, descendants of his father's people, and scattered Mono and Kuzedika Paiute tribe members. The group, numbering about two hundred, was an unpredictable and contentious lot that included many outlaws and malcontents.

Teneiya's band prospered in Ahwahnee, where the chief grew old and his three sons became men. These Native people had a passionate and spiritual attachment to Ahwahnee; their sense of place defined who they were. But a medicine man counseled Teneiya that intruders could threaten their survival. So he and his braves remained vigilant and were prepared to fight any encroachers.

—◦—

AFTER GOLD WAS DISCOVERED in California, miners flooded into the foothills. Native American tribes tried to defend their land and villages (called rancherias) from gold-seeking intruders, while Indian braves in turn plundered and pillaged the white man's camps. In one murky incident, a trading post on the Fresno River owned by a Major James D. Savage was raided. The settlers rightly or wrongly blamed the Yosemites, even though the post was quite distant from their normal range. Vengeful miners called for "wiping out the Indian savages."

To bring the Yosemites and other Indians to the treaty table, Savage organized the Mariposa Battalion, a volunteer military unit consisting of about two hundred mostly rough-hewn men. Accompanying the party on their first foray to Yosemite was Lafayette Houghton Bunnell, a twenty-seven-year-old educated and fair-minded medical adviser. He took extensive notes and later wrote an account of his experiences, *Discovery of the Yosemite*, that became a valuable historical record. Bunnell recalled that when he first entered the concealed valley, "a peculiar exalted sensation seemed to fill my whole being, and I found my eyes in tears with emotion."

Across two years, the Mariposa Battalion succeeded in killing, capturing, and driving the remaining Indians out of Yosemite. Chief Teneiya and a small group fled and took refuge with the Monos. After the soldiers left, they returned to Yosemite, intent upon living there in secrecy. But he and the others were ultimately vanquished one last time. Whether battalion soldiers or members of the Mono tribe produced their demise is not clear.

Bunnell and soldiers in the Mariposa Battalion named many of Yosemite landmarks: El Capitan, Mirror Lake, Clouds Rest, Little Yosemite Valley, Vernal Fall, Nevada Fall, Ribbon Fall, and Bridalveil Fall. A beautiful, high-country lake where the battalion captured a holdout band of Yosemites became Lake Teneiya. (The spelling of this and other namesakes evolved into *Tenaya* over time.) Tenaya Canyon and Tenaya Creek also honor the chief. Several names refer to incidents involving the Yosemites: Three Brothers, Lost Arrow, and Indian Canyon.

Half Dome originated from the first impression of a battalion soldier as he entered the valley. "I looked a good long while at that split mountain," he reportedly said, "and called it a 'half dome'"— a name that had become firmly established by 1865. Earlier it was known as Tis-se-yak and then, for a few years, as South Dome. (North Dome was on the opposite side of the valley.)

—◄o►—

IN 1860, YALE GRADUATE Josiah Dwight Whitney was appointed California state geologist and charged with studying the state's geology to locate mineral deposits in the Sierra. His influential *Report of the Geological Survey of California* was published five years later. Whitney described Half Dome as "a new revelation in mountain forms; its existence would be considered an impossibility if it were not there before us in all its reality . . . nothing even approaching it can be found except in the Sierra Nevada itself."

Despite his growing reputation as a geologist, Whitney proved way off the mark on two counts: first, his assumption that "Half Dome is perfectly inaccessible, being probably the only one of all the prominent points about the Yosemite which never has been, and never will be, trodden by human foot"; and second, his conclusion that Half Dome "had been split in two, one half having been engulfed at the time of the formation of the chasm at its base . . . the lost half having gone down in what may truly be said to have been the wreck of matter and the crush of worlds."

Another individual who came to Yosemite in the 1860s and who lived there on and off across fifty years was a Scotsman by the name of John Muir. Muir's conservation legacies have shaped the very character of America. Among his many accomplishments, he was instrumental in having Yosemite preserved as a national park. He also helped found the Sierra Club in 1892 and became its first president. In fighting many battles on nature's behalf, his sword was the written word. He wrote ten books and more than three hundred articles in some of the most eloquent and compelling language ever penned.

Although he was one of this country's greatest naturalists ever, John Muir incorrectly attributed Half Dome's shape to glacial forces. He correctly deduced that glaciers carved out the canyons and valleys of the Sierra, but he erred in concluding that glaciers sculpted the domes, at least those more than four thousand feet from the Valley floor. According to various studies, Half Dome protruded five hundred to nine hundred feet above the highest glaciers.

Exfoliation and erosion formed the rounded domes as forces, in a process also called sheeting, cast away successive thin, granite slabs called spalls over time, much like the peeling away of onion layers. Scoured by the weather—ice and frost wedging and heaving, and lightning strikes—the granite top progressively lost mass and hence weight. As the load decreased, the granite expanded outward, creating the spalls. Originally, the mountain may have been angular, but exfoliation shaved off the corners of the spalls.

Half Dome's sheer face extends twenty-two hundred feet from its base of jumbled rocks to the crest. It was formed by the progressive removal of thin rock sheets from a zone of nearly vertical joints. Indeed, this process shaped many of the landforms in Yosemite that glaciers didn't sculpt. (In Yosemite's high country, the jointing process is evident among other granite domes with partial vertical faces.) Much of a granite monolith like Half Dome consists of solid rock that is highly resistant to erosive forces. But often present in the rock are parallel cracks or fractures called joints. Weathering forces, especially ice, cause the jointed segments to break off eventually. In the case of Half Dome, the fractures are vertically aligned; that produced the mountain's distinctive vertical face. However, one prior form still remains, at the apex of this northwest side: the Visor, a prominent protrusion that resembles the beak of a giant bird or an observation booth.

To the surprise of many, there never was another half to Half Dome. Up to 80 percent of the famous northwest side may still be intact, despite references to the "missing half." Indeed, the Dome's appearance is more illusory than real. That shape prevails in views from the Valley floor, but a view of Half Dome from Glacier Point or Washburn Point reveals that only the top of the southeast side is rounded; the remainder is almost as vertical as the northwest face.

◄o►

AS IF ON A GRAND PEDESTAL, Half Dome stands at the far end of the Valley, on the divide between Tenaya Canyon and Little Yosemite Valley. At 8,892 feet in elevation, its summit juts almost one mile above Yosemite Valley. Of all the eminences in this part of Yosemite, only the lofty, two-mile-long granite ridge called Clouds Rest, with an altitude of 9,929 feet, surpasses it. Half Dome's location and height bestow upon it a visual prominence and allure that any visitor to Yosemite Valley takes in. They also account for yet another of this monolith's features—its susceptibility to weather systems to unleash their torrents there. Storms that build over Clouds Rest inevitably move down Tenaya Canyon and take aim at Half Dome. The same holds true for ones that develop in lower Yosemite Valley.

If there is any such thing as a "granite lightning rod," Half Dome is it.

◄o►

EVERY MOUNTAIN BECKONS to climbers for a host of personal reasons. And contrary to Whitney's assessment that Half Dome would never be scaled, its summit lured the adventurous early on. Several first attempts ended in failure. But on October 12, 1875, George Anderson—a former sea captain, carpenter, blacksmith, and one of Yosemite Park's early trail builders—set his sights on the top and would not be denied. The challenge: ascending a rounded slope of polished granite with a grade of forty-five to sixty degrees. First, Anderson tried applying pine pitch to the bottoms of his bare feet as an adhesive. That didn't work. Then, summoning his trade skills, he drilled a six-inch-deep hole into the granite slope every five to six feet and drove in an iron bolt, which he used as a foothold to drill the next hole. The Scotsman thus painstakingly proceeded up the six-hundred-foot incline over several days. When he finished, he descended on the same bolts and spliced together sections of rope to connect them. That enabled Anderson to pull himself back up to the top of Half Dome.

What he found was a vast, mainly flat surface covering about thirteen acres (the equivalent of approximately seventeen football fields), with a higher knoll in the middle of the dome. The side overlooking the Valley had a sheer edge; the other sides had rounded slopes before they, too, became almost vertical.

Delighted with his accomplishment, Anderson returned to the Valley. He thought about constructing a staircase to the summit.

Within a week, six men and a woman wearing a skirt successfully made the ascent using Anderson's rope. The woman, Sally Dutcher from San Francisco, a twenty-eight-year-old assistant to the famous photographer Carleton E. Watkins, demonstrated that mountaineering was not strictly a man's sport. On November 10 of the same year, right after a snowstorm that would have discouraged anyone else, John Muir became the ninth person to accomplish this feat.

Muir described his first view from the summit of Half Dome as "perfectly glorious. . . . A massive cloud of pure pearl luster . . . was arched across the Valley from wall to wall. . . . My shadow, clearly outlined, about half a mile long, lay upon this glorious white surface with startling effect. I walked back and forth, waved my arms and struck all sorts of attitudes, to see every slightest movement enormously exaggerated." The German word for this rare optical illusion, in which a vast shadow or apparition is projected on the mists of a mountain, is *Brockengespenst* or the "specter of the Brocken" (Brocken is the highest of the Hartz Mountains in Germany). Atop Half Dome, Muir identified plants such as spirea, cinquefoil, alpine daisy, buckwheat, goldenrod, Sierra onion, penstemon, and three species of "repressed and storm beaten" pine—white-bark, western hemlock, and lodgepole.

Since Muir's time, the rare Mount Lyell salamander, a lungless amphibian that sustains itself on a diet of spiders and other insects, has been spotted on the summit. The only mammal living there before the arrival of humans was the golden-mantled squirrel, often referred to as a "chipmunk." It still exists there, along with other small furry creatures that undoubtedly followed the parade of humans to the top.

Anderson's rope trail attracted only those willing to pull themselves up a perilous slope using a system that could fail at any time. In fact, snow and ice during the winter of 1883–84 broke the rope and ripped out spikes. A new rope broke in 1895 and again in 1901. In 1908, a climber inserted new pegs. Such patchwork repairs continued until a more permanent trail could be built. Anderson, who died of pneumonia in 1884, never realized his dream of constructing a staircase.

—◄o►—

TO ASCEND ANDERSON'S ROPE, of course, you had to reach the base of Half Dome. The effort then and now typically begins on the renowned Mist Trail, built in the late 1850s. Consisting largely of granite steps, it starts at Happy Isles at the far end of the Valley and winds alongside the Merced River up a narrow canyon. The trail leads hikers first to Vernal Fall, where crashing water sprays off rocks, creating swirling mists—hence the trail's name—that engulf those who pass by at the closest point. Vernal Fall drops only 317 feet, but the sheet of water is unbroken from top to bottom and as wide as 80 feet when the Merced is full, thus making it one of the most symmetrical falls in the world.

Mist Trail continues up the steep ravine to the top of Nevada Fall, not quite three and a half miles from the trailhead. Nevada Fall, like Vernal Fall, plummets over a granite platform, one of many steps in the "Giant Staircase." The full staircase, encompassing less distinguishable platforms, reaches from the Valley floor to the base of Mount Lyell—a distance of twenty-one miles and an altitude gain of seventy-six hundred feet. Glaciation quarried away the massive vertical joints of granite formations at roughly right angles, leaving stair-like platforms in its wake. Trail builders tried to duplicate nature's work, although on a much smaller scale, in the tight canyon below Nevada Fall. Using only manpower, they placed more than two thousand granite steps; some of the risers are nearly fifteen inches, others barely one.

At the lip of Nevada Fall, the Merced River surges through a narrow opening in the granite and plummets 594 feet to a projecting ledge that splays the massive falls slightly outward. Nevada Fall, unlike Vernal's even drop, begins as a constricted blast of water and then widens dramatically as it drops, resembling a giant horsetail.

From Nevada Fall, the Mist Trail follows the river to Little Yosemite Valley, which is slightly less than four miles from Half Dome's shoulder—a steep, six-hundred-foot hump that had to be surmounted on somewhat perilous footing before one reached the base of Half Dome's eastern side and the start of Anderson's rope trail. For decades, the shoulder was informally called quarter dome, a designation that conflicted with that of nearby formations formally called Quarter Domes. (Today the shoulder is referred to as Sub Dome, a name that some people find less than endearing.) In 1919, the Sierra Club funded the construction of more-permanent climbing aids up Half Dome. A train of about a dozen mules carried two coils of connected steel cable from the Valley to the base of Sub Dome. There a civil engineer named Lawrence Sovulewski took over; his crew manually hauled the coils to the top of the hump, then up the slope of Half Dome.

The revamped pathway consists of a cable handrail on each side and wooden footholds, a design that hasn't changed much since 1919. The cables are thirty inches apart—close enough to grip with both hands yet far enough apart that hikers can squeeze past each other—and above average shoulder height to accommodate the steep incline, which obliges climbers to lean forward as they pull themselves up. The cables are attached to steel posts set in sockets drilled into the granite every ten feet and fortified by heavy chains bolted into the rock every hundred feet. Two-by-fours secured to the steel posts provide a foothold—and frequent opportunities to rest.

In 1934, a crew from the Civilian Conservation Corps, an outgrowth of President Franklin Roosevelt's New Deal, replaced the cables as part of trail-building projects nationwide. The National Park Service did the same in 1984. Most of the steel posts with the exception of those along the very upper part are removed each fall and laid on the granite in order to prevent destruction from snowslides. They are then returned to their holes in early spring.

The early trail builders also constructed a granite stairway up Sub Dome. The "Rock Stairway," as some publications refer to it, has roughly 600 steps, most of which are manmade. Then the trail descends a short distance to the beginning of the cables.

The trail from the Valley floor to the summit—the Half Dome Trail—has been recognized in the National Register of Historic Places since 1988. Thousands of people from around the world hike to the top every year.

—◁o▷—

Among those who made regular pilgrimages to Half Dome's summit were Adrian Esteban and Tom Rice. For them and a coterie of companions, the Dome took on a meaning far beyond that of other outdoor adventures.

YOSEMITE NATIONAL PARK

Thunderheads eclipsed the lowering sun as it dipped toward the western horizon. The storm had swept down from Clouds Rest past Tenaya Canyon and was now massed over Half Dome, where arrows of lightning pierced the darkening gloom and caused the air to smell as if it were burning. While thunderous detonations rocked the heavens, rain began pounding Half Dome's granite slopes and raced downward in ever-thicker rivulets.

Nothing in the experience of the frightened backpacker who was caught out on Half Dome's summit had prepared him for this. Lashed by sheets of rain, barely able to make out the surrounding ridges between lightning flashes, he was growing desperate when he stumbled upon a human-made rock enclosure. He scrambled inside, spread out a sleeping pad, and scrunched himself on the ground against one of the low walls. Clutching a tarp around him, he prayed he'd survive. His imagination, perhaps stoked by the thunder blasts and rushing wind, conjured the voices of vengeful demons.

Then he thought he heard a different sound.

Amid the reverberations ripping through the sky and rolling off Yosemite's domes and spires, he could have sworn he heard laughter.

Human laughter.

He raised his head and peered cautiously over the wall. In a sustained flash that lit the surrounding terrain, he saw a pale figure a few hundred yards off, toward the area atop Half Dome known as the Visor. His brain, in shocked disbelief, registered the image of a dancing man. A dancing naked man, head thrown back, arms spread wide, hooting up into the rain.

The light died away but the shouting did not.

The backpacker rubbed his eyes. He hadn't hallucinated because, in fitful illumination from successive bursts of lightning, he saw the figure again, his skin chalk-white in the eerie light, spinning and bending with reckless grace on the exposed rock as if it were a dance floor. Another patch of darkness, then a new shock: Four figures now

circled the naked man. They were sodden, dark, clothed shapes, slap-
ping at each other and seemingly exchanging high fives, weaving like
drunken acolytes of some mountain Bacchus, their disregard a mock-
ery of the deadly forces playing around them.

But in the next dark interval, they all vanished.

The observer stared. It was as if they had dropped into the moun-
tain. Or never been there at all. Yet he was certain that he'd seen and
heard them. What mortals would dare expose themselves on the bare
summit of Half Dome, which, in a fierce storm, was essentially a
gigantic lightning rod?

At the first sign that the storm was dissipating, he rose to his feet,
troubled. He quickly stuffed his gear into his pack and hurried toward
the cables, his lifeline to a safer refuge below. As he dropped down the
granite incline, the cables burning his hands from his swift descent,
the image of the dancers remained with him.

Who were they?
Where had they come from?
Where had they gone?

—AN ANONYMOUS OBSERVER ON HALF DOME, JULY 27, 1985

1

THE LEADERS

*A large granite mountain cannot be denied—it speaks
in silence to the very core of your being.*—Ansel Adams

FOUR YEARS EARLIER
MAY 23, 1981

ADRIAN ESTEBAN FOLLOWED TOM RICE on a hillside path edging
a tributary feeding the Merced River, a spring-fed creek that
tumbled down from high in the rugged foothills outside Yosemite
National Park. Yellow oak, foothill pine, chaparral, and poison oak
formed dense clusters in the ravine below. Half a mile up the narrow trail, just before the open terrain steepened abruptly and

where the distant top of the mountain was visible, Rice stopped. Through erosion, the creek had created beds of polished red stone here, their hue the result of oxidized iron deposits. The particular pool they were looking at was set within a rock grotto, one side vertical and slick. It was known as Paradise. On the hot summer days common in the Sierra foothills, local residents were fond of jumping from the surrounding rock platforms into the cold water, sliding otter-like down a natural chute into the pool, and sunbathing on the smooth stones.

Which was fine for the locals. But Esteban knew very well that Rice had not brought him here for restful play.

There it is, Rice said. Up there.

Shading his eyes from the morning sun, Esteban peered where Rice was pointing to a ledge high above. With a rising sense of unease, Esteban shrugged free of his army-surplus rucksack and removed the green bandanna from his head. He unbuckled the military belt that held his metal canteen—Esteban's outdoor wardrobe was greatly influenced by Vietnam combat films—then pulled off his boots and, finally, his camouflage pants with multiple pockets. The tank top he liked to wear to show off his sharply defined muscles stayed on, as did his shorts. Rice, meanwhile, had stripped off his pack, old low-cut sneakers, and mandala-emblazoned T-shirt and was moving up toward the ledge.

It was morning on their first trip together to Half Dome. Rice had already informed Esteban that he had to complete a test before they would do the Dome. It was to jump from the ledge here at Paradise into the pool. To Rice, this initiation ritual was an integral part of the Half Dome experience. It would demonstrate that a companion was able to overcome his fears—a central piece in Rice's beliefs about how to reap life's rewards.

When they stood on the ledge together, Rice told Esteban it was exactly forty-four feet to the surface of the pool. He knew this because he'd previously measured the distance with a rope. The pool's depth was fifteen feet—plenty deep for their purposes.

As Esteban looked down, his stomach felt queasy, his legs weak. The swimming hole, which had seemed about the size of a small backyard pool when he stood near it, looked considerably smaller from up here. He felt himself recoiling inwardly at the thought of leaping from the ledge. In fact, he couldn't remember ever feeling so intimidated. He glanced sideways at Rice but found no reprieve in the other's set features.

He would have to do it.

Forty-four feet is higher than a four-story building. The high-diving platform in diving competition is ten meters, or roughly thirty-eight feet, above the water. Jumps of twenty to twenty-five feet challenge most thrill-seekers. To throw yourself into a small pool forty-four feet below requires extraordinary nerve—there's little margin for error. As soon as you jump, the gravitational force generated by accelerating thirty-two-feet-per-second-per-second sends your stomach upward, causing a sudden constriction of the chest and lungs, and a loss of breath. When your body reaches the water 1.7 seconds later, it's traveling about fifty-three feet per second, or thirty-six miles an hour. At that speed, water becomes a hard surface, especially if you don't slice into it just right. (Increase the height to 120 feet and you hit the concrete-like plane three seconds later at sixty mph, which explains why suicidal leaps from high bridges are mostly successful.) Impacting the water at the wrong angle could snap your neck or back.

To conquer personal fear, Rice liked to say, you had to believe in yourself. As if to prove it, he assumed a diver's stance, arms at his side, toes curled over the edge. He took a leisurely breath, raised his arms, and sprang. He wrapped himself into a tight ball in midair, spun one and a half times as he descended, uncoiled just above the water, and neatly broke the surface in a headfirst finish.

Rice paddled to the pool's edge and looked up questioningly.

Esteban's feet remained anchored to the rock. Jump or fail. As the minutes passed, his right leg started to tremble uncontrollably. Rock climbers call this sewing-machine leg. It's caused by fear.

Jump or fail. He would not—*could not*—back down.

Rice yelled up, You can do it. Trust me!

Esteban made a move to jump. Then stopped. He peered down at the water. More minutes passed.

Rice shouted, Just do it!

Esteban realized that was the key, the only solution. Just do it! With a gulping inhalation, he jackknifed his legs, then thrust himself outward. Bellowing as he plunged (good for releasing air and thus reducing pressure on the lungs), arms overhead to prevent them from smacking the surface, he felt the soles of his feet slam, stinging, into the water. Gravity drove him to the bottom, the water slowing and cushioning the impact. The late-spring, fifty-degree water seemed to clutch at his chest and squeeze his lungs. He pushed hard off the bottom and shot to the surface, emerging in a watery explosion. Looking straight at Rice, he raised his arm in triumph.

Rice nodded and smiled. Esteban had passed his qualifying test and proved himself worthy.

From this point on, Esteban knew what it took to make the leap: Just do it!

Now they could tackle Half Dome together.

As they gathered their gear, Esteban hesitated. He pointed to the mountaintop overlooking Paradise and said he wanted to go up there before they left this place; he felt this mountain calling to him.

Rice gave him a questioning glance, wondering what was going on with his buddy. Then he nodded again, pleased with the words and seeming to attune himself to Esteban's exhilaration after making the jump.

Rice told him to lead the way.

As they neared the crest, Esteban spotted something white on the ground.

Stop! he called out.

Rice froze, thinking he was about to step on a rattlesnake.

Then, looking where Esteban pointed, he composed himself with a sheepish look—Rice tried never to show fright—and bent down to pull a partial set of antlers from the thick grass.

After a quick examination, Rice handed over the antlers, the left side of a young buck's rack. He told Esteban to keep the trophy; after all, he'd spotted it first.

They were the first antlers Esteban had seen in the wild. He studied them appreciatively, then tied the prized find to his pack. Moments later, when they reached the summit, Rice discovered the other half of the rack—the carbon-copy right side—at the mountain's very highest point. To the two young men, these finds held great meaning. The buck had needed to shed his old antlers before he could grow new ones. He'd visited the hill's apex to make a symbolic passage into a new phase—adulthood—and it struck Esteban and Rice that, with this initial trip to Half Dome together, they, too, were entering a new phase in their lives. The antlers seemed to signify their deepening bonds of friendship.

There on the crest, they made a pact: Each would keep his half of the antlers, thus linking them forever.

After they descended and were driving toward Half Dome, Esteban told Rice with quiet intensity that he felt the mountain had been beckoning him the whole time; he'd needed to go to its summit to answer the call.

Rice offered a one-word explanation: *Karma.*

—◄o►—

ADRIAN ESTEBAN AND TOM RICE HAD met five years before, when Rice was a senior and Esteban a sophomore at Peterson High School in Santa Clara, about forty miles south of San Francisco. On the surface, the two teens hardly could have been more different.

Rice was the youngest of four children in a well-to-do, supportive family. His father was a Chevron Corporation executive. Two of Rice's siblings were considerably older, which may have accounted for the lack of parental supervision he'd received while growing up. Although intelligent, Rice was hardly a dedicated student. Nor was he a dedicated athlete. Very much his own man, he mostly avoided team sports, preferring instead to concentrate on his diving abilities, which he pursued on the school swim squad. At five foot nine and 160 pounds, with a diver's lithe and well-honed body, dirty-blond hair, and striking blue eyes, he looked like the quintessential California surfer. Slightly prominent teeth gave the appearance of a constant smile. Rice was amiable, outgoing, and charismatic—traits that gave him a wide circle of friends.

But at heart, Tom Rice marched to his own beat. He resisted any hint of constraint placed on him by "the system" or anyone else. Much of his free time was spent hanging out, both with the athletes or "jocks," and with the drug users or "stoners." (Such stereotyped groupings were of course typical of high school campuses.) Rice was one of those rare kids who could comfortably mix with either group. It was at parties that he and Esteban first got together, with drugs and alcohol a standard connector. As uncontested holder of the "killer stash," Rice was a fixture at all the so-called best ones, which prompted some of his friends to call him The Legend and led his classmates to designate him "most likely to party" in their yearbook. Often the first thing Esteban asked him—even before "How ya doin'?"—was "What's going down this weekend?" To Esteban, Rice was indeed the man to know, his "in" to the social world that mattered most to him.

Unlike Rice, who enjoyed all the upper-middle-class advantages and could fit in wherever he chose, Adrian Esteban was a disadvantaged minority in the mainly white schools around Silicon Valley. His grandparents had left the Philippines in the 1920s for Hawaii, where they worked in the pineapple fields and where Esteban's mother and father met and married. Believing the mainland offered more opportunity, the couple moved to San Francisco in 1957. The first of their five children, Adrian, was born in 1959. Mr. Esteban worked as a materials handler at Hunters Point Naval Shipyard in South San Francisco. When it closed, he moved his

family south to Sunnyvale and took a job at the Mare Island Shipyard across the Bay. His modest income, coupled with a gambling
addiction, often left the family financially strapped.

To Adrian, his peers always seemed to have more money, better clothes, and, long before he had one, their own cars. His parents never saw college as a worthy goal, so they didn't push their
children academically. Mr. Esteban seldom showed love or emotional support; nor did he provide much in the way of positive
guidance or discipline. Mainly he pressured his son to be an outstanding athlete, to adopt a *win-at-all-costs* mentality. Adrian also
could not connect with his mother on a very deep level because
in their culture it was considered less manly for a son to be too
close to his mom; he didn't want to have an image of being a
momma's boy.

As the eldest son, Adrian felt particularly harassed. He rebelled
against his father's badgering early on. At age thirteen, he drank
some beer. And he liked it—a lot.

Despite little parental encouragement, Esteban managed to
earn outstanding grades. He also demonstrated impressive physical gifts. At five foot six, he was small for an athlete, but he packed
160 solid pounds on his frame and had powerful legs. He worked
out religiously, pumping weights and using resistance machines to
build leg strength. In his junior year, he led the football team in
rushing and was a standout in baseball, with strong potential to
play at the next level.

But by then, Esteban had added marijuana to his growing alcohol intake—a combination that, increasingly and inevitably, mud-
dled his judgment. Entering his senior year, thinking he had it
made as an athlete, he didn't bother to train or work out over the
summer in preparation for football. He partied most of the night
before the first practice. Then, in a mile run with others to test
their fitness, he could barely finish. The coach chastised him for
his poor physical condition and lack of dedication, a rebuke that
only fueled Esteban's rebelliousness. Although he'd been heralded

at the start of the season as one of the league's best running backs, he consistently failed to produce.

Outside football, things weren't any better. Esteban's parents were divorcing, which heightened his anger and sense of isolation. He cut classes excessively, causing his academic performance to plummet. He found solace—and escape—in beer and pot. His main objective in life was to go to the best parties.

With the approach of spring, the baseball coach lectured Esteban on his lack of discipline and bad attitude. Seeing Esteban goofing around in the batting cage at one of the first practices, he warned him to shape up or risk being a flop on the diamond.

Esteban, stung and resentful, waved contemptuously at the field and told the coach this was all a crock of shit.

The coach replied that if he kept up that attitude, he may as well not stick it out.

Fine, snapped Esteban. I quit.

So much for baseball.

Joining the U.S. Marines after graduation seemed like a promising option. Military images had long fascinated Esteban. His favorite entertainments involved war movies, books, and games, and he fantasized about being in combat himself. But Esteban was not yet eighteen. His father refused to give the necessary consent and instead threatened to disown him if he tried to enlist. With Korea and Vietnam in mind, Mr. Esteban didn't want his son killed. But somehow that concern got lost in the fray. A shouting match erupted. Enraged at being denied, Esteban stormed out of the house.

In following months, apart from working at a gas station, he mainly hung out. He had moved his bed and belongings to a room in his parents' garage and spent much of his time partying with buddies who congregated there. His life became increasingly aimless.

At age nineteen, Esteban bought a "crotch rocket"—a gleaming new Yamaha 350 racing motorcycle engineered for top speed. The very next week, a car pulled in front of him on a sharp turn.

Esteban hit the brakes hard, causing them to lock, and slid under the car, his head banging the pavement. Had he not been wearing a helmet due to cold weather, he would have been totaled like his mangled Yamaha. Nonetheless, undaunted and seemingly uncaring, he seldom bothered with a helmet thereafter.

Two more bike spills followed, which he again survived with no major injuries. Then, driving a car home late one night from a party while drunk, he foolishly dared himself to cover the intervening two miles without disturbing the cruise control. On a curve where he should have braked, the vehicle sped straight ahead, slammed through a fence, and crashed into a house under construction. Mrs. Esteban reported herself as the driver to protect her son's insurance and driving record.

Deep down, recognizing the fatal course his life was taking, Esteban longed to change. At age twenty, he saw an ad for a free personality assessment and mailed in a questionnaire. The Church of Scientology invited him weeks later to come to a meeting and discuss his personal needs. Esteban enlisted in the program soon after. He liked Scientology's emphasis on uncovering the roots of behavior patterns and its technique-oriented strategies for dealing with his problems: a dysfunctional family, self-destructive actions, reliance on drugs and alcohol. What he didn't like was the escalating cost of this help and oddities such as using a meter to gauge his reactions to stress.

Esteban eventually dropped Scientology. He still found meaning in religion and the concept of a supreme being. Esteban often looked to such an outside force—"the gods"—to account for happenings in his life. Moreover, he had long believed he possessed paranormal powers, a sixth sense. Once, on deck in a ball game, Esteban suddenly just "knew" he would hit a home run. At the plate, on the second pitch to him, he blasted the ball over the centerfield fence, the longest drive he'd ever hit. During that experience, he felt an unusual clarity, as if he were looking down on it all from an astral plane. On another occasion, after he suspected an object had been stolen from him, he somehow sensed that it was still in his house—and "saw" it in the attic hidden beneath a pile of boxes. That's precisely where it proved to be, to the astonishment of his housemates. Esteban was also convinced he'd had more than one brief, out-of-body experience.

◄○►

AS HE MATURED, Esteban's interest in psychic phenomena and metaphysics grew. Movement in that direction was catalyzed by Tom Rice, who bluntly questioned Esteban's attachment to Scientology and encouraged him to look inward to deal with problems. *Trust yourself, trust your own instincts,* he argued incessantly. Rice himself embraced a Buddhism-tempered philosophy, which held that *the real god is within the self;* every individual controls his own destiny.

"I'm my own church," Rice was fond of saying. He espoused a strict moral code from which he seldom strayed. He openly shared his judgments with those around him and didn't mince words or try to shade the truth—Esteban and others knew they would always get the "full Tommy." In purely practical matters, Rice could be equally inflexible. For example, he insisted on driving only Volvo sedans because they were the safest cars around—a concern that must have amused some of his companions, given Rice's extreme risk taking in other respects.

Esteban and Rice shared a passion for pondering these and numerous other topics, generally under the influence of marijuana. Characteristically, Rice used only "natural" drugs such as pot or mushrooms. If it didn't come from the ground, he proclaimed, he couldn't be sure what was in it; even in a drunken state, he shunned LSD and other synthetic concoctions. "Sez Buds" (sensimilla) from Humboldt County frequently were their drug of choice. Also popular was the cheaper, generic, more readily available "skunk weed" from Mexico. Anything especially effective was respectfully dubbed Buddha Bud.

Rice had access to it all.

Their minds thus frequently in altered states, Esteban and Rice spent long hours together musing about the nature of humankind. Central to Rice's beliefs—his close friends referred to these as "Tommy's philosophies"—was the idea that fear prevented people from achieving their potential. In order to live life to the fullest and gain bountiful rewards, you had to overcome inhibitions and mental blocks. Only by taking risks and regarding all obstacles as tests of character could you conquer personal fear. Rice summarily rejected negativity, excuses, and rationalizations. If a companion struggled, if he faltered and grew discouraged, Rice tried to buoy him by saying, "Conquer it—it's all in your mind." *Face your fears* was his constant litany. *Only by so doing can you achieve your full potential.* In his view, because fear was created by the mind, it could also be discarded by the mind. That was life's challenge.

A tall order for most—but one that carried tremendous appeal for Esteban. Such discipline and self-reliance seemed to address a void he had long sensed in his own world. From his older friend, Esteban received the sort of guidance he had never gotten—or been able to swallow—from his father or coaches. Rice saw life as akin to a military mission, too—an element extremely potent for Esteban.

The men engaged in long discussions, usually with Esteban sharing his innermost thoughts and feelings, while Rice listened and offered advice. And Rice proved able to get beyond his dogma while offering his friend comforting personal advice.

Esteban: "When I had questions about life, Tom was someone whom I could talk with on a deep level, about women and relationships, about problems that I had at home like the bad communication between me and my parents and my father's gambling addiction, things that I was learning in Scientology that were giving me some interesting and different perspectives on life. I also sensed that he was able to relax his guard around me when it was just the two of us. He had this image of always being tough and unafraid, and able to handle any situation. To people who knew him just casually he could come off as arrogant and standoffish. But when we were by ourselves Tom could be very kind and sensitive. He told me that of all his friends he trusted me the most and that I was the most honest. With Tom it was all about truth. He did not like people who were 'plastic,' people who were fakes and not true to themselves. He did not like liars and people who did not respect themselves or others. He always told me to be true to my heart, to be honest to myself and my true feelings, no matter if everyone else wanted something else. This is the greatest attribute that I admired about Tom—the ability to always be true and honest to oneself no matter what other people thought."

ENHANCING RICE'S AUTHORITY was his aura of mystery. Few won entry into that private, inner world—not even Esteban, who by this time was probably his closest friend. To all, Rice remained an enigma, and that was the way he wanted it. He didn't discuss his innermost feelings, his personal struggles, his many relationships with women. He spoke about human issues mostly in the abstract. To those who knew him best, he seemed unattached on a deep emotional level—a closed person. The more you hung out with Rice, some claimed, the less you knew about him.

Yet it could be argued that Tom Rice craved attention and feedback. Although he seemed to respond little, if at all, to external influences, his attire—outrageous tie-dyed garments favored by acidheads; T-shirts with logos of obscure rock bands—and his extroverted persona seemed to cry out for attention. More than one of his peers suspected that beneath Rice's veneer of flamboyant confidence was insecurity.

Whatever the case, Rice above all sought to control—*expected* to control—his and friends' agendas and whatever physical challenges he took on. Rice believed that he alone was always in charge.

Increasingly, he and Esteban took their personal quests to natural settings, especially those offering unique vistas. At night, they often climbed a towering tree and sat on a high limb, fueling their talk with beer or tequila. One time Rice chose a tree in the middle of a cemetery at midnight to put them in the presence of spirits; relating to the dead, he figured, was an excellent way to confront fear. Another night found them high up in a century-old oak, the tallest in San Jose. Esteban had played in it while growing up and carried a scar on his chest from where one of its branches had broken his fall and saved his life after he lost his grip higher up. The interior of this grandfatherly oak was hollow, burned out from a lightning strike. At the time, they gave its charred black surfaces no particular thought.

Years later, they would have abundant cause to.

Another favorite place was "Acid Rock" in the foothills above the Bay Area, a huge formation rounded on one side and with a steep vertical cliff on the other. A "mini Half Dome," Esteban called it. The top provides a panoramic view of South San Francisco, the South Bay, and even much of the East Bay and Oakland. The two often went up there at night to enjoy the necklace of shimmering lights surrounding the dark bay waters, all of it encapsulated by star-filled heavens. Sometimes they stayed until sunrise.

For larger social gatherings, usually on the beach in Santa Cruz and often involving women, Rice prepared his "famous guava juice," a potent blend of fresh cantaloupe, honeydew, watermelon, oranges, lemons, limes, seedless green grapes, mangoes, pineapples, nectarines, peaches, and a "sacred" guava, all submerged in massive amounts of Hansen's Natural Soda in a huge ice chest and laced with at least two bottles of Bacardi rum 151 proof. After a caveat from Rice that the "inspired chef" was not responsible for any actions that might result after downing two glasses of this concoction, the juice was duly imbibed and the "enriched fruit" eaten. The recipe's natural sugars tended to keep everybody up all night; happily, few got sick. It was, in Rice's lexicon, "the original nectar of the gods."

Rice often provided an enormous chuck steak as well. To properly prepare the meat, he first elevated it above his head and then walked into the ocean until both he and the steak were submerged. This "sacrifice to the gods," he claimed, also seasoned the meat with spices from the sea.

The ocean figured in another of Rice's rituals. With Esteban, he would swim out to the quarter-mile buoy in apparent disregard of the frigid water and its powerful riptides and undertows—not to mention the possible presence of sharks—while each swimmer held a joint above his head. At the buoy they smoked the joints, then swam back stoned—a good test of their basic manhood and survival abilities, Rice believed.

Their thrill seeking sometimes bordered on insanity. Once, en route to Santa Cruz on Highway 17—aka Blood Alley—Esteban sped his motorcycle perilously close to Rice's car so they could pass a joint back and forth. The road is a winding, treacherous, two-lane speedway (center dividers would be installed years later) where few weekends passed without a major accident. On another occasion, Rice misjudged and strained his back diving off a cliff. On yet another, he damaged his teeth when his truck slammed into a telephone pole. Esteban suffered mishaps of his own but accepted them as the price for being an outdoor soldier: Minor wounds were inevitable and should be disregarded or serve as proud emblems of missions during which fear had been conquered.

Esteban came to believe that, together, he and Rice were invincible.

Eventually, Rice focused on the grandest of all locations—Yosemite and its crown jewel, Half Dome. He himself already had hiked to its summit several times. Now Rice, twenty-four, judged Esteban, twenty-two, ready for the granite monolith.

—◄o►—

WHEN THEY ARRIVED IN Yosemite Valley on that Saturday afternoon of Memorial Day weekend in 1981 and saw Half Dome, its striking image reflected in the Merced River, the moment was a defining one for Esteban. Still exhilarated from the leap into Paradise and the discovery of the antlers, he now felt an irresistible new power tugging at him.

The two had decided to backpack four miles into Little Yosemite Valley and spend the night above Nevada Fall, braving the company of insatiable mosquitoes and pesky bears. The next day they would hike the remaining four miles to the top of Half Dome. Leaving the Valley floor, Rice set off at a fast pace. He and Esteban took pride in their fitness, the drinking and drugging notwithstanding. They swam vigorously, hiked long distances, scaled heights. Esteban lifted weights. On all such adventures, each tried to outdo the other, and neither would admit weakness or back away from a challenge. Once, on a backpacking trip in the rugged Big Sur coastal region, Esteban had fallen way behind. Rice told him his fatigue was mental, something he could overcome if he wanted to. He branded Esteban a puss, gutless, a laggard, all of which inflamed Esteban, who then somehow pushed his spent legs in an effort to exceed Rice's pace.

And so it went between them.

On this day in Yosemite, the two sped up the easiest part of the Mist Trail to the bridge, where they savored Vernal Fall in its full spring glory. Then it was up the constricted canyon, where they attacked the high granite risers, sucking in ever-larger quantities of ever-thinner air as they ascended. A two-thousand-foot elevation gain in that narrow ravine was a push even for someone without a backpack. For Rice and Esteban, the physical demands and muscle burn added zest to the experience.

Above Vernal Fall, Rice tried to climb faster yet. More steps had to be navigated, but most of them were low and graduated. For Esteban, the tramp up what they called staircase canyon was more than just a test of stamina and strength. He felt his spirit absorbing powerful energy from some distant source.

Atop Nevada Fall, their hearts pounding, they stretched their legs out for long minutes to ward off cramping. Their quadriceps ached and their inner thighs were as taut as bass fiddle strings.

But pain was transmuted by a heady sense of conquest. "Doing the staircase" would thereafter become one of their mandatory rituals.

At midmorning on Sunday, they struck out for the Dome.

As he marched upward for what seemed like unending miles, it became evident to Esteban he was not prepared for the hike's relentless demands. Without a sports regimen to keep himself in top shape, he had allowed his body to deteriorate. The constant partying, done to mask his many failings, was now taking its toll. To escape the pain his body was experiencing, he turned inward, contemplating things going on in his life.

By this time he deeply regretted his lapses in high school, mainly his not fulfilling his potential in sports. He knew he should have repeated his all-league performance in football his senior year, and that he could have played baseball at the college level, perhaps even professionally. His self-destructive ways ultimately had robbed him of success in the most important area of his life, and nothing else offered that sense of personal worth and accomplishment. A huge vacuum now existed, which he filled by hanging out with a bunch of alcoholics and drug addicts, and even a criminal element.

He realized that he had accomplished nothing of real worth or importance in his life. And he had no clue on what he would do next.

But this trek to Half Dome felt right.

Rice paused halfway up at a stream bubbling out of the hillside, a tiny flow in a gully off the trail. The water was refreshing and cold, tasting like the granite rock of Yosemite. As the only source of fresh water along the trail, the partly concealed outflow attracted many hikers. But for Esteban and Rice it was their secret good-luck spring of artesian water, an obligatory pause to quench thirst and replenish spirit. On the descent, Rice would refill his canteen and carry the precious contents home, a gift of nectar from the gods to cleanse and sustain his body between quests.

The trail took them to Half Dome's shoulder (then informally called quarter dome, and now known as Sub Dome). The steepness of the abrupt hump surprises most first-timers. Traversing it required climbing the nearly six hundred steps put in place by Yosemite trail crews over the years.

Beside the stairway at the base of Sub Dome was a metal sign in both English and Spanish in bold red letters:

DANGER
IF A THUNDERSTORM IS ANYWHERE ON THE HORIZON
DO NOT PASS BEYOND THIS SIGN.
LIGHTNING HAS STRUCK HALF DOME DURING EVERY

MONTH OF THE YEAR.

PELIGRO
SI ESTA EMINENTE UNA TORMENTA
NO PASE ESTE PUNTO.
EL RELAMPAGO CAE SOBRE HALF DOME

CADA MES DEL ANO.

Esteban and Rice, preoccupied with their push to the top, proceeded up the stairs with nary a glance at the sign. In any case, the sky was clear. By this point Esteban's physical condition was nearing its limits. With his stamina exhausted and legs that both ached and felt like butter, it was as though he were pushing against an immovable wall. He didn't think he could continue up this steep grade, never mind the final push to the top of Half Dome. After taking a few steps he stopped and leaned on his legs, his hands pressing against his knees to support his upper body, all the while gasping for breath.

Rice looked at him and told him that he didn't have what it took to do the Dome with him; he was weak.

Once again, Esteban had to dig deeply to meet Rice's challenge. He forced his legs to move, one step at a time, fighting back the muscle burn, and made it to the top of Sub Dome where Rice waited.

There the two looked across a low saddle at cables running high up the granite slope of Half Dome. The daunting sight usually triggers an adrenaline rush in newcomers. Esteban was no exception. It was the last hurdle, now only six hundred feet away, and when he surmounted it he would stand at the apex of that wondrous pinnacle that had stared down on him just the prior day. At that moment, Esteban felt powerful vibrations emanating from Half Dome and resonating deep inside. He knew that this mountain would change his life. What he couldn't know was the extent to which this granite temple would affect not only his life, but also that of the companion who'd brought him here this day, and those of others who'd follow in their footsteps.

AFTER CROSSING THE SADDLE and now at the base of Half Dome's final steep slope, Esteban and Rice stared at the parallel steel cables leading skyward. Most mountain trails—Mount Whitney's, for example—have switchbacks to maintain a fifteen-degree gradient. The typical home staircase rises at an angle not exceeding forty degrees. But Half Dome's incline from that point is around forty-five degrees for the most part, and up to sixty degrees along certain portions. More intimidating are the steep, rounded slopes off to the sides of the cables; without something to hold on to, a hiker would likely slide to oblivion. So the cables provide essential grip. Gloves help, both to protect climbers' hands and to enhance their grasp.

But even with the cables and gloves, the prospect of pressing on is simply too fearsome for some; they go no farther. Some who do proceed suffer leg cramps or muscle strains from the high leg lifts that are necessary; they quit, too. Still others lack the upper-body strength to pull themselves up the cables, which, strung on metal poles, are above the heads of many hikers bent forward to counteract the incline. Despite the rigors, most who get as far as the cables manage to complete the ascent by pushing their bodies in a last supreme effort. Waif-like women shorter than five feet complete the climb, as do hikers in their sixties, in a few hardy cases seventies, and even on occasion eighties.

The usual climbing mode is an accelerated driving of the legs coordinated with determined pulling on the cables, a rest at one of the horizontal two-by-four boards affixed at ground level to the vertical iron poles at ten-foot intervals, and another spurt up the grade to the next board, followed by another rest. Sometimes, if there's a traffic jam, faster climbers go outside the cables, gripping just one of them. Even when the way is clear, only the strongest and fittest attempt nonstop ascents.

Arriving at the top of Half Dome is a memorable achievement, and those who climb the rock are quick to congratulate themselves. But the looming journey back down casts a shadow over the minds of many, particularly those who have even the slightest fear of heights. The mountain climber's credo, *Going up is optional, coming down is not*, applies in this case, too. In practice, though, the descent doesn't live up to the dread of it. Again, the cables are key. Although some hikers go backward down the mountain so they don't have to look at the frightful depths just beyond the granite curvature, many others, emboldened by their success up until then, slide down rapidly, allowing the cables to whiz through their gloved hands.

With the successful descent comes relief and a strong feeling of fulfillment, but there's still that eight-plus-mile trek back to the Valley floor. By this time, the legs of all but the best conditioned of hikers are wobbly. The trail's unrelenting downward course stresses your knees, and if your footwear lacks room to absorb the pounding, you may end your outing with painful and blackened toenails.

Esteban and Rice attacked the granite incline with resurgent energy. As if the duo were racing—which, in a sense, was true—they bulled their way up along the cables without halting. Esteban found strength that he didn't know he had. Whatever fatigue he had previously felt was now overcome by his resurgent motivation to get to the top.

In a final burst, Esteban pulled at the last of the cables and eclipsed the final rock barrier before arriving at the summit where Rice waited. There a sign—tucked among the rocks and easy to miss—read:

DANGER

IF A THUNDERSTORM OCCURS WHILE YOU ARE HERE,
THESE ARE THE SAFEST THINGS TO DO:

1. STAY AWAY FROM THE CABLES.
2. GET RID OF ANY METALLIC OBJECTS.
3. STAY AWAY FROM CAVES, OVERHANGS, AND
   LARGE CRACKS IN THE ROCKS.
4. GO TO THE LOWEST PLACE ON TOP AND SIT
   ON ANY NONMETALLIC OBJECTS YOU HAVE TO
   INSULATE YOU FROM THE ROCK.

WAIT. STAY THERE UNTIL THE STORM HAS PASSED.

The two men barely glanced at the sign, as though such warnings didn't apply to them.

Once on the summit, the broad expanse of the mostly flat surface surprised Esteban, as it does most. From down in the Valley, he hadn't grasped how large an area would greet him here. As expected, the summit was barren other than for a single gnarled, weather-beaten pine tree clinging to the rock and half a dozen or so low rock enclosures that previous climbers had constructed as shelters from the wind. Over toward the edge overlooking the Valley, the surface was covered by stone slabs resembling giant pancakes. The section known as the Visor jutted out about twenty feet from the edge.

What consumed Esteban, however, was not what he found on the summit. It was the 360-degree vista that greeted his eyes.

To the west towered El Capitan, the earth's largest granite mass, its three-thousand-foot face double the height of Gibraltar. Across the Valley—native Ahwahneechees called it "the place of the gaping mouth"—Yosemite Falls stumbled down the canyon wall in two majestic spills. The Upper Fall registered 1,430 feet, the Lower Fall 320, the intermediate cascade 675—a total of 2,425 feet, which makes it the highest waterfall in the United States and the eighth highest worldwide. Just then, the tumultuous torrent was swollen to its greatest volume from spring runoff.

Across the narrow Valley, lower than Half Dome, rose the polished granite of North Dome. To the east lay vast Tenaya Canyon, where glaciers in past eons emerged and sculpted Yosemite Valley. Jutting above the canyon, two miles long and one mile tall, rose the mammoth exposure of granite bluffs known as Clouds Rest. Nearby, to the south, stood Mount Starr King, among the park's tallest domes. Finally, nearly a mile directly below Rice and Esteban, lay the floor of Yosemite Valley, where lush meadows, dark groves, and the sun-sparkled river, with massive canyon walls as a frame, teased the senses like a real-life masterpiece.

Now Esteban realized beyond any doubt why Rice had wanted to bring him here. We are on top of the world here, he thought. The gods are talking to us.

Rice wasn't finished with his exhibitions for the day. As Esteban stared in fascination at the Valley floor far below, Rice approached a stone slab known as the diving board* that extended some five feet out from the Dome's sheer face. Not only does the projection bank ten degrees, but its width narrows from four feet at the cliff face to a scant fifteen inches at the tip.

Beneath this lies twenty-two hundred feet of empty space.

---

*Not to be confused with the formally designated Diving Board, a Yosemite rock formation shown on maps. The latter is a craggy rock tower extending from the west shoulder of Half Dome midway between the Valley floor and the summit. Here, two thousand feet up the steep granite, a twenty-five-year-old by the name of Ansel Adams unloaded forty pounds of photography gear in 1927 to get a shot of Half Dome's face. The striking result, *Monolith: The Face of Half Dome*, changed Adams's understanding of his medium and launched his career as one of America's most innovative photographers. Things might have gone differently had he not, with only one plate remaining, used a deep red filter to darken the sky and shadows dramatically. The result gave him what he wanted—"not the way the subject appeared in reality but how it *felt* to me." Thereafter, photography became for him a supremely creative process that transcended mere recording.

Esteban watched in horror as Rice, barefoot now, stepped onto the small slab. He inched his way backward to the tip, paused to intensify his focus, then slid his heels carefully over the edge until only the front half of his feet remained on the rock, his body leaning forward and arms extended before him. He held this position, his balance perfect, as if he were preparing to dive backward into the depths behind. Then, still balanced and with breathtaking composure, he slowly lifted a foot and stood on one leg.

After several seconds, Rice lowered his foot and walked calmly back. Esteban, transfixed, felt limp and nearly sick with relief when Rice ended his stunt. Rice's theatrics also had mesmerized others on the Dome that day, many of whom at first gaped at Rice's outrageous act and then shut their eyes in dread. His performance on that gargantuan stage suggested that, given a ready audience, there was no risk he was unwilling to take.

About then, a premonition began haunting Esteban.

He feared that someone he knew would fall from Half Dome.

2

THE DOME

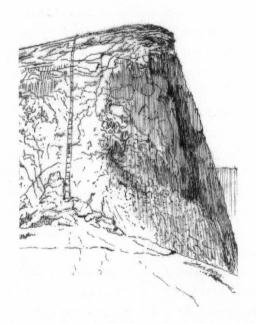

Was there ever so venerable, majestic, and eloquent a minister of natural religion as the grand old Half Dome?—Joseph LeConte, *A Journal of Ramblings Through the High Sierras of California*, 1875

E STEBAN AND RICE RETURNED to Yosemite later that summer, and again over Labor Day. Their agenda was literally carved in stone: Hike to the top of Half Dome.

For both men, treks to the Dome were far from routine events. It was as if some mystic force kept luring them back time and time again. Each year, they returned faithfully on the Memorial Day and Labor Day weekends—and whenever the urge struck. Sometimes Rice phoned Esteban out of the blue and said, "Let's go do the Dome." Esteban would drop everything, no questions asked, to join his buddy for yet another odyssey to that granite monolith.

Yosemite's natural wonders and the invigoration that came from immersing themselves in the wild made these outings a rebirth of sorts for Esteban and Rice. They always returned from Half Dome with their "karma batteries" recharged, their spirits rejuvenated, their ties with each other and the natural world more securely fastened.

However, a complication arose in Esteban's budding love affair with the granite mistress: marriage. In the spring of 1981 at age twenty-one, he had met a nineteen-year-old waitress and immediately fallen in love. Within a month, they had eloped to Reno. Unfortunately, she lacked any interest in the outdoors, preferring to stay at home. She also wanted to start a family. Neither of these priorities squared with those of Esteban, who wanted to do what he pleased, mainly with Rice.

As the months passed, it seemed to her that Esteban valued Rice and their forays together more than he valued her and their marriage. She was right. Esteban ultimately concluded that marriage had been a mistake—he just wasn't ready to commit. After a mere eighteen months together, he and his wife separated and, a year later, divorced.

◄○►

A FAILED MARRIAGE was only one of Esteban's woes. He had been attending San Jose Community College on and off since graduation from high school in 1977, taking a class or two each semester with the goal of earning an AA degree. After he and his wife split, Esteban dropped out of college in order to "get my stuff together mentally." He also considered quitting his job as a laser tech—mainly because he felt he didn't measure up—and launching a new career. The marriage fiasco made him wary about diving into another intimate relationship.

The one solid entity in his drifting life was Half Dome.

Each time Esteban arrived in Yosemite and peered up, his life took on meaning and direction. Half Dome rendered no judgments about who was worthy to scale its flanks. It asked nothing of anyone but gave everything—the universe on a platter. Deep down, Esteban knew this was something he could fully commit to. He also knew the Dome would always be there, beckoning. There were few guarantees in his erratic, stale world, but Half Dome was one of them.

On the trail in Yosemite, Esteban absorbed the air's crispness, which cleared his mind. The everyday demands and entanglements weighing down his life seemed less burdensome. He lost himself in the natural surroundings as physical pain from the unrelenting push upward stirred an inner dialogue. Initially, the mundane problems—work, college tests, and the like—roiled his brain. But with each passing mile, they melted away. His thoughts became more dream-like, and fantasies bubbled up. He imagined himself a bear, an eagle, a deer. What, he wondered, do these creatures sense? Or he imagined himself a Navy SEAL assaulting a great fortress. It was all part of the mental cleansing, the flushing out of trivial stuff, that freed his mind to ponder bigger issues: What's life? What does it all mean? How do I fit in?

Marveling at the beauty and power of waterfalls he passed, Esteban pictured himself crawling to the edge of one of these tumbling chutes and peering over the edge. One small slip and he'd be fatally swept down. Such intense, frightful images of death had a hypnotic effect on him.

He felt a bond with strangers on the trail, most of whom radiated a spirit of engagement and humanity. When he looked into their eyes, a mutual understanding flowered. Out here, masks weren't necessary; rank vanished. Everyone was on equal footing as they pressed toward the summit.

Esteban's confidence grew with each journey to and from Half Dome. He saw these outings as a blueprint for life: Identify a goal, lay plans to achieve it, then execute the plan. The treks required both physical and mental preparedness. That meant no late partying the night before; rising at dawn; apportioning his time, food, and water on the trail; avoiding cramped or pulled muscles by taking breaks in proper sequence and of appropriate length; and overcoming bodily pain. The payoff: million-dollar views at the top, the camaraderie of fellow hikers and rapt discussion of life's many unanswered questions, a storehouse of adventures to share with others, and that sweet sense of success.

Accomplishing this agenda energized Esteban. It made him feel good about the world and was a powerful antidote for his low self-esteem. It also helped him conquer the demons within, to get past his travails.

On return hikes to Yosemite Valley and gazing back up from the Valley floor at that majestic rock face as it held the day's last rays of sun, Esteban felt that he belonged here. He was both exhilarated and let down about leaving. But the brief respite from nagging reality stoked his enthusiasm. He was recharged and ready for life back home again. The image of Half Dome remained fixed in his mind long afterward. When difficulties arose, he could simply recall the Dome and find peace.

Esteban knew Rice harbored similar feelings. If anything, Rice revered the Dome more than anyone, though, unlike Esteban, he chose not to verbalize his sentiments. Rice let his actions do the talking.

Over the years, traveling to Yosemite evolved into pilgrimages for these best of friends. The Dome became their mecca, a sacred place. They called it "our mountain."

◄○►

ESTEBAN AND RICE COMPETED fiercely to see who could go the farthest and fastest. But they took even more pride in their accomplishments together. Leaping off the ledge at Paradise, scaling the staircase up Nevada Fall, driving their legs up Sub Dome and the cables . . . each of these achievements testified to their personal well-being but also cemented the bond between them. Rivalry melded into deep loyalty and trust once they arrived on Half Dome's summit.

Up there, camaraderie is magnified and spreads widely. For many climbers and hikers, something intangible happens on a mountaintop—what John Muir described as the "mysterious enjoyment felt there, the strange calm, the divine frenzy." Human frailties—prejudice, envy, selfishness, egotism—tend to dissipate in the thinner air, and all human emotions boil down to the joy of the moment. Many people feel infused by a spirit of kinship and kindness. They are more apt to touch someone else, provide assistance, share. Much of this fellowship flows from the energy everyone had mustered to reach the summit. In collective consciousness, they savor this special place.

That feeling of connectedness may also stretch into Yosemite's past. You can almost sense the many American giants—Chief Teneiya, John Muir, Joseph LeConte, Teddy Roosevelt, and Ansel Adams, among others—as well as countless foreign dignitaries and notables from all walks of life and nations who have visited its hallowed grounds. Place-names, plaques, photos, exhibits, and the captivating scenery call attention to individuals who helped preserve Yosemite and contributed to what it is today. Esteban often remarked that he felt the presence of the original Native dwellers. He envisioned them making one last stand in Yosemite Valley, where their souls elected to stay. That, in his view, explained the sacredness permeating the site.

At least initially, Rice was much more attuned than Esteban to the outdoors. He knew about poisonous snakes, bears, and poison oak, and how to filter water, tie knots, and navigate by the stars. He was familiar with campground etiquette, fishing techniques, survival strategies, and a host of other things related to the natural world. He taught Esteban many outdoor crafts and skills. And he respected the environment. His family had taken him camping and read books about John Muir, Ansel Adams, and other conservationists. As an adult, Rice practiced good environmental ethics in the wild, picking up trash left by others, leaving each campsite cleaner than he'd found it, and urging his companions to do the same. He railed against stinky horsepack trains in the high country and ugly pizza stands, hamburger joints, and housing units on the Valley floor, "one of the most beautiful places on earth."

John Muir's penchant for taking risks in the wilderness and his seeming invincibility probably resonated with Rice. Indeed, Muir had an insatiable lust for learning and a relentless desire to probe the inner depths of the natural world—in effect, to be part of it. In his quests, he had numerous brushes with death. To sense the immense power of whitewater rushing over Yosemite Falls, Muir crawled perilously close to its brink. He ventured behind a small waterfall between Upper and Lower Yosemite Fall at night to "see the glory of moonlight through the meshes of the denser portions of the fall"— and almost got trapped there. He clambered up a four-hundred-foot ice cone at the base of the falls, formed by plunging water, so he could look down inside. He was caught in a snow avalanche while trying to study it. Muir also provoked a bear into chasing him so he could see how it ran; took refuge in a hollow tree trunk to observe a forest fire; rushed outside when a "noble earthquake" shook Yosemite, hoping to learn something; climbed a hundred-foot ponderosa pine during a fierce thunderstorm and clung "like a bobolink on a reed" to the slender top, which swung wildly in the wind; was stranded for more than thirteen hours on the summit of Northern California's Mount Shasta in a driving hailstorm, where temperatures plunged below zero; and, while exploring a bay in Alaska, fell into a glacial crevasse that immersed him in icy water.*

Muir pursued most of his adventures alone.

---

*The Muir Glacier in Glacier Bay honors him as its discoverer.

—◄○►—

PART OF THE TOTAL EXPERIENCE for Esteban was reciting the wonders of the Dome and recounting his adventures to workmates and
buddies. These included Bill Pippey, who was always up for a challenge. To his friends, "Bip," who had brown hair and hazel eyes
that were more blue than green, seemed bigger than his five feet,
ten inches, and 155 pounds, probably because of his outgoing personality and high excitability. He often spoke loudly to compensate for deafness in one ear; that and his high, raspy voice got
others' attention. Everyone liked Bip.

Born in 1958 and a single child, Pippey was only six years old
when his mother died. From then on, his father neglected him,
often disappearing for days. Pippey had spent weekends with his
grandparents from the time he was nine until his grandmother
died when he was twelve. His grandfather then moved into
Pippey's house and looked after him. He died two years later—so
the young teenager had to learn to fend for himself. He reached
out to others in his East Bay neighborhood, particularly the nearby
Jordan family. The Jordans, who had three daughters and two
small twin sons, watched over Pippey, took him on family vaca-
tions, and treated him as one of their own. Still, the young teen
lived mainly alone. His father came and went at whim.

About this time, while Pippey and his best friend were walking
together on the way to a bowling alley, his companion was hit and
killed by a car when he tried to cross the street. This tragedy—the
death of another loved one, this time witnessed firsthand—almost
destroyed him.

Pippey worked odd jobs to support himself and to partly cover
his share of house payments, as his father demanded. In high
school, he succumbed to drugs—mainly pot—and often was truant.
An insensitive school dean told him in his sophomore year that
before he could return to school, a parent conference would be
necessary. Pippey's problems worsened. In the eleventh grade, the
dean expelled him and sent him to a continuation program for

problem students. There he enrolled in a technical course and found he had good skills. He earned straight A's. But the program didn't prevent him from dropping out of high school for good by the end of his junior year. To Pippey, it seemed the entire world was aligned against him. He didn't have any close friends, was extremely shy, never went on a date, and had little hope of success.

In 1976, Pippey read *The Power of Positive Thinking* by Norman Vincent Peale. It changed his life. "For the first time," he recalled, "I felt as though I could succeed." He worked diligently, paid his bills, saved money, and got a girlfriend. In 1976, he began working as an assembler at Quantra-Ray, a laser manufacturer across San Francisco Bay in Mountain View.

But two days before Pippey's twenty-second birthday, his father split for good, taking money he had been hoarding from his son's contributions, including three months of back rent and cash for other bills. That same day his girlfriend also broke up with him. Pippey hit another low. He began drinking and abusing drugs even more heavily than before, abetted by co-workers and others. It wasn't unusual for him to consume four shots of liquor at lunchtime and half a pint of bourbon in the evening—just enough, he said, "to still be able to function at work the next day." Plus he regularly used pot, methamphetamine, acid, and coke. By this time, he had moved into an apartment with a Quantra-Ray co-worker in Sunnyvale, near Mountain View.

Pippey took his first backpacking trip in the summer of 1982 and discovered the power of the mountains. He began backpacking frequently. It was an activity he quickly came to value and respect, and one that provided an energy outlet. Time in the outdoors reduced the stress in his personal life and the workplace. It helped heal wounds. To get in top shape for these outings, he initiated a physical conditioning regimen, which included jogging ten to twenty miles on most days.

Pippey's life had turned the corner.

‑◄○►‑

AFTER HIS FIRST TRIPS WITH RICE, Esteban recruited Pippey for a trip to Half Dome the following summer. In addition to Rice, Esteban's three younger brothers, Alan, Andrew, and Alex, and two of his young cousins, Sean and Eric, joined them. Esteban wanted as many of his family and closest friends as possible to "gain the magic of a Dome expedition." To him, it was a rite of manhood and an initiation into the "Dome brotherhood."

When the party of eight arrived at a small camping area called Red Bud on Highway 140 near the town of El Portal just outside of Yosemite, at midnight on a Friday in midsummer, they consumed two six-packs of beer while relaxing after the long, tiring drive. Then, instead of bedding down in the campground, they loaded their gear and took off in pitch darkness for Paradise. Esteban and Rice, always quick to fantasize, likened this nighttime foray to a "midnight assault in 'Nam requiring total silence."

With only one flashlight among them, no one could see more than two feet ahead on the narrow, hillside pathway. At one point, Esteban lost his footing and went rolling down the slope, crashing through brush and almost landing in a stream. Although uninjured, he lay there motionless in the dark to see how his companions would react. Pippey started shouting in panic, until Rice punched him to hold him to the code of silence of their military fantasy. Satisfied with his charade, Esteban eventually made his way back up to the trail, and the group marched on.

At Paradise, Sean, a scrawny young teenager who carried a sleeping bag under each arm, slipped on the polished rock and fell into the water. He reemerged without the bags, which rested at the pool's bottom. Although they retrieved them, the bags were soaked. Esteban's two cousins had to pass the night without them.

The next morning, they all watched as Rice climbed up to the ledge resting forty-four feet above the pool.

Esteban: "To see Tom on a rock, perched high like an eagle, waiting for the exact right moment to dive into the wind and execute perfection . . . that's what Tom was all about. He would wait until all eyes were keyed on him, for this was what his ego demanded. Then he would delay, as though he were part of the stone itself, seeking the perfect vibration that resonated from his inner universe. Only then would he launch into his beautiful, flawless dive."

Rice spun his tightly compacted body two and a half times on the descent, straightening out just in time for his hands and head to break the water.

It was Esteban's turn. He knew what he had to do. He climbed to the ledge and leaped off without hesitation. By this time, however, he had adopted a new approach when jumping: He kept his arms close to his sides to protect them from slapping the water, all the while cupping his groin area to thereby "protect the family jewels," as he put it. No one else wanted any part of this exercise. However, Rice expected Pippey to jump. None of them knew that Pippey was terrified of heights.

Pippey realized he couldn't refuse Rice. He climbed up to the ledge but, paralyzed by acrophobia, couldn't even go near the edge. For more than fifteen minutes, he dawdled up there, frozen with fear, while everyone waited. Pippey finally clambered down to a lower, twelve-foot ledge and jumped.

Returning to the high perch, he told himself, Whatever it takes to throw myself off this ledge, I'm going to do it. Rice gave him a thumbs-up, Pippey sucked in a full chest of air, launched himself, and hurtled down into the pool.

Pippey was ecstatic—he nearly came out of his skin with glee. It was a great personal victory.

Rice was impressed. Pippey had gazed into those frightful depths and conquered his terror. He had passed Rice's test. From that time on, Rice referred to Pippey as one of the bravest people he knew.

After the sleeping bags had dried in the sun, the eight packed up, returned to their vehicle, and left for Yosemite.

On the Mist Trail, Rice set his usual fierce pace up the granite stairs. Pippey was close behind and Esteban held his own, while the others lagged. The men were sweating profusely by the time they reached the top of Nevada Fall, where they performed another ritual that marked their Half Dome excursions: plunging into the Merced River to cool off. In mid-July, the river's flow was not strong, but it was a very cold fifty-six degrees.

◄o►

THE MERCED RIVER BEGINS on the glacial slopes of Mount Lyell, Yosemite's highest peak at 13,114 feet. After crashing down Nevada and Vernal falls, the river meanders through Yosemite Valley where the current remains strong, especially in spring and early summer. That and its frigid water have accounted for several drownings over the years. With additional volume from Yosemite and Bridalveil falls and a host of smaller cascades, the Merced surges again by the time it leaves Yosemite, tumbling down steep chutes and cascading for several miles over and around boulders the size of cars and houses. Then it drops more modestly—a long run of swift current, intermittent rapids, and deep pools that attract kayakers, whitewater rafters, swimmers, and anglers. From Happy Isles in upper Yosemite Valley to the Lake McClure Reservoir, the Merced flows 135 unobstructed miles.*

Swimming in the Merced's chill water and treacherous current can be exceedingly dangerous at any time. The risk is many times greater above a waterfall. From 1975 through 2000, there were 37 drownings in Yosemite, which made up 22 percent of the park's 166 accidental deaths during that period. Twenty-nine of the thirty-seven occurred in and around waterfalls. Five happened in the Merced River directly above Nevada Fall, and four of those individuals were carried over the falls. Ten drownings took place

---

*The natural beauty and assets of the Merced River were given added protection when its upper seventy-one miles from Yosemite to the town of Briceburg, and the forty-three-mile-long South Fork of the Merced, were designated National Wild and Scenic Rivers in 1987. The lower part of the main stem was given this federal designation in 1992, thus preserving the free-flowing state of this spectacular waterway.

near Vernal Fall—three of those victims went over. Another three people lost their lives at Yosemite Falls, while one got swept over Bridalveil Fall and another over Ribbon Fall. Hidden Fall was the scene of four deaths.

Several common denominators characterized the drownings in and around Yosemite's rivers and waterfalls. People who misjudged the current may have been swept off their feet or unable to swim out of it. Some may have lost their footing in the water or slipped on a rock and fallen in, only to be carried downstream. In other cases, the force of the current pinned them under a downed tree, rock, or other obstruction in the river. Hypothermia as a result of the Merced's frigid temperature can quickly sap a person's strength and make it almost impossible to escape the current. (Hypothermia is a drop in body temperature caused by exposure to cold conditions. Depending on the circumstances, it can set in slowly or rapidly. You lose your ability to function and, without countermeasures, can die from hypothermia itself or from the loss of bodily function that leads to drowning, a fall, or other fatal mishap.)*

-◄o►-

RICE AND PIPPEY STRIPPED off their clothes and dove into the icy water fifty yards upriver from Nevada Fall. Esteban and three others joined them but kept their shorts on. Given the gentle, midsummer flow, this exercise wasn't too risky. They all swam the few feet out to a large, flat boulder and sunbathed. Despite other hikers and campers nearby, Rice and Pippey weren't the least self-conscious

---

*A classic example of misjudging river hazards is the twenty-nine-year-old man who parachuted illegally from El Capitan on June 9, 1999. He was BASE jumping, one of the most dangerous of all sports, which entails parachuting from Buildings, Antennas, Spans, and Earth. It has been illegal in Yosemite since 1980, mainly because jumpers violated the rules when it was legal. In this case, the jumper had planned his escape in advance. He landed safely, quickly removed his gear, and, before the authorities could snare him, dove into the Merced River in the hope of reaching a getaway vehicle on the other side. But the man disappeared, surely overcome by hypothermia and the current's strength and turbulence. His body was found nearly a month later three or four hundred yards downstream, pinned horizontally in the upstream undercut of a large boulder and out of view.

about being naked. Rice seldom hesitated to flaunt his body; for him, it was all part of overcoming inhibitions and gaining freedom. On Half Dome's summit, he regularly strolled about and sunbathed in the nude.

Returning to the riverbank, thoroughly cooled and refreshed, the men got dressed and ate lunch.

They left for Half Dome after eating. At the bottom of the cables, Pippey totally freaked when he saw the steep grade and cable handholds, which looked perilous. He kept his fear to himself, though, hoping he could make it up by focusing on the stone at his feet. He waited until the others were ahead before starting. One hundred feet up, he glanced to his right and saw nothing but emptiness. Panic seized him. His body trembling, his face ashen, he retreated inch by inch, unable to look left or right and gripping the cables with a steel hold. He collapsed at the base of the cables, still trembling as he embraced the ground.

Esteban and Rice retreated down the cables to check on Pippey. They encouraged and cajoled him, but Pippey, convinced he'd never reach the top, told them to go on ahead. After a few minutes, Rice lit a joint, inhaled deeply, and passed it to Pippey, who took a couple of hits and then several more. Soon stoned, eyes glazed, he bounced to his feet raring to go—anywhere. He tackled the cables again, with gusto, bellowing the *Batman* theme song all the way up the granite slope.

Pippey survived his first journey up the Dome and, his dues paid, was henceforward a Dome regular. Being with close and supportive comrades filled a longtime void in Pippey's life. He became Esteban's housemate. He also was swayed by Rice's leadership and charisma, and counted him among his best friends, though he tended to be more cautious than Rice about taking risks.

Pippey: "To me, taking risks is like confronting a fence. Some individuals stop when they see an obstacle and stay safely on their side. Others might go to the top of the fence, to at least see what's on the other side before deciding. And then some just jump over

the fence without knowing what's on the other side. I saw myself
as the second type, one who looks first and, if things appear too
dangerous, stops. Rice was the latter type, one who is willing to
plunge into something without sizing up the possible consequences if anything should go wrong."

PIPPEY OFTEN DROVE his outlandish, souped-up truck on these trips,
including that first one to Half Dome. After purchasing it in 1981,
he invested more than seven thousand dollars and much of himself in creating what everyone called the "Bip Mobile," totally
reconstructing the half-ton, extra-long-bed '72 Ford inside and
out. Pippey disassembled the cab, then built a frame from half-
inch steel tubing and covered it with sheet metal rippled with
dents. He painted the metal blue, interweaving stripes of silver,
gold, and copper. He fashioned a wedge-shaped and tilted front
end with a big hood scoop, including fenders and radiator, that
all opened as a unit, like a big-rig truck. He installed two square
headlights and a square fog light below each to form a triangle.
The cab interior had gold-colored, diamond-tucked crushed vel-
vet on the headliner, side panels, sun visors, and seat, which also
sported foot-long strips of brown- and gold-patterned crushed vel-
vet. Brown shag carpeted the floor. A T-shaped console on the
interior ceiling housed four lighted switches for dual gas tanks,
dual fuel pumps, dual batteries, fog lights, and a stereo. There were
eight speakers in the cab and two in the customized aluminum
camper shell Pippey had installed. Inside the shell were side pan-
eling, brown- and gold-patterned crushed-velvet strips where the
sides and headliner intersected, gold crushed-velvet headliner with
a 110-volt outlet in the center and two lights, and more brown
shag, beneath which lay a four-inch-thick foam-rubber mattress
pad. To rev up performance, Pippey overhauled the 302-horse-
power, V-8 engine and converted the manifold to four barrels from
two. He raised the compression ratio to 1.5:1, balanced and blue-

printed the short block, and installed a new carburetor, recreational vehicle camshaft, headers, dual exhausts, power brakes, power steering, and automatic overdrive transmission.

When he finished, the truck weighed a hundred pounds less than the original and was more efficient, enabling him to cruise at a hundred miles an hour and get twenty-three miles to the gallon. Pippey often drove that fast late at night on Highway 395 in the eastern Sierra Nevada en route to Mount Whitney, another of his favorite haunts. The Bip Mobile could accommodate eight people—three in the cab and five in back. Including the many trips to Yosemite and Mount Whitney, it logged more than two hundred thousand miles. The truck's roar and dual exhausts caused heads to turn in Central Valley towns—and drew the attention of police, who sometimes pulled him over, mostly out of curiosity.

In the spring of 1984, Pippey proposed to Pam Skog, his girlfriend of three years. He and his buddies drove to Paradise for a bachelor party, for one last fling before that big leap to the altar. Pippey urged his best man, Tom Rolf, to jump from the high ledge. Just before Rolf hit the water, he assumed a sitting position—a common technique for creating a huge splash in a swimming pool, but not a smart maneuver while plunging thirty-six miles an hour into a creek pool. According to Pippey, Rolf "banged himself up pretty good" and, for weeks afterward, including at the wedding ceremony, suffered from a sore and bruised underside.

◄O►

RICE AND A HALF DOME expedition were inseparable in everyone's eyes. He was the organizer, the motivating force, the one who planned everything down to the last detail, including the timeline and all logistics. He even prepared the menu, which emphasized good nutrition: veggie sandwiches, gorp, PowerBars, fruit, and lots of water. Plus beer, especially a choice microbrew when the guys could afford it. Everyone else had only to show up and pay his share.

Sometimes, instead of stopping at Red Bud after their long drive from the Bay Area, the men ditched at Camp Curry in Yosemite, where they slept behind a big rock so park personnel wouldn't see them. Or they broke into an unoccupied tent-cabin, occasionally with help from an employee whom Rice had befriended and perhaps partied with. Rice knew a woman who worked in the cafeteria; she prepared custom-made sandwiches for the gang, filling them with avocado, sprouts, tomatoes, peppers, onions, lettuce, and cheeses, and plastering them with mayo, mustard, and black pepper. The men referred to these as Dome-wiches. A gallon-sized mini keg of imported beer they lugged into the backcountry was a Dome keg.

Every trek had an element of competition and challenge: Who could race up the staircase, Sub Dome, and cables the fastest? Who could pack the heaviest load? Who could get closest to the edge? There was little tolerance for the timid—slackers were taunted. And Rice always tried to set the highest bar.

Esteban: "Tom was one of the most competitive persons I've ever known. He would make everything into a game of competition, and he always had to win. If he could not be better than you physically and athletically, then he would try to be tougher than you mentally, which included not showing any emotional signs of weakness."

On the trail, Rice scrambled way ahead, stopped, and waited for everyone else to catch up. Then he set another killer pace to the next milestone. He drove everybody to keep on schedule so they could ascend the summit and descend before dark, if they weren't camping on the top. Rice knew what it took to motivate Esteban: question his courage. He prodded others differently. If anybody questioned him, he just growled and said, "Eat shit and die."

His own personal frailties lay beyond anyone's reach.

On the summit, Rice typically gravitated to the diving board. There, occasionally wearing only his briefs, he assumed the diving position and inched backward until he stood at the end of that naked rock pedestal. The more people who watched, the more fearless he seemed to be. Sometimes his companions refused to look, either out of terror or to deprive him an audience.

Esteban: "Every time we climbed the Dome, you knew Tom would do it. It always scared the shit out of us and yet we were drawn to it, and it was inescapable, his closeness to death and sheer will to overcome his fear of it."

In this and his other stunts, Rice was betting as always that he controlled the outcome.

—◁o▷—

TYPICALLY, RICE CONCEIVED a plot to make each Dome outing special. It became part of the ritual.

Once, on a "nighttime assault," they drove to Glacier Point and hiked in the dead of night to Little Yosemite Valley. Pippey brought his wife. She slowed the group down considerably, which enraged Rice, who didn't hide his displeasure or mince his disapproving words. Rice was adamant about excluding females from these forays into the wilderness. On this trip, they unwittingly placed their sleeping bags next to a steep drop-off and didn't realize their peril until daylight.

For their Memorial Day trip in 1984, accompanying Rice and Esteban was "Half Dome Jerome," a summer employee in Yosemite National Park and friend of Rice, who bestowed the moniker. Half Dome Jerome was built like a shotputter. The threesome brought a case of San Miguel, a premium Filipino beer. The twenty-four bottles weighed just over thirty-three pounds, and to avoid breakage they carried the case in a separate backpack. Each hiker took a turn hauling it along with all his other food and gear—akin to adding a sack of bricks to an already oppressive load.

When they reached the summit and saw unmelted snow in shaded areas, Esteban interpreted this as a "great message from the gods." The snow guaranteed ice-cold beer.

Part of their routine on top was to circulate among other campers, strike up conversations, and share stories and tangibles.

On this overnight outing, the three men indeed had something special to share: cold beer, a few bottles of which they sold for five bucks each to some of the two dozen campers on the summit. With others, exchanges transpired. One camper, for example, invited everyone to peer through the giant lens of his telescope while he described the constellations. Elsewhere, a cheery fire stoked by wood that a camper had hauled up was attracting a friendly group. And there was a chef from a New Orleans restaurant who cooked up a killer stew and shared it with Rice and his buddies. They reciprocated with beer.

Esteban met a camper who offered him LSD. In the drug world, this particular acid—"Orange Sunshine"—allegedly was the best, concocted by the Harvard professor and drug guru Timothy Leary. Esteban downed it and soon was tripping. Lying on his back, he watched the flaming stars twirl about the moon in a gargantuan pinwheel pattern. He jumped to his feet and sauntered toward the western horizon, along the Dome's surface that sloped ever downward. As Rice and others watched, Esteban, playing a game of chicken with himself, disappeared below the skyline as though he would continue into the abyss. Just before gravity started to overcome the grip of his hiking boots, Esteban stopped and turned back.

Then he strolled toward the Dome's sheer face. The full moon cast Half Dome's image over the Valley. To Esteban, the shadow on a distant wall was an eagle, symbolizing his own powers, and the silhouette of Clouds Rest a giant pyramid. He tight-walked along the mountain's edge feeling totally in control, invincible. He stepped down to a three-foot-wide ledge and walked along it with only a dark void on his left. He dropped to another narrow ledge. In front of him a rock structure jutted out, like the beak of a giant bird. On its facing side was a black hole—an opening in the granite, the eye of the bird. He climbed to this mysterious cleft, peered in, and saw a rock chamber.

Later that night, after midnight, Esteban showed Rice and Jerome the cave he had discovered. They accessed it through an opening amid the jumble of rock slabs that covered this part of the summit. The chamber's interior was conical: fifteen feet long, three to four feet wide, and six and a half feet at its highest point, close to where they stood. It dropped to four and a half feet in the middle and to four feet at the farthest end. There Yosemite Valley was visible through the small portal Esteban had stumbled upon.

In the chamber's outer side—actually its own separate cubicle, which extended still farther out—was another four-foot-wide, five-foot-high opening that looked out to the upper Valley and Tenaya Canyon. Just beyond the gap was a ledge about four feet wide and thirty inches deep. You had to clamber over a two-and-a-half-foot boulder, then lower yourself down, to reach it. Esteban, Rice, and Jerome each slid over the boulder in turn and eased himself into a sitting position on the ledge, which conveniently tilted back slightly. A stone slab provided back support. Sitting there was like occupying the open cockpit of an airplane with only empty space in front of and below your legs.

Squeezed together, legs dangling over the edge, each swigging beer, the trio took in Yosemite's northern ridges and domes, all bathed in moonlight. The stars danced above, and a vast empty space loomed immediately before them.

They dubbed this bench-like perch the King's Chair.

—◁o▷—

KARL BUCHNER WAS ANOTHER Dome compatriot whom Esteban recruited from Spectra Physics, a company that had bought out Quantra-Ray, where Esteban, Pippey, and Buchner still worked. Although an outdoorsman, Buchner wasn't a regular on Esteban's and Rice's outings. He and Esteban had met while playing together on a softball team. Buchner's friends called him Beach Boy or Surfer Dude. He looked and acted the part—blond hair, blue eyes, almost six feet tall, a muscular 185 pounds, laid-back. He did in fact surf and was active in a variety of other sports as well.

Esteban's descriptions of Half Dome and the King's Chair persuaded Buchner to join him and Rice on a Memorial Day weekend trip in 1985. On the summit, they smoked pot, mingled with other campers, and swapped stories. Buchner likened the communal spirit to that of a cult gathering, a mini Woodstock. As the sun disappeared beyond the granite pinnacles to the west and darkness settled in, Rice and Esteban led him to the cave, where they wedged together on the King's Chair and passed around a jug of "bug juice"—Gatorade and vodka. "Totally awesome" was how Buchner described this experience. The three men talked about returning later that summer. They would invite others and somehow make the outing really special. Buchner wanted his best friend, Steve Ellner, to join them and experience what he had. Esteban would invite his new supervisor at work, Bob Frith, whose passion for the outdoors was just getting ignited. Pippey would surely join them. He'd likely recruit the young Jordan twins, whom he had wanted to include on a Dome journey for quite some time.

They set the date for the same weekend as Rice's twenty-eighth birthday: July 27–28.

3

THE HIKERS

*I was lying in a great solemn cathedral, far vaster and
more beautiful than any built by the hands of man.*
—Theodore Roosevelt, Yosemite, May 1903

Among the multitude attempting to reach Half Dome's summit
on Saturday, July 27, 1985, were three parties, their fates
destined to merge there on the top.

Rice and Esteban headed their contingent. Esteban had recruited
his work supervisor, Bob Frith, a recent East Coast transplant. Frith,
in turn, had enlisted his best friend, Bruce Weiner, also from the

East Coast and newly arrived in California. Bill Pippey brought along sixteen-year-old twin brothers, Bruce and Brian Jordan. The boys were drifting into chronic substance abuse, and Pippey hoped that exposing them to nature would redirect their lives in more promising directions. Rounding out the group were Karl Buchner and Steve Ellner. Buchner had persuaded a skeptical Ellner, his closest buddy, to join the outing. The group would backpack to the top, camp there, and celebrate Rice's birthday the next day in style.

Leading the second group was Mike Hoog of Santa Rosa, a town one hour's drive north of San Francisco. His party included Linda and Dan Crozier, Rick Pedroncelli, and Jennie Hayes. A Half Dome veteran himself, Hoog wanted the others—all of them Dome first-timers—to spend the night up there so they could experience its full impact.

The third group consisted of six men in their twenties from San Jose, five of whom worked for high-tech companies and lived in the same apartment complex. Their experienced leader and organizer, Brian Cage, had logged at least ten journeys to Half Dome's summit.

The leaders of all three groups shared deep ties to this granite temple—feelings of wonder and devotion that would infuse their companions as well. Staring up at that stone mass and realizing you'll be trekking to one of the most remarkable places on earth is enough to jump-start anyone, even veteran outdoorsmen.

There were twenty hikers in all, eighteen of them men who, to varying degrees, were risk-takers and self-styled outdoor warriors. They all had the same agenda: spend the night on Half Dome.

◄○►

IN 1985, FOLLOWING two decades of upheaval, the nation was mostly unruffled. It had returned to conservative values in politics, education, entertainment, and social affairs. The 1960s began with high hopes and idealism inspired by a young president, John F. Kennedy. But his assassination in 1963 and then the assassinations in 1968 of two other revered public figures—Martin Luther King Jr. and Senator Robert F. Kennedy—mired the country in prolonged grief and despair. The escalating war in Vietnam, moreover, ignited more protests than ever before. Intense demonstrations rocked college campuses, where students took control of administrative offices and, in some cases, shut down all operations. Police brutality sparked race riots and fires in several cities. Trust in government and institutions spiraled downward.

Questioning authority and convention became de rigueur. Individualism and alternative lifestyles flourished, symbolized in part by male hairstyles—shoulder-length manes, ponytails, Mohawks. Use of marijuana spread among the young. The advent of birth control pills in the 1960s liberated women and led to greater sexual license and promiscuity. The credo of the times was *Do your own thing*. These and other newfound mores coalesced at Woodstock in upper New York State in August 1969, a mammoth throng devoted to rock and roll, drugs, sex, and lawlessness.

At the dawn of the 1970s, anti-establishment activities—fueled by the Nixon administration's Watergate shenanigans—gathered even greater momentum. Drug use soared—not only of pot, but also of LSD and cocaine, the drugs of choice among the rich and famous. Violent underground movements took form. The Black Panthers, the Charles Manson cult (which murdered actress Sharon Tate), the Symbionese Liberation Army (which kidnapped and brainwashed newspaper heiress Patty Hearst), and other radical groups lashed out against what they saw as a corrupt system, but did so mainly to wreak destruction for its own sake. America's withdrawal from Vietnam and the resignation of President Nixon didn't immediately reverse Americans' cynicism. Slowly, however, extremism ebbed. Even some of the most radical protesters realized they still had to earn a living.

By 1980, an across-the-board retrenchment of mores was under way. Many people heralded conservative family values. And many in the new generation aimed to earn lots of money. Meanwhile, men's hair got shorter and inflammatory words and phrases like *pig, racist, anarchist*, and *burn, baby, burn* faded from the lexicon. *Cool, awesome, gnarly*, and *dude* reflected the more laid-back times. In schools, it was "back to the basics"; innovations from the '60s— flexible scheduling, individualized learning, inductive and prob- lem-solving curricula—were curtailed. The spread of sexually transmitted diseases decelerated sexual promiscuity. Patriotism once again came into vogue. Spearheading this conservative move- ment was the new president, Ronald Reagan, elected in 1980 and reelected in 1984.

—◄〇►—

ESTEBAN, RICE, AND CREW at mid-decade were among the era's "upwardly mobile" crowd, the original "twenty-somethings," the "me generation." Succeeding in their Silicon Valley high-tech jobs and making money were important, but enjoying life came first. For these guys, parties, drinking, drugs, and raucous gatherings were a way of life. Theirs was a true-life *St. Elmo's Fire* sans Demi Moore.*

The big ritual for Rice's crowd was attending the happy hour that most major nightclubs in the area—the Baja, The Rodeo, Terrace, Saint James Infirmary, P. J. Mulligan, D. B. Cooper's— held on Friday evenings. To entice customers, the clubs served up not only cheap drinks, but also free food. The group hit several venues every week, an activity they called upper hoboism.

The upwardly mobile were cool and had that *Miami Vice*/Don Johnson look—designer jeans, sport coat, casual dress shirt, no tie, tennis shoes, no socks. The exception was Pippey, who often

---

*Interestingly, the film's title refers to a type of lightning discharge. When the buildup of opposite charges is insufficient for lightning to form, a coronal discharge, a circular bluish glow, or even a mass of sparks may appear over a high, sometimes pointed object. The phenomenon, first noted at the top of ships' masts, is called St. Elmo's fire, for the patron saint of sailors. The movie's title connotes the turbulent energy of the characters as they approach adulthood.

showed up with ripped or stained clothes, sometimes both. Those who frequented the clubs were mostly singles, the last of the baby boomers. AIDS had not yet stormed into public awareness, so the pursuit of casual sex was still mainstream; booze and pot remained rampant; and smoking indoors was not only legal but hip.

By this time, the frenzied disco beat of the '70s was giving way to '80s pop. Culture Club, Prince, Dire Straits, and the sassy, unconventional Madonna hit the airwaves and distributed their music in a newfangled format, compact discs. Radio tunes in 1985 were likely to include Madonna's "Like a Virgin," "Material Girl," and "Crazy for You." Nevertheless, hard rock persisted and a guy needed to know how to dance to have a chance with the free-spirited young women who frequented local clubs.

Rice's charisma and often outrageous behavior attracted many followers, including a parade of females. Pippey, who often shouted across a crowded room to snare someone's attention, was loud and boisterous. Esteban, on the other hand, was usually laid-back and low-key. However, his hair-trigger temper could erupt if anyone annoyed him or he sensed disrespect, especially after a few beers, giving rise to the occasional parking-lot brawl. The group's other members were the more sedate Buchner and Ellner.

A newcomer was Bob Frith. He had moved to California that April to work as a laser tech supervisor at Spectra Physics. The youngest of eight children, with six older sisters, Frith had grown up outside Arlington, Virginia. He held a bachelor of science degree in engineering from the University of Rochester in New York, with a major in optical engineering. Only twenty-four years old in 1985 when he took the supervisory job at Spectra Physics, Frith was bright and had good business and people skills—definitely a young man on the move.

Frith charmed everyone he met with his sparkling personality and good looks accentuated by a strong chin, clean-cut features, and rich dark hair. A happy-go-lucky type who was always ready with a quick joke, Frith loved life and having a good time. He plunged enthusiastically into everything he did and always with a smile. He could arrive at a party not knowing a soul and, by night's end, be friends with everyone there. Plump at 190 pounds for his five-foot, eight-inch height, he nevertheless had a way with women. Between his and Rice's charm and good looks, the other guys would, as Esteban put it, "hover around like vultures waiting for scraps!"

◄O►

EXCEPT FOR THE MORE culturally inclined Ellner, the main bond among these men was sports. They competed fiercely in pickup basketball and touch football contests. After each game of the high-flying San Francisco 49ers, Esteban typically hosted a barbecue bash on the pool deck at his apartment complex that often blared long past midnight. In January 1985 Coach Bill Walsh and quarterback Joe Montana led the team to their second consecutive Super Bowl title by shutting down Dan Marino and the Miami Dolphins.

The men tracked most other sports as well. In the National Basketball Association, Larry Bird was voted the most valuable player for the 1984–85 season and a young player, Michael Jordan, was crowned rookie of the year. And in a rarity for major-league baseball, two Missouri teams, the St. Louis Cardinals and Kansas City Royals, were riding high and would later meet in the World Series.

Rice, Esteban, and company paid little attention to politics and international affairs, which were fairly low-octane at the time. There was no hint of a warming trend in the Cold War when Mikhail Gorbachev took the Soviet helm in 1985, but subsequent events—the fall of communism and the Berlin Wall, and the dissolution of the USSR—would make Gorbachev one of the most significant political figures on the twentieth-century world stage.

Aside from *St. Elmo's Fire*, movie hits included *Back to the Future* and another youth flick, *The Breakfast Club*. *Out of Africa*, starring Robert Redford and Meryl Streep, won Best Picture for 1985. Redford also launched the Sundance Institute that year and organized the first Sundance Film Festival in Park City, Utah.

The Half Dome crew may have read Tom Clancy's blockbuster *The Hunt for Red October*, but most likely didn't pick up two other big sellers that year: *The Color Purple* and *Lonesome Dove.* Treasure hunters located the *Titanic* on September 1, sparking renewed interest in the tragedy seventy-three years earlier and culminating in the monster film hit *Titanic* in 1997. Another tip of the iceberg that shocked the nation was the announcement on July 25 by movie star Rock Hudson that he had AIDS. This revelation and Hudson's death six weeks later generated big headlines. In recognition of the unfolding AIDS plight in Africa, music stars convened to record "We Are the World," which won a Grammy.

—◄o►—

IN THEIR QUEST for adventure at Yosemite, Rice, Esteban, and compatriots probably didn't realize that beneath the beauty and splendor of this famed national park simmered many long-standing sociopolitical issues.

Ever since the first national park—Yellowstone—was established in 1872, questions had swirled regarding the proper mission of national parks. Did America want them to be preserves for nature? Havens for tourists and recreationists? Resources for both private and public consumption? As much as any park, Yosemite reflected the conflict of priorities that buffeted these national treasures.

Yosemite was first designated a national park in 1890 (the state of California managed Yosemite Valley and the Mariposa Grove until 1906 when those land grants were receded to the federal government and made part of the national park around them.) Despite this protection from exploitation, powerful pressures to accommodate tourists and develop recreational amenities seethed. The Curry Co.—and other lodging and food operations—got started in 1899. In 1903, state officials reinstituted a nightly entertainment spectacle that began almost thirty years earlier: an evening bonfire at Glacier Point followed by hot embers dumped over the edge, which created a flaming firefall to the Valley floor.*

The elegant, stone Ahwahnee Lodge opened in 1927, offering a golf course, tennis courts, and a swimming pool. The park's Badger Pass Ski Area began operating in the winter of 1935–36. Over the subsequent three decades, gas stations, motels, gift shops, apartments, restaurants, houses, garages—all told, more than a thousand buildings, a few thousand campsites, and thirty miles of roads and parking areas—sprouted in the Valley, resulting at times in suffocating human and automobile congestion.

The surge of environmentalism that swept the nation in the 1960s and '70s carried over to the nation's parks.** The preservation of nature became the National Park Service's chief mission. Increasingly, science rather than recreational values directed the efforts of park managers. Their new philosophy was to let nature exist on its own terms to whatever extent possible in these high-use public settings.

That put an end in 1968 to Yosemite's nightly firefall, a small but symbolic change. To reduce congestion, park managers closed the upper end of the Valley to automobiles, built a one-way road system, and introduced shuttle buses to transport visitors throughout the Valley. The main parking area at the visitor center was converted to a pedestrian mall.

In addition, certain meadows in the Valley became off-limits in order to allow restoration of natural habitats, while in others, boardwalks were installed to accommodate walkers. The Ahwahnee golf

---

*The firefall was ended by an Assistant Secretary of the Interior in 1913 and reinstated by the Secretary in 1917.

**This era produced the Federal Wilderness Act (1964), the National Wild and Scenic Rivers Act (1968), the Federal Clean Air Act (1970), the Federal Clean Water Act (1972), and the Federal Endangered Species Act (1973).

course was removed. Stocking Yosemite's historically fishless streams and lakes with hatchery-reared trout would eventually be phased out.

A General Management Plan for Yosemite was established in 1980 with five broad goals: reclaim Yosemite's priceless natural beauty, allow natural processes to prevail, promote visitor understanding and enjoyment, markedly reduce traffic congestion, and ease crowding. But by July 1985, little progress had been made. Too many groups had vested, often conflicting interests in the park's future. For example, those whose livelihoods depended on the arrival of millions of tourists each year, businesses both inside and outside the park, opposed restrictions on cars and any reductions in lodging and other visitor amenities. Environmental groups wanted the priority on preservation, while others insisted that the resources existed primarily to be used by the public.

Although the management plan favored letting Mother Nature take her course in Yosemite, shifting political climates and disagreements in subsequent years impeded timely progress toward that end.

—<o>—

IN THE SUMMER OF 1985, backpacking and extreme outdoor sports such as hang gliding, aerial skiing, and BASE jumping were riding a wave of popularity. Few aficionados were as intense in their quest for adventure as Esteban, Rice, and especially Pippey, whose newly discovered love for the outdoors was toughening his body and spirit. Pippey liked nothing better than a grueling backpacking trip. He set a fierce pace way ahead of others, as if he were leaving behind years of family neglect and abuse. Pippey's favorite destination was Mount Whitney, offering one of the most spectacular hikes in the country.

Summiting Mount Whitney—at 14,494 feet, the highest peak in the lower forty-eight states—involves eleven uphill miles and an elevation gain of more than six thousand feet, mainly on a steady, 15 percent grade. Fortunately, there are countless switch-backs—a hundred of them just between Trail Camp at twelve thousand feet, where backpackers overnight, and the crest of the ridge at fourteen thousand feet.*

In early July, three weeks before the upcoming Half Dome event, Pippey organized a backpacking trip to Mount Whitney with Esteban and Frith. The plan was to hike to the summit, which is located in Sequoia National Park, then descend the other side and camp at the eastern end of the Park. It would be a major test for Frith, who had been in California less than three months, and who was overweight and a smoker. Frith may not have been in the best of shape, but his boundless enthusiasm usually carried the day.

En route to Mount Whitney, the Bip Mobile cruised east across the Central Valley, through Tuolumne Meadows in Yosemite, over Tioga Pass, and south down Highway 395 for a hundred miles. The three men crawled into sleeping bags alongside the parking lot at Whitney Portal (elevation: eight thousand feet) and slept. At sunrise, they set out for Trail Camp, where they spent the night before the final ascent.

Adding to the physical stress of lugging a fifty-pound backpack up more than six thousand feet are the risks posed by high altitude. As you climb higher, each breath contains fewer oxygen molecules due to decreasing barometric pressure; blood becomes increasingly inefficient as an oxygen supplier, so your body must work harder. Any exertion during the first couple of days at high elevation—even going up a typical staircase—causes shortness of breath, a normal response.

---

*Hulda Crooks is evidence that such an accomplishment requires more will than muscle. In 1962, at age sixty-six, after her doctor recommended that she begin exercising in the mountains to combat breathing problems caused by pneumonia, Crooks successfully hiked up Mount Whitney. She made the trek almost annually for the next twenty years, twenty-three times in all, climbing it one last time in 1987 when she was ninety-one. That same year she also scaled Mount Fuji in Japan. Crooks's feats earned her the nickname Grandma Whitney. One of Mount Whitney's needles is named Crooks Peak. She died in 1997 at the age of 101.

What isn't normal is altitude sickness, an unpredictable and imprecise affliction that generally can occur above five thousand feet. The first signs include headache and perhaps some dizziness or queasiness. Under the same conditions and regardless of age, gender, physical conditioning, or prior climbing experience, one hiker may experience altitude sickness while another feels nothing. Untreated, it can lead to acute mountain sickness (AMS), the body's intolerance of a hypoxic (low-oxygen) environment. AMS symptoms include headache, nausea or vomiting, fatigue or weakness, dizziness or light-headedness, confusion, and staggering gait. A hiker with these symptoms should stop and descend immediately. Practically speaking, ascending to eight thousand feet—the altitude at which Pippey, Esteban, and Frith launched their trek up Mount Whitney (and approximately the same elevation as the top of Half Dome)—shouldn't cause major problems. But above that level, and certainly above fourteen thousand feet, AMS becomes a serious, potentially life-threatening concern. If it occurs, you cannot get enough oxygen no matter how fast you breathe. That leads to brain swelling, a condition called cerebral edema, which can be fatal.

Hikers and mountain climbers usually can avoid AMS by acclimatizing over several days. The most stringent recommendation is one day of ascent for each thousand feet above eight thousand feet elevation. Pippey, Esteban, and Frith did acclimatize over two days on this particular journey; they spent one day at eight thousand feet and a second at twelve thousand. Nevertheless, thin air was still a threat.

Soon after the threesome left Whitney Portal and headed up the mountain, Pippey, a veritable hiking machine, was way out in front. The first three-and-a-half-mile leg meanders through a pine-scented forest of Jeffrey pine and red fir, and leads to Outpost Camp in a wildflower-filled meadow, the first of the two camping areas on the trail. From there, it is another three and a half miles to Trail Camp. Here backpackers have built low rock walls to ward off piercing winds, and resident marmots either beg for food or steal it from campers. The pica, a high-elevation-dwelling mammal that looks like a huge mouse but belongs to the rabbit family, also populates this area.

After Trail Camp, where the trio bedded down for the night, the trail becomes steep. But the vistas up ahead, to the left and right, more than compensate for the uphill grind. Tufts of sky pilot—one of the most beautiful and fragrant of alpine wildflowers—garnish the trailside. Then come the hundred switchbacks leading up to Trail Crest, a mountain pass that is still two miles from Whitney's summit. From this ridge is a view of the upper Kern River Basin to the west, a gigantic bowl beyond which lies another range of snow-covered peaks—the Great Western Divide and the Kaweah Range. To the east are sweeping vistas of lakes, the Owens Valley, and the Inyos Mountains beyond, home to bristlecone pine trees, some more than four thousand years old, maybe even six thousand.

Esteban and Frith struggled, their party lifestyle taking its toll. Ever the warrior and despite his fatigue and increasing light-headedness, Esteban pushed onward. So did Frith, who wore a bright red bandanna around his neck. At Trail Crest, Frith got a headache and nosebleed, but he trudged on, describing the adventure as "bitchin', bitchin'." (This was a standard phrase in Frith's vocabulary, one he applied to various marvels. He may have learned it from "Bob Bitchin'," a popular character on the TV show *Saturday Night Live*.)

When they finally reached the summit, as many as fifty other people were milling about, smiling, holding hands, and a few just meditating. Esteban felt very woozy—all he wanted to do was lie down. An instant later, or so it seemed, Pippey was shaking him awake. Actually, Esteban had been out for about thirty minutes, oblivious to the sheer drop-off just a few feet away.

The three men departed down the other side of Whitney to a grassy meadow bordering Guitar Lake, so named because of its shape. During this long descent, Esteban sweated profusely. When they arrived at the small lake, it was in shadows and the temperature had dropped. Esteban began shivering uncontrollably—the first sign of hypothermia. Pippey and Frith stripped his wet clothes, put him in his sleeping bag, and heated soup for him. While Esteban dozed, they stripped off their own clothes and jumped into the ice-cold lake, which they could tolerate only for a few seconds.

That evening, they saw two other backpackers camped nearby. In his customary fashion, Frith sauntered over and struck up a friendly conversation. He later returned with freshly popped popcorn his newfound friends had given him.

Esteban, Pippey, and Frith met a solo backpacker named Joe the next day. He was, as Esteban characterized him, a "1960s hippie type." Joe and Frith hit it off right away, and soon the four were a band of brothers. When the group had settled down for the evening, Joe broke out a few joints and Esteban produced a bota bag containing 151-proof Bacardi rum, which served as not only refreshment but also antiseptic, mouthwash, and fire starter. Between shots of straight rum and hits of Joe's weed, the happy campers soon forgot all about their physical ailments. Still to come were a dinner of Top Ramen noodles augmented with salami and cheese, and then "killer cigars" that Esteban kept in a waterproof pouch. Evening passed into night.

They realized the next day there was little food left. Checking his topo map, Pippey pinpointed a stream five miles away—a ten-mile round trip—where they might catch fish. It was either that or go hungry, so off they went. Both Pippey and Frith loved to fish and had brought along telescopic rods. At the stream, they saw many smallish trout, but the fish weren't biting. Pippey, hiding behind a small waterfall, finally managed to coax out about a dozen wary little rainbows with salmon eggs, and the men snared their dinner.

The party arrived back at camp just as darkness settled. That night, amid breathtaking wilderness rimmed by snowcapped mountains, they savored the fish fried in butter and lemon. More Bacardi, more pot, more cigars, and a cozy fire and fabulous view of Mount Whitney's crest . . . all left the three men quite mellow and very appreciative of the great outdoors.

For Frith, this outing confirmed his love of the Sierra Nevada. He already was looking forward to Half Dome.

─◄o►─

FOR THE HALF DOME OUTING, Frith recruited Bruce Weiner. Not only did he want his friend to experience California at its best, but he expected the trip to reignite their deep friendship.

Frith and Weiner had met at the University of Rochester in New York, where both were optical engineering majors. They were the same age—twenty-four. In contrast to his friend's heft, the five-foot, nine-inch, Weiner was on the lean side, weighing 165 pounds. He had thick, curly black hair. After college, Weiner was employed for a little more than a year by Inspex Corporation in Waltham, Massachusetts, but he was less interested in career than recreation—skiing, biking, golfing, beaching, gambling, party-ing—and scouting for female companionship. He worked out with weights three times a week and played racquetball most days, so he was in reasonably good physical shape. Although not as extroverted as Frith, Weiner was easygoing and friendly, and had a subtle sense of humor.

In letters he wrote to Weiner after moving to California in April, Frith reported "lots of jobs, lots of sun, lots of women in bikinis here in the West." The report quickly persuaded Weiner to pull up stakes. He began job hunting in the Bay Area and accepted an engineering position at Lockheed Missiles and Space Corporation in Sunnyvale, near where Frith worked.

Weiner had just arrived in California in early July; he'd moved all his boxes into his new apartment the very day he left for the Half Dome trip, leaving him no time to unpack. The Yosemite outing would be Weiner's first mountain adventure—in fact, his first real hike of any substance.

Steve Ellner—a single child who, by his own admission, could be stubborn, opinionated, and uncompromising—was a greenhorn, too. Unlike the others, he had zero affinity for the rugged outdoors. But Buchner was certain that the beauty of Yosemite and Half Dome would captivate the twenty-seven-year-old Ellner, as they do most first-time visitors. Buchner wanted his pal to experience the summit "happening," particularly sitting in the King's Chair at night. Because Ellner was Esteban's roommate (Esteban had moved out of the house he shared with Pippey when Pippey's girlfriend moved in), the wonders of Half Dome had been already drilled into him.

He agreed to go, despite considerable misgivings. In the preceding days, Ellner's co-workers kidded him about lightning on Half Dome. Aren't you the tallest? You'll probably be the one who gets struck, they joked. Ellner, the only six-footer in the group and a self-avowed coward, would carry those thoughts with him throughout the trip.

An unlikely pair would accompany the seven men: the sixteen-year-old twins Brian and Bruce Jordan. Pippey hoped the mountain might work its magic on these two drifting teens, his "little brothers." The youngest of five children, with three older sisters, the Jordan twins were just six years old when Pippey, then fourteen, "adopted" the Jordan family as his own. Mr. Jordan was an easygoing, affable guy who wrestled with an alcohol problem. He and Pippey often sat in the garage until very late at night, talking and drinking. Sometimes Mr. Jordan passed out in a drunken stupor.

He and his wife neither closely supervised nor firmly disciplined their two sons, who attended school in a low-income neighborhood in the East Bay city of Hayward and were surrounded by drugs and other temptations. Of the two, Brian was more outgoing and assertive. He often spoke of becoming a big success someday. Unfortunately, some activities, such as using and selling marijuana, were just too tempting. Bruce, who had blonder hair than his brother, was more reticent and quiet. He also got into drugs early on, but, unlike the enterprising Brian, didn't sell them.

Both good-looking young men, Brian and Bruce were mainly interested in girls and cars, like many teenage boys. But smoking pot contributed to their excessive truancy, and that prompted the high school to drop both from classes and send them to continuation school—the same thing that had happened to Pippey when he was their age. Recalling his own troubled past, Pippey realized that Brian and Bruce were surely headed for trouble, so he tried to steer them back on course. In order to do that, he believed he had to gain their trust. The linchpin in this scheme was fishing, an activity the twins had taken up at ponds around the East Bay and truly loved.

Pippey first took them on a backpacking trip near Mount Whitney, where they camped and hooked golden trout, a beautiful native species. The twins themselves got hooked, and more outings followed. Pippey was heartened to see the boys soak up these experiences and get high on nature. When it came time for the July pilgrimage to Half Dome, Pippey seized the opportunity to bring them along. It would be another major step in their reformation.

—◦—

AT 2 P.M. ON FRIDAY, July 26, Weiner picked up Frith at Spectra Physics in his rental car, courtesy of Lockheed. They bought various camping supplies, freeze-dried meals, and trail mix, then drove to Rice's home near Santa Cruz, where he and Esteban waited.

Pippey and the Jordan twins would drive in the Bip Mobile and rendezvous with others at Red Bud that night. Buchner and Ellner planned to meet the group on Saturday somewhere on the trail or, later, at the top of Half Dome. First, Buchner wanted to show Ellner as much of Yosemite as possible.

The caravan from Santa Cruz—Esteban and Rice in Esteban's truck, Frith and Weiner in the rental car—left for Yosemite around

5 P.M. They headed east across the Central Valley—listening again and again to the number one hit at the time, "Brothers in Arms," by the Scottish group Dire Staits—and stopped at nine thirty in Merced for a Chinese dinner. Esteban couldn't get the song's lyrics out of his head. On a dark stretch of road somewhere between Merced and Mariposa, Weiner noticed that Esteban's truck, just ahead, started to swerve. He flashed his high beams and honked until Esteban, who was dozing off at the wheel, pulled over. They switched drivers; Frith drove the truck and Rice joined Weiner. At Mariposa, they cranked up on caffeine and quickly hit the road again, arriving at Red Bud around midnight.

The Bip Mobile pulled in thirty minutes later. Despite the late hour, everyone was pumped up about the forthcoming hike. Some drank beer, others smoked pot, and everyone jabbered about the coming day. Weiner turned in before the others. Lying there among the pines, listening to his friends' chatter and the incessant chirping of cicadas while watching shooting stars streak across the sparkling sky, he thought it was one of the most peaceful and relaxed moments of his life.

The others eventually rolled into their sleeping bags, too. For most of them, it would be their last peaceful rest for a long time.

◄○►

MIKE HOOG'S GROUP—Jennie Hayes, Rick Pedroncelli, and Linda and Dan Crozier, who was a year younger than his twenty-two-year-old sister—reached the entrance to Yosemite on Highway 120 just before midnight that same Friday. They continued a few more miles to the Crane Flat Campground and bedded down.

The group rose at six thirty the next morning, gobbled down breakfast, quickly packed up, and left for the Valley and their big day of hiking. They were on the trail to Half Dome two hours later.

Hoog, twenty-one years old, was a passionate outdoorsman, and a fitness buff. He ran marathons and competed in triathlons. A lithe, 160-pound man who stood five foot eleven, he sported shoulder-length blond hair often tied in a ponytail and boyish good looks. His easygoing and fun-loving manner belied an inner intensity that drove him to achieve. He had spent a lot of time with the Crozier family since the third grade, including vacation time. The youngest of five children, Hoog had at eighteen experienced his father's death, an event that deeply affected him. He saw firsthand how fragile life could be, so his attitude was, *Savor the moment.* He had gone to Half Dome on several earlier trips and become a self-described Dome freak.

Hoog had just earned an associate of arts degree in emergency medical services from Santa Rosa Junior College. His close friend Linda Crozier also had recently graduated—from the University of California, Davis—with a bachelor of arts degree in physical education and had enrolled in a master's program in exercise physiology. In 1974, with her father's encouragement, Crozier became one of the first girls in the nation to play Little League baseball. In 1982, the nineteen-year-old and her father rafted down the Snake River in Idaho. She fell in love with whitewater rafting and the outdoors.

Crozier, who had a close and supportive family, was a straight-A student in high school. She thought about becoming a doctor but chose sports medicine and physical therapy instead. At Davis, she earned certification as an athletic trainer and worked as a student athletic trainer for several teams, which exposed her to all kinds of injuries. She also joined the Outdoor Adventures program there, learning to guide a raft through whitewater and gaining the requisite skills and mental toughness for whitewater rescues.

At 115 pounds, she was slim for her five-foot, five-inch, height—and distinctively pretty, with shoulder-length, feathered dark brown hair, hazel eyes, and olive skin. Crozier was self-confident, extroverted, and content—qualities that accented her Eurasian attractiveness (her father was Caucasian, her mother Chinese). Most of the time her face held a smile.

Hoog and his troupe arrived at Nevada Fall shortly after noon. Several trails converge there, bringing together day visitors, backpackers, and hikers; more than fifty were sprinkled about. Hoog's upbeat and friendly group ate their lunches and joked with each other and those nearby, radiating good spirits. They stretched out on the rocks in their swimsuits to soak up sunshine and rest before the final leg of the trek.

Hoog and Crozier were alike in many ways. But one common trait would prove most serendipitous on that particular Saturday— each was a trained emergency medical technician.

—◄o►—

THERE ARE SEVERAL PROGRAMS that prepare people to handle medical emergencies. The most elementary is Basic First Aid, offered by the American Red Cross. It entails two hours of training in fundamentals—bandaging, cleansing wounds, treating burns, and the like. Another Red Cross course (six hours) teaches cardiovascular pulmonary resuscitation (CPR), or how to treat a victim whose breathing or heart function has stopped. The Red Cross also offers a more extensive, fifteen-hour Public Safety Program that includes CPR. It's designed for firefighters, lifeguards, and others who respond to public emergencies.

Courses leading to emergency medical technician (EMT) certification are much more extensive.

Three levels of EMT certification are available in California: EMT-I, EMT-II, and EMT-III (paramedic). EMT-Is complete 114 hours of classroom and clinical training on diagnosis, treatment, and quick transportation of victims to the nearest medical facility. They are not certified to administer medications—except, in certain locations, oral glucose and epinephrine autoinjectors— nor to administer intravenous substances. EMT-IIs train for at least 306 hours. This certification level is uncommon in California, however; EMT-IIs work mostly in rural counties where the case numbers do not justify using paramedics. EMT-IIIs undergo 1,032 hours of instructional and clinical training to become paramedics. The training is broad—how to take blood samples; how to perform emergency interventions, such as intravenous procedures; how to administer a large assortment of prepackaged drugs, such as morphine and nitroglycerin; and more.

After Hoog completed his EMT-I certification in Santa Rosa, he considered studying to become a paramedic. Linda Crozier also had undergone a rigorous EMT-I course that spring. Her teacher, Dr. Ben Shrifrin, was an expert in wilderness emergency medicine and rescue; he had lots of experience in outdoor-related medical emergencies and was an avid mountaineer. A co-teacher in Crozier's class was Bill Bryant, a good friend of Shrifrin's who had a similar background in mountaineering. Bryant and Shrifrin had served together on the Tuolumne County Search & Rescue Team.

Their instruction would be put to good use on Half Dome.

‐◄○►‐

AT RED BUD, Rice's group of seven awoke to a crystal-clear summer sky. A full day of hiking was on tap, ruling out a side trip to Paradise. They tossed their gear into the vehicles and left for Half Dome.

The caravan entered Yosemite Valley thirty minutes later. Accustomed to the low, rounded mountains of the East, Weiner was awestruck by Yosemite's granite spires and domes. Then, at the distant end of the park, there it was—Half Dome. He had difficulty visualizing himself atop that overpowering mountain, and wondered silently if he could really accomplish such a feat.

They gorged themselves on a buffet breakfast in the cafeteria at Camp Curry, then loaded their backpacks with gear, clothing, and food. It was a two-mile march to the trailhead at Happy Isles.*

The sky was blue when the group headed out except for a single cumulus cloud floating above Clouds Rest.

---

*In earlier years, hikers could drive to and park at Happy Isles at the far eastern end of the valley. The General Management Plan of 1974 established a shuttle-bus system to replace cars and reduce congestion in that area. The trade-off, however, was diesel fumes spewed by the buses.

Each hiker hefted a full backpack. The exception was Weiner, who carried the only pack he had, a book bag with two shoulder straps; it contained a few food and clothing items. Frith packed forty-five pounds of his and Weiner's gear, a load they would take turns shouldering. The seven hikers reached the trailhead and began their journey. Fifteen minutes later, they were at the bridge where Vernal Fall is first seen, and hoofed it up the Mist Trail, "doing the staircase."

By the time they eclipsed Vernal Fall, a few cumulus clouds had formed in the sky to the east.

Meanwhile, Buchner and Ellner were a good thirty minutes behind the others when they reached the trailhead after their quick tour of the Valley's sights. At the bridge, Buchner chose the John Muir Trail along the canyon's side. It was a longer but more scenic route, and not as steep as the Mist Trail, an important consideration for Ellner, who had become increasingly dubious about this undertaking.

Rice, Esteban, Pippey, and the Jordan twins arrived at Nevada Fall around twelve thirty. Frith and Weiner, struggling with the altitude and arduous ascent, showed up several minutes later. Rice greeted them at the top of the trail; he was standing on the rock right at the lip of Nevada Fall, his toes inches from the river before it careened over the edge in a torrent of whitewater. Weiner and Frith couldn't believe what their eyes were telling them.

Frith and Weiner joined the others on a sandy beach alongside the river. Rice and Pippey then stripped off all their clothes, dove into the chill water upriver from Nevada Fall, and swam out to a large flat rock. So did Brian and Bruce Jordan, and then Weiner, who thought, This skinny-dipping is cool! On the rock, the swimmers hooted, shouted, and yelled obscenities while tussling like schoolboys to push each other off. They returned to shore and, still nude, lounged about while eating lunch and drinking beer.

Several cumulus clouds in the eastern skies now had combined and were massing over and around Clouds Rest.

-◄O►-

BRIAN CAGE, CLU AND Zip Cotter, and Steve White left work in the Bay Area on Friday and drove east until they reached a popular campground off Highway 120 outside Yosemite National Park. The plan was to rendezvous the next day at Glacier Point with Paul Kolbenschlag and Monroe Bridges, who would depart from San Jose at 4 A.M. on Saturday and drive straight through. Cage had persuaded the group to take the Glacier Point route to Half Dome, explaining that because the trail starts at about seven thousand feet, there is less elevation gain. In fact, the 4.6-mile hike from Glacier Point (at 7,214 feet) to Nevada Fall (at 5,900 feet) isn't all downhill. The Panorama Trail does descend to Illilouette Fall at 5,850 feet, but then it winds back up to 6,600 feet before dropping down again to Nevada Fall. The distance from Glacier Point to Half Dome is just under nine miles, or more than half a mile longer than the Mist and John Muir trails.

In the summer of 1983, while hiking along the Little Sur River south of Carmel on the Pacific Coast, Cage had slipped, fallen into the river, and fractured his right patella. He was evacuated by helicopter. After that debacle, his knee always ached on long hikes.

How dangerous is hiking in Yosemite? It's quite safe on the trails. Nonetheless, falls—while hiking or climbing boulders and rocks—account for most of the park's accidental deaths. Some hikers are killed by rocks cascading from above. Others die when they leave the trail to command a better view. Many trails in Yosemite traverse steep terrain littered with loose rock, such that one misstep may lead to a slide and fatal plunge. Ironically, there haven't been any recorded deaths on Half Dome's heavily traveled trail, despite the hazards. For those who might lose their grip on the cables, the sloping granite apparently allows sufficient footage and time to recoup.

Cage's party assembled in the Glacier Point parking lot shortly before noon on Saturday. After they donned hiking boots and organized their gear, everyone gathered for a group photo, with a side view of Half Dome in the background. Five of the men wore shorts, one wore jeans, and they all sported ratty T-shirts. Steve White wore his signature bandanna on his head. To the east beyond Half Dome a mass of cumulus clouds blanketed the mountain ridges. Before they departed Glacier Point, Clu Cotter bought a postcard showing a lightning bolt striking Half Dome.

Within the first half mile on the trail, the six men spotted two five-foot rattlesnakes about ten feet off the path, writhing together in mating behavior.* Few things get the adrenaline flowing on a hike like seeing one of these creatures, which do their best to avoid humans and keep the peace. These reptiles were exceptionally huge. Much to the dismay of his companions, Kolbenschlag waded into the bushes to get a photo of these specimens, but he kept a safe distance.

And then the six hikers resumed their march toward Half Dome.

—◄o►—

HOOG'S GROUP PAID LITTLE attention when Rice and his buddies arrived at Nevada Fall. However, when Rice, Pippey, and others shed their clothes and began shouting vulgarisms, Linda Crozier and Jennie Hayes were stunned and offended, especially with families, young teens, and other females gathered at this popular hiking destination—the standard terminus for most Mist Trail day-trippers.

Let's get out of here—we don't need this, Crozier told her friends.

So they hoisted their backpacks and left. It was 1:30 P.M.

---

*The author experienced the first of his many rattlesnake sightings in California very near Glacier Point over forty years ago. Contrary to popular belief, rattlesnakes inhabit elevations of up to ten thousand feet—even higher in warm climates. That's probably their uppermost range in the Sierra Nevada around Yosemite. According to the Yosemite Medical Clinic, about two persons suffer a rattlesnake bite in the park each year; there has been one known snakebite death in Yosemite, in 1931.

By that time, a thick, dark cloudmass hovered above Clouds Rest. The first rumbles of thunder could be heard off in the distance.

The threatening weather prompted Rice and his companions to pack up. Rice and Esteban assured the others that once they were on the summit, they would be safe and dry in the cave if a thunderstorm hit. That's where we're heading, Esteban said as his fellow hikers prepared to move out.

It would be a race to the top of Half Dome: Who could get there first? Pippey and Bruce Jordan didn't wait for the others; they hefted their packs and pounded up the trail, with Esteban, Rice, and Brian Jordan not far behind. Frith and Weiner brought up the rear again.

After the surprise encounter with rattlesnakes, Cage's party had proceeded down Panorama Trail to Illilouette Fall, then gutted out the uphill leg, which slowed their progress. Beyond that point, they set a good pace en route to Nevada Fall and a much-anticipated break. The six arrived at the falls shortly after Rice's crew had left. Everyone stripped down to their shorts and swam out to the same big slab in the river, where they performed their own distinctive ritual: an air-guitar rendition of the Jimi Hendrix classic "Purple Haze."

Refreshed, they returned to shore, got dressed, packed up, and headed out through Little Yosemite Valley as the thunderstorm brewed.

Buchner and Ellner didn't arrive at Nevada Fall until nearly two o'clock, and stopped only briefly amid the steady rumble of thunder. Ahead lay darkening skies. Buchner desperately wanted to make up for lost time. Ellner followed his friend up the trail but wondered if it was wise to keep going. In fact he didn't like anything about how the day was shaping up.

The phalanx of menacing clouds forged down Tenaya Canyon, taking direct aim at Half Dome.

4

THE CLIMBERS

Go climb a rock!—Yosemite Mountaineering School

ON LATE FRIDAY AFTERNOON, July 26, 1985, while scaling the northwest face of Half Dome, rock climbers Ken Bokelund and Rob Foster were halfway to the summit. Bokelund was nineteen years old, Foster eighteen. The previous summer, both had completed their first Yosemite climb, the south face of Washington Column. Throughout that modest, one-day ascent, the face of Half Dome had stared at them from directly across the Valley, never leaving their sight. Its peerless image seared their minds and beckoned their souls. When they left Yosemite the next day, they were already planning their next climb—of Half Dome's face, one of the most famous big-wall climbs in the world.

And now, a year later, here they were.

In the preceding days, the weather had been unstable, with clouds building up and thunderheads forming. As Bokelund and Foster scaled Half Dome on Friday, a fierce thunderstorm broke out in late afternoon. This storm was particularly intense; frenzied rain pounded them. The two climbers wore rain pants and jackets, and hard yellow helmets to protect their heads from fatal head trauma in the event of a slip or fall. To escape the sprays and sheets of water blasting down off the rock, making it almost impossible to see, Bokelund and Foster sought refuge at a rock structure called the Chimney. They wedged themselves into the flue between this spire and the mountain's face, their feet butted against the spire and backs against the face. Runoff funneling down through the surrounding crevices drenched them while the thunderstorm roared overhead. Lightning flashes and thunder cracks soon became almost simultaneous.

Bokelund and Foster were, in their own words, "scared shitless."

They heard the air around them crackle and then, almost immediately, a bright flash from above momentarily blinded them. A lightning bolt had just thrashed the summit. Its electrical current streaked down the water on the granite surface and shocked the two climbers leaning against it. Within minutes, another strike hit the mountain, delivering another jolt to their bodies. Foster felt as if the electrical charge were driving his tongue out of his mouth. For the next several minutes, the two men bore repeated electric shocks. Fortunately, the voltage was not high enough to injure them seriously.

Foster screamed, We've got to get off this mountain!

◄○►

THE SPORT OF ROCK CLIMBING first became fashionable in the French Alps and the Italian Dolomites. Its popularity had skyrocketed over the years, especially in Yosemite, where granite monoliths challenged the world's best climbers like no others. For starters, some of the most continuous vertical surfaces anywhere on the planet were found there. Climbing them required supreme skill, strength, and endurance. Unlike European granite, Yosemite's rock was extremely smooth, as a result of glacial polishing and the processes of exfoliation (sheeting) and erosion, all of which shaved off corners and angles and left the rock slick and curved. Jamming hands and toes into vertical cracks—natural avenues to the top—was the standard mode of ascent. Some of the climbing was friction climbing that entailed the smallest of fingerholds. Clinging to these holds often had less to do with technique than faith.

As sports go, rock climbing is a world unto itself, a vertical wilderness of sheer rock. A climber packs not only everything a backpacker carries—food, cooking gear, sleeping bags, and all the rest—but also huge coils of rope, carabiners, hammers, pitons, wedges, blocks or camming devices, headlamps, webbing, and a bag of chalk to keep fingers dry and gritty. And water—lots of it. The standard rule is two liters per day per climber; three if the weather is hot. Each liter weighs 2.2 pounds. So a four-day climb means each climber must lug a minimum of nearly eighteen pounds of water.

Overnight climbers prefer to sleep on ledges and always tie themselves in. When there's no ledge, they snooze on the face in a hammock-like sling, or portaledge, that is anchored at the belay or tied in.* Mice, rats, and squirrels live in the cracks on Yosemite's walls. These rodents, as well as ravens or crows, may raid precious food supplies or ravage gear such as sleeping bags; the helpless climbers can do little else but watch such thievery. There are unique procedures for relieving oneself on a mountain face and packing out excrement so it doesn't contaminate the environment.

---

*A belay is a means of securing the climber by using a rope and usually a belay device to prevent or minimize falls. The rope is attached to a pin or cleat anchored in the rock, to the climber, and to the belayer below. A belayer is the person on the ground or at the belay station who secures the lead climber, feeding out rope as the climber ascends or gathering up the slack as he descends.

The climber's main companions are vertical rock, empty space, and vertigo-inducing depths.

◄○►

AMONG THE PANTHEON of granite megaliths, Half Dome has long been seen as special. Early on, would-be climbers viewed this unique structure as the most difficult climbing challenge in Yosemite, if not the world. George Anderson was the first to hoist himself to the top with rope and spikes, in 1875. He subsequently established a trail for others that was more of a hike than a technical climb. Almost sixty years passed before anyone climbed Half Dome via another route.

John Salathe, a Swiss blacksmith in Yosemite, accomplished that feat in 1946 when he and a companion scaled the southwest face. Much like Anderson, Salathe applied his occupational skills to forge a climbing breakthrough. He had climbed on many of the best routes up Yosemite's rock walls but found that the soft metal pitons available at that time were inadequate; they bent and mushroomed when driven into granite cracks.* By cannibalizing the axle of a Model T Ford, Salathe fashioned pitons out of hard steel, which he and his partner Anton "Ax" Nelson used to ascend the Dome's southwest face. His innovation became the standard for Yosemite climbers who followed, and for climbers across the globe.

Salathe proved there was more than one way to ascend Half Dome, but the southwest face wasn't anywhere near as challenging as the northwest face, the nearly vertical wall staring down at visitors on the Valley floor. Up to then, few believed it was possible to scale the eighty-degree slant that characterized much of the

---

*A piton is a metal spike with an eye on one end that climbers place in the rock to secure their rope. The rope is attached to the piton placed by the lead climber. If the leader falls from ten feet above the nearest piton below her, she would fall a total of twenty feet before drawing the rope tight, assuming the piton holds.

cliff's twenty-two hundred feet. A few of the world's best climbers in the mid-1900s thought otherwise.

In 1954, three climbers attempted the ascent but were thwarted just two hundred feet up. The following year Royal Robbins, Jerry Gallwas, Warren Harding, and Don Wilson also tried but made it up just 450 feet. Nonetheless, they surveyed a possible route to the top. Two major obstacles were a smooth section more than a hundred feet high and about halfway up, and the overhang at the summit known as the Visor.

More than a year after the Robbins team's failed attempt, Robbins, Gallwas, and Mike Sherrick laid new plans to conquer the northwest face. In this increasingly competitive arena and hoping to scoop any other would-be climbers, they launched their try up the face in early summer 1957. Inch by inch, they lifted up their hundred pounds of gear in a haul bag suspended below them by ropes. The climbers used a flashlight to signal their progress every night to companions on the ground—but, to avoid publicity, only during the firefall spectacle, when the attention of everyone in the Valley was riveted on Glacier Point. A fourth companion had hiked to the top and posted a sign warning people not to throw rocks over the edge—a popular and innocent activity among Half Dome summiteers, who were completely unaware there might be climbers below.

On day two, the three men confronted the 125-foot-high smooth section. To continue, they had to reach a series of chimneys and flakes three hundred feet off to the side. Robbins managed to climb fifty feet up the smooth granite. There he placed three pitons. He fixed his 150-foot climbing rope to these anchors and lowered himself back down. Then, in a display of daring and skill, he gripped the rope and launched into an explosive horizontal charge across the seemingly unassailable barrier, swung back, and charged again. At the outermost reach of his fourth pendulum swing, he grasped a narrow ledge with his fingertips and secured a hold. He now had a route to continue up. His two companions executed the same maneuver. (This part of the climb—a signature move that Robbins pioneered on several other climbing routes in Yosemite—has since been named the Robbins Traverse.)

The three climbers continued up until they were three hundred feet from the top, directly below the Visor. Securing meager foot- and handholds, they inched their way up another hundred feet, only to encounter another slick, insurmountable section. But to their surprise, they came upon a walkable ledge—virtually a climber's highway—that circumvented the barrier. At the end of what has since been dubbed Thank God Ledge, the climbers found more foot- and handholds.

The trio completed their feat by executing a series of mantle maneuvers, pulling their bodies up to a point where they could then push down with their palms, jack themselves up, and gain a foothold. After five days on the wall, Robbins, Gallwas, and Sherrick had surmounted the "unclimbable" northwest face of Half Dome. They completed the climb in twenty-three pitches. A pitch is the distance between one belay stance and the next, usually 100 to 150 feet, with the maximum distance being the length of the rope, or about 165 feet. Thus, the vertical length of their route was about twenty-two hundred feet.

The next successful ascent of the northwest face didn't take place until three years later, and it entailed only two nights in bivouac. A one-night ascent quickly followed. Then, in May 1966, Jeff Foote and Steve Roper completed the climb in a single, long day.

In 1967, Liz Robbins, wife of Royal, became the first woman to climb Half Dome; she followed the same route as her husband's first ascent of the northwest face a decade earlier. Her accomplishment signaled the revolution in women's climbing that would soon follow. Greg Lowe and Rob Kiesel made the first winter ascent in January 1972, overcoming a fierce storm with howling winds. Their hands were nearly frozen.

The route that Robbins and his mates blazed is called the North-west Face Regular Route. By 1971, that and three other routes up the northwest face—Arcturus, Northwest Face Direct, and Tis-se-yak—were active. Today rock climbers can choose from among a dozen technical climbing routes to reach Half Dome's summit.

—◄o►—

THE CLIMBING WORLD, in which scaling big walls had become the ultimate measure, needed a way to grade the difficulty of ascents. As early as the 1930s, a five-point grading system was devised to rate hikes and climbs in the Sierra Nevada. Technical free climbs were consigned to Class 5. But because they varied widely in the level of difficulty, Class 5 was subdivided in the 1950s into nine ratings—5.1 to 5.9. As climbers became more accomplished and skillful with each passing decade, this Yosemite Decimal System* was extended up to 5.15, the most difficult climb ever completed up to that time. Subcategories (a through d suffixes) in each numer-ical category were added to delineate the variations even further.

Up to 1970, the adventure in climbing was conquering virgin vertical terrain. Fierce rivalries took root on the floor of Yosemite Valley. Tested Yosemite climbers jealously guarded their turf and were contemptuous of others who didn't meet their standards. For them, it wasn't just a question of which route someone climbed; it was also a matter of technique and speed. Some of the world's greatest climbers—the so-called granite astronauts—achieved major breakthroughs on Half Dome and that larger, even more imposing mass of granite nearby, El Capitan, with its thirty-two-hundred-foot face—"the Crown Jewel of American Rock Climbing."

---

* This system is not to be confused with the decimal system in common use. Under the Yosemite Decimal System, the levels following 5.9 are 5.10 (not the same as 5.1), 5.11, and so on. The original Sierra Club grading systems also had a Class 6 for artificial and aid climbing, but it is no longer used. Artificial or aid climbs are graded on a separate A0 through A5 scale.

These breakthroughs included many first ascents on new routes. Among the climbers in that Golden Age of Climbing were Royal Robbins, Yvon Chouinard, Tom Frost, Warren Harding, David Brower, Galen Rowell, George Whitmore, and Allen Steck. Some parlayed their success into business ventures, such as sponsorship or work in commercials and movies. Robbins, for example, established a successful line of clothing; Chouinard started an outdoor equipment retail firm, Patagonia, which was initially based on climbing devices he invented.

Yosemite climbers settled in a campground in the park and made it their own. Camp Four was a much-abused place where a motley assortment of climbers hung out and slept, a number for the entire climbing season. Some lived on as little as fifty cents a day and ate mainly oatmeal. Like a gypsy camp, Camp Four had its own subculture whose members felt they owned Yosemite. Its scruffy ambience and characters aside, Camp Four gave birth to the sport of rock climbing as the world would come to know it.

IN THE EARLY DECADES, nearly all climbing involved the use of aids, particularly pitons and expansion bolts. When Warren Harding completed the first ascent of El Capitan—the Nose Route—back in 1958, he hammered in more than one hundred bolts. The entire climb, which involved many descents to the Valley floor and returning to the spot where he had left off, took forty-five days over a year and a half. But the sport had become so popular by the mid-1970s that piton scars and abandoned hardware and bivouac webbing were degrading the formerly pristine rock walls. So climbers sought ways to reduce the impact. Purists used as few aids as possible, heeding John Muir's exhortation to "leave no mark except your shadow." As Royal Robbins said, "It isn't getting to the top that's primary, but how you climb there." Not all climbers bought in to this newfound sensitivity, however.

Climbers invented new kinds of low-impact aids that could be wedged into rock crevices to prevent a fall and then removed, leaving no trace. These included a variety of metal chocks, stoppers, and hexes—essentially, rectangular or hexagonal pieces of metal—that are still in use today. In clean climbing, as this approach came to be called, climbers didn't hammer any new protective devices into the rock; they employed only removable items.

A natural progression in the sport of rock climbing was free climbing—climbing without any gear that you could stand on or use to pull yourself up, including rope. Free climbers used only the natural rock surfaces to ascend; they adapted themselves to the rock rather than trying to shape the rock with mechanical devices. Free climbing had its own techniques* and demanded a higher level of gymnastic flexibility and fitness (especially for the most difficult climbs), along with exceptional strength and unique muscular development. Climbers in Yosemite developed new techniques that revolutionized so-called crack climbing. Previously, climbers relied on gaston—putting their fingers in a crack and pulling outward, as if opening a sliding door—for support. Now they were jamming hands and fingers into cracks, squeezing them to create tension within, then hanging by that limb, a technique that required far less strength than gaston. The skeleton rather than muscles did the work.

Free climbing the major walls in Yosemite wasn't really where the action was up until the mid-'70s, mainly because few thought it possible. Events on June 15, 1976, dispelled that notion.

That day, two Colorado climbers, Jim Erickson and Art Higbee, launched an audacious attempt to free climb Half Dome's Northwest Face Regular Route and thereby scoop the Yosemite fraternity

---

*These techniques are perhaps best illustrated by the one-finger pull-ups that climbing legend Wolfgang Gülich made famous. No mere party trick, this incredible maneuver enabled Gülich, a shy German, to complete some of the world's most difficult climbs, a number of which have not been duplicated to this day. Actor Sylvester Stallone was so impressed by Gülich that he got him a job doing stunts in the 1993 movie *Cliffhanger*.

in its own backyard. Beginning in 1971, Erickson had attempted this climb nine times and failed. Still, he believed it could be done. Underlying his latest venture was a movie project. Cinematic technique, like climbing technique, was undergoing its own revolution of sorts. It had evolved to the point where a crew could capture an ascent on film from above, below, and the sides.

Everything began as planned. Erickson and Higbee inched their way up the face. From Ericksons's previous attempts the two climbers knew they could not free climb the Robbins Traverse. In order to circumvent the smoother section, Erickson spotted a possible option. He climbed straight up two hundred feet, and when he couldn't go any further, he traversed forty feet to the right, and then he descended forty feet, arriving at the ledge at the end of the Robbins traverse. Higbee followed suit. This free variation approach has since come to be known as the Erickson Traverse. The pair contined up to Big Sandy Ledge, where they spent the night.

In the morning, staring down on them from above were the Zig Zags, a four-hundred-foot course of narrow cracks that offered the smallest of toe- and fingerholds. Indeed, cracks in the third Zig Zag were so tight, only fingertips could squeeze in. Previous climbers always relied on aids here. Erickson and Higbee each fell several times trying to surmount this stretch. But eventually, Higbee, taking to heart his belief that a climber "has to push himself through the doubt," found one more crack to wedge his hands into, one more potato-chip flake to crimp with his fingertips, and the strength to pull himself up onto Thank God Ledge. Erickson followed. Success seemed to be within grasp. After thirty-four hours on the face, after twenty-two pitches, after twenty-one hundred feet of successful climbing, only one hundred feet remained. This last leg would take thirty minutes at most.

However, Erickson and Higbee were shocked to encounter yet another granite slab blocking their ascent, not very high but smooth and slick. They scoured the rock again and again looking for something to grasp but came up empty. Finally, an exhausted and feverishly hot Erickson used aids to scale this one last obstacle, thereby ending the free climb. Although the two men called their effort a "magnificent failure," the climbing community called it a "magnificent achievement." They had showed the climbing world what was truly possible. From then on, free climbing took center stage.*

Erickson returned to Yosemite later that summer. First he went to Half Dome's summit and affixed a top-rope that hung down over the northwest face. Then he repeated his and Higbee's climb. When he reached that last troublesome slab, Erickson free climbed it with the top-rope for his protection, thus completing the task he and Higbee had set out to achieve. Technically, however, the top-rope compromised the ascent as a pure free climb. Recognition for that feat would go to Leonard Coyne in 1981.

◄○►

SMOOTH GRANITE, OVERHANGS, unstable granite flakes, bivouacs on the narrowest of ledges—all of these and much more test the tenacity, skill, strength, and endurance of climbers. The commitment is such that, beyond a certain point, the only escape is up. Mountaineers live for—and sometimes die for—this challenge.

Each year there are more than a hundred climbing accidents in Yosemite. Nearly all of the 51 climbing deaths between 1970 and 1990—an average of 2.5 per year—were due to trauma injuries; hypothermia caused 4 of them. In the intervening years, the fatality rate has slipped to two per year. Yosemite's search and rescue division typically performs fifteen to twenty-five rescues of rock climbers annually.

In addition to the obvious risk of falling, there are numerous weather hazards, including thunderstorms that seemingly erupt out of nowhere. Torrents of rain may fall. Often the rain is near freezing and intermingled with hail. Sheets of runoff soak climbers, reducing

---

*The film documenting Erickson's and Higbee's feat, *Free Climb*, won many awards.

visibility and rendering the granite slick. If a storm rides in on a cold front, packing chill winds, potentially fatal hypothermia can overtake unprepared climbers.* Sometimes the wind is so fierce, it whips climbers from their moorings or sends their tent and supplies flying into the void.

Another serious danger is lightning, which imperils anyone exposed on a rock face. A direct lightning strike is unlikely, but lightning branches may lash the granite, shooting deadly electrical charges in any direction.** Stifling heat and insufficient water can also be dangerous. Some climbers become so dehydrated, they can't continue. Absent more water or a rescue, they die a slow death.

Anyone climbing Half Dome is particularly prone to weather attacks, because a system can slide into lower Yosemite without causing a disturbance, then unleash raw fury when it hits the Dome. Two climbers got trapped on its south face in October 1968 when a storm brought snow and freezing conditions. Hypothermia and a shortage of supplies threatened their lives. Expert climbers flown to the summit by helicopter rappelled down the face and rescued the pair.

DESPITE THE DANGERS and discomforts, climbing is for many an all-consuming passion. They interrupt, end, or never start their careers, focusing exclusively on completing the next climb. Climber Todd Skinner said free climbing means "going right to the edge" of your capabilities. For many climbers, this closeness to death—the risk of dying—produces an adrenaline rush that

---

*On October 21, 2004, a fierce, early-season snowstorm hit Yosemite and snared two Japanese climbers who were about two-thirds of the way up El Capitan. They were unprepared for such brutal conditions and died from exposure. Another climber was rescued.

**On June 25, 2000, four climbers were struck by lightning while climbing on Yosemite's Cathedral Peak. Three of the climbers lost consciousness and all of them suffered burns. One went into respiratory arrest. A rescue team reached the stricken party and, by ground evacuation, carried out the most seriously injured climber, who survived.

most other life experiences simply can't. It is what keeps many of them married to the sport. Probably no other sport creates such a feeling of oneness with Mother Nature. Attached to a mountainside by fingertips and toes, the climber necessarily becomes part of the rock—or else. One climber says that while scaling a granite face, she felt close to God, so intense was her relationship with the natural world.

Climbers speak of "floating" or "performing a ballet" over the rock, each placement of foot and each reach into a crack creating unity with the mountain. The sport is one of total engagement with the here-and-now, which frees the mind from everything else. Climbers' concentration is complete and focused. Their only thought is executing the next move.

Rock climbing has been called the King of Sports, not only because of the skills, courage, and mental conditioning it demands but also because it takes place in the grandest of places. There is no stadium, court, diamond, gym, field, or track that can rival nature's arena.

Ken Bokelund, who was on the face of Half Dome the day Rice, Esteban, and company battled nature at the summit, and who went on to become a highly accomplished climber, said: "Climbing for me has always been the strength of the body over the weakness of the mind. If you train so that you are very strong physically and you have mastered the techniques, then all that's left is believing. Freeing your mind of fear is the key. This is very difficult to do, but when you can achieve it, then you are in true harmony with the rock. Fear is just one more thing to worry about and is very distracting. It can make you fall.

"What sometimes happens when fear enters the climber's mind is sewing-machine leg—a leg that starts shaking out of control. It happens to all climbers at one time or another and obviously is very dangerous when one is clinging to the side of a rock. But when you know you are strong enough to complete any maneuver, once that level of physical confidence is achieved, then you are able to put fear out of your mind. Climbing becomes a very simple pleasure. It's just you and the rock. It's a total clarity of being, a time when nothing matters, you're moving without any thought, you're in a place where time stands still. Even when you're on a wall for days, when you get down, everything seems exactly the same, as though time never passed."

◄○►

BOKELUND AND ROB FOSTER, his climbing buddy, first hooked up at Burlingame High School in Burlingame, California, just south of San Francisco. Bokelund was five foot eight and weighed 140 pounds, undersized for most sports but just about perfect for rock climbing. A mountaineering school introduced him to the sport when he was in elementary school. In short order, he became a very good climber.

Before Foster got involved in rock climbing, he was generally unmotivated. He hung out with a group of other anti-establishment types in high school who cut classes, didn't do homework, smoked pot, and earned poor grades. Then Foster discovered climbing through Boy Scout camp. It changed his life. Like Bokelund, he was slim: 150 pounds on a five-foot, ten-inch, frame. He began eating well, exercising to build muscle, and climbing instead of bumming around. His schoolwork improved.

Rock climbing brought Bokelund and Foster together. With only a modest amount of climbing gear, the two started clambering up trees, buildings, rocks, stone bridges—whatever was available. Then they put their budding skills to the test at Castle Rock above the town of Saratoga in the South Bay, a big training rock for climbers. Each took a few falls and got banged up. Foster's mother insisted they get climbing instruction, so the pair enrolled in a two-day course at Lovers Leap near Lake Tahoe, where they learned technique and safety skills. After that, as Bokelund put it, their commitment to rock climbing soared "off the Richter scale."

They saved money and bought more equipment, and built a plywood climbing wall in Bokelund's backyard.

After graduating from high school in 1983, all Bokelund lived for was climbing. His lifestyle for many years was spartan; he earned just enough money at various jobs to pay for shelter and food. Unemployment checks sometimes filled the gaps. He played guitar for enjoyment.

Foster, a year behind Bokelund in high school, was also addicted to climbing. When few climbing challenges remained in the Bay Area, he and Bokelund set their sights on Yosemite. They developed climbing muscles—in their forearms, triceps, and lats—and worked religiously on technique. The pair was ready to tackle a big wall.

In summer 1984, they successfully scaled the south face of Washington Column, one of Yosemite's easier wall climbs. The next summer they planned to climb the face of Half Dome.

Their intent was to complete the ascent of the Northwest Face Regular Route in three days, beginning on Thursday, July 25. The two teens possessed the zeal of youth but not much in the way of sophisticated gear or clothing. With little money to fuel their passion, they scrimped and scrounged to get by. For the Half Dome ascent, they decided to go light, carrying only the bare necessities. All of the climbing gear weighed about thirty pounds. They chose not to bring their sleeping bags, which were too bulky and heavy. And they couldn't afford new, lighter ones. So each packed a canvas sack to sleep in, along with rain gear, wool pants, a synthetic shirt, and sleeping pad. They didn't pack gloves, although later they would be grateful to discover a stray pair in the bottom of a pack. Their single haul pack was an old army duffel bag. It contained their sleeping sacks and other items plus ropes, food, and climbing paraphernalia. By packing lean, they could lug eighteen liters of waters, which weighed about forty pounds—half the total weight of their stuffed haul bag.

Bokelund and Foster planned to employ several climbing techniques. Portions of the ascent would entail clean climbing—that is, using pitons and bolts already hammered in the granite, and their own removable protection. For sections rated above 5.10, they would do aid climbing—ascending their ropes using nylon ladders (called etriers), slings, and daisy chains. Otherwise, the pair would free climb—use only their hands and feet on the natural rock features while hitched to rope in case of a fall. They arrived in Yosemite on Wednesday, July 24.

Just reaching the base of the northwest face poses a physical challenge for climbers who are carting loads of gear. There are two approaches.

One involves hiking to Sub Dome, as do those headed up Half Dome via the cables, and then skirting the hump and traversing the base of the cliff to its bottom. This stretch alone takes more than six hours. Some climbers, especially guides with clients, rent mules to haul their gear—including cushy sleeping bags, portaledges, wine, good food, and other comforts—to the staging area.

The second approach entails a three-hour scramble through the slabs, a rocky jumble at the bottom of the face where the footing is treacherous and the route so confusing that climbers may not arrive at their intended destination. A spring at the base supplies drinking water.

That first day, Bokelund and Foster hiked the eight-plus miles to the base of Sub Dome and then descended the circuitous route to the bottom of the face, where they camped for the night. They began their climb at sunrise on Thursday.

Their first day on the rock went well. The only others ahead of them were a guide with his female client, about half a day up. Clouds materialized, but no storm. Light showers doused the mountain that night. Although it was midsummer, moisture, wind, and low mountain temperatures made for chilly nights on Half Dome's face. Bokelund and Foster slept tied in on a sloping ledge, snuggled in their canvas sacks and wearing wool pants and synthetic shirts for additional warmth. Each wore one of the two gloves from the stray pair that fortunately showed up; each tucked the other hand inside his clothing.

On day two, after thirteen pitches, they reached the halfway point by midafternoon. They had successfully executed the Robbins Traverse and were on schedule. However, a storm was building. By 3 P.M., the sky had darkened. Then it unleashed a deluge. For the next hour, rain hammered the two climbers, soaking them to the bone despite their rain gear. Not wanting to get caught on the exposed rock directly above, they sought protection at the Chimney, where they could wait out the storm. When lightning zapped the summit, though, both absorbed several electrical shocks. An extremely frightened Foster wanted to rappel down and get off the face, while Bokelund urged calmness. In the back of his mind was the potential loss of their meager but cherished equipment, all two hundred dollars' worth, if they retreated down the mountain without it.

But as savage lightning bolts flailed Yosemite's granite, repeatedly shocking the two men, Bokelund had second thoughts. Maybe it wasn't so wise to hunker down after all; maybe they should retreat. On the other hand, a descent would require thirteen rappels down the thirteen pitches that had taken them half a day to complete, not the least of which was Robbins Traverse. Rappelling down that stretch wouldn't be quick or easy, much less safe. Indeed, rappelling under any conditions is dangerous. Most climbing fatalities occur on descents rather than ascents, when climbers don't rappel properly or rappel off the end of their rope or slip off a steep trail while hiking down from the summit. Bokelund and Foster stayed put. They were trapped.

Patches of sky soon appeared among the rain clouds. The end of the storm was in sight. When the rain stopped and sun broke out, Bokelund and Foster committed themselves to completing the climb as the best of two bad choices. Water still poured down the mountain through chutes and crevices. To decide who should lead the climb at that point, they played the game ro-sham-bo, or rock-paper-scissors. Foster lost. Up he went, out onto wet granite and the bare section. Meanwhile the guide and female climber far ahead had boogied up the face as fast as they could to reach the summit, leaving only Bokelund and Foster on the wall by late Friday. That night it rained some more. Bokelund and Foster, hunkered down on a ledge to sleep as best they could, were wetter and colder than they had ever been.

On Saturday, July 27, with Foster still leading the way, they scrambled up the granite. Only six pitches separated them from the top. Frantic to reach the summit, they wedged their fingers and toes in crevices, and balanced on tiny ledges and whatever rock protrusions were available. Storm clouds began building again—this time, later in the afternoon. Again, the situation became risky. Although the climbers were farther up the face, they were even more vulnerable closer to the summit. Fear drove them—they were desperate to evade another lightning barrage. Bokelund and Foster willed their bodies to work harder, to overcome exhaustion. Their physical conditioning was pushed to the limit.

At 4 P.M., menacing storm clouds were moving toward the Dome. Flashes of lightning and rumbling thunder carried a very clear message. The pair traversed Thank God Ledge, pulled themselves up the remaining smooth face on ropes, and, by means of hasty mantle maneuvers, surmounted the last section of rock around 5 P.M. But there was no time for celebration. They felt terror rather than glee. Foster spotted a small rock enclosure in the Visor and wanted to take cover there until the storm passed.

It was the same enclosure awaiting Esteban and Rice, who at that moment were gunning for the summit.

Nothin' doin', said Bokelund. We need to get the hell off this mountain!

In a frenzy, they stuffed the gear in their packs and raced off. Bokelund and Foster scurried down the granite slope so quickly, half slipping and sliding, that they burned their hands on the metal cables. At the base of Half Dome, they ran across the saddle, up to the top of Sub Dome, and then down the granite stairs. Farther along, two backpackers—Esteban and Rice—were coming up the trail.

Bokelund and Foster warned the two older hikers not to go up there, it was way too dangerous. They then scampered down the trail with one goal in mind: to put as much distance as possible between them and the ferocious storm brewing over Half Dome.

5

THE STORM

When the glorious pearl and alabaster clouds of these noonday storms are being built, I never give attention to anything else. No mountain or mountain-range, however divinely clothed with light, has a more enduring charm than those fleeting mountains of the sky. . . .—John Muir

S torms were brewing across the Sierra Nevada, threatening any sightseer or wanderer who was ignorant or dismissive of their power. Mounting thunderheads accompanied the hikers pressing on toward Half Dome, each intent on reaching the summit.

Hoog's contingent departed Nevada Fall and hiked as a tight unit. Pippey and Jordan left shortly afterward and quickly passed them on the trail. Also skirting by them were Esteban, Rice, and Brian Jordan. Frith and Weiner lagged; the forty-five-pound pack they took turns hefting was bogging them down. Buchner and Ellner were nowhere in sight.

Cage's party was farther back. Their later start and slightly longer hike from Glacier Point meant they would arrive on the summit around 6:30 P.M. if they stayed the course.

The mounting storm soon would require that the hikers respond in some fashion. However, none really knew the capacities, behaviors, and dangers of thunderstorms. On that particular day, they would base their decisions more on misinformation, happenstance, and emotion than knowledge.

-◄o►-

THUNDERSTORMS HOLD massive quantities of energy, one of the most powerful of which is lightning—a random, chaotic, and treacherous phenomenon. Every thunderstorm demands respect. One may occupy a confined cloud mass and appear quite tame. A distant observer might see telltale gray streaks directly below the cloud, indicating rain. Perhaps a streak of lightning flashes within the cloud, followed by a peal of thunder. This confined type of storm represents, in John Muir's words, a "Sierra mid-summer thunderstorm reduced to its lowest terms." Yet it can form abruptly and then suddenly unleash a deadly lightning bolt that strikes objects directly below or several miles away where the sky is blue.

A mountain thunderstorm spanning thousands of acres can be a violent, tumultuous affair. Driving, flooding rains accompany sheets of hail and terrifying lightning bolts that lash out from anywhere at any time, savagely blasting whatever stands in the way. Explosive cracks of thunder shatter the atmosphere as though it were made of fine china, prompting sheer terror in anyone caught in the inferno. As lightning strikes here, there, and everywhere, the thunderbolts bring ear-piercing booms so intermingled with sheets of blinding light that it can be difficult to pair each flash with each roar. This is Mother Nature in one of her most overwhelming displays of power.

Watching a thunderstorm from a safe haven can be glorious beyond words. It is a symphony of mesmerizing sounds, sights, and smells.

◄o►

IN CONTRAST TO weather systems that originate over the Pacific Ocean, Sierra Nevada thunderstorms develop inland. The moisture comes from the Pacific, but initially it is stored in the air rather than in clouds. The air flows across California's Central Valley, rises, and accumulates in thermals, or ascending currents of air. As the thermals drift toward the mountains, warm air from the foothills propels them upward. At higher elevations, infusions of warmer air from canyons and valleys send the thermals spiraling farther aloft, where they meet colder air. This mixing destabilizes the atmosphere; countless crystals and droplets combine to form a puffy, white cumulus cloud—frequently the first harbinger of a thunderstorm.

If other cumulus clouds develop in the vicinity, they often combine into a single, large cloud or sometimes clusters of clouds. This mass may hover over one mountain peak in an otherwise clear sky but can move in any direction.

Because air surrounding the cloud is cooler, the warmer air within keeps funneling upward, creating the cloud's vertical shape. In the troposphere (the lowest, densest part of the atmosphere), this ascending parcel encounters lower air pressure, which causes the cloud to expand and cool as its interior air mass becomes saturated with moisture. Ice ultimately forms within the cloud. When this mass becomes too heavy to keep rising, precipitation falls as rain, hail, or snow—sometimes all three. When the mass reaches the tropopause (the boundary layer between the troposphere and stratosphere above), where the temperature is constant, it stops rising and the cloud top flattens into a fearsome anvil shape. This is a cumulonimbus cloud, or thunderhead.

Cumulonimbus clouds are vast, dark, moisture-laden, and formidable. They may tower twenty to forty thousand feet into the atmosphere—even, in the case of a super thunder cell, sixty thousand feet. Ragged formations called scuds hang down menacingly from tops that push up against an invisible ceiling. Within the thunderhead, violent updrafts and downdrafts generate enormous power and energy, resulting in fierce winds and torrents of rain. Sometimes the updrafts break through the flattened cloud top and punch into the stratosphere. This so-called overshooting of the top usually portends the most severe of thunderstorms.

Often accompanying such fury is a frenzied but usually short-lived barrage of hail. Hail is formed by water droplets freezing as they climb within a cloud, dropping back down and picking up more water, then rising again. The frozen droplets may repeat this cycle hundreds of times, adding layer upon layer and increasing in size until, too heavy to remain aloft, they fall to earth. Hail can be as small as a pea or, in midwestern states, as big as a baseball or even a volleyball. Hail in the Sierra Nevada seldom exceeds half an inch in diameter.

At any given moment, nearly two thousand thunderstorms are happening somewhere on earth. More than forty thousand occur every day, sixteen million each year. They keep the planet's heat stores in equilibrium: The vast quantities of moisture in the air that result when sunlight reaches and heats the earth, causing evaporation, are returned to the earth by thunderstorms. The moisture evaporates into the air again, and the cycle begins anew.

A thunderstorm may develop quickly, although not without advance notice. Especially in the afternoon, cumulus clouds can darken and thicken fast and then rapidly evolve into more menacing cumulonimbus clouds. The one-cloud storm, or single-cell thunderstorm, doesn't linger for long. Larger thunderstorms have multiple cells—clusters of storms that combine and feed off each other and that widen and prolong the turbulence. This process sometimes occurs in a predictable pattern, as it does over Florida, where thunderheads form on many afternoons.

Thunderstorms have three stages: developing, mature, and dissipating.

The developing stage, amid high convection turbulence and air movement, is very dangerous, especially for people who are caught unprepared (as frequently happens) or don't take precautions quickly. Lightning can strike ten miles ahead of the storm where skies are still blue—hence the phrase *a bolt out of the blue.* Because every bolt originates in a storm cloud, one can exit from a concealed cloud—a cloud behind a mountain ridge, for instance—and literally streak sideways to hit something miles away. It seemingly strikes from out of nowhere.

The heaviest precipitation, winds, and lightning take place in the mature stage, which can last from a few minutes to several hours. Surprisingly, fewer people are killed or injured during the raging chaos of this stage than during the developing phase, maybe because fewer people are outdoors and exposed.

In the dissipating stage, rain and lightning activity decreases as the storm winds down. But even as thunderheads move away from the immediate region, lightning bolts may continue to strike it. The safety rule is to wait at least thirty minutes after a storm has passed before venturing out.

During the summer in mountainous regions, thunderstorms typically develop between 2 and 6 P.M., the hottest time of day. That's also when the descending angle of the sun's rays prompts a temperature drop higher up in the atmosphere, which in turn creates atmospheric instability. The storm's precipitation snuffs out the warm updrafts of air—its fuel—and the thunderstorm ends. Once again, nature has achieved the homeostatic balance it seeks.

The wise mountaineer follows this rule: *Up high by noon, down low by two.*

—◄○►—

A STORM CAN GENERATE lightning, its most menacing element, only when hail and ice form in a cloud. When turbulence causes these icy particles to collide, the electrical charges within the cloud divide. Positive charges usually travel to the top and negative charges to the base, thereby creating a giant storage battery. Because the earth below a thunderhead also becomes positively charged, there is a potential for cloud-to-ground electrical transmission. It's the attraction of these opposing charges—also within a cloud and between clouds—that produces lightning. Again, nature equalizes opposing forces and achieves stability.

Various forms of lightning play out. The flash from a discharge within a cloud or between clouds, which often resembles a bursting bomb or fireworks, is called sheet lightning. A single jagged bolt from cloud to ground is streak lightning, and a bolt with multiple branches or "leaders" is forked lightning.

Strong, horizontal winds can cause streak lightning to appear as parallel luminous or blurred bands with multiple flashes, a phenomenon known as ribbon lightning. When parts of a lightning streak are longer lit or brighter than other parts, it is bead lightning, or rocket or chain lightning. Ball lightning is just that—a sphere that seems to float in the air and then disappear in a loud explosion. Typically the size of a baseball, ball lightning can be as much as a foot in diameter. People have seen such lightning balls bounce off walls within a structure or tumble down mountainsides.

When the buildup of opposite charges is insufficient for lightning to form, a coronal discharge or circular bluish glow—or even a mass of sparks—may appear over a high, sometimes pointed object. This phenomenon, first noted at the top of ships' masts, is called St. Elmo's fire, for the patron saint of sailors.

About one in four lightning bolts strikes the ground. These spectacular exchanges between cloud and ground occur when tremendous negative charges of static electricity build in the bottom of a cloud, and positive charges accumulate on the ground.

Their strong attraction to each other creates an electrified or ionized atmosphere that can make the air buzz and crackle, and a person's hair bristle. When the potential for a discharge overwhelms the insulating air's ability to keep them apart, the negative charges shoot down toward the positive charges in an invisible, jagged, zigzag pattern called a stepped leader.

An object on the ground—usually one that is elevated, such as a tree, building, or rock—may launch a discharge, or lightning streamers, to connect with the leaders, thus triggering a lightning bolt, which neutralizes the opposing charges. This process can recur tens or even hundreds of times in a storm. An observer usually sees the discharge shooting upward—manifested by upward branching —to meet the downward-moving stepped leader.

In mountainous areas, where clouds are close to earth, the lightning bolt may be shorter than three hundred feet. In flat country with high clouds, a cloud-to-earth flash may be as long as four miles and, in some extreme instances, twenty miles long. The intensely bright lightning core is extremely narrow—as little as half an inch, according to some authorities. The core appears to be wider because it is surrounded by a glow discharge, or corona envelope, that may be ten to twenty feet wide. The speed of the lightning discharge varies between a hundred and a thousand miles per second for the downward leader track and up to eighty-seven thousand miles per second for the more powerful return stroke. More than one discharge can happen in the same lightning bolt, a process that causes lighting to flicker until the charges have dissipated.

Sometimes the polarity within a cloud is inverted: Negative particles ascend and positive ones descend. In inverted polarity, positive charges in the bottom of the cloud first rush to the ground and create a lightning channel. Electrons then flow from the ground up through the channel back to the cloud. Such reversed, "positive cloud-to-ground" lightning strikes usually carry more charge, last tens of milliseconds longer, and are less branched than the more common negative to-ground lightning. Why or how this reversal of charge occurs is unknown. Indeed, there is much about lightning that remains a mystery.

One hundred lightning bolts strike hit the earth every second, or more than 8.6 million a day. Annually, twenty million lightning bolts strike the ground in the United States.

A lightning bolt can contain an electrical potential of one hundred million volts and reach a temperature of fifty-five thousand degrees Fahrenheit, which is five times hotter than the sun. The average flash is brighter than ten million, hundred-watt lightbulbs. A single strike can generate more energy than all U.S. power plants combined at that instant. Theoretically, a thunderstorm could meet the nation's electricity needs for four days.

Lightning has an impact on more than just the atmosphere: Its electrons can travel beyond the upper atmosphere and affect the radiation belt in the ionosphere for several hundred thousand square miles. A lightning strike in Texas, for example, might influence the radiation belt over South Dakota.

It all happens in a brilliant, single one-thousandth of a second.

WHEN INTENSE HEAT generated by lightning causes the surrounding air to expand explosively, the resulting shock wave, also referred to as a sonic boom, is thunder. Sound travels at about eleven hundred feet per second, so it takes five seconds for the sound of thunder to reach someone a mile away. In contrast, light travels at 186,300 miles per second; anyone near or far who has a clear view can see a lightning flash instantaneously. Counting the seconds between a lightning flash and thunderclap is an easy way to gauge how far away the lightning is. Importantly, the distance between one lightning strike and the next in a sequence of strikes can be six to eight miles. If someone hears thunder forty seconds or less after the flash, the lightning is eight miles or less away—in other words, within striking distance of that person. Whenever you can hear thunder, the next lightning bolt can strike you.

When a lightning strike will occur is completely unpredictable. Moreover, there is no safe interval between one bolt and the next; the second may follow almost immediately. *Where* a lightning bolt will hit is more predictable, although still a crapshoot. Lightning usually assails the closest and most accessible object, not necessarily the highest point, as many people believe. It's more a matter of which objects *respond* to electrical charges in the cloud. The downward-moving stepped leader from the cloud draws a reaction or discharge from the closest point, which often is the highest object around, such as a tall tree, rock outcropping, or mountain summit. And contrary to popular belief, metal does not attract lightning. It does, however, concentrate and conduct electricity far more efficiently than most other materials.

After a lightning bolt hits something directly, the electrical charges may then shoot off in multiple directions, conducted by receptive matter such as water or damp ground, rock, or trees.

◄o►

LIGHTNING CAN DEVASTATE a human being. Except for floods, it kills more people in the United States annually than any other weather event. In each of the last thirty years, on average, lightning killed sixty-seven people and injured about three hundred in this country. However, these are only documented cases. The true number of fatalities may be closer to a hundred and the number of injuries well in excess of five hundred—there is no requirement that lightning injuries be reported, and many victims don't seek treatment.

Based on reported data, the odds that people living in America will be struck by lightning are about one in seven hundred thousand. Including the additional estimated deaths and injuries puts the odds at 1 in 240,000. The odds that you will be struck in your lifetime are one in three thousand, while your chance of being affected by someone who has been struck is one in three hundred. Those who live where there are numerous thunderstorms and who spend a lot of time outdoors are at much higher risk.

From 1990 through 2003, the most lightning deaths each year occurred in Florida—twice as many as in any other state—followed by Texas, Colorado, Ohio, and North Carolina. Eighty percent of all lightning fatalities are male. A man playing golf in Florida is at high risk. Tampa Bay has been dubbed the nation's lightning capital.

There are four ways lightning can injure: by striking directly, by striking an object that someone is in contact with, by using the human body as a pathway, and by ground current, also known as step voltage. In each case, injuries may result from the electrical discharge itself or from mechanical trauma—in other words, if the victim is "thrown" by a muscle contraction or suffers a fall. The shock wave from a lightning strike can hurl a person many feet. Those who are thrown on the ground or against a tree, boulder, or other hard obstacle may sustain contusions, internal organ damage, bleeding, fractures, or concussions.

Lightning hits people indirectly much more often than it does directly. A person standing under or near a tree usually is injured or killed by an indirect strike, sometimes referred to as splashing or a side flash. Someone in an enclosure, such as a cave or crevice, or under an overhanging rock, or in a chimney on a rock wall, might be at greater risk: If lightning strikes in the vicinity, the charge can travel on the ground or rock—especially when it's wet—and streak within the enclosed space. Because rock is solid and therefore highly resistant to penetration and the flow of current, lightning shoots across its surface. A person in contact with that surface draws the whipping electrical charge because the human body is far less resistant than the rock.

Some lightning injuries and deaths occur indoors. Lightning can enter homes and buildings directly, through externally exposed wires or pipes, or through the ground. Once inside, electrical, telephone, plumbing, and radio/television systems, and any metal wires or bars in the walls or floor, can conduct the charge. If these things aren't grounded—that is, able to conduct the charge into earth, where it dissipates—the lightning may jump through the air as it seeks a better or different path. A person nearby could become the new conductor. Lightning has claimed the lives of people who were washing dishes, taking a shower or bath, talking on the phone, or standing near an appliance.

Critical to any electrical shock, whether from lightning or a home outlet, is the degree to which it passes through or over a human body. A body's condition can either enhance or minimize that passage. Dry, clean skin tends to resist electricity, while wet skin—say, from rain or sweat—offers little or no resistance and easily becomes a conductor. Even ten to fifty volts, which normally causes only a mild tingling, can generate a strong shock if you have damp, sweaty, salty hands. Increase the voltage to beyond 50 volts and touching a live wire will give you a good jolt—and possibly kill you if you're immersed in water, such as a bathtub. A shock from 220-volt wiring, which is standard in American homes, can cause severe injury or even death. Shocks from industrial accidents (responsible for about eight hundred deaths a year in the United States) typically involve a range of twenty thousand up to sixty-three thousand volts.

But that pales in comparison with one lightning bolt, which typically packs an electrical potential of fifteen million volts.

—◄○►—

PERHAPS SURPRISINGLY, only about 10 percent of those struck by lightning die. The most dangerous and potentially fatal injuries involve the cardiovascular and neurological systems. The only cause of immediate death from lightning is cardiac arrest or the complications thereof, partly because electrical energy tends to travel through the least resistant parts of the body, especially blood vessels, which lead to the heart. Normally, only immediate and effective cardiovascular pulmonary resuscitation, followed as soon as possible by emergency medical treatment, can save cardiac-arrest victims or help them counter the serious consequences of cerebral hypoxia, a lack of oxygen in the brain. If lightning victims' hearts don't stop, the chances that they will die from any other cause directly attributable to the lightning injury are low—but only if medical care is readily available.

Fortunately for lightning victims, most strikes aren't fatal. Despite the enormous voltage, the current passes over the surface of their body, a process called external flashover. Minimal current enters it. Additionally, the extremely short duration of a lightning shock, measured in milliseconds, results in a very brief flow of current internally or externally. The result: little, if any, skin breakdown. Burns or tissue destruction may be insignificant.

Even though lightning injuries may not be lethal, however, they can be severely traumatic and damaging to the victim and also very stressful for the family. Because such injuries are primarily neurological, they may entail sleep disturbances, memory and attention deficits, dizziness, chronic fatigue, irritability, depression, severe headaches, anxiety attacks, acute pain syndromes, peripheral nerve damage, and fear of storms. A person's "software" gets scrambled. Some victims develop an intense pain syndrome from injury to the nervous system, a condition that is almost impossible to cure. These symptoms may make it impossible for the victim to hold a job, which poses dire financial consequences for the family.

When lightning strikes near the head, it can enter orifices such as the eyes, ears, and mouth. That may explain the myriad eye and ear maladies related to lightning injury. If lightning does flow internally, it can short-circuit the body's electrical systems, leading to temporary tinnitus, blindness, confusion, amnesia, cardiac arrhythmias, and vascular instability. Other indirect consequences may include severe brain damage and seizures caused by hypoxia during cardiac arrest.

Some people have been zapped by lightning more than once. Roy "Dooms" Sullivan, a former ranger in Shenandoah National Park in Virginia, holds the somewhat dubious record. Between 1942 and 1977, he allegedly survived seven lightning strikes—at a campsite, while fishing, in his front yard, backyard, in a fire tower, inside a ranger station, and while driving a Jeep. Sullivan committed suicide in 1983 because someone he loved rejected him.

Far behind this record holder are several people who have been struck "only" three times.

-◄o►-

ALTHOUGH LIGHTNING and mountains go hand in hand, the numbers of deaths in mountainous national parks have been surprisingly few. (Data on lightning injuries in the parks are largely unavailable.) Still, even under routine circumstances by park standards, lightning has brought grief to a number of individuals and families.

Most visitors to Yellowstone National Park are aware of the frequent thunderstorms there. Yet lightning deaths since Yellowstone opened in 1872 have totaled only five. One occurred on Yellowstone Lake beneath a blue sky when a bolt from a cloud hidden behind a mountain ridge struck a boater directly in his head. The other four were a canoeist on Lewis Lake, a sheepherder standing next to a lake, a hiker on a mountain ridge who fell two hundred feet after he was struck, and a twenty-one-year-old man who had left his broken-down truck and taken refuge under a large tree during a rainstorm.

Sharing a border with Yellowstone is Grand Teton National Park, with mountain peaks towering above thirteen thousand feet that entice hikers and climbers. Grand Teton, designated a park in 1929, has recorded fatalities since 1950. Lightning has caused just one death there. (Another one occurred just outside the park's boundary on 11,101-foot Table Mountain.) The fatality happened in July 2003 among a party of thirteen climbers. Nearing Grand Teton summit, the climbers began a hasty retreat when a thunderstorm erupted. Six reached a ledge called Friction Pitch, and one, a twenty-five-year-old mother of two tots, settled down alongside a large puddle of water. Suddenly a buzz filled the air; then a colossal lightning bolt lashed the mountain. A climber on the ledge was toppled and plummeted fifty feet before a safety rope arrested his fall; he dangled out in space upside down. Seated next to the woman at puddle's edge was her husband. The lightning knocked him momentarily unconscious. When he awoke, his wife wasn't breathing, her lips and throat were black, and her clothing was shredded. The puddle was gone; lightning had completely vaporized it. Despite intensive CPR, the woman couldn't be revived. In all, seven hikers suffered injuries, five seriously. The clouds parted about three hours later, and two private companies carried out a dangerous two-helicopter rescue operation. In gusting winds one helo picked up the dead and injured one by one from Friction Pitch and whisked them down to a second helo holding at Lower Saddle, where they were flown to the meadows below and then transported to a hospital.*

Rocky Mountain National Park, with its high mountains, numerous trails above ten thousand feet, and frequent thunderstorms, has been the scene of ten lightning deaths. The park boasts the nation's highest continuous paved road—Trail Ridge Road— much of which is above the tree line. The road crosses the Continental Divide at Milner Pass at 12,183 feet. All but two of the fatalities happened above eleven thousand feet, including three alongside Trail Ridge Road. Another three involved climbers on or near mountain peaks. The two exceptions were a motorcyclist and a hiker, both of whom got stuck at about seventy-five hundred feet in elevation.

You might think that lightning is a killer on 14,494-foot Mount Whitney in Sequoia National Park. In fact, there have been only two deaths. The first occurred in 1904 when eight federal fish commissioners were researching golden trout in the region. A thunderstorm broke out, and all but one in the group sought shelter under a rock shelf near the summit. A direct lightning strike killed the exposed man standing on the rock; two of his compan-

---

*The two helicopter pilots, Laurence Perry and Rick Harmon, were both honored with the Pilot of the Year Award for 2003 by Helicopter Association International.

ions were knocked unconscious but survived. The second fatality happened on a July afternoon in 1990 when a thunderstorm battered the summit. All thirteen people there felt the ground zinging; their hair stood on end. They took shelter in the Smithsonian Hut located on the summit, a historic structure with rock walls, a cement floor, and a corrugated iron roof. While inside, the hikers heard the rock walls and concrete humming, followed by several booms and a bright flash. Then, according to eyewitnesses, a white and yellow ball of lightning one foot in diameter bounced off each of the four walls before exploding in a loud crack. One person was knocked unconscious, another suffered third-degree burns, and the rest incurred minor burns and numbness. The unconscious victim, a twenty-six-year-old man, stopped breathing and had no heartbeat; intensive CPR by those in the hut failed to revive him. A helicopter evacuated him to a hospital, where he was pronounced dead.

His family and three people who were injured filed suit against the National Park Service, contending it should have posted a warning about the danger of occupying the hut in a storm. The court upheld their claim.*

Sequoia National Park was the site of another lightning fatality. It took place on Moro Rock, a 6,725-foot granite dome that juts out from the forested surroundings like a giant thumb. Much as on Half Dome, a quarter-mile trail follows Moro Rock's contour and leads hikers up a 325-foot elevation gain to the summit, which offers a sweeping view of the Great Western Divide to the east. Some sections of the human-made, five-foot-wide trail are concrete, and large granite slabs have been placed elsewhere as steps. An iron railing traces the outer side of the trail, while a rock wall borders the other side.

On August 20, 1975, about twenty-five people—half of them children between seven and fifteen years old—were on the Moro Rock summit trail. The day was clear—only three cottony cumu-

---

*The disposition of this lawsuit will be covered in chapter 10, Aftermath.

lus clouds occupied the distant sky. But the clouds consolidated, enlarged, and started moving swiftly toward Moro Rock. Soon a sea of black loomed over the dome. It started to sprinkle. Several hikers felt electricity in the air; hands tingled and hair bristled. The sprinkles morphed into a deluge of rain, then a barrage of hail, prompting most of the hikers to retreat hastily to their cars.

One party halfway up the trail included Lawrence Brady and his wife, mother, and two sons (ages seven and nine), along with the wife's brother and mother. To escape the driving hail, they hugged the rock wall while heading back down. Brady's shoulder was leaning against the granite when a ferocious lightning bolt struck, illuminating Moro Rock in a spectacular flash. Electrical charges streaked about the dome, blasting stone into fragments wherever the trail's iron pipe touched it and sending rock splinters and dust into the air.

Brady exclaimed, "My God, we've been hit by lightning!"

His wife checked first on their two screaming sons, then him. By then, the thirty-one-year-old man was lying facedown on his mother-in-law's lap, unconscious. The electrical charge must have struck his shoulder before it shot across his body, giving him just enough time to utter something. When his wife turned him over, she saw his pupils beginning to dilate and his tongue in a gag reflex. She hit him hard in the chest a couple of times, then cleared his airway and mouth with her fingers and began mouth-to-mouth resuscitation. A trained nurse arrived to help with CPR. After several more minutes, two park officials appeared and took charge. They administered oxygen.

Meanwhile, two other rangers came racing up the trail to check on another victim, Edward Schieler, a thirty-eight-year-old man who had been struck directly in the head while snapping photos on the summit. The lightning whizzed down his entire body, shredded all his clothes, exposed even his genitals, and blew off his left hiking boot. Only the cuff of his pants clung to the shod foot. The blast threw him beyond the railing, where his convulsing body teetered near the edge, about to topple over to certain death. Fortunately, his uninjured cousin was able to lift him back. He and another man grasped Schieler's arms and legs and began carting him down the trail. When the two rangers met them, the victim's eyes were slightly dilated, his pulse was weak and fast, and his coloration slightly bluish. He was incoherent and his body shook violently, but he was still breathing. Blood oozed from his ear and nose, and burn wounds and cuts covered his entire front side. A hole the size of a quarter perforated the bottom of his left foot. On the stretcher, he twisted and turned. His arms lashed out reflexively, and at one point he grabbed the railing. He vomited twice, which forced the rangers to stop and turn him on his side so he wouldn't choke. They doubted he would survive.

In the case of Brady, rangers continued administering oxygen and CPR to the man where he lay, despite the still-raging storm. At one point, his pupils constricted back to normal, his lips and ears became pink, and his tongue relaxed. But soon, his pupils began dilating again and his skin returned to a bluish tint. He had "doll's eyes"—completely blank. Further efforts to revive him were futile. More than an hour after the lightning first struck, the rangers concluded that he was gone. They asked the family to go to the nearby visitor center so the two young boys would be spared the sight of their father, then hoisted him down to the parking lot. An ambulance took him to a hospital, where he was pronounced dead.

Schieler also was taken to a hospital. Doctors there determined he had a severe skull fracture, probable brain damage, and injuries to his arteries and organs. He remained in critical condition for several days and was hospitalized for three weeks. According to his physician, Schieler's exceptionally strong heart kept him alive. But he sustained a total loss of hearing in one ear and a 90 percent loss in the other. A hernia protruded into his bowel; the resulting blockage caused severe hemorrhoids that eventually had to be surgically removed. Ever since the episode, he has suffered bouts of acute depression and fits of imbalance that have prevented enjoyment of most physical activities. Kidney and prostate problems also developed years later. He was unable to work again, and his family endured financial hardship.

Mr. Schieler and Mrs. Brady each filed suit against the National Park Service. They argued that a sign should have been posted warning hikers about the danger of hiking on Moro Rock in thunderstorms. The courts did not uphold this lawsuit.*

—◄○►—

UP TO 1985, only three lightning deaths had definitely occurred in Yosemite, with a fourth possibility. The first happened in May 1921, when lightning struck a worker at Hetch Hetchy Reservoir, and the second in July 1936, when a middle-age man was killed at the Tuolumne Meadows garbage dump.

The third took place on August 27, 1972. Randall Boone and Edward Williams were on the first leg of a two-week camping adventure when they departed Yosemite Valley at midmorning en route to Half Dome. These best of friends, both in their late teens, had graduated the previous year from Serramonte High School in Daly City, just south of San Francisco.

Only one downy-white cumulus cloud drifted in the west as they ascended the trail past Vernal and Nevada falls. The sky directly above was still blue when Boone and Williams started up Sub Dome. But by that time, the single cloud—behind Half Dome, out of view—had joined other cumulus clouds to form a giant thunderhead that eclipsed lower Yosemite Valley and was moving rapidly.

Atop Half Dome, they encountered a gray, leaden cloud mass, its furls folding over one another like ocean waves. As Boone and Williams savored the sweeping vistas at 3:30 P.M., the dense cloud suddenly unleashed a torrent. The pair weren't prepared for rain, so they frantically sought cover in and around the rock forms

---

* The disposition of this lawsuit will be covered in chapter 10, Aftermath.

sprinkled about the smooth granite surface. Near the edge, they peered down into a crevice and spotted refuge—a chamber tucked within a jumble of rocks. A solid stone ceiling kept it dry.

Nearby, a hollow, two-foot-high iron pipe jutted up. Someone had drilled a hole in the granite and planted the pipe there for an unknown reason.

Boone and Williams slid into the shelter. It was the driest place on Half Dome, aside from a tent. Within minutes, two other damp hikers squeezed in. The four men huddled together while the storm played out its drama. Through openings in the rock, they saw lightning slice occasionally through the thick, wet air.

Boone reached for his camera in the hope of snagging a photo. That's the last thing he remembers. Lightning hammered the Dome and shot through the cave, slamming his head against the stone wall and knocking him out.

When he regained consciousness, Boone saw Williams slumped over, not breathing. The other two occupants, who also had been knocked unconscious briefly, were alert by then, too. No one knew CPR. Boone frantically attempted to breathe air into his best friend's mouth, and when that didn't revive Williams, the three men hastily carried him a couple of hundred yards over to where other campers were. One tried unsuccessfully to find a pulse. Boone again tried mouth-to-mouth resuscitation but finally gave up. Williams was dead.

Park officials attributed Williams's death to the iron pipe. Lightning had struck the pipe, they theorized, zoomed into the chamber via wet granite, entered the back of Williams's head where it rested against the rock, and exited from his foot. Rangers ultimately sawed off the iron pipe, leaving a protrusion less than two inches long.

Yosemite's records on a fourth fatality possibly due to lightning are not definitive. The case is instructive nonetheless. In June, Timothy Clark, 22 years old, had been hiking in Yosemite's high country when he got caught in a lightning storm. Desperate, he abandoned all of his gear, descended the mountain and hiked five miles back to Merced Lake High Sierra Camp, where he told persons he got struck by lightning. Observers noted during the next couple of days that he behaved strangely and was somewhat disoriented about his location. After another two days had passed, Clark set out on the four-mile hike back to Yosemite Valley. He left the trail at one point, walked onto a grassy ledge, and apparently fell to the switchback below. Hikers later stumbed upon his body and notified a trail crew working at Merced Lake. Authorities later confirmed that Clark had died as a result of the fall. But if he had indeed been struck by lightning as he claimed, then it may have been the true culprit by causing erratic behavior that led to the mishap.

◄o►

ON SATURDAY, JULY 27, 1985, as the Rice, Hoog, and Cage parties, along with other hikers, tramped toward Half Dome, another tragedy was unfolding just to the south.

Kings Canyon National Park, which borders Sequoia National Park, is only forty miles from Yosemite as the crow flies. It took John Muir several weeks to travel there from Yosemite Valley with a pack mule named Brownie. His purpose was to locate groves of giant sequoia trees, an effort that eventually led to their protection from timber mills. Today the drive from Yosemite Valley to the lower reaches of Kings Canyon takes three or four hours.

James Wunrow, twenty-seven, who worked on a park survey crew in Kings Canyon, left early that Saturday morning for a day hike by himself. He didn't tell anyone where he was going; nor did anyone see him leave, including the ranger who at 7 A.M. opened the Roads End Permit Station at Cedar Grove, located at the eastern end of the canyon. Wunrow must have started up Bubbs Creek Trail before the ranger arrived, aiming for the high country.

In 1984, while trimming trees for the Forest Service in Superior National Forest in Minnesota, Wunrow had touched a live power line and received a severe shock. Ever since, he had been prone to intense headaches. His co-workers and supervisors in Kings Canyon found Wunrow to be extremely introverted and often depressed, even disoriented at times. Wunrow wasn't a skilled or knowledgeable outdoorsman. He took only day hikes, always alone, and stayed on maintained trails.

The weather pattern that week had been consistent—warm, clear mornings followed by a buildup of midafternoon storm clouds, then an hour or two of heavy rain and some lightning. On that particular Saturday, however, thunderheads began building earlier, around midday. By one o'clock, a severe thunderstorm had moved east from Kern Canyon into the Bubbs Creek drainage. At one thirty, Wunrow was hiking back when, about four miles from the Cedar Grove trailhead, a violent thunderstorm swept in, producing high winds, drenching rains, fierce hail, and frequent lightning bursts. He was on a moderately forested hillside at sixty-three hundred feet in elevation, about three hundred feet below the ridgeline and up from the gully where Bubbs Creek flows. Wearing only a T-shirt, jeans, and baseball cap, Wunrow donned a long-sleeved wool shirt that he had wisely brought along. He hurriedly searched for shelter and spotted a rock formation just off the trail. On the side of the formation away from the trail was an opening formed by two boulders and covered by a large stone slab—a small, cave-like structure about five feet wide, four feet deep, and two and a half feet high. He crawled in and lay down to escape the downpour.

Around ten the next morning, a woman backpacking up the trail saw Wunrow's boots and part of his day pack sticking out from the rock shelter. Only someone ascending the trail could have seen them. But she assumed that the person inside was napping, so she continued on. The same thing happened an hour later when another backpacker came up the trail. He didn't stop, either.

Backpackers Steven King and Marvin Talbert set out on the Bubbs Creek Trail later that afternoon. Three miles up, they met a ranger coming down who, citing a bear nuisance, advised the two men to stow their food properly. It was around five o'clock when they approached the rock structure and saw Wunrow's boots. At first, like the two earlier hikers, King and Talbert assumed someone was resting inside. But on second glance, the feet seemed to be at an odd angle, so they decided to investigate.

Wunrow lay on his left side in a semi-fetal position, steel-rim eyeglasses askew on his face, his right arm at his side, and his left arm resting on the ground.

Hey, buddy. You okay?

No response.

They noticed that Wunrow's fingernails were purple, a condition that King, a police officer, recognized as being caused by a lack of blood circulation. He looked closer and concluded that Wunrow was dead. King's training had taught him that any death could be a homicide, so he didn't touch the body. On the left side of Wunrow's head was a wound—it looked liked a bite of some sort—and there was a small rip in the back of his shirt. These signs and the ranger's earlier warning triggered a question in King's mind: Had a bear killed this man?

King and Talbert marked the spot with handkerchiefs and returned immediately to Cedar Grove, where they called the ranger dispatch office. The park dispatcher, in turn, contacted rangers Debbie Bird and Richard Fishbaugh, who packed overnight gear and headed up the trail. They arrived at the fatality scene around 10 P.M.

Illuminating the body with their flashlights, Bird and Fishbaugh didn't see any evidence of an animal attack. In any case, fatal attacks by black bears were very rare. The rangers considered hypothermia, although Wunrow's wool shirt should have provided adequate warmth. Then they detected a singed hair on the victim's scalp, which raised the specter of lightning. But the evidence wasn't conclusive. They could only speculate that Wunrow had died of hypothermia or from a natural cause such as heart attack, or had been struck by lightning. They radioed in their report and pitched camp.

The next morning, a helicopter brought Fresno County coroner Robert Hensel to the scene. He examined the body and noted a small puncture with dried blood in the victim's scalp, behind his right ear. Hensel thought it might be a gunshot wound, but then quickly determined it was superficial and probably caused by an ear loop on Wunrow's wire-frame glasses. However, on the left side of the head were numerous burned and singed hairs, and almost imperceptible wounds that looked like tiny hemorrhages. Body hairs on the right wrist, lower back, and just above both knees also were singed. Midway down and in the center of the back was scarred tissue, as if someone had bored small holes in the skin and created little craters with black, cauterized edges. Hensel concluded that lightning caused the wounds—that the electrical charge had entered Wunrow's head, traveled through his body, and sparked a fatal cardiac arrest.

Exactly how Wunrow had been struck wasn't at all clear. There weren't any signs of a lightning strike in the vicinity, nor any high trees or jutting rock formations nearby to attract a bolt. But surely lightning had hit somewhere, perhaps on the ridge, and streaked across the moist ground into the rock enclosure where Wunrow lay. The damp conditions, including his wet clothes and skin, obviously placed him at greater risk. His death, a chance occurrence, illustrates the fickle nature of lightning.

The savage storm that had erupted in Kings Canyon and claimed Wunrow's life was part of a larger, intense weather system rumbling north toward Yosemite.

◄◌►

BILL PIPPEY AND BRUCE JORDAN were setting a furious pace, hoping to outrace the burgeoning storm. Close behind, Tom Rice and Adrian Esteban made a quick stop at their secret spring. Brian Jordan soon joined them. Meanwhile, Mike Hoog's party leapfrogged ahead. The hikers weren't unfriendly with each other, but neither did they mingle or banter back and forth in good spirits, as hikers often do. Those with Hoog still viewed Rice's band as rowdy and crude. Back at Nevada Fall, someone—maybe Pippey—had jokingly referred to Hoog's party as a "bunch of weenies."

Leaving Nevada Fall, Weiner felt encouraged that the remaining distance wouldn't be as steep. Still, he and Frith plodded. The pair fell behind again, in part because they stopped every ten to fifteen minutes to trade off carrying the forty-five-pound backpack but also because Weiner was fast becoming exhausted, especially his leg muscles, which were cramping up due to dehydration. They gulped down the last of their water. Esteban had told them about the secret spring, but Weiner and Frith couldn't locate it. Other hikers they asked didn't know its whereabouts, either. Though Weiner wanted to take a longer rest, Frith, gung-ho as ever, urged that they push on and catch up with the others.

Pippey and Bruce Jordan were shooting to reach the top first. For Pippey, it was more than a competitive thing; he was proud to be in good physical shape. So, despite the intimidating weather, the two hikers plowed ahead, never stopping. They ignored the danger warning at the base of Sub Dome and never once pondered the potential hazards as they scrambled up the cables on Half Dome.

But a hundred feet up, Pippey's stomach suddenly became bloated.

Pippey: "One minute, I'm fine. The next, I can barely keep my bowels from exploding."

In a voice loud enough for Jordan to hear, he uttered, Yes, God, I understand.

Clearly, Pippey thought, a very powerful force was trying to discourage him from going up there. He and Jordan retreated down the cables so Pippey could relieve himself.

ESTEBAN AND RICE, with Brian Jordan not far behind, were putting on steam to reach the summit ahead of the storm. Two wild-eyed young climbers—Ken Bokelund and Rob Foster—scampering down the trail advised Esteban and Rice, Don't go up there—it's too dangerous, then continued on down toward the Valley, obviously in a rush to get off the mountain.

The warning sparked rather than doused Esteban's and Rice's motivation to pick up the pace.

Esteban: "If there was one trait that set Rice apart from everyone else, it was his strong will. When he committed himself to something, it was all or nothing."

Esteban, of course, was Rice's alter ego—just as tough mentally, just as unswerving in grit and determination. Neither was likely to cower when he faced a physical challenge or risky situation on his own. Together, such a response was unthinkable.

Buchner and Ellner still poked along somewhere far behind. A fearful Ellner wanted no part of a lightning storm. His snail's pace and constant complaining angered Buchner, who didn't like being held back. When the two were about halfway between Nevada Fall and Sub Dome, lightning flashed ahead and thunder growled. A shaken Ellner slowed even more. The next lightning burst prompted him to turn around abruptly and pound back down the trail.

Buchner dropped his pack and ran after him, arguing, It's crazy to go back down now!

He persuaded Ellner to hike toward Half Dome. If necessary, Buchner said, they would camp at the base.

◄o►

HOOG'S GROUP METHODICALLY clawed away at the miles between them and Half Dome. In addition to all of his camping gear and supplies, Hoog hauled a three-gallon water container weighing more than twenty-five pounds. The five hikers arrived at the camping area beneath Sub Dome soon after the retreating Pippey and Jordan. Although dark clouds were moving in, the blue sky directly above still glistened.

Without hesitation, Hoog led his group up Sub Dome but didn't get far before he encountered a gentleman descending the granite stairs. The older hiker, who was fiftyish and carried a staff, said a storm was about to hit and strongly advised Hoog and his companions not to continue up.

Heed the sign, he said, referring to the public warning that Pippey and Bruce Jordan had ignored.

Hoog badly wanted to spend the night on Half Dome. Initially, he dismissed the man's cautionary words and was about to press on. On second thought, however, the advice seemed wise. Hoog stared at the stairs for several long seconds, deliberating. Then he and his four cohorts turned around and retraced their steps. The gentleman had already disappeared from view.

The third party back was Cage's, which held a steady pace. All members of his troupe were experienced backpackers, so they didn't think much about the oncoming storm, a familiar phenomenon in the Sierra Nevada. They would continue hiking through the forest, and if the weather got nasty, the group would simply stop, wait, and decide what to do next.

Esteban and Rice charged up the trail. Just below Sub Dome, they encountered Hoog's group in retreat. Dan Crozier repeated the gentleman hiker's precaution.

Rice brushed by Crozier, muttering, Someone's gotta do it.

He and Esteban pushed on.

Adrian Esteban
on outdoor outing,
pre-1985.

Bill Pippey on Mt. Whitney trip, pre-1985.

Adrian Esteban makes the leap at Paradise.

Ken Bokelund
climbing
Half Dome.

Rob Foster
on the face of
Half Dome.

View from inside the cave.

View looking out past the King's Chair.

Rick Pedroncelli, Linda Crozier, Mike Hoog, and Jennie Hayes waiting out the storm.

Linda Crozier's view up the cables early into her climb.

Standing left to right: Zip Cotter, Steve White, Clu Cotter, Monroe Bridges. Brian Cage in foreground.

Ranger Colin
Campbell on his
horse, John Paul.

Half Dome on the evening of July 27, 1985, after lightning had struck.
(photo by Ken Bokelund)

Medi-Flight pilot, Al Major.

Medi-Flight helicopter on Half Dome's
summit during rescue operation.

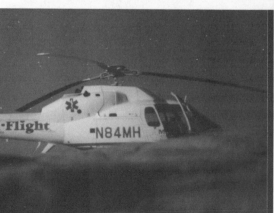

Mike Hoog pointing to
cave, summer of 1986.

Bruce Weiner undergoing physical therapy weeks after
the episode.

Adrian Esteban revisits the King's Chair fifteen years later.

Mike Hoog, Linda Crozier, and Jennie Hayes revisit Half Dome the following summer

6

FIRST STRIKE

*Zigzag lances of lightning followed each other in quick
succession, and the thunder was so gloriously loud and
massive it seemed as if surely an entire mountain was
being shattered at every stroke.*—John Muir

Well ahead of their companions, Esteban and Rice reached
the bottom of the cables at 5:40 P.M. and appraised the
impending storm. Heavy dark clouds in multihued layers already
blanketed the sky and sagged into the mountain cavities. Lightning continued playing over the ridges and spires, and thunder
rumbled like battleship guns nearby.

They stared up at the top of Half Dome six hundred feet away, shrouded in mist. Nobody else was in sight. Their take-no-prisoners pace had put them ahead of the pack when Bill Pippey forfeited the lead due to a bilious stomach.

Rice and Esteban now had to weigh their next move. A strong climber could ascend in less than fifteen minutes; they had done it themselves many times. Their thirty-five-pound backpacks would be a hindrance, but the threat of lightning would spur them on. At the top, they'd reach the cave's shelter in less than five minutes.

Roughly twenty minutes in all, then. Risk it or not?

While a lightning bolt might possibly strike the granite slope near them or even hit the cables they would be clinging to, a strike higher up, on or near the summit, was far more likely. The trouble was, even if lightning struck at the top, a potent charge could streak anywhere on wet surfaces. Anyplace on the mountain would be dangerous if Half Dome were coated with water.*

As Esteban measured the sky, he felt drizzle on his upturned face and blinked. Hard rain, he sensed, wasn't far off.

Neither of them spoke as they peered up the cables. Rice was the undisputed leader, and Esteban, ever the good soldier, would accept his decision. If Rice expressed doubts or caution, Esteban would mull them, but he didn't really expect dialogue. When the pair faced challenges, they seldom resorted to reasoned deliberation and judgment. Instead, they trusted their guts and seized opportunities for adventure. From that standpoint, this storm was no different from past hazards. Together they would improvise to meet all threats. The two exchanged a glance and Esteban knew the decision had been made.

Fuck it, Rice muttered. This is our mountain—let's just do it!

Okay, Esteban replied.

---

*In June 1963, a lightning bolt struck rain-dampened granite near the top of the cables, streaked across the rock, and hit the cables and approximately fifteen hikers gripping them. They screamed as the electrical charge clutched their hands and whipped across their arms and chests. No one was killed, but several incurred severe burns.

He realized nothing would deter Rice now. Nor, despite some apprehension, did he really want to deter him. The two were connected by karma, were brothers in arms. Esteban wouldn't let his brother down. The others would have to look out for themselves while they waited out the storm.

It's you and me, Esteban said, believing that only he and Rice would be heading into the vortex.

Shirtless despite the growing coolness, Rice moved rapidly toward the cables, Esteban immediately behind him. As if cued by their movements, a mosaic of jagged lightning streaked the sky followed by rolling claps.

Before the thunder had faded, Esteban's sixth sense kicked in with a sensation of foreboding. He took a few more steps, then stopped and called to Rice.

Whatever happens, he said, I want you to know I love you, man.

Rice turned with a quizzical expression. After a moment's hesitation, he gripped Esteban's outstretched hand and said he loved him, too. Then he attacked the slope.

Their legs drove hard against the granite and their arms strained at the metal cables. Atmospheric energy seemed to draw them magnetically as they ramped upward in a fury. Esteban imagined the scene as a vast battlefield, explosions drawing nearer, the thunder a precursor to combat. Despite his repressed fear, or perhaps because of it, Esteban felt more alive at that moment than at any time in his life. His senses seemed heightened far beyond their normal range. Perhaps, he thought, this is the kind of rush other extreme thrill-seekers experience when they surf a twenty-foot wave, bungee jump off a high bridge, skydive, rock climb a big wall, or ski off a cliff. Never before had he and Rice felt this level of intensity.

He became aware of Rice talking, of words spilling out quickly. Rice offered dire calculations about what could happen to them if lightning zapped the cables. Maybe he was just trying to ratchet up the thrill level. Or maybe he was indulging his engineer's mind.

In any case, they both jerked their hands off the steel cables each time deadly brilliance lit the skies.

As if it mattered.

With lightning, there was no margin for last-second adjustments.

◄o►

THE STRAGGLERS IN THEIR GROUP were spread out some distance behind. Closest to Rice and Esteban, and at that moment approaching the top of Sub Dome, was Brian Jordan. He'd split from the others early on, content to hike at his own pace. Proud of the stamina he was displaying and eager to impress the older men and make his mark as a budding outdoorsman, he followed in Rice and Esteban's footsteps without a second thought.

Farther back were Frith and Weiner. The warning sign at the base of Sub Dome stared at them as they approached the stairs. A concerned Weiner wondered aloud if they should stop and wait out the storm. Frith assured him that refuge—the cave—awaited them at the summit. Once there we'll be safe, he said, repeating Rice and Esteban's mantra.

Weiner's legs were still cramping. He doubted he could make it up those stairs. If he delayed much longer, however, his muscles might tighten further and completely rule out a final ascent, even after the storm passed. Soon it would start raining. Where could they find shelter in a drenching downpour? As the newcomer in the group, Weiner didn't want to hold anyone else back, especially Frith, whose heart and soul were committed to summiting Half Dome on this day.

We're close, Frith urged. We'll be able to dry off and rest in the cave.

Believing he had little choice at this point but to continue, and mustering every last bit of his physical strength, Weiner forced his aching legs to move step by step up the punishing staircase.

Once atop Sub Dome, they caught a glimpse of Rice and Esteban nearing Half Dome's summit just as clouds unleashed pouring rain. There it is! Frith said excitedly. One last push and we've made it! The two donned ponchos, dropped down to the base of the cables, and started up the granite slope.

The possibility of mortal danger occurred to neither of them.

◄○►

RICE AND ESTEBAN surmounted the final incline and hit the summit running. Though they had ignored the signs warning of danger, they still were acutely aware of their vulnerability. Lightning would strike the Dome—it was only a matter of when. In effect, the pair had engaged nature in a round of Russian roulette. But the rain-drenched air remained mercifully free from that terrifying flash as they dashed across the summit toward shelter.

They dropped their packs at the cave entrance and scrambled in. We made it! they yelled jubilantly and high-fived each other, then reclined on the rocky floor, energy and emotions spent.

It was 6 P.M.

Minutes later, Esteban heard someone yell his name. He clambered back out and was astonished to see Brian Jordan standing on the summit and peering around, a worried look on his face. Esteban beckoned to him, motioning urgently. As the boy hustled over, Esteban saw Frith and Weiner appear at the summit's edge. Esteban and Rice's presumption that they alone would challenge the storm by summiting Half Dome was flawed.

Come on! Esteban yelled.

It's absolutely bitching! Frith gushed when he reached the cave entrance. It's everything you said it was!

Rice, who had stripped his drenched clothes in the cave, emerged nude to greet the new arrivals. Laughing, he broke into a dance of celebration, feet jigging on the rough granite, rain pelting his body. Caught up in his euphoria, the others slapped hands and shuffled their feet; that is, except for Weiner, who was near collapse.

Bring on the lightning show! somebody yelled as they settled down in the enclosure.

The newcomers cast off their backpacks and sought space in the tight quarters. After pushing so hard up the mountain, they were relieved to be in the cave's shelter; in their minds the thick granite walls and ceiling provided an invincible fortress against the raging storm. Later, when the storm ended and the others rejoined them, they would celebrate their accomplishment in full.

Brian Jordan was flush with pleasure. The youngster had demonstrated he could aim high and hit his goal. If he could climb Half Dome in the face of a storm, he could accomplish just about anything. He sat squeezed between two backpacks, savoring the glow of his triumph and pleased to be there with the veterans Esteban and Rice.

Bruce Weiner had amazed even himself. He'd completed his first hike—to the top of a famous mountain, no less. Though practically numb from pain and fatigue, he felt supremely proud. The easterner had proven he could measure up when it counted. Best of all, he'd done it in the company of Bob Frith.

If Frith was tired, he didn't show it. He exuded his customary jovial spirit. Being there on the top of Half Dome, he told everyone, was the high point of his twenty-four years. Now that he'd discovered the wonders of mountains, he intended to make these marvelous treks many times. Nowhere but in California could he experience something like this. He and Weiner would share many future adventures. Life was very good indeed.

In his quiet manner, Esteban also enjoyed a sense of profound fulfillment. He believed he was right where he belonged, having journeyed once again to his personal mecca. While he couldn't find the precise words to describe this feeling, he was one with the elements in this spot, no question about it. Others might find their mystical connections elsewhere, but for Esteban, those connections were here, with Rice. Sharing the sanctity of the moment with newcomers only deepened his appreciation.

Rice, too, had reason to be pleased. He'd seized the moment and led the way up the granite monolith. He'd inspired the others to confront their fears and challenge the storm. More than ever before, Rice's bond with this mountain seemed firmly cemented. The Dome was sacred, a primal link to nature. What he found here transcended the material realm and imbued him with a higher purpose: to remain physically and morally fit.

The rain turned colder. Hailstones began clattering on the rocks. The five men dug into their packs for dry clothes—long pants, sweatshirts, sweaters. The small cave obliged them to huddle, which generated a soothing body heat. Some broke out trail mix and granola bars. Rice, now clothed in shorts and a sweatshirt, reached into his pack for a small head of broccoli to munch on.

Anyone got beer? Esteban asked.

Only Pippey, somebody answered, which drew laughter and speculation about how long it would take their usually hard-hiking companion and the other Jordan twin to join them.

Esteban slid over near the cave's entrance and lit his camping stove. He brought water to a boil, then carefully carried a tin cup of tea with him out to the ledge. The hail had ceased and the rain slackened.

Come check out the greatest scene in the world! he called back to Frith as he settled down on the King's Chair.

Frith crawled over the boulder and came face-to-face with the twenty-two-hundred-foot drop to the rocky slabs. He swallowed nervously and cautiously lowered himself down beside Esteban. With his legs dangling over the edge and nothing but emptiness before him, Frith confessed he'd never experienced anything like this before.

This is unreal, he said, searching for the right words. It was worth everything to get here.

Esteban nodded pleasurably.

We're on top of the world, man, he said. The gods are smiling on us.

The time was 6:25 P.M.

◄O►

EARLIER, BILL PIPPEY, having voided his stomach and intestines, finally was ready to move on. With Bruce Jordan he retraced his steps up Sub Dome and started up the cables in the chill rain, dense, ominous clouds overhead. The two men were only twenty feet up the cables when an enormous bolt lashed the rounded surface of North Dome directly across the Valley. Like a laser light show, the jagged streak shuddered in place for almost a full second.

Jordan halted and said he was scared and wanted to stop. Pippey studied him. Under normal circumstances, he might have cheered the youngster on. But now, dehydrated and severely weakened from diarrhea, he was in a different frame of mind. And this was hardly a normal situation.

Got no quarrel with that, he said agreeably.

Actually, he thought, it's damn sensible.

They headed back down to the base camp, where they quickly pitched their tent. At about six fifteen, they hunkered down to wait out the storm. Pippey fished beer from his pack. While consuming it, they had little concern about the tremendous light show flashing all around them outside, feeling secure in their shelter. The pyrotechnics peaked at six thirty with a ferocious explosion that lit up their nylon tent as if a billion flashbulbs had detonated.

FARTHER DOWN, Brian Cage and his group reached tree line during the storm's crescendo. The edge of the forest provided a good view of Half Dome. In disbelief, they spotted men moving above the cables, seemingly among the storm clouds.

Shaking their heads, Cage's group put on all available rain gear and gathered under the arms of a big Jeffrey pine. There they clustered against the trunk, fairly warm and dry and in good spirits, although not as protected as they might have assumed.* They broke out crackers and salami, passed around a bottle of Yukon

---

*Tall trees, like other high spires, are natural targets for lightning. During this storm, a female hiker took refuge under a tree. A stringer from a lightning bolt struck the tree and the electrical charge shot down the wet trunk and along the exposed roots under her feet, delivering a jarring shock to her and searing each of her fingernails.

Jack, and settled back to wait. There was still plenty of daylight to get to the summit if the storm let up. If it didn't, they would camp somewhere near their present position.

From beneath the Jeffrey pine, they watched the lightning grow ever more intense as flash after flash illuminated the sky. It seemed to pinpoint Half Dome. Suddenly an enormous, radiant blast shattered the air, followed immediately by a piercing *boom*—the loudest thunder crack Cage had ever heard. Another flash arrived moments later. He watched as the bolt shot across the summit of Half Dome, then made a 180-degree turn to strike at the lip of the overhang there. Though he had grown up in Oregon and seen his share of electrical storms, Cage was awestruck. Never had he seen lightning take such a radical path. Nor had he ever heard anything to match the brain-splitting *craack-boom* that resonated off the granite walls.

He later described his group's reaction:

Frankly, it scared the crap out of us.

—◄o►—

MIKE HOOG'S GROUP made shelter in an open area by spreading a plastic sheet on the ground and covering it with a large tarp overhead. The hikers lay under the tarp in their sleeping bags and ate trail mix, salami, cheese, and crackers. Although they were close to Half Dome, they had decided to complete their hike the next day. Meanwhile, the storm raged. Linda Crozier felt as if the clouds were closing in around them, which made everything murky and ominous. The pounding thunder was louder than ever, a relentless assault on her ears. Lightning, it seemed, was striking everywhere at once.

In fact, though, at the eye of this hell broken loose stood Half Dome.

—◄o►—

THE OPENINGS IN THE CAVE afforded eerie, fleeting images cast in ghostly hues. Lightning tracers glowed—the veins of an irate god?—as thunderclaps battered the granite formations again and again. Inside the enclosure sat Rice, Weiner, and Brian Jordan. For the moment, Rice had little to say. The youthful Jordan was sandwiched between two pack frames. Weiner was bent forward, adjusting his bootlaces.

Outside, Esteban and Frith sat in the King's Chair.

Did you hear that? Esteban asked suddenly.

What? Frith looked at him. Hear what?

That funny buzzing—it seemed to fill the air.

You must be high, Frith told him. I didn't hear anything.

Esteban laughed. Whatever, he said. True, he was high. But not on drugs. No drug could produce the kind of elation he was feeling.

He sobered slightly as the buzzing sounded again. This time, Frith heard it. Their hair bristled. The air seemed to crackle, like sizzling bacon, but neither man grasped its portent. Frith relaxed and began to say again how unbelievably bitching all this was, just awesome, the greatest experience of his life.

Distracted, Esteban turned to crawl up over the boulder back into the cave. With his left hand on the rock for balance, he pushed off on his left leg, his right poised in midair. At that instant, the cave exploded with a cataclysmic roar as lightning ripped across its surfaces.

Esteban was slammed against a wall, his left hand pinned there as if by an electromagnet. He thought he saw his arm inflating and warping and twisting like something grossly overcooking in a microwave oven. He felt as though he was imploding, being fed into a vacuum. He screamed but didn't hear his voice. Everything grew dark. He was somewhere above his body, peering down at himself and those in the cave. He was being transported far away.

No! he bellowed.

Suddenly, somehow, he was back in his body. But it was numb and couldn't move.

I'm dead, he thought.

Electricity had entered through a single knuckle and shot down his body, departing simultaneously, as buckshot might, from the cheeks of his buttocks, left thigh, and left heel. Esteban had no way of knowing then how lucky he'd been. At the instant of the strike, his limited contact with the granite had confined the charge to the left side of his body.

Weiner also had been lucky. Bending to adjust his laces, he was touching the wall only with his buttocks and thighs. As the lightning whipped about the enclosure, residual moisture on his clothing and skin served as a conductor and restricted the charge to the surface of these two body parts.

When the cave exploded, Weiner felt that the detonation was in his head and he was being sucked into a vacuum, his body being wrenched in a thousand directions simultaneously. For one long instant he couldn't feel, see, or hear anything. Everything was black; he didn't know where he was. When he regained his senses, he heard himself screaming. He had no feeling from the waist down. His first thought was that Esteban's portable stove had blown up. But then he heard Esteban moaning:

Oh, my God, we've been struck by lightning. I'm dead, I'm dead, I'm dead.

Weiner looked at Brian Jordan next to him. Eyes vacant, Jordan deadpanned, We've got to get out of here. His chin then dropped to his chest.

In hoarse tones, Weiner tried to convince Esteban he was still alive. The message didn't register right away. In Esteban's blurred consciousness, everything was taking place in extremely slow motion. A strong odor like burning sulfur filled his nostrils. Objects and sounds drifted in and out of focus. At length, as though he were fiddling with the image and volume controls on a TV monitor, the picture began to clear. He discovered he could move his arms.

Turning his head to scan the cave, he saw Rice slouched sideways against the granite wall in a fetal position, his body jerking and twitching. His bare legs were badly charred, the blond hairs blackened. Lightning had shot into Rice's back where it rested against the rock wall and out through his thighs and legs. His glassy eyes were expressionless.

Esteban looked over at the youngster, Jordan, who was slumped forward, his still form reeking of burned flesh and hair. The two packs flanking him bore basketball-sized holes, as though there'd been a grenade attack. Conducted by the metal frames, the lightning had passed instantly from them onto Jordan's right shoulder and out his left pectoral.

The sixteen-year-old appeared lifeless. This realization unleashed a crushing sense of tragedy in Esteban—almost as if he'd suffered a second lightning bolt. Injuries, no matter how severe, were one thing. But death meant finality, hope extinguished. Nature had an answer for those who dare challenge her preeminence. With sickening clarity, Esteban now saw that the risks had been miscalculated, limits exceeded—and it was too late for corrections.

He pulled himself forward painfully, dragging his still-paralyzed legs behind. Twisting to glance out at the King's Chair, he was horrified by what he saw: Frith contorting on the stone perch, vomit and froth gurgling from his mouth, eyes rolled back and showing their whites. His forehead bore a dramatic, cauterized-looking gash no more than an inch long, as if someone had plunged a white-hot dagger into his skull. In this case, though, the thrust probably had come from within. Frith's lower body had absorbed the violent charge, which apparently rocketed up through him and out his brow. Or had lightning traveled through the air and pierced him directly in the head? It didn't matter now. He was making dreadful noises. His thrashing body threatened to catapult itself off the narrow ledge.

Esteban maneuvered his upper body over the boulder. Grabbing frantically at Frith's pants, he managed to snag the waistband. He pulled him back from the lip, but Frith's body continued to convulse toward the edge, as though seeking the void beyond. Esteban strained to hold on. With a monumental effort, he tugged Frith back again. He tried to pull him over the boulder and into the chamber, but Frith's writhing, 190-pound bulk was too much for him.

Fighting off panic, Esteban yelled over to Weiner, You've got to help me, man! He's gonna fall off the ledge!

Seeing his friend's peril energized Weiner. His legs still numbed, he struggled to where Esteban was, leaned over the boulder, and managed to grip the sweater on Frith's left arm while Esteban grasped the right. Together they pulled Frith back so he lay more securely. They tried to raise him off the ledge and over the boulder, but with their legs useless, they couldn't exert enough leverage.

Momentarily releasing his hold on the sweater, Weiner gripped Frith's hand with all his strength, hoping that he might return the grip.

Wake up! Weiner yelled frantically at Frith.

A chilling awareness that another bolt could strike at any moment seized Esteban.

Convinced he could do no more, his brain shrieking at him to seek safety, Esteban let go of Frith's right arm and allowed him to slump on the ledge, desperately hoping he would stay there. Esteban started to drag himself past Weiner, who had renewed his grip on the sweater. As he did so, a violent convulsion arched Frith and propelled his legs over the edge. Weiner desperately held on.

Frith slid farther, his weight yanking Weiner closer to certain death.

Weiner had no choice but to let go.

In horror, he and Esteban watched as Frith disappeared over the precipice to the rocks twenty-two hundred feet below.

Weiner screamed *No! No! No!* then clamped his eyes shut and began to sob.

◄o►

DRAINED OF EMOTION by what had happened, Esteban felt remarkably dispassionate as he looked over at Rice, whose left leg was twisted beneath a dislodged rock. Rice retched and gagged on regurgitated broccoli, unintelligible noises issuing from his mouth. Dragging himself over to where Rice was, Esteban propped his friend up slightly, cleared his mouth of food, shook him gently in a vain attempt to restore consciousness, and wondered what else he should do. Severe burns scorched Rice's legs, which even then were smoking. His wounds were bloodless, cauterized by the searing electricity, and blanched, like acid burns. To Esteban they resembled the insides of charred, split-open frankfurters. He lifted Rice's shoulders to turn him and was alarmed to see a fire-blackened hole in the back of his shirt. Through the hole he saw a skinless depression about six inches in diameter. Esteban slowly let Rice down again, thinking maybe there was spinal damage. Rice's eyes were open but unfocused. Minute seizures—aftershocks—still wracked his body. Esteban stared into his friend's eyes. Was it just his imagination, or had he seen a flicker of expression? Was Rice trying to communicate?

An ominous, atmospheric crackling sounded outside. The hairs on Esteban's arms stood upright. His newfound calm vanished in a torrent of fear. He screamed to Weiner, to all of them, conscious or not:

We've got to get the fuck out of here!

Weiner heard the terror in Esteban's voice and tried to stand but fell back again, the muscles in his legs severely knotted. Knowing he couldn't get very far, he hoped and prayed that lightning would not strike the same place twice.*

Esteban, convinced that he was in mortal peril, could think only of escape. He turned away from Rice, gripped Weiner's shoulder in passing, and pulled himself toward the cave's entrance. His legs were inept, but with his powerful arms and upper body he thrust himself up onto the summit and then powered his battered frame across the granite, his elbows clawing the unyielding rock

---

*A naive hope, actually, because lightning follows no such rule. A case in point is the Empire State Building, which has been hit by lightning dozens of times in a year and several times during a single storm.

like a belly-crawling soldier. His sights were on a crevice called the outhouse that was about 150 feet away in a depression obscured by rocks. Campers used it as a toilet, but that was the least of Esteban's concerns at the moment.

His senses, leavened by fear, told him another bolt was coming. Crawling frantically, rolling down a decline, scrambling even faster, he finally reached the depression. Another blast shattered the heavens just as he scrunched himself into the crevice. The granite around him shuddered. His body absorbed a charge from the moist rocks, but this one seemed no more potent than from a household outlet.

He had been spared.

Giddy with relief, Esteban blended tears with shrill laughter. He was alive!

And for an instant, that was all that mattered.

7

SECOND STRIKE

The Half-Dome possesses one feature in particular that I always found remarkable and charming,— the strange manner in which it catches and holds the last light of the day. Often for a full hour after the valley has sunk into shadow, this high Alp, over-looking by two thousand feet the intervening heights, receives the western glow, and like a great heliograph reflects the peaceful messages of the evening over all the quiet valley.—J. Smeaton Chase, author of *Yosemite's Trails*, 1911

Although Weiner was shaken to the core by the catastrophe that had befallen him and his companions, and despite his weakened legs, he survived the first electrical blast with no apparent major injuries. Amazingly his body was slowly coming back to where it was before the lightning blast. Whether Rice would come out of it alive, however, was not yet clear; he was still unconscious, his head sagging to the side.

Fearing the worst, Weiner thought that he wasn't going to make it.

Weiner possibly could have mustered enough strength to scramble out of the cave, as Esteban had. But getting down those cables with legs still immobilized—more from fatigue and cramps than from the lightning—was unthinkable. And he wanted no part of being out there on the bare summit, a human lightning rod, during another killer strike. So, desperately praying that lightning wouldn't strike the cave a second time, he stayed put.

Buzzing and crackling suddenly filled the air. Weiner didn't have time to budge before another blinding explosion blasted the granite and ripped through the enclosure. Unlike the first strike, when the electrical arc streaked across his bottom half, this one engulfed most of his body.

Weiner immediately found himself floating in inky nothingness. In the next instant, he was halfway outside his body, watching it convulse once, then slowly sink into a relaxed state. He was drifting away. He sensed that if the connection between his body and fleeting spirit were broken, it would mean death.

Then he started flowing smoothly and effortlessly back into his body. He was in the cave again, lying on the cold stone floor, his entire physical being seemingly frozen. He became aware of a cool breeze blowing across his bare skin, suggesting that indeed he was still alive. He also felt a deep, pervasive, excruciating pain in his chest, as if that cavity had been blown wide open.

All Weiner wanted was for it all to end. A seductive, soothing thought fleetingly entered his consciousness: If I crawled to the King's Chair, I could throw myself over the edge and join Bob Frith in blissful death, forever free of pain.

For several minutes, he lay motionless. His fogged mind slowly cleared. He knew now that, in the wake of the second strike, he was seriously injured, that perhaps these were his final breaths. Charred remnants of his shirt, which had been burned open by the electrical blast, stuck to his exposed skin. Though the outside of his chest seemed to be intact, his ribs felt broken, tormenting him each time he sucked in air. And searing pain shot through his legs whenever he moved even slightly. The hiking boot on his left leg had been completely blown off.

Soon after the second blast, Rice gradually regained consciousness—almost as if the jolt had recharged his brain. He moaned, then screamed in agony from the weight of Weiner's body on his stricken leg. Rice's other leg was bent grotesquely under a rock. Weiner rolled off him. He removed his belt and, using it for leverage, he and Rice in turn pulled each other to an upright position, both experiencing excruciating pain in doing so.

Next to them was Brian Jordan, his face bluish, his body slumped over and as still as the surrounding granite.

By now the rain had slowed to a drizzle, the mass of storm clouds was marching eastward, the thunder and lightning were now just lingering remnants of their former rage. Weiner peered through the cave opening and saw the clearing sky.

He began yelling for help.

◄o►

IN HIS CONFUSED STATE, Weiner thought the second strike had happened mere seconds after Esteban had left the cave and that he had probably been struck dead. In fact, Esteban's frantic roll down the slope to the outhouse crevice surely saved him. As he lay there, Esteban thought only of his own miraculous survival and thanked God over and over for sparing him.

But the reality of what had just happened—the Jordan kid killed, Bob Frith spilling over the precipice to certain death—doused his momentary relief. Tragically, Esteban's long-standing premonition that someone he knew would fall from Half Dome had come to pass.

His thoughts turned to Weiner and Rice in the cave. He heard screams coming from that direction but was too frightened to leave the crevice.

Minutes passed. The unfolding clouds in the tumultuous skies above Half Dome, like the last wild leaps and thrashes of spawning salmon, were releasing their final charge before weakening and then dying. Soon, patches of evening sky showed between the fast-moving billows, their tops now illuminated by the emerging evening sun. Only faint rumblings of thunder persisted from afar.

In this part of the Sierra Nevada, the storm was over.

Esteban's feet were numb, but he had feeling in his lower body. Finally, believing that the danger had sufficiently subsided, he left the crevice and began crawling back up the slope toward the cave.

Nearing the summit, Esteban saw someone coming over the ridge at the top of the cables. He waved his arms and shouted to attract the hiker's attention.

It was Mike Hoog.

━◄◦►━

THROUGHOUT THE DOWNPOUR, Hoog and his four companions had stayed mostly dry under their tarp below Sub Dome, where they planned to camp for the night. Hoog wanted a sunset photograph from the summit now that the sky was clearing. He asked if anyone cared to join him, but no one made a move. So he took off by himself, hustling up the stone stairs of Sub Dome and then up the incline to the top of Half Dome. Black clouds still hovered above, casting sinister shadows on the mountain. To the west, a light blue sky was dappled with wispy clouds. A distinct line separated the darkness of the departing storm and brightening skies.

On the summit, Hoog saw someone frantically waving and shouting at him. It was Esteban, whom he recognized as a member of the rude, boisterous group at Nevada Fall. That earlier encounter made Hoog suspicious now. Was this guy high on drugs? Were he and his pals playing a joke, hoping to scare Hoog or, as a dark inner voice warned, push him over the edge?

He approached cautiously. When Esteban told him his buddies were injured, Hoog followed Esteban to the cave but avoided getting too close to the brink, his senses on heightened alert. Bending down and peering into the enclosure, he first saw a frenzied Weiner, screaming for help and begging that someone remove him from the cave. Close by was a second man, Rice, his body inert, his face pallid, his eyes glassy. Smoke wafted from the legs of both men. Farther in, there was a boy slouched to one side; a breeze tussled his light brown hair, the only thing on him that moved.

Odors of burned hair and flesh hung in the air.

Hoog was a trained emergency medical technician, or EMT, but this was the first time he would treat injuries in the field. The seriousness of it all and his place in these unfolding events dawned on him: Lives might be at stake.

He was scared.

The first emergency response in such cases is to ensure the scene is safe, that whatever caused the mishap has passed. Only then, after appropriate triage (providing priority assistance to patients, if there's more than one, either immediately or as other resources become available), should an EMT proceed with medical care. Triage often entails a color scheme to denote the order for giving attention. Black typically represents someone beyond help, in most cases dead; red denotes someone who is in critical condition but might be saved; yellow means serious but not critical; and green signifies that a person is injured but capable of getting by on his or her own. The EMT does a quick assessment and then treats the red victim first, followed by the yellow.

Other than the nearby cliff, Hoog didn't detect any lurking dangers now that the storm appeared to be over. He inhaled deeply and steeled himself against his own nervousness so it wouldn't prevent him from doing what he had to do.

Esteban told him about Frith falling over the edge and how Brian Jordan hadn't stirred since the lightning strike. Trying his best not to freak out, Hoog lowered himself into the cave and squirmed past Weiner and Rice and over to Jordan. With two fingers, he felt for a pulse in one of the two large arteries—the carotids, which deliver blood to the head—in the young man's neck. No pulse. That indicated a stopped heart and probable death. Hoog concluded there was nothing he could do.

Then he turned to Weiner. First he checked to see if Weiner had any feelings in his legs. If he didn't, that could mean a spinal injury, possibly caused by a violent impact against rock or a severe muscular contraction. Weiner would then have to be immobilized and stabilized right there; improperly moving a patient with a broken neck can prove fatal. Fortunately, Weiner confirmed that he could feel and move his feet. In a quick inspection, Hoog detected no other immediate life-threatening circumstances. He focused on Rice.

Although Rice's leg muscles were very tight and swollen, he, too, had feeling in his legs and toes. He also could move his upper body, so a serious back injury seemed unlikely. But his pallor suggested the likely onset of shock.

Esteban, who now had full use of his legs, approached the cave to assist.

When Rice saw him, he started yelling: Adrian, get your fuckin' ass in here and get me out. Don't leave me behind to die like you did!

A shaken Esteban crawled to Rice and slapped and then shook him, shouting: Goddamn it, I was going to die! I had to go. It wasn't my fault! Esteban couldn't cope with this accusation, and his body began trembling. He had to get out of there.

Outside the cave, he stomped around, violently upset. Esteban pleaded to himself: How could he accuse me of leaving him to die?

What more could I have done? If I had stayed, I probably would have been killed by the second bolt. Then no one would know that anyone was in the cave, no one would be helping him now. I had to leave—I had no choice. Can't he see that?

Still highly agitated, Esteban lowered himself back into the enclosure to help Hoog, who was grappling with choices, among them whether he should move the two men.

He knew he shouldn't if there were any possibility of spinal or neck injuries. On the other hand, the cave was cramped, with insufficient space for both of them to lie comfortably on their backs and be treated. Hoog concluded that the chance of spinal injury was remote; he would remove both victims from the cave.

First he pushed the rock off Rice's leg. Then he and Esteban shifted the four backpacks and other odds and ends out of the way. The pair lifted Weiner, one supporting his upper body by holding him under his armpits, the other grasping his legs. With much careful and strenuous maneuvering, they managed to get him out and up onto the open granite, and gently laid him down. Hoog took off his own jacket and covered Weiner with it.

In similar fashion, Hoog and Esteban retrieved Rice and placed him near Weiner. Both men lay there, groaning and twisting in anguish. To Hoog, it looked like either or both could slip into shock, a potentially fatal development.

Shock is a downward spiral of bodily functions triggered by the inability of the circulatory system to send an adequate supply of blood to tissues. Infections, burns, heart attack, spinal cord damage, and rapid blood loss from an injury or wound can cause it. With impaired blood flow, valuable resources are shunted toward the more vital brain and internal organs. Surface blood vessels constrict, leaving the skin pale and clammy. Heart rate increases, breathing becomes more rapid, and digestion slows and ultimately halts. Body temperature is erratic, with hypothermia a threat. If blood pressure drops, mental functioning deteriorates. First the victim experiences a sense of impending doom, then apathy and weakness, then disorientation and incoherence. The final result is coma. If the regression in bodily functions isn't diagnosed, halted, and reversed early, the patient is likely to die. Even in hospitals, the mortality rate for acute shock is 50 percent.

Hoog, who knew that a potential shock victim must be kept warm, returned to the cave to gather warm garments from the men's backpacks. He reexamined Brian Jordan and, despite his extreme queasiness, searched his body for a pulse. He couldn't feel one anywhere. The boy was indeed dead, becoming one of the 10 percent of lightning victims who perish.

◄○►

WHILE HOOG was doing what he could for the victims, Rick Pedroncelli, having decided to follow him to the top after all, was making his way up. Once there, he spotted Hoog and others off in the distance, near the edge. When he got closer, he saw his friend attending to one of two individuals lying prone. A third, Esteban, was sitting and looked dazed.

When Pedroncelli approached, Esteban leaped up and said: We need to get help!

Initially, Pedroncelli was quite reluctant to get involved, for reasons that had to do with another death—that of his mother. She had died unexpectedly when he was only twelve years old. The event left him with deep-seated feelings of insecurity and made him less willing to take chances. Still, it was evident something terrible had happened, that Hoog needed help.

After Pedroncelli got a quick update on the situation, he asked if he could do anything. Hoog told him to retrieve the men's sleeping bags and air mattresses from inside the cave. Pedroncelli slipped down through the opening and crawled to the backpacks near the body of Brian Jordan. Shaking uncontrollably, he hastily snatched a couple of bags and mattresses, and retreated outside as fast as he could. He and Hoog positioned Rice and Weiner on the mattresses, and covered them with the bags.

By this time, both Weiner and Rice were fully delirious, squirming and moaning under the sleeping bags, obviously in acute pain. Esteban appeared to be stable but extremely distressed and understandably panicked about his companions. Pedroncelli didn't see any way for these two men to get the medical assistance they clearly needed. Here they were on top of a mountain with nightfall approaching, far away from the Valley and possible assistance. He felt powerless.

Hoog said: We have to get Linda up here.

◄○►

LINDA CROZIER, eager to finally see the view from the top that her good friend Hoog had long touted, had already decided to climb to the summit to join him and Pedroncelli. Wearing only running shorts, a T-shirt, and a sweatshirt tied around her waist, she struck out for the Dome, the time now being around 7:30 P.M.

At the base of the cables, alone, she gazed up the rock incline wrapped in shadows and total silence. The scene, in her words, was "very moody."

She began the climb feeling more than a little intimidated by the steep, black, wet slope and the absence of other hikers to lend psychological support. Pulling on the cables with sufficient arm strength to keep moving upward taxed her to the limit. She stopped halfway to take a photo looking up the cables, and as she pointed her camera, Pedroncelli suddenly appeared in the viewfinder where the cables ended. He was beckoning her with his arms and calling out. Sensing something was wrong, Crozier put away the camera and yanked even harder on the cables, making her legs respond in kind.

As she drew nearer, Pedroncelli shouted: Hurry! Lightning killed two guys and three others are badly hurt!

On top, heading over to Hoog and the others, Crozier rehearsed in her mind the basics of cardiopulmonary resuscitation. Then she saw Weiner and Rice lying on the stone surface. Hoog told her about the dead boy in the cave and about the hiker who had vanished over the cliff. The irony of it all didn't escape Crozier: These were the very men whose behavior she had found so distasteful back at Nevada Fall. Her brother Dan had conveyed to their two leaders, Rice and Esteban, the older hiker's warning about not scaling the summit with a storm brewing. But whatever negative feelings she may have had regarding this crew evaporated amid the tragedy that now engulfed them.

Her first reaction—why, she doesn't know—was to peer down over the edge. There, in the rocky jumble far below, was something white—probably Frith's body. She was also thinking about what Hoog had said about the dead boy in the cave. Up to this time she had never seen a dead person before, and she felt squeamish about confronting that possibility now. With this chilling consideration kicking around in her head, she accepted Hoog's conclusion, cleared her head of distractions, and returned to where the injured lay. Hoog gave her a quick rundown of the treatment he had provided so far. Crozier, who had more experience than Hoog in emergency medical care, took charge at that point.

A teacher in Crozier's EMT training had emphasized the importance of problem-solving skills in addition to knowledge of standard medical applications. Absent medical equipment in an outdoor emergency, you must be able to improvise and use all available resources. Although the curriculum included electrical injuries, the instructor had touched only briefly on those caused by lightning.

Without any medical gear or medicine on Half Dome, Crozier's medical training would be supremely tested. Yet it was her more intangible qualifications—knowing how to deal coolly with various athletic injuries as a trainer, for example, and how to take decisive action in life-threatening situations as a whitewater guide—that would be brought to the forefront this night.

She moved right away to the third phase of emergency care—assessment—which entailed checking the life-essential functions, or ABCs: airway, breathing, and circulation. In EMT terminology, this is a primary survey. If either victim had an ABC problem, such as a blocked airway, it would have to be dealt with immediately.

A quick inspection showed that neither man had any major breathing obstructions or bleeding. Given Rice's unmoving and quiet state, he appeared to be the most critically injured at this juncture, so Crozier examined him first. She noted extensive burn lesions, cauterized by the lightning's searing heat, and knew that such traumatic wounds could produce shock. She felt for pulses at his wrists and elbows but found none, which signaled low blood pressure and the probable onset of shock. Reaching up into his shorts, she checked the femoral artery in his groin and was relieved to feel a pulse. So, at least for now, Rice had some circulation to vital organs. Crozier would tap this particular pulse in follow-up checks as a baseline reference, and use it to assess the rate, rhythm, and strength of his overall cardiac system. If the pulse diminished, it would mean Rice was slipping deeper into shock.

Crozier detected a pulse on Weiner's wrist, but it was weak. Judging from his intense writhing, his pain seemed all-encompassing. His murmurings suggested that he believed he was going to die.

Esteban suffered only a few dime-sized blisters on his left elbow, hip, and knee where the lightning had exited. By this time, he had regained all feeling in his entire body and was fully coherent.

Two new hikers appeared on the summit. They said they, too, were EMTs and offered to assist. One, Renee Miller, was in her early twenties; the other was a man who only gave his first name, Brutus. They were camped below the summit and, like the others, had climbed up to enjoy the sunset. Crozier, thankful for their presence, enlisted Miller's help in assessing the victims. She asked Hoog and Brutus to examine Brian Jordan yet again.

Inside the cave, the two men found that Jordan's face had turned a cyanotic blue, the result of insufficient blood oxygen. They also noted a wound in his upper right shoulder where the lightning most likely had entered. On the left side of his chest, just above the nipple, were signs of electrical burns—probably the exit wounds. The electrical charge appeared to have flashed across and possibly through Jordan's chest near his heart, shocking it and causing ventricular fibrillation, a chaotic twitching of cardiac muscle that completely disrupts the pumping of blood. Only immediate CPR and an electrical jump start from a defibrillator (a device that restores normal heartbeat), followed as soon as possible by emergency medical treatment, might have saved him.

Crozier wanted a head-to-toe examination of both Weiner and Rice to ensure there were no injuries to the neck, spine, or back, no broken bones, and no other wounds or injuries requiring prompt attention. This is a secondary survey, in EMT parlance. While she examined Rice, Renee Miller did the same for Weiner. The two women worked in tandem and compared findings, each advising the other what to look for as they scanned the men's bodies.

Now more awake, Rice complained of severe pain in his legs and feet. Crozier spotted a wound in his left ankle—the lightning probably exited there—that resembled a bullet hole. His legs looked as though a potato peeler had scraped sections of skin off of them and left white blotches of burned flesh. He also had burn wounds on his arms; he could barely move the left one.

Miller discovered that Weiner's wounds were almost identical.

As Rice's and Weiner's wounds made clear, lightning not only had scorched the outside of their bodies, vaporizing any residual moisture from the rain and thereby causing severe burns, but also seemingly had penetrated their backs—hence, the gaping, leathery lesions there—and blasted out through the feet.

This had triggered a cascade of calamitous and potentially fatal physiological events. The burns caused swelling in the legs, which in turn shut off circulation to lower extremities, just as a tourniquet would. That explained the pair's whitish blue feet. Though Rice and Weiner still had some feeling in the legs, the swelling, if untreated, threatened to starve tissue of the oxygenated blood it needs to stay alive. Because dying muscle tissue releases toxins that can cause kidney failure or damage other bodily systems, the legs would have to be amputated if it reached that point.

On an impulse, Hoog abruptly left to see if any more hikers were coming up the cables who could turn tail and summon more help. Meanwhile, Pedroncelli thought of another strategy—sending an SOS by Morse code with his flashlight to campers in the Valley.* He went to the edge, in line of sight of the campgrounds far below, and began flashing SOS, which he remembered from war movies. The evening sky was still light, however, and Pedroncelli doubted that anyone down there could see the flashes. So, after several attempts, he stopped.

At this point, other than the small contingent on top of Half Dome—those few who were giving and receiving aid—no other people in all of Yosemite had any inkling of the calamity.

◄○►

ROCK CLIMBERS KEN BOKELUND and Rob Foster made it to the Valley floor by 7:30 P.M., physically and emotionally spent but grateful they had survived their brush with lightning uninjured. Rainwater immersed the parking lot at Camp Curry. Bokelund gazed up at Half Dome as the last rays of sun bathed the famous rock face they had just scaled. A shimmering golden glow radiated from it, framed by turbulent, multihued clouds. It was the most striking image Bokelund had ever seen. He snapped a photo.

The climbing duo tossed their gear into the car and headed out, not once thinking of the two hikers they had warned about

---

*Morse code, widely practiced for decades, is now rarely taught, except in pilot training and in the military. The emergence of cell phones has rendered this form of emergency communication even more passé. We can confidently conclude that with this new technology, the 1985 Half Dome episode would have proceeded quite differently.

going up there and unaware of the life-and-death drama that was playing out on the summit at that very instant.

◄o►

BRIAN CAGE'S PARTY of six remained under the giant Jeffrey pine at the base of Half Dome, waiting for the storm to pass. After the rain stopped and as the clouds began to disperse, early-evening sunlight filtered through. Splashes of blue punctuated the western sky, and to the north, just beyond Half Dome, a rainbow arced across the heavens. The six agreed there was still time to reach the summit. They removed their ponchos, hoisted their backpacks, and headed up the trail toward Sub Dome.

As they plodded along, Steve White remarked how good he felt after the extended rest. Zip Cotter, who was taking long, slow strides, responded in his usual laconic manner that all he wanted was to get to the top. They had already hiked nine miles from Glacier Point that day lugging forty-pound backpacks. Though dog-tired, the hikers were intent on finishing the climb; they could rest on Half Dome.

They reached the base of the cables at 7:50 P.M., dropped their backpacks, and rummaged through them for gloves to better grip the cables. Given the fading light and slick surfaces, the climb was going to be tricky this evening.

Just as they were about to start up, a man with long blond hair—Mike Hoog—appeared at the upper cables and shouted down to them: Go get help! Two guys got hit by lightning!

Then he disappeared, before they could get more information. They weren't sure if he was serious, and if he was, what kind of help did he want? Not knowing what to make of all this, the hikers decided to scurry up there and find out.

Clu Cotter led the way up, closely followed by Steve White. The other four—Cage, Zip Cotter, Paul Kolbenschlag, and Monroe Bridges—lagged behind. Clu Cotter, a Half Dome first-timer, was taken aback by the steepness of the grade and the far distance between stepping boards. Fearful of heights as well, he didn't look down. When he and White reached the top, they saw people bent over individuals in sleeping bags at the point overlooking Yosemite Valley.

White's first thought was: God, it really happened!

He and Clu Cotter waited for their four companions to catch up. As all six men reached the scene, Weiner and Rice were howling and squirming in pain.

Cage: "I specifically remember one calling to the other by name and screaming, 'My God, my God, we're going to die, we're going to die!' And frankly, my buddies and I were thinking that one or both might very well die."

The new arrivals shed their backpacks and offered to help. Those loaded packs would prove to be a lifesaver, because they were stuffed with valuable supplies—sleeping bags, food, stoves, clothing, and, especially important, water. Linda Crozier immediately put Brian Cage's party to work, requesting that they move Weiner and Rice to a more level spot. With three on a side, the six men gently lifted each victim where he lay on a mattress, carried him a short distance, and set him down. When they finished, Weiner and Rice were at right angles to each other, their heads about six feet apart.

Crozier then asked Cage and White to try to find a pulse anywhere on the victims' feet. Cage pulled the boots off Rice and was astonished to discover that the bottoms of his socks on both feet were missing, as though they had vaporized inside the boots. The bottoms of his feet seemed okay—cold and pink-white, not burned in any way—though the edges of the remaining sock material were charred. Cage and White couldn't locate a pulse in either Weiner's or Rice's feet. Cage leafed through a pamphlet from his first-aid kit for information on how to treat lightning injuries and found nothing there on the subject.

Kolbenschlag and Zip Cotter walked a short distance away to another part of the Dome, unnerved by the obvious pain and anguish of the two injured men. Kolbenschlag was so physically beat, he could do little more than collapse on the granite. He was in poor shape for the hike and had barely made it to the summit.

As the dampness and frigid stone stole warmth from their already compromised bodies, Weiner and Rice both complained of feeling chilled. Crozier didn't observe any deterioration in their vital signs, but she was still very aware of the threat of severe shock and the extreme danger it would pose. Getting and keeping them warm was crucial. At her request, Clu Cotter, White, Bridges, and Cage pulled sleeping bags from their backpacks. Bridges went into the cave to retrieve more bags. When he shone his flashlight in the dark enclosure, the sight of Brian Jordan's body made him recoil.

Bridges emerged with two more sleeping bags, deeply traumatized by the image of the boy whose brief life had been abruptly extinguished. Crozier placed one bag under and two more on top of Weiner and Rice; each was now enveloped by four bags.

It was 8:30 P.M. The victims' weak and rapid pulses indicated to Crozier that their blood pressure was dangerously low. In her assessment, one or both might perish if they spent the entire night there. She and the others could continue to treat for shock, maintain the ABCs, periodically monitor the pair's condition, and try to make them comfortable, but both needed advanced medical treatment.

One option crossed her mind: Could a team of hikers somehow transport Weiner and Rice down to the Valley floor? Not likely. Even if they had enough agility and strength to do so, how could this maneuver take place without causing further injury?

Meanwhile, the clock was ticking. In little more than thirty minutes, darkness would fall.

Crozier fought back against the panic rising within her. Weiner's and Rice's fates were squarely in her hands—she and she alone had to make the right decisions. She desperately wanted someone to lift this burden from her shoulders, to have the park rangers take over.

But no relief was in sight.

◄○►

HOOG WAS A long-distance runner, and whenever life became stressful, he turned to running as an outlet. Confident that Linda Crozier could manage with the others' aid, he announced that he would go and get help. With that he left, intent upon sprinting to the ranger station in Little Yosemite Valley over four miles away. Pedroncelli, sensing he was no longer needed, followed Hoog down the cables.

Crozier accepted that no other help was forthcoming anytime soon. In her mind, she needed more control over the situation, more continuity in the care of the two victims. So she organized teams. She, White, and Clu Cotter would attend to Rice, and Miller and Brutus to Weiner; Bridges would remain at Esteban's side. If any of the injured took a turn for the worse, Crozier reasoned, those who were closely attending him would be more apt to spot it. To supply nourishment for the group, Cage boiled water and cooked food on his camp stove.

Given the extreme pain in Rice's right leg, Crozier feared it might be fractured or broken as a result of the severe muscle contractions that often accompany electrical injuries. His right foot was angled. She gently pulled the foot to straighten it out and then instructed White how to hold it in traction. Squatting, he grasped the foot with both hands at the ankle and lightly drew it toward himself by leaning his weight back, thus producing tension in the leg. This relieved Rice's pain somewhat.

White asked Rice why he and his buddies had risked coming up there in the storm.

Rice proved as unyielding as ever. What he felt and was thinking he would keep to himself. That had always been Rice's way, and apparently even this tragic incident would not dislodge him from his long-rooted stance. His clipped, muted response: We wanted to dance in the lightning.

Off to the side, Bridges sat with Esteban, who by now had become morose and stoic. He, too, was not talking, not respond-

ing to Bridges's questions about what happened, and why. He'd
withdrawn, tormented by the disastrous turn of events precipi-
tated by their dash up the mountain. With brutal awareness, he
now realized how wrong he and Rice had been in thinking that
together they could meet any challenge; that overcoming fear was
the way to reap life's rewards. The suddenness, unpredictability,
and ferocity of lightning were unlike anything they could have
ever conjured up or overcome. He sat there, plagued by the harsh
penalties wrought by their misjudgments. Two people had been
killed. How would he ever get over that?

His outer face was indeed a stoic mask, but inside was the deepest pain anyone could ever feel.

There was nothing he could do now about what happened,
except pray that neither Rice nor Weiner died as well.

BILL PIPPEY AND BRUCE JORDAN had wisely stayed below Sub Dome
after the sixteen-year-old said he was afraid of the lightning storm.
Karl Buchner and Steve Ellner also stayed below due to Ellner's
fears. Now they all hooked up and prepared to join their companions on the summit. They repacked their backpacks and began
the ascent.

While climbing the stairs, they encountered a frenzied Hoog
dashing down. He blurted out that hikers had been hit by lightning up on top, that he was going for help.

Ellner said: That's it, I'm not going any farther. I'm out of here.

He headed back down. Pippey initially thought Hoog meant
the strike had occurred some time ago, but Buchner told him no,
it must have just happened. Pippey refused to believe that the incident involved anyone in his group. As he later stated, "I simply
blocked that notion out of my mind."

On the cables they met Pedroncelli coming down. Stammer-
ing, he reported that two guys got killed and one was a young kid,

that two others were badly hurt. Pedroncelli also said he thought the group was from San Jose but wasn't sure.

Those words stunned Buchner, Pippey, and Jordan. Buchner acutely felt Bruce Jordan's presence right behind him; it was probably his brother who had been killed. In silence, the three continued their climb, the full weight of the unfolding tragedy now hanging over them like a landslide about to give way from above.

Dan Crozier, Linda Crozier's brother, remembers that Hoog had a ghostly look on his face when he reached the camping area below Sub Dome and explained what had happened and where he was going. Like Hoog, Dan Crozier was in excellent physical shape and said he'd go with him. By this time, Pedroncelli had arrived; he remained with Jenny Hayes as Hoog and Crozier bounded down the terrain in dimming light with little regard for the trail.

As soon as Buchner, Pippey, and Bruce Jordan arrived at the summit and Rice saw them coming his way, he shouted: The kid's dead, man, the kid's dead! Frith fell over the edge!

Buchner absorbed the full impact of the news, then said: I can't handle this.

He retreated back down the cables.

When Buchner joined Ellner at base camp, he couldn't speak. His eyes, according to Ellner, were glazed over and blank, zombie-like. Ellner waited for Buchner to say something, anything. Then, as though a third person was speaking through him, Buchner told Ellner about the two deaths and how Weiner and Rice were all messed up.

Referring to Esteban, Ellner asked: How's Adrian?

He seemed to be okay, Buchner replied.

Ellner: "At that point, I was just glad he was alive and that I was, too."

He and Buchner chose to stay put for the night, out in the open without setting up their tent, but neither slept much. Each attempted to digest the horrifying news about their comrades whose care, whose very lives were in the hands of strangers.

On the summit, meanwhile, Pippey rushed up to Esteban and asked: Is it true? Is it true? Oh my God, oh my God, oh my God.

Pippey was responsible for Brian Jordan coming on the trip. Now he was dead and so was Frith, and it looked like Weiner and Rice were going to die, too. The enormity of it all crushed Pippey. He stood planted in place, crying uncontrollably.

Bruce Jordan, as if he hadn't heard the news, just stared blankly at the ground. Although the reality had dented his consciousness, a world without his twin brother hadn't fully penetrated yet.

◄○►

IT WAS 8:45 P.M. Darkness was settling over Yosemite Valley. On Half Dome, efforts to keep Weiner and Rice alive and as comfortable as possible continued unabated. Those caring for the stricken hikers also attended to each other.

All the activity was taking place just feet from the precipice. Pippey and Bruce Jordan were the most shaken by what had happened, and their mental states were the most unpredictable. White noticed that Jordan stood off in the shadows by himself, his blond hair, white shirt, and ashen face illuminated by remnants of the evening light, all of which made him look ghostly. He had shown no emotion so far. Given the psychological impact of what had transpired, there was a danger that yet another hiker might plummet over the edge, either intentionally or accidentally.

Crozier went over to Pippey, who was still sobbing, and grabbed him by the shoulders, shook him, yelled at him to get control of himself. It was important, she said, that he look out for Bruce Jordan. She told Pippey to take him to the middle of the Dome, a safe distance from the edge, and sit with him, comfort him, and keep him away from the first-aid area. She stressed that the pair were not to hike back down in the dark.

His shoulders still shaking, Pippey put an arm around Jordan. Together they ambled over to the broad granite saddle between two elevations on the summit.

Kolbenschlag, who knew Morse code from his pilot training, came up with the same idea Pedroncelli had earlier that evening. He stationed himself near the edge with a direct view of the camp- grounds below and began sending an SOS with his flashlight. Fatigued from the climb and stress, he reclined in a sandy spot with his upper body braced against a rock and flashed a signal every ten minutes or so, closing his eyes and resting between trans- missions. Zip Cotter, who had retrieved two cups of hot choco- late, spelled Kolbenschlag, and together they sent SOS's intermittently over the next hour. It still wasn't dark enough, how- ever, for anyone down in the Valley to readily notice a faint emer- gency signal from Half Dome.

While dozing at one point, Kolbenschlag was startled by some- thing on his hand. He reflexively flung his arm up and out, and glimpsed a furry object—a chipmunk or similar creature—hurtling off the mountaintop with a pathetic squeal. When he came to his senses, Kolbenschlag felt awful about what he'd just done.

-◄o►-

LINDA CROZIER continued to check Weiner's and Rice's pulses periodically to monitor their condition and stay alert for any sudden change. Every twenty minutes, she and Renee Miller also did a serial exam of the two men: Does this hurt? Do you have feeling here? Are you warm enough? Because the lightning strike had knocked Rice unconscious and because he was com- plaining of neck pain, Crozier feared that perhaps he had suf- fered a head or neck injury after all. She had Clu Cotter take over in keeping Rice's leg elevated, and told White to hold Rice's head immobile.

The leg wasn't broken, Crozier concluded; rather, his pain— like the severe ache in Weiner's legs—was due to burn-related internal problems aggravated by repeated cramping and swelling. The inflammation was stealing fluids from the rest of their bod- ies and made them crave water. But Crozier wouldn't give them anything to drink because she worried their stomachs couldn't absorb gulps of fluid. If they threw up, they might inhale vomit and suffocate, which sometimes happens to shock victims. Instead, to slake their thirst and prevent dehydration, she offered them T-shirts partially soaked in water to suck on.

Weiner cried out that he had to pee. Crozier asked Brutus to get a plastic bag so they could collect the urine for later examination by doctors. But when they helped Weiner into position, he couldn't relieve himself. Although his bladder was full and his need to urinate overwhelming, the lightning probably traumatized his sphincter muscle, causing it to spasm and block his urinary tract. A more remote possibility was the blockage of his kidneys with burned blood cells, a condition that can trigger kidney failure. Weiner screamed in agony. Alarmed that his organs might be damaged, he became frenzied.

Rice yelled at him: Get fuckin' control of yourself! You're going to be all right!

The words had a calming effect on Weiner.

It was crucial that neither of them fall asleep, slip into semiconsciousness, or, worse, lapse into a life-threatening coma. By staying awake, they could respond to questions and communicate how and what they were feeling—a barometer of their worsening or improving condition. If either sank deeper into shock, Crozier would have to try a different medical tack. She called over to Esteban and asked him to come closer and make sure Weiner and Rice remained conscious.

This snapped Esteban out of his own mental distress. He crouched near each victim and turned first to one, then the other, saying over and over: I love you, man. You're going to be okay. You're going to make it.

By now, Pippey was more composed, too. He offered to help Crozier. She inquired about Bruce Jordan, whom Pippey said had fallen asleep in his sleeping bag. Crozier asked Pippey to heat water for coffee, tea, or hot chocolate for anyone who wanted refreshment. It was important to keep him busy, she knew—to make him feel like he was contributing.

Nine o'clock. Only a faint glow silhouetted the western mountain ridges. As darkness took command, Kolbenschlag's and Cotter's more visible SOS signals by flashlight began to elicit responses from the Valley floor. Soon there were tens of lights blinking back from the campgrounds. But did anyone down there really know Morse code? Might campers be thinking this was merely a gambit, a playful exchange of light beams? Actually, in his exhausted state, Kolbenschlag had been flashing the wrong signal. In Morse code, SOS is dot-dot-dot, dash-dash-dash, dot-dot-dot. He had been transmitting dash-dash-dash, dot-dot-dot, dash-dash-dash, or OSO.

Pippey wandered over to where Kolbenschlag and Zip Cotter were and observed their signaling efforts. Like Pedroncelli, Pippey knew from movies what the proper SOS was. He detected the error and told Kolbenschlag, who promptly started flashing the correct signal. Soon one light brighter than the others began flashing in return. It was what Kolbenschlag was looking for—SOK, the code for "I acknowledge your call, will get help."

When Zip Cotter shouted to the others that the SOS had been seen and rangers would be told, loud cheering erupted. Someone in the Valley now knew of their plight.

◄O►

THE SENDER OF THE SOK contacted a park ranger, who quickly forwarded it to Jim Reilly, the supervising ranger that evening. He in turn dispatched John Dill, a park search and rescue technician, to investigate.

Dill drove to a parking lot near Mirror Lake, where there is a good view of Half Dome's summit. He had no idea what this emergency was all about, but using a bullhorn amplified by a battery hook-up, he could gather clues by shouting questions to those on top. This was a standard communication mode for Yosemite's search and rescue division when rock climbers got into trouble on a mountain face. Communicating this way with someone on the top of Half Dome was a first, however.

At 9:25 P.M., through his bullhorn, Dill instructed the signaler (Kolbenschlag) to blink the light once for "yes," twice for "no" as he posed questions. Cotter was the relay man: He yelled the questions to Linda Crozier, fifty feet away, who shouted back answers for Kolbenschlag to translate into one or two blinks of the flashlight.

Is this emergency for real?

Yes.

Is anyone dead?

Yes.

How many?

Two blinks.

Is anyone injured?

Yes.

How many?

Three blinks.

Are the injuries the result of a fall?

No.

Is anyone bleeding?

No.

Are there broken bones?

No.

If you don't receive help, will someone die?

Everyone on the summit could hear the exchange among Dill, Cotter, and Crozier, and everyone zeroed in on Crozier when Dill shouted up this last question.

Crozier: "I knew that if I said no and someone died that night, I would blame myself for it, that I didn't do all I could have. Until I had to respond to this question, I hadn't needed to think this way. When I shouted yes, it was as if we all accepted that, yes, it could happen."

Kolbenschlag flashed one blink to Dill. Moments passed without a response.

Then Dill repeated: If we can't get to you tonight, will someone die?

Cotter again relayed the question to Crozier. Why had Dill asked it twice? Did it mean they weren't going to send help?

With all eyes on Crozier, she hollered more resolutely this time: Yes!

There was an extended pause down below. Dill then shouted up that he would get back to them.

When Cotter relayed Dill's final statement, a collective sign of relief could almost be heard from those on top. Help was in sight —park rangers and medics would arrive soon.

The nightmare was about to end.

—◀◉▶—

THE OPTIMISM on the summit soon gave way to the immediate realities. Weiner's and Rice's legs had become increasingly numb. Crozier couldn't detect circulation in their feet, which were turning white. This indicated that capillaries in the feet weren't transporting blood, a bad sign. So she and Miller vigorously massaged the pair's legs and feet hoping to boost circulation.

Weiner seemed to be in worse shape at the moment, both physically and psychologically. He reported more pain throughout his body and was more incoherent than Rice. He still had to pee urgently but couldn't, and that caused agony. At one point, he gasped that he was having trouble breathing. Crozier, listening to his chest, heard a slight gurgling in his lungs—a possible indication of pulmonary edema, or fluid in the lungs, which could drown him. Treatment for pulmonary edema is oxygen delivered through nasal prongs or a facemask; sometimes a breathing tube is inserted into the windpipe or the patient is hooked up to a ventilator. But, of course, Crozier had no such equipment.

Rice became more demanding and hostile, which is typical behavior in trauma cases. He demanded water. Crozier relented but gave him and Weiner only about two tablespoons' worth. Rice craved more.

Fuckin' bitch! he yelled.

After almost three hours of lying in the same position on his back, one foot elevated and held in traction, his head immobilized, Rice was extremely uncomfortable. He wanted to move, wanted more to drink, but Crozier refused. His verbal abuse turned more vociferous—he called her one nasty name after another. She placidly accepted his tirades, realizing they stemmed from agony and frustration, and were a good sign that he was coherent and stable and gaining strength.

Esteban told Rice: Listen to Linda and do what she says. You'll be okay. I love you, you're the greatest.

Esteban also reassured Weiner, who at one point muttered he wanted to die. He appeared to be fading.

Crozier later recalled that Esteban proved to be a bulwark in this crisis. "He was like the Rock of Gibraltar, absolutely the greatest. Except for Pippey and Bruce Jordan, he was the only one there whom Rice and Weiner knew. He stayed by them, talking to them, telling them they were going to be all right and to thank God they were alive. He was able to calm them down and sustain their spirits."

AT 10:20 P.M. there was still no more word from Dill or anyone else in Yosemite Valley. Why hadn't authorities followed up by now? The joy that everyone had felt forty-five minutes earlier had evaporated. As interminable minutes dragged by, Linda Crozier's confidence ebbed. More doubts crept into her mind about the sole responsibility she had assumed for decisions, whether she was making the right ones, whether others should continue to defer to her judgment, whether she could keep this up.

She thought: How did I ever get into this position, being responsible for two men, either of whom could die at any moment? Outwardly, despite her inner turmoil, she projected a sense of coolheadedness, self-assurance, and resolve.

To help the others stay alert, she rotated their assignments while they still cared for the same victim. They also checked with each other and provided mutual support and encouragement: How are you doing? Are you okay? Do you need anything?

As time passed, the temperature fell and a cold breeze swept across the bare granite. Still under cloud cover, the dome's cast was dark, almost pitch black. Crozier, skimpily clad, was becoming increasingly chilled. Sitting, she stuck her bare legs, riddled with goosebumps, under the edge of the sleeping bags covering Rice. Others also clustered next to Rice or Weiner. Warm clothing was parceled out. Anyone who wanted a hot drink could tap Cage's and Pippey's ready supply of boiling water.

Slivers from a partial moon finally peeked through scattered clouds, diffusing the thin light that now reflected off granite and that illuminated, in eerily gray hues, the Dome and everyone huddled there. Zip Cotter described the scene as "surreal, what I imagined being on the surface of the moon would be like."

Group morale was of concern to White. What would happen if there weren't a rescue that night? He told jokes in an effort to perk everyone up and bolster their spirits. He didn't want anyone to become disheartened or lose their focus if they had to spend the entire night on Half Dome. It was White whom Crozier leaned on most for support. He kept asking her how she was, telling her she was doing a great job and not to take Rice's insults to heart.

White had a strong opinion about the tragedy—that sheer stupidity and craziness had kindled it. But he kept his thoughts to himself.

White: "While I felt deeply sorry about what happened to these guys and tried to do everything I possibly could for them, I also became very angry about what they did. In the face of extreme danger, they acted like there was none, almost in defiance of the storm and lightning. Just unbelievably reckless. It was all so unnecessary, a waste."

Every now and then, a semidelirious Weiner called out: I can't feel my legs! I can't breathe! I'm going to die!

Again Rice yelled at him to get a grip, that he'd be all right, and again the words soothed Weiner. Rice's inner strength was helping Weiner—and himself—survive the crisis.

It was now 10:45 P.M. Physical as well as mental fatigue overcame Esteban. Crozier urged him to try to sleep while Bridges sat nearby, nudging Esteban periodically so he wouldn't drift into a coma. But Esteban couldn't sleep. Numbed, he just closed his eyes and wrestled with distressing thoughts about the day's events.

Rice suddenly exclaimed he was going to throw up. Crozier went into emergency mode, enlisting White and Cage to help her swiftly turn Rice on his side so he wouldn't choke on vomit. The three grasped his sleeping bag and carefully rolled him over, avoiding any movement that might jar his neck or back.

Then Rice coolly announced: Just kidding. I wanted to see if you know what you're doing.

White and Crozier looked at each other, incredulous. But as she regained her composure, Crozier reckoned that Rice, in his own twisted manner, was probably just trying to loosen everyone up, show he could roll with the punches, counterattack, take control again. The incident, however irritating to his caregivers, once more revealed his unflagging and indomitable spirit.

Eleven o'clock came and went without additional communication or sign of help from below.

Was a rescue under way or not?

And what had happened to Mike Hoog?

Stillness descended upon the Dome. When they weren't conferring about the status of Weiner or Rice, everyone was silent, and the silence aggravated their anxiety and stupor. The hikers were drained. They were cold and weary and somber, and just wanted to curl up inside a sleeping bag, though if Weiner or Rice made the slightest noise, someone rushed to attend to him. How much longer could the two injured men hold on without a bodily collapse of some sort?

As Linda Crozier's morale began to sink, too, her fears increased. The thought of what might happen to Weiner or Rice under her care was almost unbearable.

She quickly suppressed another surge of panic. The voice in her head said: Get a hold of yourself, Linda. You can't be the one who gives up hope—the others are depending on you. If you despair, the whole group will lose confidence. And that would be disastrous.

Esteban: "One of the most heartwarming emotions I felt and that sustained my will on this terrible night was watching these unknown persons comfort and care for me and my fallen buddies in our most dire hour of need. I remember people giving me their food, water, clothing, blankets, attention, caring, and human warmth throughout that night, which seemed to last forever."

Rice became more clearheaded as the night deepened, though he still complained vehemently about everything. Crozier made a pact with him: If help doesn't arrive by midnight, we'll move you into a more comfortable position. At this point, she had concluded privately that Rice probably would survive until morning if there were no rescue before then. He was stubborn and belligerent, intent on getting his way—a good omen.

However, the deterioration in his legs meant that without some kind of enhanced treatment, he would probably lose one or both of them to amputation.

The outlook for Weiner was bleaker. He lapsed into longer and longer periods of quiet punctuated by whimpering and sobbing, and into and out of consciousness. His injuries seemed more critical, his pain and unease more intense. Moreover, Weiner didn't have Rice's dogged determination. His fragile mental state might make him less inclined to resist death.

It was now 11:45 P.M., more than five hours since the lightning strikes.

Where were the rangers?

8

RESCUE

The age-long stability of nature—my God, you can depend on it! There's eternity in these rocks.
—Carl Sharsmith, Yosemite ranger, 1930–94

Ranger Colin Campbell felt uneasy that no one was on duty in Little Yosemite Valley; the assigned ranger had left earlier that Saturday morning due to illness. Many hikers and campers frequented this area—especially now, at the end of July—which meant that any number of issues involving campers, bears, injuries, and the like could demand the ranger's attention. Campbell told his supervisor, Dan Horner, that he thought he should cover the station, at least for the night. Horner agreed. So Campbell saddled up his horse, John Paul, gathered some toiletries and a rain slicker, and departed for Little Yosemite Valley in late afternoon. He expected to return the next day.

Campbell, an assistant horse patrol supervisor, was thirty-five years old, married, and the father of a two-year-old daughter. More than six feet tall and husky at 195 pounds, he had held several National Park Service jobs, all in Yosemite. He'd received his bachelor of science degree in natural resource management from California Polytechnic College in San Luis Obispo in 1980 and, the prior year, had begun working for the National Park Service manning an entrance station at Yosemite for the summer. The next season he worked in campgrounds, mainly handling campsite reservations. Then he patrolled the park in a vehicle as a ranger. After two years in that position, he settled into the horse patrol division. This was the post Campbell occupied in 1985, his first year as a full-time ranger.

At 4 P.M. on July 27, as John Paul plodded up the John Muir Trail, a storm was building over Tenaya Canyon. It's going to be a real douser, Campbell thought. And, his experienced eye told him, unusually menacing. Moreover, it was sweeping right smack toward this part of Yosemite. Ordinarily, he gave hikers and backpackers freedom and space to enjoy the backcountry as long as they obeyed the law. Campbell kept a sharp eye out for potential problems, but he usually played it low-key and attempted to stay in the background. This time, though, his instincts made him uneasy. Something about this storm seemed different. So, with John Paul's hooves clacking on the granite, Campbell told people he passed not to take any undue risks, not to get caught out in the open, to be particularly careful in case of lightning.

When he reached Little Yosemite Valley, Campbell first stopped at the ranger station there, which consisted mainly of two wall tents. He then made rounds throughout the area to make sure everything was all right. Back at the station, he settled down for the evening. Scott Jackson, a trail maintenance employee who lived here in one of the tents during summer, soon returned from a day of hiking and joined him.

Lightning and thunder started blasting the heavens as they sat. When heavy rain began falling around 6 P.M., Campbell and Jackson took cover in the tents. Sheets of rain hammered the canvas for the next forty-five minutes, accompanied by barrages of lightning that left a distinctive scent, like burned gunpowder, in the drenched air. Ferocious cracks of thunder sent shock waves more powerful than Campbell had ever felt reverberating in the very ground under their feet.

By seven o'clock, the storm had passed. Campbell fired up a propane gas stove, opened a can of SpaghettiO's from the station's food stash, and spooned it into a pot to heat. He and Jackson then plunked down in a couple of chairs and ate their meager dinner.

Mike Hoog and Dan Crozier reached Little Yosemite Valley a little before 9:30 P.M. It took them a few minutes to locate the ranger station in the dark. When they did, Campbell was in front of a tent brushing his teeth, while Jackson was seated by the campfire. Hoog gushed out the details: Five guys hit by lightning, two dead, one fell over the edge, three guys injured, two seriously, they could die, need medical help fast!

Campbell now knew that his decision to man Little Yosemite Valley had been a good one—and that it was going to be a long night.

On his walkie-talkie, he reported the information to the ranger at the dispatch station down in the Valley. He and Jackson then hastily loaded a couple of packs with gear kept there at the Little Yosemite Valley station: oxygen canisters, a breakdown litter, ropes and anchors, climbing hardware, flashlights, and a "blitz pack" of emergency medical supplies. Campbell's walkie-talkie would keep them in close contact with the Valley. Because John Paul wasn't equipped with a pack saddle, Campbell decided to leave him teth-ered at the station and go on foot, a decision he would later regret.

Without further delay, each man hefted his forty-pound pack and, in pitch darkness, they departed up the trail for Half Dome.

—◄o►—

AT THE VERY TIME Hoog was spilling the news to Campbell, John Dill was shouting questions via his loudspeaker up to Paul Kol-benschlag on the summit of Half Dome. Just after Dill repeated the question, Will anyone die if help doesn't arrive? his walkie-talkie came on. It was the park dispatcher relaying Campbell's report. Now Dill knew what had caused the emergency.

Dill yelled up to Kolbenschlag that he would get back to them, leaving those on top clueless about what would happen next. He himself didn't know.

As in most of the country's national parks, hundreds of emer-gencies occur in Yosemite every year—crises involving injuries, fires, climbers in trouble, lost hikers, lawbreakers, and more. When something potentially serious happens, the news is first reported to the central dispatch station. The ranger on duty there then for-wards it to the shift supervisor. Usually the supervisor assigns each case to an "incident commander," who then assumes operational responsibility for that emergency.*

The standard response to an emergency, if at all possible, is to move a ranger or team of rangers—a "hasty team"—quickly to the scene to assess the situation and report back to the shift supervi-sor. Regardless of whether a site report comes in, the supervisor and incident commander assign resources and brainstorm on

---

*In 1985, the National Park Service had five divisions in Yosemite: protection, resource management, maintenance, interpretation/education, and administration. Only per-sonnel in the protection and interpretation/education divisions were referred to as rangers. Protection rangers were generally responsible for fee collections, law enforce-ment, emergencies, and search and rescue operations, while interpretation/education rangers handled public information activities.

strategies—including contingency or backup plans—to deal with the emergency. *Reach, treat, and evacuate* is the approach in most cases, *reach* being a ground action typically.

The shift supervisor this night was James Reilly. Rangers wouldn't be able to reach the top of Half Dome anytime soon, so he would have to make decisions without valuable information from the scene. Given the extreme nature of this particular incident and potential rescue attempt, Reilly chose to keep matters in his own hands rather than assign the case to an incident commander, at least until things became clearer.

Campbell and Jackson would be first on the scene, but they would need at least two hours from Little Yosemite Valley, placing them on the summit sometime around midnight. For support after their arrival, Reilly dispatched a team of rangers—Dan Horner, Mike Mayer, and Paul Ducasse, each a park medic capable of providing advanced medical care, such as starting IVs, administering medications, immobilizing limbs, and using MAST (Military Anti-Shock Trousers)—inflatable pressure pants to increase blood pressure and ward off shock. They would go on horses.

Reilly also sent a crew of seven, headed by top-notch rescue climber Dimitri Barton, in case anyone had to be removed from Half Dome. That would require team skills, such as lowering a victim by rope down very steep sections of rock. If victims couldn't be evacuated this night, Barton's team would establish a support camp in Little Yosemite Valley. Medical and other supplies could be brought there from the Valley for transport to the summit by runners.

By the time Horner, Mayer, and Ducasse rode off on their mounts, it was already 11 P.M. Barton's team soon followed on foot.

The wild-card strategy was an air rescue, a long shot at best. The park helicopter wasn't designed for night flying, plus it took a skilled and experienced pilot to carry out such a complex assignment after dark. The only real option was to summon a helicopter from a commercial service in San Joaquin Valley to the west. But even then, given the hazards of night flying at low altitudes—

power lines, trees, and other objects to avoid, not to mention possibly strong winds over Half Dome—such a mission would be dangerous and very costly. Without sufficient moonlight, it wouldn't even be considered.

Reilly was particularly conservative when he made decisions of this magnitude. He placed the highest value on the well-being of rescuers and was aware of a rash of helicopter crashes in recent years. As the clock neared 11 P.M., with clouds still filling the sky, he hadn't called for a helicopter rescue. The hikers on Half Dome wouldn't receive help anytime soon. Complicating matters was another emergency report that came in right after Reilly got word of the Half Dome incident. This one, too, was a matter of life and death.

◄◦►

THE SECOND REPORT arrived at the dispatch office at 9:45 P.M. Hikers lost in the park had used a CB radio to communicate their desperate situation to a son in Yosemite Valley, who then told a ranger.

The ranger was able to piece together this much: that four females—two adults and two thirteen-year-olds—were lost in the vicinity of Tenaya Canyon; that the adults were sisters, ages forty-five and thirty-eight; and that both suffered from epilepsy and needed medicine daily. The group had intended to hike from Olmsted Point near Tenaya Lake in the high country down to Yosemite Valley via the little-used and poorly maintained Snow Creek Trail. Because this was to be only a day hike, the women weren't carrying extra clothing or food—or epilepsy medicine. The son had planned to pick them up in Yosemite Valley at hike's end.

The foursome had left Olmsted Point at 1:30 P.M. and expected to reach the Valley around 8. This left little more than an hour of daylight after the hike—a very small margin of safety. Moreover, had they scanned the skies, they likely would have noticed the cumulus clouds building above Clouds Rest.

Staying on Snow Creek Trail can be difficult where it traverses bare granite. Indeed, midway down, the women lost the trail. They spotted a "duck"—a trail marker made of stacked rocks—and then more ducks, which they tried to follow. These occasional markers led them farther down into a canyon, which seemed like the right direction. But after some distance, they found themselves over-looking an impassable cliff.

Anxious about the dark clouds massing overhead and the looming storm, the women frantically retraced their steps in the hope of locating Snow Creek Trail. A duck here and there sug-gested they were back on course, though mainly they just headed downhill as swiftly as possible on the assumption their destination was ahead. The rain that began in early evening quickly drenched and chilled them. When they hit level ground, the hikers weren't anywhere near Yosemite Valley. They were in Tenaya Canyon, about three miles east of Happy Isles.

Exiting Tenaya Canyon is extremely difficult. Its steep, pol-ished-granite walls rise thousands of feet, and dense vegetation car-pets the floor. Rangers refer to it as the "Bermuda Triangle of Yosemite," given the many hikers who have gotten lost there.*

Amid the fierce thunderstorm, wandering in the canyon maze, the women spotted and took refuge in a rock enclosure (not unlike Rice, Esteban, and their fellow hikers on Half Dome, and James Wunrow in nearby Kings Canyon National Park, all of whom took shelter in rock enclosures on this same day, with tragic conse-quences). They stayed huddled together in the enclosure even after

---

*One high-profile case dates to 1966, when Charles Frizzell, a thirty-one-year-old sci-entist at the Bay Area's Livermore Radiation Laboratory, seemingly vanished in Yosemite. Frizzell was last seen on June 4 hiking down from Olmsted Point. In those Cold War years, government authorities feared he had been killed or kidnapped, or that he had defected to China. Park rangers searched Tenaya Canyon in vain for more than a week. Some of Frizzell's co-workers joined the hunt, a contingent that later evolved into the Bay Area Mountain Rescue Unit. The mystery wasn't solved until spring 1971, when a hiker found Frizzell's credit card and a skull in Tenaya Canyon. Later that summer, another hiker stumbled upon some bones on a narrow, tree-lined ledge. Ranger Butch Farabee returned to the site with him and discovered more than a hundred human bones, pre-sumably Frizzell's, and shreds of a backpack several feet up in a nearby oak tree. Farabee suspects that Frizzell put his pack up there as a signal for help; that perhaps he had fallen to the ledge and broken bones below his waist. At the request of Frizzell's widow, Farabee buried the remains in Tenaya Canyon.

the storm had long since passed. About 8:30 P.M. they were able to contact the son with their CB radio. By this time, the forty-five-year-old woman had had an epileptic seizure. Without medicine within ten to fifteen hours, she or her sister might die. To make matters worse, both had suffered ankle sprains.

Reilly got the report on the lost hikers shortly after the Half Dome report. He assigned only two rangers, Ron Mackie and Scott Emmerich, to the Tenaya Canyon rescue because he was short-handed due to the Half Dome mission. Mackie, a supervisory park ranger, knew the area well. Emmerich was a park medic.

At 11:30 P.M., each hefting forty pounds of gear, Mackie and Emmerich embarked on a strenuous and treacherous hike to reach the four women. Their route was Aircraft Crash Canyon, so named because of numerous airplane crashes there in the early 1940s when U.S. Air Force pilots flew practice and sightseeing missions over Yosemite. (To this day, a large engine from one of the downed aircraft remains in the canyon.) In Mackie's experience, most hikers lost in Tenaya Canyon ended up in the inner gorge, in an area informally called Lost Valley. He and Emmerich headed for that location.

When the women took refuge in the rock enclosure, they wisely left their lit flashlights perched on a high rock. A ranger "spotter" on a distant point overlooking the canyon saw the light beams and guided the two rangers via radio as they descended. After hiking in the dark and cold all night, Mackie and Emmerich reached the most dangerous part of their journey, a drop down a steep and slippery granite incline. Rather than risk a fall, the two waited an hour for dawn before continuing.

Meanwhile, the four shivering and terrified hikers lay cuddled together trying to fend off the frigid temperatures. In addition to their other medical problems, one of the teens had a sharp pain in her side—a symptom, the two adults worried, of appendicitis. The night passed. None slept a single minute, their chilled bodies approaching hypothermia. Only the shared warmth from their snuggled bodies saved them.

The women left their shelter at dawn and began walking as best they could. Mackie and Emmerich, who by now had reached the canyon floor, spotted them at around 7 A.M. Emmerich administered medicine to the more seriously impaired woman, the one who had suffered a seizure, while Mackie prepared hot food and drink on his camping stove. The severe pain in the teen's side had abated and ultimately would prove to be benign.

Back in Yosemite Valley, a rescue helicopter from Lemoore Naval Air Station near Fresno had been summoned, and when it arrived, it flew to Tenaya Canyon to evacuate the party. The chopper transported the hikers and Emmerich to the Valley, then returned to retrieve Mackie. Thus ended a successful mission.

◄o►

BY THE TIME JACKSON and Campbell left Little Yosemite Valley, it was nearly 10 P.M. Jackson, who had turned twenty-three the previous month, was in superb physical condition. A long-distance runner like Hoog, he had spent the summer weeks hiking and running the park's trails. Campbell, on the other hand, as a horse patrol supervisor spent more time getting about on horseback than on foot. And he had arrived at Little Yosemite Valley this day wearing cowboy boots rather than hiking boots, not anticipating a trek through rough terrain in the dark. Even more worrisome, how would he scale Half Dome's slippery granite in slick leather soles?

Hoog and Dan Crozier followed on the heels of Jackson and Campbell to rejoin their hiking companions at the base of Half Dome. All told, the pair would log more than sixteen miles of hiking, mostly uphill, over fourteen hours. To that, Hoog added a jaunt up and down the cables on Half Dome. As they retraced their steps, the rush of the evening's excitement overcame their fatigue.

Right from the start, Jackson outpaced Campbell, who was silently cursing himself for not having worn hiking boots. Or better, he wished he had ridden John Paul. Jackson reached Sub

Dome at 11:15 P.M. and kept on going. Campbell got there ten minutes later. By now his feet were sore and blistered. He needed hiking shoes. Approaching a tent, Campbell flashed his light, roused the sleeping occupant inside, and inquired about the man's shoe size. The startled camper surely thought this was some kind of sick joke, but then he saw the ranger uniform and concluded it wasn't.

Size twelve, he responded.

It was Campbell's size exactly—a "lucky break," he later recalled.

Campbell said he needed hiking boots. The camper offered what he had: his high-top sneakers. Campbell pulled off his boots, stashed them near the tent opening, donned the sneakers, and vanished.

It was 11:30 P.M.

◄○►

MEANWHILE, RANGERS Horner, Mayer, and Ducasse rode their horses up the John Muir Trail. The terrain blocked out moonlight in many places, making it almost impossible to see anything in the shadows. Horner, the park's horse patrol supervisor and an experienced horseman, assured his companions that their mounts knew the trail and could be relied upon to stay on it.

Mayer and Ducasse were quite leery about trusting animals to negotiate the narrow track at night, with its numerous granite steps, rocks, drainage abutments, and occasional steep drop-offs. They themselves couldn't even sense in the dense blackness whether they were going uphill or down. Flashlights were out of the question because the light might disrupt the horses' vision, creating an even greater hazard. So the riders had no choice but to place all faith in the animals' ability to grip stone with their hooves and keep a hand in front of their faces to ward off any unseen branches. All the time Horner listened to his walkie-talkie for updates on the rescue and if there would be an attempted air evacuation.

◄○►

SHORTLY AFTER 11 P.M., moonlight broke through partially clearing skies, spurring Reilly to move ahead with plans for a helicopter rescue. Although he still lacked a firsthand evaluation of the emergency scene, Reilly approved a request to dispatch Medi-Flight of Northern California, an air ambulance service from Memorial Hospital in Modesto, approximately a hundred miles west of Yosemite.

In 1985, such service was a relatively young concept, one rooted in knowledge gained from the Korean and Vietnam conflicts. In particular, army surgeons tending the 250,000 casualties of the Vietnam War saw the need for timely triage and quickly learned the importance of rapid transport and treatment of wounded soldiers. Findings showed that victims' chances of survival were best within the first hour of critical injury, the so-called golden hour. After that, the odds declined dramatically.

Also, research on heart attacks had demonstrated the value of prompt cardiopulmonary resuscitation. CPR must take place within four to six minutes of heart failure to restore cardiac function and oxygen circulation. Otherwise, the damage may be irreversible.

The emphasis on immediate treatment gave rise to a host of new emergency services. First came the expansion of emergency rooms at hospitals. Before the 1970s, many general acute-care hospitals didn't have anything like an emergency department; only a few large medical centers did, and they were mostly teaching facilities. Prehospital care was almost nonexistent, and medical treatment usually didn't begin until a patient arrived at the hospital. Typically, patients were delivered to the nearest hospital either by hearses, because they were the only vehicles available in which people could lie flat, or by an ambulance if one was at hand. At the hospital, a nurse, intern, or on-call physician would administer treatment in a room stocked only with basic medical supplies—bandages, suction, oxygen, scalpels, hemostats, splints, restraints, sutures, syringes, and a few medications. It may or may not have had any emergency equipment. If it did, this "emergency room"—now a misnomer in all but the smallest hospitals—served as the staging area for care. For serious cases, the on-call nurse would summon a staff physician, the patient's personal doctor (if known), or perhaps another general practitioner or surgeon outside the hospital.

Over time, as the importance of sophisticated emergency care gained recognition, ambulances bypassed small hospitals with limited facilities in favor of larger medical centers with better emergency services and equipment. Thus evolved dedicated emergency departments, which were common features at most hospitals by the early 1970s.* Spurring this movement was the federal Emergency Medical Services Systems Act of 1973 authorizing the secretary of the U.S. Department of Health, Education and Welfare to provide grants to states and other jurisdictions to develop and operate emergency medical services. Expanded legislation in 1976 helped promote EMS systems in rural and other medically underserved areas.

Still, high-quality emergency rooms were inaccessible to many victims within the golden hour. What these patients needed was treatment at the scene, and that meant improving ambulance services. Up to the 1970s, ambulance drivers in most areas of the country had to meet minimal standards—get their fingerprints checked, pass a special driver's test, and take a basic first-aid course. The situation called for trained professionals who could provide immediate, appropriate emergency medical care in the field, which prompted the creation of prehospital emergency medicine certification programs. Paramedics soon became essential members of ambulance teams.

Some urgent cases, however, necessitated the kind of sophisticated treatment available only at well-equipped hospitals. The solution: faster transport to those facilities by helicopter. A few

---

*In 1968, a group of eight physicians founded the American College of Emergency Physicians. In 1979, the American Board of Medical Specialties and the American Medical Association recognized emergency medicine as the twenty-third medical specialty. So board-certified emergency medical care has only been available for about thirty years.

advanced hospitals around the country therefore began offering air ambulance services with EMTs, nurses or paramedics, and sometimes physicians on board to provide expert care.

An auxiliary development in emergency medicine was trauma care—treating patients who have severe and multiple injuries at regional centers that offer a team of multidisciplinary experts and special trauma gear. Trauma is the leading cause of death among people younger than forty-four (auto accidents are responsible for about half of such deaths) and one of the country's most expensive health-care problems. While many trauma deaths happen immediately, many others occur past the golden hour for any number of secondary reasons. In response to this need, some hospitals gained designation as trauma centers.

On Half Dome this night, Rice's and Weiner's critical condition mandated transport to a trauma center. Not only can lightning injuries be highly destructive and lethal, but sometimes they aren't readily detectable, as with damage to vital organs or the brain, impairments to the nervous and circulatory systems, or a weakening of the immune system. Only a highly trained physician using advanced technology might correctly diagnose and treat such injuries. With each passing hour, the future well-being of Rice and Weiner hinged on Medi-Flight's ability to pluck them from Half Dome and deliver them to a trauma center.

WHEN MEDI-FLIGHT began operating on December 1, 1978, it was only the third air ambulance program in California and one of only nine nationally. Founder Rick Donker, vice president of Memorial Hospital, had earlier developed the statewide EMT curriculum.

When an accident report came in, Medi-Flight customarily flew directly to the scene or wherever the injured person was located. There, Medi-Flight's paramedic treated and, with the help of a flight nurse, stabilized the injured party, which typically involved inserting an IV and hooking up a cardiac monitor, then strapping the patient onto a gurney. The helicopter delivered the "packaged" victim to Memorial Hospital in Modesto.

Night flights were common at Medi-Flight. It received up to three or four calls on most nights, many from the California Highway Patrol. Each response depended on the amount of moonlight available for a safe flight, landing, and evacuation.

Given its proximity to Yosemite, Medi-Flight routinely flew there, perhaps once or twice a week in the busy summer months and maybe once a month or less in winter. However, flying a helicopter into Yosemite Valley could be dicey even in daylight, particularly on summer afternoons when the heat and thinner air made it more difficult for chopper blades to generate lift. Crane Flat, which sits above the Valley floor, gave helicopters more room to maneuver; consequently many victims were taken there for airlift out of the park.

Night flights to Yosemite Valley were less common. On moonless nights, victims in critical condition were transported by ambulance to Crane Flat to await air evacuation if and when conditions permitted.

Medi-Flight became especially cautious about night flights after a tragic mission on June 23, 1982. Just after 1 A.M., a Medi-Flight crew that included a top-notch pilot, paramedic, and nurse took off from Modesto for Sonora Pass in the Sierra Nevada to retrieve an auto accident victim in critical condition. In scant moonlight, while trying to manuever the craft for landing, the pilot was disoriented by a patch of darkness. Helicopter lights don't provide adequate illumination in pitch dark, with no objects to illuminate. All the pilot sees is bright light and a black backdrop. In effect, he can't see.* Airplane pilots can navigate by instruments when flying in utter darkness or obscured conditions, but helicopter pilots don't use instruments in tight places like Yosemite Valley. For them, it all comes down to visibility. They need ambient light to see objects, landmarks, and the horizon—reference points for

---

*The improvement in night vision goggles spurred on by the first Gulf war in the early 1990s has greatly assisted helicopter pilots in their night flying.

keeping the craft properly oriented. When visibility is poor, a helicopter pilot may be unable to sense if the machine is turning, tilting, dropping, or ascending and can quickly become disoriented, lose control, and begin an "uncontrolled descent"—or even flip the craft. That's what happened in this case. When the Medi-Flight pilot hit a dark patch, he couldn't see and, hence, couldn't navigate. The craft began swerving and dropping, its tail rotor hit a tall cedar tree, and the machine crashed. All three crew members perished, including paramedic Dan Donker, Rick Donker's twenty-eight-year-old brother.

In 1982 alone, nearly twenty air ambulance personnel were killed nationwide. So when authorities in Yosemite requested a nighttime evacuation from Half Dome on July 27, 1985, Medi-Flight was understandably guarded about accepting the assignment.

The pilot on duty at the time was Al Major, thirty-five years old. Major had learned how to fly helicopters in U.S. Army Flight School at age nineteen. Immediately after graduation in April 1969, he left for Vietnam, where he was stationed at Tay Ninh northwest of Saigon on the Cambodian border. Major flew UH-1Hs (Hueys) and AH-1Gs (Cobras), first as a pilot, then as an aircraft commander, fire team leader, and ultimately air mission commander. During his nineteen-month tour, he logged close to seventeen hundred combat flying hours. Although several times he returned to base with his chopper "limping" from enemy fire, Major escaped injuries or wounds. By the time he was discharged in 1970, he had received the Bronze Star, Distinguished Flying Cross, and fifty-three Air Medal awards, each one awarded for either twenty-five hours of combat flight or fifty hours of noncombat flight. Most of Major's were the former.

Before he agreed to fly the Half Dome mission, Major contacted the FAA's Flight Service Station in Stockton for moon information. The station reported a quarter to third moon that would set behind Yosemite's ridges at 1:42 A.M. Medi-Flight's protocols called for departure within six to ten minutes after a call came in. The flight to Yosemite Valley would take approximately thirty-seven minutes, if all went well, and arrive shortly after midnight. It would be a tight window, but a rescue attempt was possible—if the moonlight held. Because he would need to refuel on this extended mission, Major also requested confirmation from Yosemite that he could access the fuel in the Lemoore Naval Air Station's cache in the Valley (its helicopter search and rescue squadron sometimes performed rescues in Yosemite).

With these matters resolved, Medi-Flight accepted the assignment. Major took off from Modesto at 11:23 P.M. in the company's TwinStar, a large, French-made helicopter geared to the demands of the air ambulance trade.

Whenever he flew, Major conversed sparingly and showed little humor. His main concern was the safety of his crew and helicopter. He strived to make each mission as routine as possible; he remained cool and detached while focusing only on immediate tasks. Major imposed a steadfast rule: When a call came in, he wasn't to receive any information about the victims. That way, his decisions would be free of emotional influence.

Accompanying Major were flight nurse Maggie Newman and paramedic Bill Bryant. Because nurses undergo more training than paramedics do, the flight nurse is in charge of medical care on air ambulance flights. But such training focuses on hospital care, so nurses typically relinquish authority in the field to the paramedic, who usually has more experience with field traumas.

As a hospital nurse, Newman once witnessed a helicopter rescue; the high drama captivated her. After that, she wanted to be part of an air ambulance team. She got her wish and soon became, as she says, a "trauma junkie," her adrenaline racing while dealing with life-and-death situations—from knife and gunshot wounds to car accidents, falls from precipitous heights, and other human calamities. Although Newman was scared to death most of the time, she tried never to show it. To achieve calm, she sometimes slept in the helicopter en route. Major didn't like that; he wanted crew members to be on the lookout for other aircraft and obstacles.

Newman occasionally donned sunglasses and a cap so Major couldn't see her sleeping.

The nurse on the ill-fated flight that crashed in 1982 had been Medi-Flight's chief flight nurse. Newman suffered panic attacks following the accident. After time off to reflect on whether this was really the right career for her, she returned to work as chief flight nurse at Medi-Flight, the position she held in July 1985.

In all of her experiences, however, she had never treated a lightning victim.

Paramedic Bryant received his EMT certification when he was only a high school senior, in a class that Rick Donker taught. Bryant had been scheduled to man the doomed 1982 flight but wanted to go to Mexico on a getaway and got Dan Donker to cover for him. Others sometimes perceived Bryant as arrogant and a "cowboy" who often ignored protocols and instructions if he thought something should be done differently. He didn't hesitate to correct doctors when he thought their actions were wrong.

Field emergencies often involve head traumas, broken necks, and excessive bleeding, each of which can cause shock. Among environmental injuries are hypothermia, frostbite, drowning, and snakebite. Logistical issues may complicate these medical problems, something that few nurses or physicians have experience handling. A patient with chest pain, for example, might be given oxygen and receive an IV and morphine—standard medical procedures. But if a victim is pinned inside a car that's upside down in a muddy ditch, what then? Bryant insisted that fellow paramedics at Medi-Flight learn how to rappel, make an accident scene safe, fight fires, extricate people, carry out search and rescue operations, and perform other important nonmedical tasks.

Ironically, Bryant had taught segments of Linda Crozier's EMT class. But as the copter lifted off in Modesto and headed toward Yosemite, he had no idea that Crozier was the very person who'd taken charge of administering emergency treatment atop Half Dome.

-◄◦►-

AS CAMPBELL HIKED up Sub Dome, he got a report on his walkie-talkie that an air ambulance was on its way, which meant he had to reach the top of Half Dome in time to establish a landing zone (LZ). Quickening his pace, he arrived at the bottom of the cables at 11:45 P.M. as Jackson's silhouette appeared against the sky beyond the ridgeline above.

On the summit, it took Jackson a few minutes in the blackness to locate the group huddled around the two victims. His sudden appearance, seemingly from out of nowhere, surprised everyone. A greatly relieved Crozier assumed he was a ranger and immediately began reporting on the injured. But Jackson stopped her, explaining he was in park maintenance and there to help only with logistics.

When Campbell reached the summit, Jackson shouted to him. This time, the arrival of a uniformed ranger gave everyone a huge psychological boost. Crozier briefed Campbell on the victims, once again believing that, finally, she would be able to hand off the care of Weiner and Rice to someone else. Campbell quickly assessed the pair, checking mainly for any loss of vital functions and signs of trauma. He administered oxygen to Weiner, who appeared to be in worse shape. Then he told Crozier to carry on while he established a makeshift helicopter pad for a possible air evacuation.

Campbell: "I concluded right away that some good stuff happened this night in terms of how the emergency was handled. Linda was able to provide accurate information on the injured and a sense of stability about the situation. I felt I could leave her in charge and go set up the landing pad. The best care for the two victims was to get them off the mountain as quickly as possible."

Campbell radioed his report to the dispatch center in the Valley. Experience told him that an air evacuation was still a long shot, given the moonlight's small window of opportunity and the unpredictable sky. There were only two other options, neither of them good: A ground evacuation by Horner and his team, or an air evacuation at dawn. Next, Campbell radioed the Yosemite Medical Clinic to say the victims would need to be brought there as soon as possible after the rescue. One was in very bad shape, he reported, with labored breathing and compromised vital signs.

After Campbell gave Crozier a stethoscope and blood pressure cuff, he set out with Jackson to find a suitable LZ.

Crozier took Rice's and Weiner's blood pressure. She couldn't get a reading for either of them, which indicated their conditions were very precarious. The stethoscope told her that Rice's breathing was okay but that there still was gurgling in Weiner's lungs, an early symptom of deadly pulmonary edema.

A calmer Rice again wanted to move now that help was in sight. Crozier said no. Esteban urged Rice to trust her judgment and told him he would be okay if he could just hold on a bit longer.

As seconds ticked away, the helpers entered a suspended state, as if they were holding their breath underwater while waiting to surface. It was a race between the descent of the moon and the arrival of a helicopter. With each passing minute, an evacuation this night became more unlikely.

◄○►

CLU COTTER SCANNED the western horizon, trying to estimate how long it would be before the moon disappeared. To him, it looked like there was less than two hours of moonlight left. Something had to happen soon.

He peered into the darkness. All of a sudden, a speck of light appeared far off in the distance. He fastened his gaze on the light—it was getting bigger. An aircraft was entering the Valley! He shouted the news. A resounding cheer erupted on the summit, all eyes now focused on the light coming toward them. The speck grew brighter and brighter as the helicopter's searchlight swept back and forth to illuminate the ground.

As the copter drew closer, the *whop-whop-whop* sound of rotor blades became louder, amplified by the granite walls. Surely everyone in Yosemite Valley heard the noise, but for those on the summit, the roar of the rotors seemed to lift a mountain of weight off their backs.

It was just after midnight when Major landed his aircraft in Ahwahnee Meadow, only a few hundred feet from Yosemite Village and the famed Ahwahnee Hotel, where bedded guests no doubt wondered what was happening.

Campbell and Jackson had located a mainly level site on a high part of Half Dome that was separated by a saddle from where the victims lay almost three hundred feet away. They hastily removed rocks and swept away small gravel and any other matter that the copter's downdraft might kick up.

Campbell returned to the group of rescuers to gather flashlights. Six of the hikers returned with him to the landing zone. Campbell arranged the flashlights in a circle on the ground around the LZ to outline the area where the helicopter should land. The others positioned themselves far back from the circle while Campbell got ready to guide the copter in, using his two flashlights as a mark to direct Major in his approach.

Down in the Valley, Reilly quickly briefed Major. Time was crucial. If Major landed on the summit and the moonlight vanished, he and his crew might be stuck up there overnight. Gary Colliver, a ranger and park medic, joined Major and Bryant for the ascent. Newman remained on the Valley floor; her skills would come into play when the crew and victims returned.

Major stayed tightly focused on his mission. Flying up to Half Dome and landing on top in the dark would be hazardous, but if there was some moonlight and few obstacles, he considered it an acceptable risk. The greater challenge would be taking off from the summit and dropping down into the Valley with trees all around. His concentration had to remain razor-sharp. True to his code, Major didn't want any information about the victims. In his view, "a pilot can't be influenced by such factors—they may cause him to make a bad judgment, such as trying to go too quickly."

In a roar of the engine and twirling rotors, the helicopter lifted off from Ahwahnee Meadow at 12:35 A.M. Major would have to fly forward in a spiraling, circular course, rather than climbing straight up, to make the most efficient use of the craft's horsepower at that altitude. Such a course would also provide needed visibility. Those on board couldn't see the mountain they were ascending— a "very eerie experience," in Colliver's words—as they departed the Valley and passed through a dark zone devoid of any reference points.

After about a ten-minute climb and nearly a mile of elevation gain, there it was, the summit of the Dome, a circle of flashlights off in the distance. Following Campbell's guidance, Major maneuvered his machine over the LZ for a "pinnacle approach," or one from directly above. Then he gently brought it down. When the craft got near the ground, Bryant jumped off wearing his communications headset with a cord long enough for him to remain safely away from the spinning rotors. Although Major was concerned about landing on an uncertain surface, he hovered only briefly as Bryant directed him to move the aircraft a few feet or inches this way or that for the most level spot. Major placed the landing skids lightly on the rock, barely "feeling" them settle, and shut the engine down.

Major: "This type of helicopter likes to be either solidly on the ground or sufficiently airborne, and not in between. The in-between part—that is, close to but not on the ground—can set up a sympathetic vibration or ground resonance that can destroy the aircraft, literally shake it apart, so we obviously tended to avoid that flight regime."

Bryant scuttled over to where the injured lay. After Crozier's thorough report, he concluded there was little more to be done medically on the summit.

Bryant: "There was just no time to waste. At that point, I thought it was fifty–fifty at best that we would get both patients off the rock that night. If the moon disappeared, the rescue was probably off until daylight. The priority was to move as quickly as possible to get one—and, if we were lucky, both—patients to the Valley."

Given the amount of floor space a patient strapped in a gurney required, the helicopter could only take one patient at a time.

If only one of the victims could be evacuated tonight, Bryant asked Crozier, who should it be?

Weiner, she answered.

Jackson, Brian Cage, Steve White, and Bryant lifted Weiner onto a stretcher and moved him to the helicopter. Meanwhile, Colliver checked Brian Jordan's body in the cave and determined that nothing more could be done. The body would remain there for the night.

Once Weiner was strapped in the helicopter, Colliver, with no medical issues to attend to, climbed aboard for the flight down. Bryant stayed behind.

Rangers in the Valley had positioned park vehicles, their red and blue lights flashing, as a beacon for Major. One vehicle's headlights faced Ahwahnee Meadow to illuminate the landing zone. Spotlights shone on the highest pine trees nearby to help Major avoid them.

Major fired up the helicopter, lifted off, and flew away from the summit. Past Half Dome's edge, he began the one-mile descent, which he would have to execute very deliberately, especially on this first flight. The only available light came from a sliver of moon, which reflected off the high granite, and from the vehicle beams and other lights far down on the Valley floor.

Colliver: "On the summit, the moonlight illuminated the granite and the nearby ridges, and my eyes were adjusted to the light. However, what lay beyond Half Dome looked like a black hole. When we dropped into this void, with no horizons or reference features other than an occasional floating point of light on the Valley floor, it produced for me a sudden sensation of blindness, disorientation, a loss of breath, and fear for what might be out there in the pitch darkness. It was only when we got close enough to the Valley floor to see light reflected off the ground or nearby objects, and could get a sense of relative motion, that I felt safe and could breathe normally again."

Unnerved by the descent, Colliver prayed that Major had a better sense of the surroundings than he did. In fact, Major considered the flight down quite normal and manageable. He had flown hundreds of more demanding and dangerous missions, his eyes had adjusted to the darkness, and he had little difficulty charting the route. Plus, as Major said later, "Yosemite officials had the landing zone lit up like a Christmas tree."

After a rightward-spiraling descent and keeping the helicopter centered over the illuminated target, Major brought his craft down in Ahwahnee Meadow at 1:07 A.M. Weiner was immediately transferred to a waiting ambulance and brought to the clinic. Although park physician Bill Bowie was in charge, Newman took over Weiner's care. She connected him to a cardiac monitor and inserted an IV and Foley catheter, or tube in his penis, to collect urine. This helped alleviate his urinary tract blockage.

Back on the summit, Crozier again reviewed Rice's and Esteban's injuries with Bryant. Only then did she and Bryant realize they knew each other from her EMT class. Bryant's knowledge, experience, and calming influence finally brought Crozier the relief she desperately needed. At last, someone else was in charge—she could give her mind and body a rest.

As the rescue activities buzzed around him, Esteban, watching in silence, felt a flood of emotions and thoughts. He was tremendously relieved that Rice and Weiner had survived the many hours on Half Dome, and were now in good hands. Still, big uncertainties remained. Would they live? And if they did, what future impact would their injuries have? Would his buddy Rice be crippled for life? Thankfully, his own fate didn't depend on an air evacuation. His wounds were primarily mental—anguish over what had transpired, psychological fragility, not to mention complete exhaustion. He had been thrashed by lightning, been deprived of sleep, and was emotionally spent from bolstering Rice's and

Weiner's spirits across several hours. Over and over he replayed the day's decisions in his mind: Why did this happen and why did we challenge the gods? What if we had done this instead of that? He couldn't stop dwelling on his leaving Frith on the ledge. What about Frith's loved ones, and those of the Jordan kid?

But one fact superseded all this and took center stage in his awareness: He was alive! Outwardly, Esteban appeared to others to be shell-shocked. Inwardly, he was screaming with joy that he'd escaped his companions' fate. He wanted to jump up and kiss the sky! At that instant, he felt more in touch with life than ever before—far more than he had while racing up the cables with Rice, which seemed like eons ago, and experiencing the rush of living on the razor's edge. Esteban wanted to freeze this moment so he would never forget what it felt like to cheat death and get another chance.

AT 1:15 A.M., Major launched the helicopter a second time, intent on flying to and from Half Dome as fast as possible. Over the Dome and now familiar with the landing zone, he circled it, landed with little delay, and kept the copter's engine running. Bryant was attending to Rice on a nearby stretcher. Though Rice seemed reasonably stable, Bryant knew the often hidden health risks from lightning strikes. He also believed that if the rescue had to be aborted, Rice's condition would only deteriorate, and Bryant didn't look forward to spending the night with him on the rock. He was very thankful that the highly skilled Major was the pilot this night.

Before Bryant and Jackson placed Rice in the helicopter, Steve White told him to enjoy the ride because he would never get another one quite like it. This comment seemed to boost Rice's spirits. With Rice and Bryant on board, Major took off and, his route now clearly established, descended more rapidly than before. The copter set down in Ahwahnee Meadow at 1:25 A.M. Except for the Foley catheter, Newman tended Rice the same as she had Weiner.

At 1:30 A.M., only twelve minutes of moonlight remained, barely enough time for one last pickup. Esteban waited nervously, thinking how cruel it would be to have survived lightning strikes only to perish in a helicopter crash. Major didn't waste any time: He took off again, flew up to the summit, and waited as Esteban, who didn't need a stretcher, was hoisted aboard. Campbell joined him. Just as Major lifted off from Half Dome, the moon was disappearing behind the ridgeline. Campbell later said the flight down was like "dropping into a black envelope, one of the most frightening experiences in my life."

Now Major had to rely strictly on the lights on the Valley floor for direction and orientation. He completed this third and final journey without mishap. The rescue was over.

With two patients strapped in gurneys and limited space, Weiner and Rice would need to be taken in separate helicopters to the University of California, Davis Medical Center in Sacramento, which had a major trauma center. During the rescue, Yosemite authorities had summoned a second helicopter from CALSTAR, an air ambulance service at St. Rose Hospital in Hayward. Major refilled the copter's tanks from the U.S. Navy's fuel trailer and, at about 3:20 A.M., he, Bryant, Newman, and Weiner, who had been strapped into a gurney with an IV and cardiac monitor in place, departed for Memorial Hospital in Modesto. They passed the CALSTAR helicopter on its way in to retrieve Rice.

The emergency staff at Memorial Hospital examined Weiner while the helicopter refueled for the flight to Sacramento. They determined that he wasn't in any immediate danger. Major had "houred out," so he was done for the night. With a new pilot and Newman and Bryant still on board, the copter departed for UC Davis Medical Center. By that time, CALSTAR was en route to the same hospital with Rice.

Medi-Flight had done its job. Now the fates of Weiner and Rice rested with doctors in Sacramento.

9

RECOVERY

Never more, however weary, should one faint by the way who gains the blessings of one mountain day; whatever his fate, long life, short life, stormy or calm, he is rich forever.—John Muir

Weiner and Rice both arrived by helicopter at the UC Davis Medical Center, Sacramento in the early-morning hours on Sunday. After Weiner gave the authorities his parents' phone number in New Hampshire, he was sedated and his world went black again. Rice, too, was sedated.

A slew of IVs delivered morphine, sedatives, vasopressors (medications that raise blood pressure), saline, and other fluids to the two men. Dr. Howard Klein, a plastic surgeon, was the attending physician.

Dr. Klein reported that massive electrical charges had shot though each of the hikers, entering at the hips and exiting at the feet. The basic injury was to microscopic blood vessels: As they clotted, tissue began to die. The sudden jolt of electrical current through the legs had also severely damaged both muscles and nerves in their lower bodies, causing leg muscles to swell. That blocked the transmission of nerve impulses and blood to their lower legs—a condition called compartment syndrome. It can produce necrosis (tissue death) of all structures in the legs and necessitate their amputation. Dr. Klein was concerned that the burn wounds would progress, which, in the case of electrical injuries, they often do.

Although he possessed feeling in his feet and could move his toes, Rice's lower body was still numbed and fraught with pain. His right leg in particular was severely damaged, his entire calf muscle split in half and exposed two or three inches deep, as if someone had split it down the middle with a knife. There was a large wound spewing pus on his back near the spine. Dr. Klein's initial prognosis was that even if he didn't have to amputate, Rice would probably never walk again.

A toxic compound released into the bloodstream by the burns continued to threaten both victims by attacking the kidneys. They were retaining fluids, which caused their body weight to increase dramatically.

After only a few hours of sleep, Weiner and Rice each underwent two hours of surgery early Sunday morning. Internal pressure on their leg muscles had to be released and the wounds cleaned out to prevent infection. Dr. Klein led a surgical team of five physicians, who performed a fasciotomy on the leg muscles: They cut the fascia, or lining that holds muscle together like a sleeve, and thus allowed the swollen muscle to bulge out. This, in turn, reduced pressure on the blood vessels and nerves, averting permanent damage. Once such swelling subsides, physicians repair the fascia and then graft skin over the affected areas.

◄o►

AFTER THE HELICOPTER rescue, postclimax letdown settled in among those who remained on Half Dome's summit. Everyone was mentally, physically, and psychologically spent. Crozier broke the tension.

Okay, guys, she said. It's Miller time.

After nearly seven hours of life-or-death anxiety, the fates of Weiner and Rice were in someone else's hands.

The adrenaline rush that had kept Crozier alert and focused for all those hours abruptly cratered. Weary and cold, she now had to descend the cables and Sub Dome and reunite with her hiking companions. Except for Scott Jackson, the trail maintenance employee, who offered to accompany her down, the others would spend the night on Half Dome as they had planned. Steve White and his fellow hikers offered to share with her their sleeping bags and anything else that provided warmth if she elected to stay on top for the remainder of that short night. She declined.

Crozier: "I desperately needed to get off that mountain—to get away from the edge, away from the danger, away from death!"

Before she left, she thanked those who had lent so much help and support throughout the ordeal. Everyone there felt the strong sense of cohesiveness and mutual affection that had blossomed during the long hours.

Jackson and Crozier began their journey down the treacherous slope. It was fully dark; the moon had long since set beyond the western ridge. Crozier clutched the cables as hard as she possibly could and half slid, half staggered down the slick granite. The descent, although dangerous, was nevertheless manageable at that point. The next leg down Sub Dome was definitely more perilous—there was nothing to cling to for support. The steps were narrow, uneven, and irregular. A slip and fall could prove disastrous. Jackson led the way with his dimming flashlight as the pair groped along. He would descend a short distance, stop, turn around, and illuminate the path for Crozier as best he could. To Crozier, the combination of shadows and faint light was almost more treacherous than no light at all.

Panic seized Crozier. Jackson was going too fast.

Maybe I should have stayed on top after all, she wondered. No, I *had* to get off that mountain!

They reached the final steps, then level ground.

At the base of Sub Dome, Crozier reunited with Mike Hoog, her brother Dan, Jennie Hayes, and Rick Pedroncelli. She gave them a somber update on what had transpired on the summit after Mike and Rick left, then collapsed into her sleeping bag, wrapping her chilled, depleted body tightly for as much warmth and comfort as possible. Jackson spent the night with them. But the evening's events proved too unsettling for Crozier to fall asleep quickly.

Back on Half Dome, it was 3 A.M. before Brian Cage's group crawled into their sleeping bags. Clu Cotter, whose bag had left the summit with Rice, managed to find a stray one. He didn't know whose it was. It was too small, and in the frigid night air he could barely keep warm. By morning, the water in the campers' canteens would be frozen.

The six men lay there, each trying to surrender to his exhaustion, each aware that the body of a sixteen-year-old boy was still slumped in the cave only a short distance away. Nearby, Bill Pippey and Bruce Jordan were battling despair.

―◦―

AT 6:30 A.M., the pilot of Yosemite National Park's helicopter prepared to retrieve the bodies of Bob Frith and Brian Jordan. He flew to the base of Half Dome and located Frith among the rocks, then returned to pick up Rangers Evan Smith and Dan Dellinges.

With them on board, the helo flew to a ledge at the base of Half Dome's face, right above the rocky jumble—a landing zone the park routinely used for rescues in that vicinity. In contrast to Medi-Flight's large helicopter, this aircraft was much smaller and better able to maneuver in tight places. The pilot carefully finessed the helo to the ledge and brought the front half of the landing skids down on it for stability. This enabled Smith and Dellinges to hop out. After they moved a safe distance away from the rotors, the helo lifted off, bound for the summit.

Smith and Dellinges followed standard procedure for a fatality. They took pictures and measurements, and surveyed the scene for evidence of foul play. As with all accidents, the rangers didn't want to assume anything, only to be surprised later on.

The helicopter flew to the summit to get Bruce Jordan and ferry him down to the Valley. There, a priest, Father Rod Craig, offered comfort. The teenager broke down, his pent-up emotions and sorrow finally spilling out.

He sobbed uncontrollably, asking over and over, Why him and not me? Why did I survive? Why didn't I save him?

The helicopter returned to the base of Half Dome to remove Frith's body, which Smith and Dellinges had placed in a body bag and wire rescue basket—a "wire coffin." Part of Frith's foot was missing and couldn't be found. They attached the basket to a rope lowered from the hovering helicopter, which rose and headed toward the park morgue.

After a long night and only a few hours of sleep at home, Colin Campbell—the first ranger on the scene the night before—returned to the Valley at 7 A.M. Someone told him a female hiker had brought his cowboy boots down to a ranger station in the Valley from the camp where he had swapped them for sneakers. According to the ranger there, the hiker had held Campbell's well-worn boots at arm's length. Campbell collected them and then joined the helicopter flight taking Rangers J. R. Tomasovic and Jim Tucker to the summit to prepare Brian Jordan's body for removal.

After the helo deposited Tomasovic and Tucker on top, it dropped Campbell off in Little Yosemite Valley. There he saddled up John Paul and rode down to the Valley floor. The helicopter returned again to the base of Half Dome, picked up Rangers Smith and Dellinges, and transported them back to the Valley.

On the summit, Tomasovic asked Pippey to identify the body in the cave, a standard procedure. It was a heart-wrenching moment for Pippey; he confronted the tragedy all over again. The body of Brian Jordan lay before him, more than seventeen hours after lightning had ended his brief life.

Jackson had since returned to the summit. He helped lift Jordan's body over to the helicopter landing site. One image that still lingers in his memory is that of a partial head of broccoli on the granite cave floor.

By noon on Sunday, July 28, the rangers and Jordan's body had been airlifted from the summit. The rescue mission was officially over.

◄○►

HOOG'S GROUP ROSE with the sun. They packed their gear and said good-bye to Jackson, who was heading back to the summit. The group spoke little on the way down to the Valley. Crozier mused that, during the long ordeal the previous evening, she'd never once absorbed the view from atop Half Dome, her reason for going up there in the first place. She and her companions promised themselves to return the next summer.

Along the trail, they heard hikers chattering about something that had happened on Half Dome overnight, but neither Crozier nor Hoog said a word in passing.

From the Valley floor, they saw a helicopter flying up to Half Dome's summit. The helo and speculative human buzz in the Valley about what was happening seemed eerie to Crozier, as though there were a locked room holding profound secrets and only she had the key.

The group went to the Yosemite Clinic to inquire about Rice, Weiner, and Esteban. The staff were reluctant to give out any information, saying only that Rice and Weiner had been transported to the UC Davis Medical Center in Sacramento. Crozier and Hoog didn't mention their role in the rescue.

Later, they spotted the park helicopter swooping away from the base of Half Dome with a body bag slung below. This was the image that stayed fixed in their minds as they departed Yosemite.

Cage's party packed up and left the Dome sometime early that morning. An unnamed hiker joined them on the somber hike out, relating a story about how, when the previous day's storm rolled in, he'd taken cover in a rock enclosure on Half Dome, fearing for his life.* Aghast, he'd watched five guys dance on the granite as the storm raged. Then they disappeared. He said he'd scrambled down the mountain as soon as it seemed safe to do so.

Now he knew what had befallen the dancers.

After the helicopter lifted Bruce Jordan from the summit, a solitary Pippey hiked down. Karl Buchner and Steve Ellner were there to meet him at the camping area below. The three trudged back to the Valley. Ellner's primary thought was that he needed to call his parents and tell them he was alive. He suspected there already had been publicity about the episode.

He was right.

Pam Pippey, Bill's wife, who was four months' pregnant with their first child, was driving home at nine o'clock Sunday morning from an appointment when she heard the radio report: *Lightning strike on Half Dome, five people hit, two killed.* Her first thought was that her husband was among the five, and she might now be a widow. Frantic, she raced home and called Yosemite. No one there could give her the names of the people involved. A park official she spoke with said someone would call her back. Three hours passed before anyone did, just shortly before her husband himself called.

---

* This individual's name and whereabouts during the episode have remained undisclosed. He was the anonymous observer of that striking scene that opened this book.

By noon, Pippey, Buchner, and Ellner had arrived in the Valley. Pippey immediately called Pam, and Ellner phoned his parents. When the three reached the ranger station, Mr. and Mrs. Jordan, whom park officials had contacted the previous night, were there with a stone-faced Bruce Jordan. Seeing the Jordans was more than Pippey could handle; he broke down yet again. Mr. Jordan's attempts to comfort him helped Pippey considerably.

Esteban doesn't remember much about what transpired after the helicopter evacuated him from the Dome, including whether he even slept. All he recalls is the flight down and then sunlight. That morning, rangers questioned him. Esteban briefly described the incident and what happened to each of the men in the cave.

"I didn't know there was a lightning rod there," he added, referring to the iron pipe that park officials had sawed off after the lightning incident in 1973, leaving a one-plus-inch section protruding from the granite.

A priest tried to comfort Esteban, who could think of nothing but Frith tumbling over the edge. The image terrified him. Later that morning, he passed a structure—the rescue cache building—where there were rangers and search dogs.

This must be where they took Frith, Esteban thought.

He wanted to see his friend one last time. A ranger told him that wasn't a good idea, but Esteban persisted. A body bag was inside, and to Esteban, its size and shape seemed odd. Then it struck him why. He stopped in his tracks, whispered a farewell to his companion, and left.

Esteban had placed a note on Pippey's windshield telling him to meet Esteban at the rescue cache. When Pippey, Buchner, and Ellner arrived, they were surprised that Esteban seemingly didn't have any injuries. Park officials interviewed the three men; Buchner and Ellner could offer little information about what had happened.

Word was circulating that a lawsuit would be filed.

Mrs. Jordan asked rangers, Why did the park allow my son and the others to go to the top of Half Dome if it was dangerous and there might be lightning?

Mrs. Jordan: "We hold Yosemite rangers responsible for the tragedy. They allowed the hikers to scale Half Dome despite the hazardous weather. How many city people realize the danger? They were permitted to go, so they must have figured it was safe."

That Sunday, Monroe Bridges and Brian Cage, two of Linda Crozier's helpers the prior night, lumbered into the ranger station in Yosemite Village, introduced themselves, and were escorted to an office. At the request of Ranger Tomasovic, the two men agreed to make a voluntary statement "for the record" summarizing what they had witnessed. At that point, both were physically beat, having completed the hike to the top on Saturday, helped with emergency care into the wee hours on Sunday, and after minimal sleep hiked back down to the Valley.

A ranger asked if they had seen the sign at the start of the stairs at Sub Dome. Both replied that they had. Then the ranger asked if either could recite what the sign said. Again, they responded yes, and repeated its warning. The ranger thanked them for cooperating and added that their statements could help the National Park Service defend itself in a potential lawsuit.

Cage: "That's when it really hit me. As much as this was an accident caused by a combination of Mother Nature and poor human judgment, there remained a looming wrongful death lawsuit against Yosemite National Park. I remember the ranger commenting that a big-money lawsuit could easily consume the entire budget the park allots for making Half Dome and other backcountry destinations accessible."

Bridges and Cage also told the ranger they were prepared to testify that the accident happened because the five men in the cave had been reckless. Esteban himself had stated as much.

That same day, Yosemite closed the trail to the summit until the electrical storms abated. According to park rangers, the hiking tragedy on Half Dome was one of the worst in Yosemite's history.

"Half Dome is probably the worst place you can be during a thunderstorm," said Bruce Brossman, director of Yosemite Mountaineering School. "It gets hit all the time. The skies that day were black, and it had been raining on and off for several days. These were the fastest-moving and most violent thunderstorms I've ever seen in sixteen years I've been in the Sierra. But they were predicted."

◄O►

WITH NOTHING ELSE to do in Yosemite, Esteban, Pippey, Buchner, and Ellner left. Pippey wanted to rejoin his wife as quickly as possible and begin his healing. He drove home alone and remembers little about the trip, his mind in a complete fog, his emotions swinging wildly. He knew that his sudden bout of diarrhea on the cables of Half Dome surely had saved his and Bruce Jordan's lives. But that was small consolation. With the previous day's events, he had suffered another severe setback in his young life.

Why, he wondered, do tragedy and death follow me?

His mother, grandparents, best teenage friend, and now Bob Frith and Brian Jordan—all dead. And Rice and Weiner might yet die.

Buchner also drove back alone, still speechless and distressed. He found solace in the fact that Esteban and Ellner, his two closest friends, had survived the ordeal. Ellner drove Esteban in Esteban's truck. Ellner talked incessantly on the journey home, hoping to boost Esteban's spirits.

Esteban was tremendously agitated. He and Rice had been the leaders that day. Others followed them and suffered grave consequences. The fates of Rice and Weiner still hung in the balance. He could not rid himself of the crushing knowledge that he and Rice were ultimately responsible for the tragedy. But further riling him was Rice's accusation that he, Esteban, had abandoned him in the cave. And Esteban kept telling himself he had done everything possible to save Frith.

Esteban: "The dilemma I faced: Do all I could to save someone else, and let myself possibly die, or save myself and let someone else possibly die."

In trying to rationalize his actions, Esteban wanted to believe Frith "told" him with the whites of his eyes that it was okay to leave him. He felt like their souls had touched, had connected. He thought he had had little choice but to leave Frith "in God's hands" on the ledge.

However, he also had fled the cave and sought safety for himself. Of the five hikers in the enclosure, only Esteban had endured the catastrophe with no major injuries. He should have felt thankful, and he did feel enormously thankful, but guilt nevertheless overwhelmed him. At the moment of peril, the self-preservation instinct took over.

Now self-doubt tormented him.

Ellner turned the radio on and began flipping from station to station, hungry for news. The story came on, although by now it had widely circulated: *Hikers hit by lightning on Half Dome.*

There were still many untold parts to this tale to dissect.

‐◄o►‐

LINDA CROZIER RETURNED to her apartment in Davis. She recounted for her roommates what had happened and called her parents to fill them in. That night, she still felt traumatized. Crozier could recite all the events but, at that point and for many days to come, felt no emotions tied to them.

"I was terrified up there, but I learned a lot about myself. Up on top, I kept my cool, but once it was all over, I was totally numbed. I was in mental shock for days afterward. For the first time in my life, I didn't like being alone at night."

Like Esteban, Crozier felt guilty. But the genesis of her guilt was how she had consciously avoided checking on Brian Jordan in the cave. She wondered if he might have been in a state of suspended animation rather than dead; if he could have been revived with CPR. She did some research on lightning injuries but couldn't find any definitive information.

Several months later, Crozier got a whiff of burned hair from her curling iron. The odor was familiar—and then she suddenly realized why.

"The smell rocketed me right back to Half Dome like a shock! I hadn't realized I had smelled burned hair up there until I smelled it that day in my apartment."

◄o►

AT HOME, ESTEBAN sank into deep depression. He had no one to talk to, no one to comfort him. There were nightmares about Frith toppling off the edge. The worst had Esteban letting go of Frith— who miraculously wakes up during the fall. This gruesome thought tortured Esteban. He sought comfort from a priest, who assured him there was nothing else he could have done.

Esteban wanted to feel better. But deep down, he had to battle these demons—and battle them alone.

He recalled his attitude after the lightning strike: Just thankful it wasn't me. Esteban had a keen interest in the military, and in his readings about it, he learned that his reaction mirrored that of soldiers whose comrade triggers a land mine: Glad it wasn't me. It was simply human nature to feel that way, he believed. Guilt, however, almost always followed.

By then, the press was calling for information. Esteban didn't take the calls; instead, he sought refuge at his parents' house. But reporters also called there, so he hid at a friend's place, where other friends joined him. They urged Esteban to go on TV, seeing this as an opportunity for him to gain notoriety and make money in the process.

Esteban: "Of course, these 'good friends' really didn't care about the feelings of the survivors and their loved ones. All they cared about was my fifteen minutes of fame on TV. And they hoped in some way to cash in, too."

Though Esteban was a poor communicator, he finally succumbed to an overwhelming barrage of requests and consented to be interviewed. A friend set up the first interview and started behaving as if he were Esteban's agent.

Inwardly, Esteban was looking to the media for a favorable judgment of his actions on Half Dome.

◄o►

AFTER A HASTILY BOOKED FLIGHT, Weiner's parents arrived at the UC Davis Medical Center on Sunday.

Rice and Weiner were still in serious condition on Monday. Doctors considered a kidney transplant for Weiner, whose kidney functioning had declined 90 percent. He gained 40 pounds overnight from retained fluids, his weight ballooning to 205. While Rice's kidney problems weren't as severe, his weight sky-rocketed, too. Blood circulation in both men's legs was still seriously impaired.

On Tuesday, Klein operated a second time to further decompress their leg muscles. Doctors wouldn't know for several days if they had succeeded in saving the legs, or if Rice and Weiner would ever walk again.

The pair underwent frequent baths to debride (scrub) dead tissue from their burns. Such tissue provides an ideal medium for the growth of bacteria that can cause infection, one of the biggest risks associated with burns. Debridement involves an instrument not unlike a cheese grater. This procedure was "extraordinarily painful," according to Weiner, despite higher doses of morphine. Meanwhile, each man wore a device that kept a foot raised and flexed. This kept the large tendons in their legs, such as the Achilles tendon running down the back of the shin, stretched, preventing them from contracting and becoming disabled as a result of disuse.

The fasciotomies had exposed Rice's and Weiner's leg muscles, which were covered by bandages extending from their toes to their backs. Incisions beneath the bandages would remain open for weeks. When Weiner's bandages were temporarily removed for bathing purposes, exposing the damage, he experienced sheer horror. Only then did he realize the extent of his injuries. He was appallingly disfigured. Large globs of what looked like ground meat protruded from six or seven surgical sites, each three to twelve inches long. His legs were swollen to incredible proportions. It was as if two huge sausages had burst open in numerous places, their contents squeezed out under high pressure.

Linda Crozier called the hospital to inquire about visiting Rice and Weiner. No one could say when that would be possible, but on Tuesday she went to see them anyway. The burn unit nurse said they had undergone surgery earlier that day and were in bad shape.

Dr. Klein dropped by and told Crozier that, absent her care on Half Dome, both men surely would have faced amputation. She couldn't tell if he was being honest or just trying to make her feel good. In any case, the scene Crozier encountered in Rice's and Weiner's separate rooms was sobering. Their bodies had swelled so much, she could barely recognize them. Both men were under medication and in much pain. Crozier whispered to each that she was thinking of them, then left.

Crozier: "Seeing the two guys in the hospital alive is when I began to feel good again."

◄○►

AMONG THE HIKERS that day, only Pippey attended Brian Jordan's funeral. To say the event was extremely sad for the Jordan family—mother and father, sisters, and Brian's twin brother—doesn't convey the agony they endured in burying their young son and brother. Pippey shared their despair but also felt great torment, believing he had been responsible for Brian's death. Being at the funeral, he recalls, was "the hardest time I ever had in my life."

Bob Frith's funeral took place in Virginia, another emotionally devastating event. Grieving parents, six older sisters, and a brother had to lay to rest the youngest member of their family. Again, the only member of Rice's band who attended was Pippey. Frith had been Pippey's dear and important friend, someone he deeply admired and had grown to love.

Pippey gutted out the two funerals—barely. He wondered about his relationship to God and, once again, why close family members and friends had been snatched from his life.

In his fragile state, Pippey resisted visiting Rice. Dealing with any more heartbreaks would simply be too much. But after about two weeks, he forced himself to go. When he arrived at the hospital, Rice was lying in bed "all torn up, with tubes everywhere," still crippled from the waist down. In roller-coaster fashion, his weight had fallen dramatically. Seeing his good friend in that condition freaked Pippey out; he just couldn't take it on top of everything else.

He didn't visit Rice again until several weeks later, long into his recovery.

Pippey visited the Jordans every weekend, and together they grieved and supported each other. In his view, Mr. Jordan had handled the tragedy with sensitivity and class, providing tremendous comfort not only to his wife and children but also to Pippey. Pippey tried to console a morose Bruce Jordan, who seemed to be sliding back into oblivion.

◄o►

NEWSPAPER REPORTERS interviewed Esteban, who also appeared on several TV news programs.

He told one reporter: "It was instantaneous, like going from heaven to hell in a second."

To another, he said: "I know what we did was totally stupid, but we're gung-ho types. We knew the dangers, but we also knew the excitement, the thrill of a challenge. We decided we were going to go for it no matter what.

"It was the thrill of being in a life-and-death situation. It was like playing Russian roulette. There was such a rush as we were going up and saw those dark clouds. The adrenaline was flowing. There was an intense feeling that you could die at any moment."

He had nothing but praise for Linda Crozier and others who treated the victims on Half Dome.

"They saved our lives," he said. "They were really noble—full of courage and sure about what they were doing. We were all so lucky that they happened upon us."

Later, Esteban reflected on why he agreed to be interviewed.

"All I know is that I had to let people know what had happened, and in a strange way this outpouring to anyone and everyone who would listen was sort of a confession that I was hoping would cleanse away the pain and sorrow I was going through. This was one of the lowest points in my life. I felt like an outcast from my 'older brother' Tom [Rice]. Without a spouse or girlfriend to share my innermost thoughts and to comfort me, I was truly lonely. My only out was to talk about it. And once I started talking, I felt better. I was not depressed anymore. The excitement of being on five different news stations live made me forget about all my mental suffering. People wanting me gave me a sense of belonging, a positive feeling. It was a cathartic experience. In the same way Tom needed a fix of attention at the diving board, I had found my fix."

In each interview, Esteban mentioned that he hadn't been aware of the "lightning rod" near the summit cave. Its sole purpose, he reasoned, must have been to draw lightning away from people up there. He related how the pipe extended into the rock chamber.

This explanation was far from accurate. The one-plus-inch pipe stub surely had nothing to do with the lightning strike or how the blast whipped through the enclosure. The iron remnant was anchored in solid granite about twenty feet away; neither it nor any other metal pipe extended into the chamber. The stub couldn't have attracted lightning—the entire summit was available. Perhaps it had in the 1972 case, when the pipe stuck up two feet, but even that scenario was dubious. Assuming the protrusion drew lightning on that fateful day in 1972, the charge could have streaked across the wet rock and through the rock enclosure. And certainly anyone who was near the iron pipe or touching it would have placed himself at greater risk, given that any metallic object is a prime conductor of electricity. So the National Park Service was correct to whittle the pipe down. However, lightning barrages had continued to batter Half Dome every year since.

Amazingly, not one reporter queried Esteban further or verified the accuracy of his statement—which, if true, certainly cast a whole different light on the tragedy.

Esteban also put a different spin on Frith's fall from the summit. He told most interviewers that he'd held on to Frith's sweater until it began to rip from his grip, that he'd had to let go when Frith was about to tumble over the edge. Actually, Esteban was recounting how, given his weakness at that instant, he tried in vain to pull Frith up and over a boulder, then into the enclosure. He couldn't hold on to Frith indefinitely, so he released his grip—not letting Frith tumble off the ledge, as he later claimed, but rather letting him slump back onto it. There, Weiner continued to grasp Frith's sweater for a few seconds before it slipped from his grasp.

Esteban: "In my interviews, it seems that I was looking at the presence of the iron pipe as a logical reason to account for the deaths of two people and the life-altering injuries to two others. I sought some external justification for the disaster. And with my overwhelming feelings of guilt, I didn't want to admit that I chose to leave Frith on the ledge. So I described how I had to let him go. This was true, but what it doesn't say is that when I let him go, he settled back down on the ledge and did not immediately tumble over the edge. That came seconds later."

In those interviews, he also stated: "Half Dome is my spiritual place, and I must go back there."

Some of Esteban's fellow hikers and others connected to the incident didn't take kindly to his media activities. In their opinion, he was exploiting the tragedy for personal gain. Karl Buchner's father called Esteban at one point and counseled him to stop, arguing that the publicity was insensitive to the victims' families. Only then did Esteban grasp the serious implications of his actions. He canceled all upcoming interviews.

◄○►

ESTEBAN WAS HESITANT to face Rice, even though the recovery period was "when Tom needed me the most." Part of him wanted to go. And he really had no excuse for not going. Nevertheless, he remained at home or at a friend's house, where he lost himself in drink. It was pure denial—in his effort to rid himself of guilt, he wanted to believe a major tragedy hadn't even occurred.

He also didn't attend the Jordan and Frith funerals. Why? He wasn't sure.

A full two weeks passed before Esteban visited Rice and Weiner. His decision to go was partly serendipitous: One of Rice's girlfriends had called to ask if they might carpool to the hospital. She had just recently met Rice and promised to do whatever was necessary to help him fully recover. She and Esteban drove to Sacramento together.

In intensive care, hooked up to IVs, Rice was very subdued. He was still receiving morphine to kill the pain. He mumbled that he was very glad Esteban had finally come to visit him. But then Rice admonished Esteban not to talk to the media, even though he surely knew that Esteban had already done so. Apparently, Rice was telling him indirectly that he had betrayed their trust. He said Esteban's priorities were all wrong, that two people had died, that he and Weiner had nearly died, too. Esteban felt wounded. Rice was scolding him—in front of his girlfriend, no less.

Esteban: "That was Tom's style. He would rip into you no matter what the surrounding circumstances were."

Rice told Esteban he couldn't remember much about the lightning incident. He did say, however, that the second bolt delivered the major blow to Weiner. This was news to Esteban; until then, he had no inkling of the second strike hitting Rice and Weiner.

Something troubled Esteban: the possibility that Rice and Weiner, either in the cave or there at the hospital, had spoken privately about his actions on Half Dome that day. He worried that they blamed him for leaving them behind in the cave.

Esteban: "To this day I do not know what Tom and Bruce may have talked about when I was not present. I have a guilty feeling that Bruce's version of what happened afterward reflected negatively on me, that I basically left them to die in that hole in order to save myself and that Bruce saw me drop his best friend Bob to his death."

In fact, Rice and Weiner never discussed it. They occupied separate rooms in the hospital as a precaution against cross-contamination and infection. Furthermore, Weiner held no affection for Rice and had no reason to confide in him. Esteban's fear that the pair had confided behind his back was totally unfounded.

He visited with Weiner only briefly on that occasion. The next time he came, Weiner had been flown to Massachusetts.

During Esteban's second visit, Rice seemed really pissed off. He stripped off his shorts and showed Esteban his testicles, which looked like a single grapefruit.

Look what happened, he said.

Rice's tone was accusatory, as though he resented the fact that Esteban hadn't suffered any injuries.

Feeling further aggrieved, Esteban stormed out.

AFTER THE SECOND ROUND of surgery, some sensation and circulation returned to Rice's and Weiner's feet. But according to Dr. Klein, a specific prognosis was very difficult because their electrical injuries were still in the early stages of healing.

He said both men were extremely lucky to have survived the ordeal so well.

Dr. Klein: "Even if they both have terrible problems with both of their legs, they're still alive, their brains suffered no damage, and their heart and lungs seem okay. Each appears to have been spared serious kidney damage, a major concern in electrical burn cases. They have a lot to be thankful for."

He cautiously told Rice that once Rice regained movement in his lower limbs, he might be able to get around—but probably "won't be able to dance again." Rice retorted, half in jest, I'm going to dance on your fuckin' grave!

During the first two weeks after the accident, Weiner also had suffered pneumonia, heart problems, and several infections. Any of these problems could have proved fatal. The two men, in Dr. Klein's opinion, would require many more operations, skin grafts, and plastic surgery. Even under the best of circumstances, both faced a long road to recovery.

Weiner remained at the medical center through August 9. A constant morphine drip into his jugular vein—the only vein big enough for that large a dosage—blurred his recollection of what transpired there. Mostly, he remembered extreme pain.

Weiner's parents wanted him at Massachusetts General Hospital in Boston as soon as transfer was safe.

Mrs. Weiner: "First we were afraid he was going to die. Then we were afraid he was going to lose his legs. Then we were just afraid."

THE NEXT TIME Linda Crozier went to UC Davis Medical Center, Weiner was gone. She promised Rice she would visit him at least three times a week.

Up to then, Crozier hadn't had any contact with the media, which reported extensively on the tragedy but didn't cite helpers' efforts in the aftermath of the lightning strike. Her dad called a TV station and relayed the story from their point of view. It sparked a media blitz that engulfed Crozier. In several interviews, she repeated the names of all those who had lent a hand on Half Dome, but, to her disappointment, the media ignored that aspect of the story. All they wanted was information about her efforts and those of Mike Hoog.

The other hikers, too, focused their praise on Crozier and Hoog.

Steve White: "They are the real heroes of this thing. I've never seen people work better under such conditions. I can't think of what would have happened if they hadn't come along."

Crozier's father proudly stated: "Our family has always been built around the kids. We told them that they can do anything if they work hard enough. Linda's always been the take-charge kind of person, from the days of Little League to today. What she did at Yosemite didn't surprise me."

She also received letters of commendation from helicopter rescue pilot Al Major, paramedic Bill Bryant, and California governor Pete Wilson.

Yet out of the spotlight, Crozier insisted that her companions deserved as much tribute. "Everybody still needs heroes in this country," she said. "These young people cared enough to get involved. They had the skills and they really saved lives. I'm very proud of them."

-◄o►-

CROZIER CONTINUED to visit Rice at the hospital right up until his release three months later. She was there when he walked for the first time.

To her surprise, Rice talked excessively, bubbling over with commentary. They spent hours gabbing. Rice spoke mainly about himself—how karma had spared his life and that henceforth he must do something to fulfill his destiny, though what that might be wasn't clear. However, neither spoke much about the incident, a subject Rice clearly avoided. Nor did he say much about his cohorts, other than that he really didn't know Frith, Weiner, or Brian Jordan very well. He repeatedly beseeched Crozier to extend his appreciation to all of her Half Dome helpers.

Rice wasn't modest when it came to showing Crozier his wounds and scars. He had lost a lot of weight in the intervening weeks. He spoke at length about his family, how he was "the black sheep." It came out that Crozier's and Rice's fathers worked at the same company, Chevron.

In all of the time Crozier visited Rice at the hospital, there were never any other visitors.

—◁o▷—

WEINER WAS FLOWN to Massachusetts General Hospital, where Dr. John Burke, chief of trauma services, treated him. He was isolated in a special room with a plastic enclosure around the bed to prevent direct human contact, an extremely depressing state for Weiner. After several days, he was moved to another room without a plastic shield and finally allowed to have some human contact. This boosted his morale tremendously.

Instead of bathing Weiner frequently (as UCD Medical Center in Sacramento did), hospital staff swaddled him in heavy layers of gauze and, around the clock, kept the gauze soaked in a diluted solution of silver nitrate, which kills bacteria. He was constantly wet from the middle of his back to his toes, like lying in a puddle twenty-four hours a day. The silver nitrate turned his toenails and fingernails black. Weiner despised these treatments.

Dr. Burke performed eight skin grafts on both of Weiner's legs and his left foot, where the lightning had exited. Initially, Burke used skin from a cadaver, which was a temporary graft, acting more like a biological bandage, and subsequently removed. In later surgeries, he lifted skin from Weiner's intact left thigh.

He commended the emergency medical technicians on Half Dome for saving Weiner. "If Weiner had stayed overnight on the mountain, he wouldn't have survived."

According to Dr. Burke's prognosis, Weiner would have sufficient strength in his legs to lead a normal life. However, some permanent loss of muscle strength was to be expected.

Weiner left the hospital on Friday, September 13, about six weeks after the episode on Half Dome. Rice remained hospitalized for three months.

-◄o►-

THE SIMULTANEOUS Half Dome and Tenaya Canyon missions carried out by Yosemite rangers on the night of July 27 and morning of July 28 involved fifty-nine park personnel in all. All of these individuals under the command of Ranger James Reilly received an Exemplary Act Award—the National Park Service's recognition for outstanding performance.

10

AFTERMATH

We are not building this country of ours for a day. It is to last through the ages.—Theodore Roosevelt, May 1903

When Weiner returned home from the hospital, he weighed 130 pounds. He was so thin, it hurt to sit on a wooden chair without a pillow. Dr. Burke instructed him to consume thirty-five hundred calories a day, almost double what an adult normally consumes.

One night several weeks after his release from the hospital, Weiner had a horrific nightmare.

"I was back in the cave and everything was happening all over again. This time, I knew we were going to be struck by lightning, but I could not convince anybody to listen. When Bob got hit and started to fall off the mountain, I could not let go of him and I was dragged over as well. I awoke screaming and my parents rushed into the room to comfort me. Even after I woke up, I could still smell burned flesh and I could still hear the screams of those around me in the cave."

In November, two months after discharge, Weiner returned to California and his job at Lockheed, determined to put his life back on track. He could work only five hours a day. Whether sitting, standing, walking, or lying down, his constant companion was pain—the "pain of healing," as he referred to it. The first thing he felt in the morning was severe pain, most likely brought on by damaged nerves attempting to regenerate.

"Sometimes it felt like there was a knife being driven to the bottom of my foot. Sometimes it felt like someone was pulling my toenails out."

He underwent physical therapy for a full year. His legs were shriveled due to the loss of muscle mass; some parts looked like raw steak. They remained stiff, causing him to shuffle around and reach with his arms and torso rather than bend his knees. He used a cane and took great care climbing stairs. He had to wear pressure bandages every day for about eighteen months; otherwise, his legs would painfully swell and the grafted skin would form into keloids, or elevated, irregularly shaped, progressively enlarging scars. For the first year, his scars were very angry looking—bright red and highly conspicuous. Several years passed before they became inert and therapy could be discontinued. To this day, the hairless scars covered by abnormal-looking skin are readily noticeable.

The accident severely scarred Weiner's mind as well. Before, he was an easygoing, affable guy who made new friends effortlessly. Afterward, he became very cautious and withdrawn. Driving made him especially nervous, and loud noises easily startled him. Expelling the Half Dome events from his mind took a long time.

One relentless torment was the image of Bob Frith slipping over the edge. It prompted him to seek professional help.

Doctors assured him there was nothing he could have done; that Frith's fate was sealed when the lightning lashed his head.

Weiner: "The first four weeks, the story ran nonstop through my mind. I visualized pulling Frith back into the chamber or Frith falling over the edge while I still held on to him. Now, months later, it's still in my mind, but I have more control over when I run the story."

During his recovery, Weiner experienced many emotional states: guilt that he survived, which others told him was a normal response; moments of elation, thankfulness, depression, despair; and everything in between. After his return to California, he was diagnosed with post-traumatic stress disorder. He tried two or three counselors until he found one he liked—a man who helped him stabilize his life.

It took a good ten years for Weiner's emotional roller coaster to grind to a halt, until a degree of equilibrium and happiness returned to his life. But issues lingered. It's still difficult for him to establish new relationships. He has made few new close friends and shies away from being fully open with anyone other than close family members.

Weiner remained at Lockheed for almost two years before he left in September 1987 to join InSystems, another Bay Area company, where he worked until late 1991. Then he returned to Massachusetts to take a position with Image Engineering Corporation in Somerville. Although he worked there during most of the 1990s, Weiner began transitioning to a more helping profession. Before Half Dome, material values hadn't really driven him; they were even less important afterward. Instead, he wanted to contribute to others in some way, to be proud of his work and feel fulfilled. As early as 1994, Weiner had started doing volunteer work at an animal hospital. He continued volunteering over the next several years at various veterinary agencies. Meanwhile, he enrolled in the School of Veterinary Medicine at Tufts University in 1995. In spring 1998, he began working full time at a veterinary clinic, thus ending his long career in engineering. He received his veterinary degree in May 2000.

Throughout his long recovery, Weiner has endured constant physical discomfort. Now, twenty years later, he still doesn't have much feeling in his feet. Pain shoots through them, then travels up his legs—a result, he explains, of severed leg nerves still trying to regenerate. The pain and suffering have made him a more tolerant and grounded person. He's more appreciative of his life and tries to express that to others. On the other hand, he is less patient when someone uses his time unnecessarily, as if he realizes the preciousness of each minute and doesn't want to waste it.

As a veterinarian, making a difference in peoples' lives and those of their animals brings Weiner pleasure and reward. His own experiences as a patient have helped him be a more caring vet. One of the things that disturbed him most in the hospital was a sense of dehumanization: Staff seemed to ignore his wants and wishes. They bathed, fed, disturbed, awakened, or left him alone at their own convenience and paid very little attention to his emotional and spiritual needs. Doctors and nurses treated him like a large burn, not as a human being with injuries. Weiner realizes as a vet that even though his charges have a physical ailment, he must treat their entire being. Before treating an animal, he always spends a few minutes just petting and calmly talking with it. He thinks this helps.

—◁o▷—

WITH ONLY A FEW exceptions, Rice remained adamant about not discussing the Half Dome episode. However, he did communicate at length with Linda Crozier while hospitalized, and the two corresponded in the months following his discharge in November. Those exchanges revealed a sentimental and receptive side to Rice that others rarely saw. Crozier respected Rice's strong desire for privacy, but she did reveal some of his sentiments to others to illustrate how the tragedy had affected him. His experiences served as a kind of instructive mirror.

After his discharge, Rice really zeroed in on earning a college degree. He enrolled at Chico State University in Chico, California, studied diligently, and kept to a tight schedule, often remaining at the library until it closed at midnight.

Physical rehabilitation was almost as intense a pursuit for him as academics. Once he was able, he began biking, hiking, swimming, skiing, and lifting weights.

In letters to Crozier, Rice shared his thoughts and detailed his progress toward full recuperation. "I'm still dancing," he wrote. He charted that progress using the Half Dome hike as an analogy and baseline. In one letter, he drew a diagram for her depicting the trail and how far his recovery had advanced along it, with an arrow labeled I AM HERE pointing to the spot. It would be great fun, he mused, to visit Yosemite with her, though "most of the park rangers probably think that I'm a cross between a stupid idiot and a crazed maniac."

Rice also expressed interest in meeting Linda's brother, Dan, but acknowledged that "I know he probably isn't too anxious to meet me." The couple of times Dan Crozier had seen him, "I was either burnt to a crisp cluttering up one of the most beautiful places on earth or stark naked around his sister. Not a good first impression."

In a rare reference to the episode, Rice described his feelings on his helicopter flight down from the Dome: "I probably would have been scared to death flying down the face of the dome if I was all there. As it was, a blur of noise and stars and then awesome, almost breathtaking silence (though I had not much breath to take), and a beautiful, calm, peaceful feeling… floating… floating… until we landed!!! Then it was time to find out if I was going to live or die. You see, being sober in an accident for the first time I finally felt the feeling of death trying to fill my body. It had already crept through my left leg and was emptying the life out of the bottom half of my body." Rice confessed that the episode had given him greater faith: "You know, it is just amazing how many wonderful stories have been written depicting the power of faith. But for a stubborn man like me it takes the pleasant shock of reality to drive the message home."

That faith reemerged in a letter he wrote to Crozier in spring 1986:

"I am very thankful for my health, the fact that I was just alive has never been enough for me and I think God knew this. Though it has been a long hard road toward recovery, I feel good, real good. My legs are getting stronger and stronger, ankle not up to par yet but I am starting to hike.... I'm starting to enjoy progress at a slower pace now. Before it was flying off of cliffs, instant gratification, standing in the winner's (he-man's) circle; basically having to satisfy my ego so I could temporarily lose that scary feeling of insecurity. But now I'm finding I am slowing myself down, gaining more over a longer period of time by steadily working toward a goal. Granted the limelight doesn't come to swoon me away; but, I feel good within myself... I can go off by myself on a nice hike, swim, workout... and feel good. This freedom is wonderful. I can feel God with me and I don't feel alone."

Rice added that he hoped "happiness has found you and spring is in your heart."

―◄O►―

THE VERY NEXT SUMMER, Esteban, Rice, Pippey, and a companion returned to Half Dome's summit. Rice may have undergone a personal transformation in the preceding year, but some things hadn't changed. Once again, he was the prime organizer and motivator, demonstrating that he still lived by his *face-your-fears* credo, the lightning episode notwithstanding.

We have to prove to ourselves we can do this, he preached.

The group called itself the "Get Back on the Horse Society."

Esteban: "Rice was still assertive and our recognized leader. Because of all the medical operations, diet, and therapy, he was much thinner than before, but he appeared to be in excellent shape. He had curbed his drinking and indulged in wine instead of beer, even diluting the wine with water. He showed no interest in partying. He was more health-conscious than ever. The only thing that showed he was ever in the accident were long black elastic stockings he wore over his feet and legs to hide the scars, which he seemed very self-conscious about, and to provide support for his calf and back-leg muscles. He had to stretch his legs every morning and before any strenuous leg activity. He followed a very rigorous routine that had been developed especially for him while he was recovering in the hospital. He said he had to do this every day for the rest of his life so he wouldn't lose the flexibility of his leg muscles and possibly the use of his legs.

"Looking back at that return trip to the Dome, I remember we were all feeling very special about the whole thing because it was the first time we had been back since the accident. I was partly scared and very excited to climb Half Dome once again. We brought flowers to leave inside the cave to honor Bob and Brian, and when we reached it, we all gathered and gave a eulogy and toast for our fallen comrades. I said how we were sorry and that we missed them and if I had to go I would like it to happen at Half Dome. At that moment, I felt a real sense of loss, how sad and useless it was for both of them to die so young."

◄O►

THE TRAGEDY GAVE ESTEBAN a new outlook on life: "I realized how short and precious life is and how quickly it can end. It was the first time I had seen death up close and personal."

The lightning jolt knocked much of the thrill-seeker out of Esteban. Before, he had been nonchalant about life, taking stupid chances without giving them a second thought. Now his attitude was: "It's not worth the risk. Nothing is."

He often returned to Half Dome in subsequent years. The tragedy hadn't detracted from its beauty, and going there continued to serve as a barometer of his physical well-being. The rock chamber, however, became for him a sacred place not to be disturbed.

Esteban: "At times, I still acted impulsively. But after a trip to the Dome, I grew more reserved and reflective. In being there, it seemed like everything was put back into perspective, that life is really not as complicated as we all make it out to be. Living and working in Silicon Valley is very stressful, but for one day I can escape all of that by going back to the Dome, where I could always find a certain peace of mind."

Life was a gift, he now realized. And he resolved to live it to the fullest.

"You only live once. If there is something that you really want to do or try, then just do it—you may never get another opportunity."

When Spectra Physics was bought out in the late 1980s, Esteban, who was twenty-seven years old by then, faced a deteriorating work situation. New management demanded higher performance. So, true to his newfound doctrine about seizing opportunities, he decided to fulfill a lifelong dream and enlisted in the U.S. Marine Corps.

Esteban: "Surviving the lightning strike gave me the spark to join the corps. All our previous trips up the Dome created a mindset to continue in the face of adversity, so on that July day in 1985, that's what we did. Even though it turned out to be a disastrous decision, I nevertheless retained the inner fire not to let obstacles deter me from going after a goal. I long wanted to join the Marine Corps. It was time to pursue it."

Like Half Dome, the marines dramatically changed Esteban's life. He enlisted in the Marine Corps Reserves instead of combat infantry—his earlier goal when he was young and more gung-ho about the military. As a reservist, he kept his job in the laser industry. The corps taught him to overcome his greatest weakness: lack of discipline. It shaped his core values and beliefs about loyalty and camaraderie. In 1985, he had been a follower mostly; in the marines he learned how to lead.

He designed a tattoo for his upper arm that celebrated more than just his status as a U.S. Marine. USMC was emblazoned beneath a big scorpio eagle whose claws gripped a red lightning bolt. In his mind, the two events—the lightning episode and becoming a marine—had merged.

Esteban served in the reserves for ten years, earned the rank of staff sergeant, and held many different jobs. The one he loved the most was military policeman. With the expert training, experience, and contacts he gained, he thought he would be a shoe-in to get hired as a police officer—his occupational goal upon leaving the corps. But when asked in a job interview if he had ever used cocaine, Esteban responded yes, believing that honesty was the best course. Instead, he was rejected. He returned to the laser industry, enrolled at several community colleges, and eventually earned an associate of arts degree in laser technology. In 1998, he enrolled in Phoenix College and, two years later, received a bachelor of science degree in business management.

◄◦►

THE HALF DOME TRAGEDY impacted—and in some cases shattered—many lives. It had driven a wedge between Esteban and Rice.

Esteban: "The Half Dome brotherhood that we felt toward each other changed in the horror of the calamity. The long-standing mutual trust and loyalty we shared were gone, and they did not return."

Ironically, Esteban and Rice became relatives. Esteban's female cousin lived in Hawaii, and on a backpacking trip Rice and Esteban took there in 1986, Rice's nephew joined them. He met and fell in love with Esteban's cousin. The two later married. While surfing and hiking there, Rice wore long socks. Whenever anyone asked about his scars, he jokingly referred to them as an old football injury. Throughout the trip, neither Rice nor Esteban mentioned the Half Dome episode. There was an underlying friction between them that sparked little arguments over trivial things. According to Esteban, the two men "never got anything out in the open."

For months afterward, Pippey's emotions were erratic, intense, and often self-destructive. The lightning strike obliterated his tight circle of friends. The estrangement between Rice and Esteban, and Bob Frith's death, left him without a hiking clique. His back-packing treks dwindled, causing his physical condition and spirit to deteriorate. He began drinking heavily again and abusing drugs. He clung to his marriage and job by a thread.

Also dashed were Pippey's onetime hopes that nature would be a therapeutic force in the lives of the Jordan twins. Bruce Jordan seemed unable to cope with the death of his brother and withdrew into a shell.

Pippey: "It's as though he descended into a darkness, where morbidity and a Gothic-like fascination with death and the occult reigned." (Bruce Jordan chose not to contribute to this book.)

"For me, nothing good came out of the tragedy. It was all just sad and terrible."

Pippey held considerable admiration for Rice's drive to enroll in college and pursue a degree. When Pippey visited him at Chico State, Rice was in great physical shape—even better than before the lightning strike. However, Pippey also noticed that Rice had-n't changed in some respects. For example, on a whitewater raft-ing trip together, they entered a dangerous rapid, out of control. Amid the mayhem, Rice and others tried to throw someone over-board in reckless horseplay. It was too much for Pippey, who demanded to be put ashore. On another backpacking trip, Rice hiked for a day and a half in the nude. Rice's exhibitionism, it seemed to Pippey, was even more pronounced than before.

For Steve White, the days following Half Dome were filled with deep sadness.

White: "I would go to work, close the door to my office, and think of how tragic it was for the two who lost their lives, and for their families, especially the sixteen-year-old twin who died and his twin brother. I've gone back up to Half Dome many times since. It has a spiritual nature for me now because of what happened there. I've never been back into the cave and don't want to go back in. Even though all of those trips have been with big groups who are thrilled to be there, I always take time to sit alone and remember. Sometimes I tell the story but tend not to because it has become more personal. I keep two pictures of Half Dome hanging in my office.

"I secured my EMT certification as a result of my involvement in the tragedy and my admiration for Linda Crozier and the other EMTs that night."

A large framed picture of Half Dome being whipped by lightning hangs in paramedic Bill Bryant's office along with the front-page story that appeared in the *San Francisco Examiner* the day after the incident.

Mike Hoog proposed to his girlfriend, Louisa Munger, atop Half Dome. Their wedding cake featured a representation of it.

Hoog: "I wanted to bring her to the Dome because that was a part of me and my life. I have a lot of wonderful memories of Yosemite and Half Dome, and also some intense ones because of the lightning strike, and I wanted her to experience the things that I did so that she could understand. When we went to the Dome for our 'dare the Dome in a day,' it was like filling her in on my experiences. I guess in a way the Dome is like a sacred place, a vortex for me. I knew that I would propose to her on the Dome."

Because of her efforts that night, Linda Crozier frequently was asked to teach emergency medial technician classes in which she recounted her experience and outlined the steps that should be taken in such situations. She met and ultimately married another EMT instructor, Mark Ghilarducci, who led search and rescue operations.

◄○►

ON JULY 28, 2001, Peterson High School in Santa Clara held a "Super Reunion" for all eleven classes that had graduated before the school closed in the 1980s as a result of district consolidation. Among Peterson's graduates were Rice and Esteban.

Coincidentally, the Super Reunion coincided with the sixteenth anniversary of the Half Dome calamity, almost to the day. On a whim, Esteban contacted Rice before the event and asked if he planned to attend. Rice wasn't sure, due to job commitments. But when the reunion rolled around, Rice was there.

Esteban: "He was the same old Tom, the best I had seen him since the accident. As usual, he was the center of attention, dressed to kill in some outrageous black leather pants and custom shirt with hair slicked back, looking like a model out of *GQ*."

The Half Dome epic, which had widely circulated during the intervening years, bestowed celebrity status on Rice and Esteban. Reuniongoers were curious: Had they really been involved in such a tragedy? Esteban, always willing to play second fiddle, just sat back and listened as Rice rattled off his typically quick and superficial account:

We were up there hiking, went into this cave when it started raining, and it was just very unlucky that a lightning bolt hit us.

Rice said he recalled very little about the accident and rescue; he had been hospitalized for four months, he hated the whole time he was in there, and he was lucky to be alive. Rice also praised Esteban: If he hadn't left the cave before the second bolt struck, and come back afterward, "we would all probably be dead."

"Esteban," he said, "saved my life and was the hero of the whole thing."

It was the first time Esteban had heard Rice talk so expansively about the incident. It was also the first time he had cast Esteban as the hero. Later that night, the two had a heart-to-heart talk. Esteban really had saved his life, Rice explained, because if he hadn't fled the granite enclosure, the second lightning bolt probably would have incapacitated him, too. Consequently, no one else would have known their whereabouts on the summit or that they were in dire need of help, without which Rice and Weiner surely wouldn't have survived the night. Rice, aware of Esteban's tremendous guilt about having abandoned his buddies in the chamber, said that in fact he was grateful to him.

Rice gave Esteban his blessing to tell their story in a book but said he wouldn't participate. And whatever bad feelings there may have been between them, real or imagined, he was willing to consign to the past and move on.

Esteban: "I think neither one of us wanted to face the severity of what had occurred, and neither of us wanted to take responsibility for the death of two human beings. And finally, over time, we just let the hurt in us die to the point that everything now was just an afterthought and we could finally acknowledge that we were happy to have survived. We never really talked about who was to blame for this."

⫷◦⫸

DESPITE THE JORDANS' initial threat to sue over the death of their son Brian, they never did. However, legal action regarding two other lightning-related incidents—the one in 1975 on Moro Rock and the other in 1990 on Mount Whitney, both in Sequoia National Park—shed important light on culpability in such cases.

The 1975 event spawned two lawsuits: one by the wife of the deceased, Lawrence Brady, and a second by Edward Schieler, who incurred extensive, life-altering injuries. Both plaintiffs alleged that the National Park Service "failed to provide any warning, guidance, or supervision with respect to the danger of being struck by lightning atop Moro Rock, or of the fact that such a storm was impending, and further failed to provide and maintain reasonable or any safety devices to de-electrify the observation area."

The court dismissed their claims. It held that:

... the National Park Service has broad discretionary power to regulate the parks in such a manner that the scenery and natural and wild life in the parks are preserved unimpaired so that they may be enjoyed presently and in the future. Placing signs throughout every area that might be potentially struck by lightning, or subject to any other dangers, such as rock slides, certainly would impair the scenery and naturalness of the parks. And, before this lightning strike on Moro Rock, there had been no prior record of lightning striking it. No injuries from lightning ever happened there before.

The outcome of several lawsuits filed against the National Park Service after the July 1990 lightning strike on Mount Whitney was quite different. (In addition to the fatality, two people were injured, one seriously.) Plaintiffs won damages totaling $1.7 million. The judge was very disturbed by the five-year history preceding the accident, beginning with an event in 1985 in which several hikers who had sought shelter in the Smithsonian Hut on Mount Whitney's summit were injured by lightning. In 1986, the safety manager for Sequoia and Kings Canyon prepared a plan for installation of lightning protection on the hut, and the park superintendent approved it. Implementing this plan, however, was a low priority for the next safety manager. Lightning struck the hut again in 1987, 1988, and 1989.

In early 1990, the National Park Service moved forward with its lightning protection plan but chose not to install warning signs until the protective equipment was in place. Thus, when lightning struck in July of that year, killing one and injuring two, the warning signs were stashed in a ranger station at the bottom of Mount Whitney.

The judge found that "the actions of the Park Service over the period 1985 to 1990 constituted a willful failure to guard or warn the public."

Given the findings in these cases, the Jordan family would have had great difficulty winning a lawsuit. In Yosemite, warning signs were posted both at the bottom of Sub Dome and at the top of the cables on Half Dome. Furthermore, Esteban and his companions had stated that they were aware of the dangers and chose to ascend Half Dome regardless. Other hikers, too, were prepared to testify that the men who took refuge in the granite chamber behaved recklessly and irresponsibly.

◄o►

MEDICAL KNOWLEDGE about lightning injuries has increased considerably since 1985. In 1992, Dr. Mary Ann Cooper and colleagues co-edited a text, *Lightning Injuries: Electrical, Medical, and Legal Aspects*, that had its roots in the late 1970s, when Dr. Cooper treated a lightning patient in the emergency room at a Cincinnati hospital. She discovered there was little information about such injuries in medical texts. Her text was an effort to pull together what medical professionals knew about lightning injuries up to that point. Today Dr. Cooper is the first to admit that much has changed since her text was published.

Based on her own extensive research, Dr. Cooper has concluded that substantial quantities of lightning probably do not enter the body. That's because, contrary to common belief and the way people speak or write about lightning, it isn't a simple, unidirectional force comparable to a bullet. Rather, lightning is a very complex wave-and-current phenomenon that behaves more like a wave washing over, around, and perhaps through some portions of a fairly large area. A lot of evidence suggests that much, if not most, of lightning energy doesn't even enter the body. It creates a flashover effect instead. This is why Dr. Cooper dismisses as inaccurate the terms *entry* and *exit*—words applied in the field of electrical burn treatment—when describing the flow of lightning. More accurate terms, she says, are *source* and *ground*.

Experimental evidence suggests that a fast flashover apprecia-
bly diminishes energy dissipation within the body, thus producing
the low percentage (10 percent) of lightning fatalities. Current
may flow internally for an incredibly short time—thousandths of
a second. When it does, it can cause the heart, respiratory centers
in the brain, and the autonomic nervous system to short-circuit,
and spark spasms in arteries and muscles. Such injuries can be
severe and in some cases fatal.

From her studies, however, Dr. Cooper has found that lightning current seldom results in significant burns or tissue destruction. A heat source must be in contact with skin long enough to
burn it. Lightning's exposure time is so brief, it can't cause substantial skin burns. Those that do occur are mostly secondary.
They happen when sweat or dampness from rain vaporizes and
the resulting steam causes red burns and blisters. Clothing, such
as a jacket, or a backpack may trap the steam, which enables it to
inflict more damage. The conversion of moisture to steam and the
resulting vapor "explosion" can blow clothing and shoes off someone's body. Metal, which holds lightning heat longer, can burn
nearby tissue. But the direct burns from the lightning current are
generally quite minor and superficial.

-◄o►-

A LONG-OVERDUE BAN on overnight camping on Half Dome took
effect in 1993. The unlikely impetus for this action was the rare
Mount Lyell salamander, an endangered species. Quantities of
human waste under the summit rocks and the many rock shelters
built there by campers were threatening the salamander's survival.
Clearly, humans' impact on the summit had become widespread
and destructive. Only one of seven trees that populated the summit for many years remained; the others became firewood.

Tens of thousands of hikers tramp about Yosemite and thousands hike to Half Dome's summit every season. So many were
cramming into Little Yosemite Valley to camp overnight that the

park began requiring reservations. The hordes on and around Half Dome can make the journey, as Brian Cage complained, "more like a trip to Disneyland than a solitary refreshing backcountry experience." The constant foot traffic widens and churns trails into dust and degrades the land. For those same reasons, Mount Whitney limits the number of hikers, a possible restriction that looms for Half Dome, as well.

The cables that put Half Dome within reach of countless persons wouldn't be installed if the decision arose today, given the current priority to keep national parks as natural as possible.

Twenty-five years have passed, as of this writing, since the adoption of Yosemite's master plan, yet implementation has occurred at a glacial pace, principally due to the park's tradition of administrative gridlock, competing interest groups, and political seesawing. Nonetheless, in 2004 Yosemite finally embarked on a $440 million plan to limit or change human activity in the park consistent with the 1980 master plan. As Park Superintendent Michael Tollefson put it, "the goal is to have a smaller human footprint." This ambitious undertaking may take two decades to complete. It involves demolishing a parking lot near Yosemite Falls; replacing another one with a grassy pedestrian promenade; rebuilding and rerouting trails near waterfalls; razing a dam on the Merced River; moving some employee housing outside the park; eliminating about 250 campsites, including those along the Merced River; limiting the number of day-visitor cars to 550 (additional visitors will have to ride buses into the park); and launching extensive remodeling projects.

Despite objections to the plan from some quarters, a broad coalition of organizations supports the overall plan as a sensible approach to preserving the natural wonders, historical values, and sublime beauty of this national treasure called Yosemite.

EPILOGUE

Think like a mountain.—Aldo Leopold, *A Sand County Almanac*

In the annals of hiking tragedies caused by lightning, July 27, 1985, ranks as one of the most calamitous dates of all time. By all accounts, the storms in the Sierra Nevada on this day were exceptionally violent; when combined with human misjudgments, this proved a formula for disaster. All told, three people in two close-by national parks were killed. These occurrences in eerily similar circumstances were most startling, like the night in the

1960s when grizzlies killed two hikers in different locations in Glacier National Park.

Three other hikers on Half Dome were stricken in 1985, with two sustaining life-altering injuries. It could have been even worse, because other hikers and rock climbers also were in extremely high-risk circumstances in Yosemite on this day.

Twenty years later, those who were involved in the episode reflect on its meaning and aftermath.

-◄o►-

LINDA CROZIER FOUND HERSELF primarily responsible for the emergency medical treatment of two individuals for over five hours. All of the other helpers that night looked to her for leadership.

"I've always marveled at the raw power of nature and am amazed when people make careless, at times reckless, decisions in the outdoors. Our natural world can at one moment be beautiful and serene, and in the next violent and terrifying. It gives warning signs—hints of what's to come—but people sometimes ignore the signs or are simply unaware of what those signs are saying. What individuals don't realize when they act irresponsibly and put themselves in a high-risk position in the outdoors is that they are also risking the lives of those who have to rescue them. I have the deepest respect for the men and women in the search and rescue community who put their own lives on the line to save others.

"On that July day in 1985, some of us rested and stared in awe at the sights, sounds, and sensations of the most intense electrical storm I have ever seen, while at the same time that very storm was taking the lives of two men and injuring three others. From this experience, I learned to love and respect nature even more, and expand my own knowledge about the outdoors. I joined a volunteer search and rescue team. I learned more about wilderness medicine and, in turn, passed along what I have learned to hundreds of others through classes and lectures. It is my hope that recounting this story will do the same."

BILL PIPPEY WAS AS emotionally affected as anyone by the episode, both at the time and afterward.

"What was revealed to me was how everybody deals with tragedy differently. That night, several courageous persons stepped up and kept it from being an even worse catastrophe. Others turned away and seemed concerned only about themselves. Some used the tragedy to make something of their lives, to chart a new direction, to finally live their dream. One devoted himself to helping others. Another retreated into a shell and allowed his life to deteriorate. One creep who wasn't even involved in the incident saw it as a chance to make money. One thing is true: No one was the same afterward and no one looked upon the other person in the same way as before. No one seemed interested in rekindling old ties.

"I took it as a major defeat, a crushing setback. I slipped back into my heavy drinking and drugging once more. I barely hung on to my life and my wife. Then one day in the mid-'90s, I woke up. I discovered Jesus Christ and became a devout, born-again Christian. I stopped abusing my body with substances. I refocused on my family, and in my work I became a laser engineer, which surely must surprise many of my old Hayward buddies."

BRUCE WEINER LIVES with the effects of the lightning strike each day of his life. It caused him to see firsthand how fragile life really is, and that it takes very little "to totally screw up one's life."

Weiner: "Going to the top at that time, I know now, was a stupid decision, but I didn't know then that it was a stupid move. How can you say you'll risk your life just so you can reach the top of a mountain twenty minutes early? That's beyond stupidity. That's just a total lack of brains. What we didn't know at the time, though, was how reckless it was to go to that cave during a raging holocaust, that we were playing with our lives.

"A big part of our decision was that we [Frith and I] were following the two leaders, Rice and Esteban. We trusted their knowledge and judgment. After all, they had been doing this hike for years and were seasoned veterans. They believed that we'd be fully safe once in the cave.

"Am I bitter about what happened? On one level, yes, I am very bitter. Rice and Esteban led us into a totally unnecessary disaster that cost my best friend his life and me my health. I guess the question is, When should one trust a 'leader' and when should one not? I'm sure there are times when one must absolutely follow a leader in dangerous situations, when he possesses the expert knowledge and skill. But this was not one of those times. There was counterinformation from real authorities staring us in the face, and still we chose to go up.

"So, in retrospect, I feel I really have nobody to blame but myself. We passed signs that gave specific warnings about not going to the summit when there are signs of a thunderstorm and not taking cover in a rock enclosure. Frith and I were adults capable of thinking for ourselves, so we had little excuse for our own actions. We were the only ones with college degrees, for God's sake! But maybe that kind of learning doesn't matter in the outdoors, when it comes down to common sense and reasoned judgment. It's a valuable lesson why someone should not give in to the pressures of the moment, to group pressures, if one's own thinking and intuition say it's not right. One always needs to think for himself—in effect, not to relinquish control over his own destiny and allow someone else to determine it for him."

◄○►

ADRIAN ESTEBAN HAS CARRIED around the tragedy in his head and heart for more than two decades and is willing to be as honest as he can in terms of confronting his role in the calamity and talking about it.

Esteban: "I can now look back and feel totally responsible and not hide from the fact that I found the cave, and that it was my idea to bring everyone else on this trip. I did not force anyone to climb the cables to the top, but Tom and I were the leaders and they were just following us. If Tom and I did not make the climb to the top, then Bruce, Brian, and Bob would not have been there and all our lives from that day on would be different.

"The thing is, Tom and I really believed that facing and overcoming your fears was the right principle to follow. For 99 percent of the time, it's a sound approach in life for realizing your potential, succeeding, progressing. It's just that it failed us that one time on the top of Half Dome. With something as powerful and unpredictable as lightning, we should have understood that sound judgment had to be part of the equation.

"Despite the enormity of the tragedy, my feelings toward Half Dome remain the same, only now they are more profound. It is still a special place for me and, if anything, the entire incident was almost like my destiny. It served as a catalyst to motivate me to do something good with my life. No matter how difficult or bad things could get from that moment forward, all I have to do is look back at the accident and remember the clarity of the actions of the many people who helped us and I gain once again the proper perspective on life. In times of distress, I have used it to help me get through and overcome tough times—for example, when my father died in 1993 and when my mother came down with cancer. The most important thing is to never give up.

"Half Dome forced me to really turn inward and find a purpose for why I am here. Because of the person I am, being very deeply involved in natural wonders and having a spiritual outlook on life, everything about the strike at Half Dome has deep meaning for me—the place where it happened, the way it happened, the time in my life when it happened, the different ways it affected people.

"I think everyone, if they live with awareness and become wise enough, will recognize some event, incident, or chance happening in their life that transforms them and drives them to live life the very best that they can from that time forward.

"For me, it was that moment."

APPENDIX

Safety Guidelines for Lightning

Of all the weather-related phenomena, lightning kills and injures more people than any other, with the exception of floods. As seen in the tragedies on Half Dome and in Kings Canyon on July 27, 1985, persons tend to seek shelter when caught in a thunderstorm and driving rains. They may also believe it's safer to be under some cover, such as rock enclosures or a tree, than out in the open if lightning strikes. (Golfers are particularly prone to do this.) But small caves, tall trees, rock enclosures and outcroppings, "chimneys" located on rock walls—each can become a death trap if lightning strikes in the vicinity. (A large cave can offer safety but only if you stay in the middle, away from the walls.) It's far safer to stay out in the open and get wet.

Here are some additional crucial safety principles:*

All thunderstorms produce lightning and are dangerous.

The outdoors is the most dangerous place to be during a lightning storm. At the first indication of an impending storm, go inside to a completely enclosed building (not a carport, open garage, or covered patio) or into a hard-topped vehicle.

Lightning can strike as far as ten miles away from any rainfall, and can travel sideways for up to ten miles.

---

*These principles of Lightning Safety are mainly those of the National Weather Service (NWS).

If you hear thunder, you are in danger from lightning.

If the air starts buzzing and your hair bristles, you are in immediate danger and should adhere to the principles below.

If caught outdoors, *seek* the lowest point and *be* the lowest point. Do not be the tallest or second tallest object during a lightning storm. Avoid tall trees (be at least twice as far from a tall tree as the height of the tree). If in an open area, crouch down on the balls of your feet.

Avoid being near or touching any metal.

If you're with a group, stay several yards away from other people.

Get out of water, and out of small boats and canoes. If you're caught in a boat, crouch down in the center of the boat away from metal hardware. Don't stand in or near puddles of water.

Wait at least thirty minutes after the last clap of thunder before leaving shelter, even with blue sky and sunshine.

The safest measures to follow with lightning are awareness and prevention. Avoid being caught in precarious circumstances.

◄○►

IF THE HIKERS IN Yosemite and Kings Canyon that day knew and followed the above principles, their calamities most certainly would have been avoided.

ACKNOWLEDGMENTS

I AM ENORMOUSLY GRATEFUL to all those persons who helped me complete this book, from the first stages of research to the final phrasing. First I want to thank each of the individuals who played a role in the events and who assisted me in telling their story. They are: Adrian Esteban, Linda (Crozier) Ghilarducci, Bill Pippey, Bruce Weiner, Mike Hoog, Rick Pedroncelli, Dan Crozier, Karl Buchner, Steve Ellner, Brian Cage, Steve White, Monroe Bridges, Paul Kolbenschlag, Zip Cotter, Clu Cotter, Ken Bokelund, Rob Foster, Al Major, Maggie (Newman) Dias, Bill Bryant, Colin Campbell, Scott Jackson, Jim Reilly, Gary Colliver, John Dill, Ron Mackie, Scott Emmerich, Dan Horner, Paul Ducasse, Mike Mayer, Dan Dellinges, Jim Tucker, Jennifer Corcoran, Marvin Talbert, Steven King, Debbie Bird, Robert Hensel, and Dr. Howard Klein. I also wish to express my deep appreciation to all those who provided information and/or critiqued what I wrote. In no particular order they are: Jim Snyder, Dr. Mary Ann Cooper, Paul Engstrom, Rick Donker, Bob Kinkead, Jim Mongillo, John Little, Jennifer Madgic, Dr. Marsh McLean, Dave Cone, Dr. Phil McLean, Jeff Rennicke, Randall Boone, Sally Howell, Liana Holmberg, Mary Heldman, John Nagle, Kris Fister, Don Coelho, Edward Schieler, Dolores Schieler, Alyza Salomon, Mike Peckner, Richard Keady, Charles R. "Butch" Farabee Jr., Mike Harding, Karen Little, Sarah Madgic, Richard Kithil Jr., Dr. Rob Hamilton, Jason Thrasher, Dave Toal, Felicia Eth, Howard Boyer, Darryl Brock, Lydia Bird, Sherry Symington, Bill Contardi, Walt Simmons, Mike Acker, Marilyn Young, Ruth Rowe, Ed Robertson, Diana Thrasher, Doug Madgic, Liz Robbins, Royal Robbins, Jim Erickson, Art Higbee, Ron Schultz, Phil Pochoda, Kirk Madgic, Richard

Baumann, Marc Soares, Jed Mattes, Linda Eade, Leonard Coyne, Buck Tilton, Sarah Rabkin, and of course my wife, Diane, who as always provided supportive companionship and sage counsel at every step of this journey.

Lastly, I wish to express my gratitude to the publisher, Peter Burford, who quickly saw the power of this story and who has been a delight to work with. I doubt an author could find a more encouraging and supportive publisher.

How to Survive

BOOKS BY JAMES HERNDON
THE WAY IT SPOZED TO BE
HOW TO SURVIVE IN YOUR NATIVE LAND

n Your Native Land

JAMES HERNDON

SIMON AND SCHUSTER · NEW YORK

ALL RIGHTS RESERVED
INCLUDING THE RIGHT OF REPRODUCTION
IN WHOLE OR IN PART IN ANY FORM
COPYRIGHT © 1971 BY JAMES HERNDON
PUBLISHED BY SIMON AND SCHUSTER
ROCKEFELLER CENTER, 630 FIFTH AVENUE
NEW YORK, NEW YORK 10020

SECOND PRINTING

SBN 671–20864–0
LIBRARY OF CONGRESS CATALOG CARD NUMBER: 70–151495
MANUFACTURED IN THE UNITED STATES OF AMERICA

FOR JAY AND JACK

Contents

James Thurber once sat by his window watching men cut down elm trees to clear a site for an institution in which to confine people who had been driven insane by the cutting down of elm trees.

PART ONE

Work, knowledge and love, Reich said, are the well-springs of human life. Who could argue with that?

—FROM Left, *by Keith Jones*

CHAPTER I

A Kite

I might as well begin with Piston. Piston was, as a matter of description, a red-headed medium-sized chubby eighth grader; his definitive characteristic was, however, stubbornness. Without going into a lot of detail, it became clear right away that what Piston didn't want to do, Piston didn't do; what Piston did want to do, Piston did.

It really wasn't much of a problem. Piston wanted mainly to paint, draw monsters, scratch designs on mimeograph blanks and print them up, write an occasional horror story—some kids referred to him as The Ghoul—and when he didn't want to do any of those, he wanted to roam the halls and on occasion (we heard) investigate the girls' bathrooms.

We had minor confrontations. Once I wanted everyone to sit down and listen to what I had to say—something about the way they had been acting in the halls. I was letting them come and go freely and it was up to them (I planned to point out) not to raise hell so that I had to hear about it from other teachers. Sitting down was the issue—I was determined everyone was going to do it first, then I'd talk. Piston remained standing. I re-ordered. He paid no attention. I pointed out that I was talking to him. He indicated he heard me. I inquired then why in hell didn't he sit down. He said he didn't want to. I said I did want him to. He said that didn't matter to him. I said do it anyway. He said why? I said because I said so. He said he wouldn't. I said Look I want you to sit down and listen to what I'm going to say. He said he *was* listening. I'll listen but I won't sit down.

Well, that's the way it goes sometimes in schools. You as teacher become obsessed with an issue—I was the injured party, conferring, as usual, unheard-of freedoms, and here they were as usual taking advantage. It ain't pleasant coming in the teachers' room for coffee and having to hear somebody say that so-and-so and so-and-so from *your* class were out in the halls *without a pass* and *making faces* and *giving the finger* to kids in *my* class during the most *important* part of *my* lesson about *Egypt*—and you ought to be allowed your tendentious speech, and most everyone will allow it, sit down for it, but occasionally someone wises you up by refusing to submit where it isn't necessary. But anyway, it's not the present point, which is really only Piston's stubbornness. Another kid told me that when Piston's father got mad at him and punished him, as Piston thought, unjustly (one cannot imagine Piston considering any punishment just), Piston got up in the middle of the night, went into the garage and revenged himself on his father's car. Once he took out and threw away two spark plugs. Another time he managed to remove all the door handles. You get a nice picture of Piston sitting quiet all evening long brooding about not being allowed to watch some favorite science-fiction program because he'd brought home a note about unsatisfactory this-or-that at school, sitting there unresponding and impassive, and then his father getting up in the morning to go to work, perhaps in a hurry or not feeling well, trying to start the car or looking at the locked doors and rolled up windows and the places where the door handles had been pried off. How did any of us get into this? we ought to be asking ourselves.

It was probably Frank Ramirez who brought up the idea

of making kites. Frank was a teacher, not a kid; we were working together. All the kids were making them suddenly; they scrounged the schoolrooms and maddened the shop teachers looking for suitable lengths of wood. Frank brought in fancy paper. The kites were wonderful. Naturally we plunged down to the lower field to fly them. They flew well, or badly, or not at all, crashed and were broken, sailed away, got caught in overhead wires, the kids ran and yelled and cried and accused one another. It went on for several days and of course we heard a lot about classes overlooking the lower field being interrupted in the most important parts of the lessons about Egypt, for after all those kids wanted to know why they couldn't be flying kites instead of having Egypt, and Frank and I were cocky enough to state aloud that indeed we also wondered why they couldn't be flying kites too, after all who was stopping them? Piston, up in Room 45, was preparing our comeuppance.

Piston had been making a kite for several days. He continued making it while others were flying theirs. It had only one definitive characteristic too; it was huge. The crosspieces were 1 × 2 boards. The covering was heavy butcher paper, made heavier by three coats of poster paint in monstrous designs. The cord was clothesline rope. It was twenty feet long. Piston was finished with his kite about the time when everyone else had finished with the whole business of making and flying kites and had settled down in the room anticipating a couple of weeks of doing nothing, resting up for some future adventure. Piston produced his finished product, which was universally acclaimed a masterpiece. It was. Pictorially monstrous as usual, its *size*, its heavy *boards*, its *rope*, aroused a certain amount of real awe. Piston was really something else, we could see that. None of us had had such a concept.

But when Piston announced he was prepared to fly it, we all hooted, relieved. It was easier to have Piston-the-nut back again than to put up with Piston-the-genius-artist. No one had thought of it as something to fly—only as something to look at and admire. In any case, it clearly would not fly. It was too big, too heavy, too awkward, unbalanced, there wasn't enough wind, you couldn't run with it—we had lots of reasons. Stubborn Piston hauled it down to the field past amazed windows of classbound kids ignoring Egypt once again to goggle and exclaim. Down on the grass we all gathered around the inert monster. If nothing else, Frank and I thought, Piston had prepared a real scene, something memorable—David being drawn through the streets of Florence.

The kite flew. Piston had prepared no great scene. Instead he had (I think) commanded the monster kite to fly. So it flew. Of course it flew. Two of the biggest and strongest boys were persuaded to run with the kite; Piston ran with the rope. Everyone participated in what was believed to be a charade. We would act as if we thought the kite would fly. It would be in itself a gas. They ran; he pulled. The kite lumbered into the air, where it stayed aloft menacingly for perhaps four or five minutes. Then it dove, or rather just fell like a stone (like an avalanche!), with a crash. When it crashed, everyone was seized with a madness and rushed to the kite, jumped on it, stomped it, tore it . . . all except Frank and I, and we wanted to. (Great difficulties at that very moment were angrily reported to us later by teachers of Egypt classes.)

The kite was saved, though. Piston repaired and repapered it, repainted it. Frank and I hung it in the room and admired it, and forgot it. But next week, Lou, the principal, approached us at lunchtime with great excitement. What about Piston? he wanted to know, and what about that Kite? Whose idea . . . ? and so on. His concern was not Egypt, but the fact that Piston and others had taken it out to the playground during lunch and flown it again. So? So!

screamed Lou, the goddamn thing was a menace! It weighed a hundred pounds. It fell down and damn near killed thirty or forty seventh grade girls, and their mothers were calling him up and was this Piston crazy or were we, or what? And he wanted it made clear that flying that kite was out! O-U-T, out! He had enough troubles with our goddamn class running around all over the place and other teachers griping and smoking in the bathrooms and parents complaining they weren't learning nothing and he'd always supported us but he couldn't have that giant kite. Couldn't have it! We soothed him, agreeing to tell Piston in no uncertain terms and so on. We walked outside with Lou, who had calmed down and had begun admiring the kite in retrospect, realizing that there was no way such a creation could fly (*aerodynamically speaking,* he said), and yet it did fly and this Piston or whatever his name was must be a pretty exceptional kid, and we were agreeing and realizing what a great guy Lou was for a principal even if, we reminded him, he had goofed up our schedule for this marvelous class we'd planned which had resulted in that extraordinary kite and other grand exploits, along with, we admitted, a certain amount of difficulty for him, Lou, and how well he'd handled it and supported us and . . . when Lou suddenly screamed Aaarrghhh! and fell back. I thought he'd been stung by a bee—we'd had a lot of bees that year, which also interrupted Egypt quite a bit, flying in the classroom where kids could scream with fake or real fear or try to kill them by throwing objects, often Egypt books, at them, exempt from retribution by the claim that they were just trying to save some *allergic kid* from *death* —but then he screamed There it is again! and pointed up, and there was The Monster From Outer Space, seventy-five feet up, plunging and wheeling and lurching through the thin air, a ton of boards and heavy paper and ghouls and toothy vampires leering down at an amazed lunchtime populace of little seventh grade girls, all with mothers and phones. Jesus Christ, look out! yelled Lou, and rushed for the playground, just as the giant came hurtling down like a dead flying mountain. It crashed; seventh grade girls scattered. (Their mothers reached for the phones.) Kids rushed from every direction and hurled themselves at the kite. They stomped it and tore it and killed it in wildest glee. They lynched it and murdered it and executed it and mercy-killed it and put it out of its misery, and when it was over and Lou had everyone pulled off the scattered corpse of the kite and sitting down on benches and shut up there was nothing left of it but bits and pieces of painted butcher paper and 1 × 2 boards and clothesline rope.

CHAPTER II

Son of ⎱
Return of ⎰ Way It Spozed To Be

About a third of the way through Kurt Vonnegut's novel *Slaughterhouse Five*, the hero became "unstuck in time" and saw a World War II movie backwards. Seen thus, every hurtful blow of war was turned into a healing act. The bombers, which took off backwards from English fields, were full of holes and wounded men. The German fighter planes they met "sucked bullets and shell fragments from some of the planes and crewmen. They did the same for wrecked American bombers on the ground and those planes flew up backwards to join the formation."

Over a German city in flames, the bombers sucked up the bombs from the ground and made the flames go out by a "miraculous magnetism." They stored the bombs in racks inside the planes and flew them backwards to England, where the bombs were unloaded and sent by rail to factories. There women took the bombs apart and turned them back into minerals. "The minerals were then shipped to specialists in remote areas. It was their business to put them into the ground, to hide them cleverly, so they would never hurt anybody ever again."

That movie, unstuck in time, showed him a world unaccountably in holocaust, showed him the familiar apparatus of war now employed to cure and heal men and cities. I suppose it to be the absolutely perfect image for us now in

America. For so many of us now see America as all wrong. If we are forty or so, we may see it—considering we were around during that same World War II—as *unaccountably* all wrong. And we hope to use the familiar apparatus of America—not only those fires, those bombs, but the whole institutional structure of America—as an agent to heal and cure, to transform by "miraculous magnetism" bad into good, horror into beauty. We dream that it will again become an agent of fruitfulness—the power which will tell us the right questions to ask in order to restore the wasted land, cause the stagnant streams to flow and fish to leap, heal The Maimed King and form, as King Arthur said, a more perfect union. We hope to become unstuck in time.

I am also addicted to another more common image, that of the road or voyage. The best expression of it is in Ortega —that man has no nature excepting the road he has traveled. So that in *The Way It Spozed To Be* I wrote a travelogue. The people who read the book and wrote me about it seemed either to recognize that land as one in which they too traveled or lived, or as one so uncharted and astonishing that they had difficulty believing in it. Only Mr. Friedenberg wanted to point out that *The Way It Spozed To Be* was an "account of the author's own gradual growth and commitment" and that it was just that commitment which put him at odds with things along that road. And that is exactly our situation, or The Problem, as they say, in America. We hope to find our work, our growth and our commitment within the institutions of our country, and in fact that is where, to some degree, we do find them—only to discover that as we do so we are more and more extruded, or if we are not, we grow to distrust ourselves.

In 1957, having spent six years in Europe, living here and there, doing this and that, I was working in a small-time military-industrial-complex-American-government agency operating in an abandoned pants factory on

17

the outskirts of Paris. Fran and I had married and were expecting our first child. We decided to go back to America.

I was perhaps happier about it than Fran. But then, I had invented an ideology for going back. Briefly, I had the idea that America needed me. The mainstream of America needed me, Jim Herndon, traveler, *voyageur*, precisely because I had traveled a different road. Certainly I would be welcome as a teacher, for instance, if only as an antidote to the kinds of teachers I had known as a child. Of course, it was possible I was misled by reading French newspapers. Who colonized the West if not those same *voyageurs*?

But it wasn't just one-way. If America needed me, I needed it in order to get serious. Besides, another good reason for going back was that I suspected we were both about to get fired and if that happened, we'd lose that free transportation back to America. We were anxious to collect it. What we were about to get fired for was the sin of not being able to get serious about our jobs. Fran especially couldn't be serious about not leaving them classified documents laying out overnight in plain sight of spies, Frogs and suspicious cats of all sorts. I couldn't get serious about revising files full of indignant letters from French contractors and complaints about airfields sinking into the mud of southern France.

Back in America, we sat in our New York hotel bar, drinking gin and tonics in the summertime, watching three ball games at once on the TV, waiting around for our government-paid plane tickets to San Francisco, via North Carolina. I'd never seen any TV at all, let alone a ball game, and here, all at once, the Yankees were playing Cleveland, the New York Giants were playing the Boston Braves, the Brooklyn Dodgers were playing somebody. Long time ago when I left America, I'd spent two days in New York, and on both days the Yankees were playing Cleveland and I went to those games in Yankee Stadium. You have to realize what all this means to someone who spent his youth lying on the sofa on sultry L.A. afternoons listening to the radio purring out play-by-play accounts of ball games from Chicago, St. Louis, New York . . . Johnny Mize hit winning homers in the ninth of both those games, the evil bastard, one of them off Mike Garcia, my idol. Luke Easter, my other idol, pulled a groin muscle in the first game—that was all he did.

When, a year after we returned, the Giants moved to San Francisco, where we lived, I felt vindicated. Mainstream America was moving in my direction. The Giants were playing in Seal's Stadium. We could go. We could sit in the bleachers for ninety cents and make bets. We could watch Willie Mays, if not Monte Irvin. I'd had a job in the mountains. Jay was two years old. I'd had a job in Oakland. We had an apartment in North Beach, where the poets were writing poetry and reading it aloud and we could hear it and mainstream America was flowing uphill. I knew that I was part of it, playing the right side of the street. I was getting serious. I had been fired. I had a job in Tierra Firma on the outskirts of town. I had work to do. I was playing ball, in America, within that apparatus.

It is hard for me to imagine now why I had such notions, but I know that I did. Perhaps my idea of mainstream America has changed. I had the idea that one could find work to do and that being able to work was what was needed. Well, we have disagreed, America and I, about the nature of the work one ought to do, yet on the whole I think I was right back then. You must find work to do in your country and you can find it, or you could ten years ago.

In *The Way It Spozed To Be* I was able to write that the book was about my "teaching, learning to teach" in a public school in America. As a travelogue it was mercifully cut short—the end of the novice traveler's voyage brought about simply, perhaps by lack of funds or by losing his

19

passport out the window of an Italian train. Returning, the traveler may describe the high points of his trip, the pleasures, the difficulties, *what it was like* and remark his determination to re-embark. He wants to do it over again, do it right this time. Perhaps he wants to stay ten years.

This book is about what it is like to work from 1959 to 1969 in America. A decade, comrades. Of course it is about schools, too, since that is where I have worked along this way. I got rather sarcastic with myself when I began to write this. What? Another school book? I'll call it *Return of Way It Spozed To Be!* I told myself; I'll call it *Son of Way It Spozed To Be!* Yet one purpose of writing, like the purpose of talking to other people, is to demonstrate to yourself that you aren't crazy. Once begun, good or bad, such a purpose becomes immune to sarcasm. So I end up with only this chapter entitled both.

I've started off about two or three years after I began to work in schools again. That is about the time when you begin to feel that you know what you are doing, when you've gotten good recommendations for doing what you are supposed to do a couple of years, and that means you are going to have a job and get paid and be able to go to work and you know you need to have those things—and so you come to work one year ready to make changes. You are confident and you know what to do and you can do it and you are going to—all of a sudden you realize that's what you have in mind—you are going to change that fucking system by demonstrating to it how to work, how to teach, what education is, really. You are going to change it by using that system itself, you are going to use those fires, bombs, machine guns, institutions, B-52's, you are going to change them instruments of death and repression and ignorance into instruments of work, knowledge and love.

So that is what I planned to write about, and I will as

best I can. But in fact the book is mostly about kites and dogs and lizards and salamanders and magic and what people I know or got to know did, on occasion, during that decade. Those things are what remain clear and they are what I know really happened and the rest is very hazy. Not only that, but the details—those dogs and so on—turn out to be the reasons for your work, and thus the very fundaments of whatever knowledge and love you get. Bonuses— unaccountable rewards. If you only work in order to change things, you will simply go nuts. I am an authority on it.

So, *Do Whatever You Think Is Right*, as Owen says in the novel *Left*—but in the meantime (I would add) keep an eye out for bees flying in the classroom, and for edible plants along the road.

CHAPTER III

Christopher Columbus

Thus: about a month before the end of one school year, Frank Ramirez and I invented a course for the next year. We thought up a simple notion. We wanted a two-hour class, and we wanted to both be there at the same time. We wanted the class to be free of certain restrictions —those regarding curriculum, those regarding grades and those regarding school behavior rules, mainly the ones about leaving the classroom.

We didn't think there ought to be any difficulties in arranging it, and at the same time we prepared to answer all the difficulties logically. The two-hour class was O.K. because the eighth grade kids had two electives anyway; they could just choose to take our class instead of two others. We would arrange to have the class the last two periods in the day (seventh and eighth); since all teachers got a preparation period (a free period, but you weren't supposed to call it *free*), we'd take ours seventh and eighth respectively and spend our *free* time teaching together in the classroom in our new class. We were making, we planned to point out, a sacrifice. The kids would enroll voluntarily and we'd notify parents about what kind of course it was. We sent out notices and held a meeting of kids who thought they might want to enroll.

Everything worked out fine. There was no trouble. We were perhaps a bit disappointed. The principal agreed. The vice-principal agreed. The counselors agreed. Perhaps the parents agreed; they abstained at least, since none sent back comment. There were really only two difficulties. First, the schedule didn't work out. When we got back to school in the fall, we found out that Lou had forgotten to schedule our prep periods right, so that we couldn't work the class in the same room at the same time for two hours. Lou merely said he was sorry he forgot it, and declined to make any changes then, at the beginning of school. He couldn't see why we were pissed off; he considered it a minor matter. We felt the whole course had been sabotaged.

The other difficulty was with the kids. About twenty-five kids showed up, clearly divided in their intentions. A few were really looking forward to having two periods of time to do stuff in—our emphasis had been on the arts, generally, and they planned to paint and write and put on plays. The rest had only been attracted by the *no assignment* and *no grade* promise in our presentation; they came in wising off and horsing around, equally clearly prepared to disbelieve and test us out. As for that great rest of the school kid population who weren't in fact there, it's clear they just considered the whole thing a trap or a shuck. They knew they could put up with the ordinary school routine, having done it seven years already, but who knew what might happen to them if they risked something new?

Besides the intentions of the kids, of course, there was also the fact of our intention—Frank's and mine. I think that is best expressed by this: we would do, as the main thing, all the stuff we did in our regular classes as a sideline when the regular "work" was finished.

Frank had been working at the school for perhaps eight or nine years. In the two or three years I'd been there, I learned from watching him how to conduct yourself as a regular teacher in regular classes in a regular school. How you could teach and work there without driving yourself nuts with boredom, rage, a sense of your own hypocrisy, without unending uproars with the administration and parents and without getting fired, which was important to me. Frank was the best at this I ever saw. He filled his room with art materials, even though he was supposed to be teaching English and social studies to seventh graders. While other teachers were complaining publicly how difficult it was in the short time of nine months to "get through" the "material" in the texts, Frank announced that the stuff you were supposed to teach in a year could be handled easily in six weeks or so, and you had the rest of the time to do other things you might care to do. He figured the other teachers dragged out the teaching of Egypt or math all year because they didn't have anything else they wanted to do or cared about, or because they were afraid of the kids once the threat of the curriculum was called off.

In Language Arts, he showed the kids how to diagram sentences, pointed out the parts of speech, showed them where to put commas and semicolons—all in quite a short time. He was the only man I've ever heard give a good answer to that old kid question, Why do we have to make these diagrams?

Why? Because they are beautiful, said Frank. What Frank understood, or knew how to work, or knew how to involve the kids in, or something . . . was a kind of inter-relationship between studies, which were supposed to be real, and fantasy, which was supposed to be not-real. So that if they were "studying" some place which was an island, they studied it O.K., read the book, answered them questions on ditto sheets, and then the kids would find themselves with big pieces of paper inventing an island, drawing and painting in its geography, describing its people, its kings and rulers, the way the people ate, or what

24

they lived in, or how they celebrated Christmas. Or they went to the library and got books and wrote to the authors, and put the authors' answers up on the board, telling where they were born and how they got the idea of writing such and such a kid's book. Then Frank might give some letters to other kids, who would write secret answers as if they were the authors and these would go up on the board too. He took kids to the Golden Gate Bridge, where they dropped off bottles with fake notes in them into the outgoing tide and the answers to these notes, from points up and down the California coast, went up on the board too, along with "environments" made from junk in cigar boxes and illustrations from books or stories which he made the kids paint left-handed with big brushes on small pieces of paper so their technique or lack of it wouldn't get in the way.

I joined him in this kind of work. In my class we wrote to the Peace Corps and got real information about the problems of various countries and the straight dope on what the Corps hoped to do in these countries, how they would work, and so on. The kids, pretending to be Peace Corps workers themselves, wrote imaginary journals of stays in Africa and South America; the idea was that they would use the official information in their writing and would solve a lot of problems. In fact, though, their journals were full of first-class air travels to and from the countries, drinking cocktails and making it with stewardesses or *white hunters* in the *bush,* torture by *natives,* escapes, liaisons with chiefs' daughters, buried treasures and elephants' graveyards. Little attention was given to the raising of chickens, the building of irrigation systems, or the growing of flax. Medical care was brought in only as accessory to a needed miracle—the chief's son cured by a shot of penicillin just when the Corpsman was about to be eaten up by head-hunting pygmies.

In English, I had the kids begin inventing languages.

25

They wrote down lists of common words and when we had the lists we'd start making a picture or symbol to stand for it, just like them Egyptians did. Then we'd choose the best symbol and make lists of those and after we had a couple of hundred or so we'd start translating simple fairy tales into our new language, or making up stories to write in it, and put the stories on huge decorated pieces of paper and send them over to Frank's class to see if they could decipher them, as if they were Linear B.

Sooner or later there would be an item in the school newspaper about it:

> The kids in Rooms 45 and 31 are making up their own languages in their class. Here is an example of it; can you figure it out?

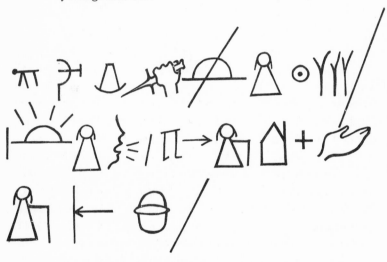

A couple of teachers would say That sounds like an interesting project and point out its relationship to Egypt to me. But, like the fake Peace Corps, where other teachers were always faintly disappointed when these journals, put on display in the library, failed to follow the government plans (the kids weren't using the information from official sources, and so it followed that they weren't learning anything, and so it wasn't social studies, but only fantasy)— the article failed to display the real point of such an activity. It failed to show the tremendous uproar when twenty kids rushed to the board to put up their symbols, the arguments of kids about which was best, and the fine look of the decorated pages when they were done. It also failed to show my pleasure at symbols which I thought just right, like these:

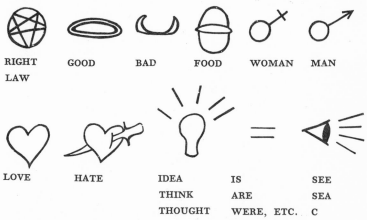

| RIGHT LAW | GOOD | BAD | FOOD | WOMAN | MAN |

| LOVE | HATE | IDEA THINK THOUGHT | IS ARE WERE, ETC. | SEE SEA C |

My pleasure was also in the process of the symbols working out. *Right* started out as a complicated drawing of a sheriff, *good* as an angel, *bad* as the devil—then they were refined into the star, horns and halo. We talked about the necessity of briefer, less complicated forms, since we wouldn't want to do all that drawing every time we Egyptians sent a note to a friend. Later on we learned from ourselves, and the symbols became simpler right away, as in *think* and *is*. We went on and made certain kinds of words different colors when we made posters, blue for things, red for actions, green for descriptions and so on, following the familiar pattern of seventh grade pedants. I pushed it a bit further, try-

27

ing to make the changeover from ideograph to alphabet, so that a symbol which once meant only *good* came to represent *G* while retaining the meaning of good.

We went on and on with it. Too much! I thought to myself all the time, full of excitement and pride, it is a great lesson. We are inventing, we are learning parts of speech and puns and structure of language and intricacies of grammar—all participating, with fun, uproar, excitement, consultant approval, letters from the superintendent saying as how Frank and I were creative teachers, A's for the kids, Frank and I coming to work feeling good and ready to go, happy parents—and we all lived through a kind of Golden Age of Rooms 31 and 45 at Spanish Main School. I mean we were a big success—more importantly *I* was; Frank had already been one for some time.

In this marvelous confident mood we approached the beginning of the year in Creative Arts. We had more ideas than you could shake a stick at.

For most of that year Frank and I agreed that CA—as the school soon began calling it—was absolutely the worst class we could have imagined. Nothing worked right. We had a lot to blame it on, griping to each other, commiserating together, telling each other it wasn't our fault. It was the administration's fault for one thing, scheduling things wrong. Then it was the kids' fault, for not being the right kind of kids. It was also the school's fault, for manifesting an atmosphere in which you wouldn't do anything unless you were made to.

In fact, another two main things—of a quite different nature, and yet quite firmly connected—were at fault. The first was what had seemed to us a detail and concerned leaving class. On the very first day we issued Permanent Hall Passes, each with a particular kid's name on it, and told the kids they could come and go in and out of our classrooms at any time, without asking permission or leave, and they could go anywhere around the school grounds. If stopped they had only to show their passes. We announced this casually; it seemed simple and obvious to us. One of the biggest drags in a school is the fact that whenever a kid wants to go anywhere, or whenever you want to send a kid somewhere to get something or do something, you have to stop and write out a pass, sign it, date it, put down the time and his expected destination. If you didn't, then the kid was sure to get stopped by some adult in the halls or wherever he was and get in trouble for being in the halls without a pass. Then the kid would come back to you, sometimes with the adult in question or with some goofy Rally Boy or Rally Girl who was On Duty at the time, and demand that you save him from detention or calling his mom for this sin, and you'd have to say Yeah, I sent him out, or Yeah, I said he could go . . . then like as not the kid hadn't gone where you said for him to go or where he said he was going, and so you had to go into that, and in the end everyone was mad and nothing had been accomplished, except maybe the kid had gotten his smoke in the bathroom, supposing that was what he wanted.

Being smart, we got around all that with the Permanent Hall Passes. The kids were ecstatic, and spent quite a bit of time that first day interrogating us as to what we really meant. They kept it up so long I finally got mad and yelled that it meant they could leave anytime, go anywhere on the grounds, that yes, once and for all yes, that was what it meant and if anyone said another word about it I was pulling back these passes and it was all off. Then they believed it.

The second thing was that all the great notions we had, all the ideas for things to do, all our apparatus for insuring a creative, industrious, happy, meaningful class didn't seem to excite the kids all that much. Most of the kids didn't want to do any of them at all, anytime. They didn't want to write to the Peace Corps, they didn't want to bring cigar boxes and make avant-garde environments, they didn't want to make plaster statuary, they didn't want to write stories, they didn't want to paint left-handed or make up new languages . . . they didn't want to do a fucking thing except use that fucking Permanent Hall Pass in the way it was supposed to be used, namely to take it and leave the class, roam around, come back in, leave again, roam around and come back in. When they went out they would say *There's Nothing To Do Around Here*, and leave, and when they came back they would say *There's Nothing To Do Out There*, and everyone would agree and say that awhile and bitch about the number of adults and narc Rally Boys who made them show their pass and brag to each other about how they told off the chickenshit narcs of all sorts . . . and for the first few days we were besieged by teachers and Rally Boys asking were those unbelievable *Permanent Hall Passes* valid and we'd say yes, and then for a few more days we were visited by kids who had invented excuses to get out of class in order to drop by and ask us urgently if it were really true that we had given out *Permanent Hall Passes* to *Every Kid* in our *Class*, and we'd say Yes! . . . and after those gripes and narratives had run out of interest someone would remember to say There's Nothing To Do In Here again, and out most of the kids would go.

Well, as a lesson plan, there is nothing I can recommend quite so highly as a Permanent Hall Pass. After a while, Frank and I, on the edge of complete despair, began to figure out what was wrong with the ideas that had worked so well in our regular classes. It was very simple. Why did the kids in regular class like to do all that inventive stuff? Why, only because it was better than the regular stuff. If you wrote a fake journal pretending to be Tutankhamen's fa-

30

vorite embalmer, it was better than reading the dull Text, answering Questions on ditto sheets, Discussing, making Reports, or taking Tests. Sure it was better—not only that but you knew the teacher liked it better for some insane reason which you didn't have to understand and you would get better grades for it than you were used to getting in social studies or English. But that only applied to a regular class where it was clear you had to (1) stay there all period and (2) you had to be doing something or you might get an F. Take away those two items, as Frank and I had done in all innocence, and you get a brief vision of the truth.

We were in a new world. Nothing can be worse than that. We had to face the fact that all the stuff we thought the kids were dying to do (if they only had time away from the stupefying lessons of other teachers) was in fact stuff that *we* wanted them to do, that *we* invented, that interested *us*—not only that but it interested us mainly as things to be doing during periods of time when something had to be going on, when no one was supposed to be just sitting around doing nothing. And not only things to be doing—it was things for *them*, the kids, to be doing. Things we wanted to see them do, the results of which we wanted to see. We wanted to see what symbols the kids would invent for English words; we didn't have much curiosity about the symbols we ourselves would invent. We didn't write fake Peace Corps journals ourselves; we only told the kids to do it. I don't mean to criticize us harshly on these points; that is, by and large, the attitude of teachers and it's a normal rationale for teaching. You want to see what the kids can do, you want to get some idea of their abilities, their intelligence, their cleverness, their ingenuity, their—creativity. You want to have something interesting to do during the class time. It was clear that many kids rather liked the writing or the painting or constructing or whatever it was,

31

once they got started (since they had to do something) and once it was finished, once the other kids expressed admiration, once they got a A, once their work was shown in the room on Back to School Night. Looked at that way, we were able to decide that we had a lot more ideas than the kids and the kids never knew what they wanted to do anyway, and if we made them do stuff we knew was interesting and exciting and all, they would be better off for it. About the sixth week of CA, we laid that out to the kids and tried to establish a hard line.

Since no one is doing anything, *then therefore*, we told them, sat down in their seats and quiet, you'll have to do assignments. We told them how great the assignments would be. That was going to be that.

Indignation, disappointment and sneers greeted my own pronouncement. I was told in plain words that I was being chickenshit. I was reminded of my brave words *when I talked them into taking this lousy course last year* (I'd thought no one was listening) and quite clearly informed that it was the same old thing—teachers promising "class participation in decision making" and then if it didn't work out just like the teacher wanted, the teacher then unilaterally changed his fucking mind. (I remind myself how things change when you give up your authority, officially, even if you really want to keep it, privately. The kids begin to talk to you just as if you are a real person, and often say just what they mean.) I was informed that the only virtue of the class was its freedom to do (to come and go) and not-do; take away that and they all planned to see their counselors and ask for transfers.

I think I would have weathered that storm, stuck to the new hard line if it hadn't been for Meg, Lily, and Jane. Meg, Lily, and Jane were our heroes. They were doing just exactly what Frank and I had figured everyone would be doing in CA, namely, they were doing stuff all the time. The first day or so, one of the things the kids had in mind was to make a newspaper, a kids' newspaper (underground papers not having been invented yet) as opposed to the boring, tendentious adult-oriented official school paper which was mostly written by the teacher in charge anyway. Having decided that, most of the kids then made use of their passes to come and go and talk about nothing to do; Meg and Lily started off immediately to make the newspaper. Meg would get the material and edit it, Lily would type and run it off and figure how to distribute it, and Jane would do the illustrations. In the end, receiving absolutely no co-operation from anyone else, they had done it all them-selves, Meg not only edited but wrote all the stories (no one else could stop coming in and out long enough to do so) and Lily talked the office into letting her use the mimeo-graph machine which was unheard of and Jane drew all sorts of stuff for it. Since that time, they had begun plans for a literary magazine to be called *Infinity,* and spent their time trying to persuade the other members of the class to write something for it. Having no luck whatsoever, they complained bitterly during that first six weeks about the other kids, how they wouldn't do anything, and how it was supposed to be a class project, and Frank and I would try to talk to the kids about writing, and about class solidarity and so on, but no use.

The point is, I had counted on support from these three in our new, reactionary notion of class. Surely they would be in favor of making the other kids write and paint and draw and so on, thus supplying them with material—but in fact, they weren't. They too threatened rebellion. Jane an-nounced she would draw or paint nothing else that year if required to. Meg agreed that it was too bad that no one else wanted to write for the magazine, but that it was obvious that "enforced writing" (she said) wasn't going to be any good. She might as well be taking *Journalism,* she said, with noticeable disgust.

I tried arguments. How about the fact that they wanted

to work and couldn't get anything done because everyone else was just screwing around? Wouldn't it be better if everyone wrote and drew for the magazine? Yes, they said, but only if they really wanted to. We went thus round and round. Meg, most brilliant and articulate of girls, told me that even in the regular journalism class there were only two or three people who really wanted to write for the paper and had any talent for it; the rest of the students, being forced to do so in order not to flunk, wrote only boring and rather stupid stuff. That, she said, was probably what caused the journalism teacher to have to rewrite most of the dull, boring stuff, and what made the whole paper thus sound like it had been written by a teacher, and after all, dull, boring stuff rewritten was still dull, boring stuff. Not only that, she said, isn't it so that good magazines are really put out by these very people who have talent and the desire to put them out? And isn't it so that most people in the world do not write, don't put out magazines, maybe don't even read them? But the magazines are good, sometimes, which was the point. Why should it be different in a class?

The fact that a magazine was good was the point. The desire of the teacher that everyone "participate" was beside the point and would surely result in a bad magazine. You couldn't have both, she was trying to tell me, and so you had to decide which you wanted.

Well, Frank and I decided without no trouble. Reaction would have to wait. Perhaps we only wanted to be reassured. The hall passes remained, and *Infinity* came out regularly. The class remained in a state of chaos, measured by ordinary school standards. Yet if I select *Infinity* as a measure (I think now), the class takes on a surprising aspect of solidarity. When an issue was ready to be put together, for instance, everyone knew it. They came that day prepared to collate the pages, staple them, serve as runners to bring twenty copies or so to every classroom (using Permanent

34

Hall Passes to do so) and when all that was over they sat down to look at and read and comment on *Infinity* and criticize it and decide if this new issue was as good or better or worse than some previous issue just as if they were really involved in it. After the first issue, in any case, Meg didn't have to write at all and Jane didn't have to do all the drawings and Lily had more offers of help with the mimeograph machine than she could handle. The offers came from other kids in other classes. They did exist. Stories poured in. There were secret writers all over the place. Kids in CA read them and judged them. *Infinity* kept coming out. The whole class took credit for it, time and time again, and they were right. *We* are doing it, they said. After all, who else was?

Well. It was the class of Piston and the kite. I think that has already told most everything else. Frank and I continued to run between joy and desperation, constantly hassled because Egypt teachers complained to us about the Permanent Hall Pass kids giving their kids the finger seventh and eighth period as they passed by, because the secretaries were complaining that the kids were using too many mimeograph blanks and cluttering up the office and arguing with them about which should have priority, page fourteen of *Infinity* or some announcement from the administration about PTA meetings, continually anxious because it always looked like no one was doing anything, and because, for example, a marvelously bright girl like Marcia should have decided to use all her free gift of time in CA doing nothing all year except going around to the boys asking them stuff like *Have you seen Mike Hunt?* (a nonexistent person whose name, translated into quick speech, turns out to be My Cunt)—a question which I'd heard asked myself a time or two when I was in the eighth grade and which had interested me then more than anything else in the entire whole wide world. We were bothered and confused and upset because the kids who never would do anything we suggested they might do were always the very kids who kept complaining to us that they were bored, that there was Nothing To Do In Here (and Out There), that We Never Do Anything In This Class and We Don't Learn Anything In Here. When we heard that complaint, we'd haul out some idea (figuring we had the kid this time!) and say *Then why don't you do* this or that? Then the complaining kid would say triumphantly, *Naw, I don't want to! Well, what about doing* this or that other thing, we'd say, and the kid would say *Uh-uh,* and then we'd say *O.K., what about . . .* and the kid got to say *No Good* and then cut out and go to the bathroom and arrive back later saying *There's Nothing Going On.*

This drove us out of our minds, and it drove us out of our minds every day. We tried to figure it out, and couldn't do it. All we could see was that the fucking kids were trying to drive us out of our minds. We did see that somehow this was the crucial issue of the course. Unaccountably, the course was not, as we'd thought, a course where students would get to do all the things we'd thought up for them to do, but instead a course where they could steadfastly refuse to do everything and then complain that there was nothing to do.

Christopher Columbus schemed and made a lot of plans and talked the principal into it and finally set sail for India, figuring that if he could get there by this new route he would become rich and famous. Unfortunately he ran into the New World first. Columbus' plans were all predicated on it being India, so he didn't know what to do with it, didn't understand it, and ended up convinced that everyone was trying to drive him out of his mind. Since there weren't going to be any spices or silks, he became obsessed with the only thing left to insure riches and fame. He thus tortured Carib and Arawak chiefs from all over, figuring from Old World premises that they knew where the gold was but naturally wouldn't tell him. It never penetrated his mind that they really didn't have any. Columbus sailed North and South and East, gold and the Old World reinforcing a vertical logic which prevented him from sailing West long enough to actually run into gold.

On one of his sailing trips, he came across several very large canoes, way out of sight of land. The canoes seemed to be full of richly dressed native businessmen, all painted and befeathered and going somewhere definite and purposive. But Columbus knew that the natives of the New World didn't go out of sight of land. He mentioned them in dispatches as an oddity, something else trying to drive him out of his mind, intimated that they were crazy, and forgot them. He didn't try to find out where they lived, or where they were going. He didn't follow them, or torture them, or try to get rich and famous from them. They didn't fit into his notion of how things were, didn't make any sense in view of his idea of what he was doing. It was too bad. I don't think Columbus ever found out that those seagoing businessmen were most likely Aztecs, possessors in nearby Mexico City of all the gold in the world. Columbus invented the New World, but its terms lay apart from his Old World logic and he just couldn't take any advantage from it.

Frank and I did a little better than Columbus. If we never quite accepted the notion that the real curriculum of the course was precisely the question What Shall We Do In Here? and that it was really an important question and maybe the only important question, we did finally understand that there was no gold in CA. We did see that if you agreed beforehand not to threaten the kids with grades, and if you agreed that everyone could leave the room at any time without asking you, that you had just entered a New World.

But quite late in the year, we did get some idea of where

we were. There was a big blond kid named Greg in the class, and Greg had maddened us all year. He wouldn't do anything at all, he complained all the time about there was nothing to do, he scoffed at all our ideas, he gave the finger to Egypt classes every day, he Took Advantage Of Freedom, he smoked in the bathroom, he encouraged Marcia and Mike Hunt, he was the original big lump of a thirteen-year-old in a canoe way out of sight of land, just trying to drive us crazy. That goddamn purposeless Greg, Frank and I often told each other, thinking frankly that if we could just get rid of him, transfer him out into some other class, then things might go right . . . Well, one day the roof finally fell in on Greg and he reaped the rewards of all his fucking around all year. The counselors, taking note of all his F's and Unsatisfactories for Citizenship, sent out forms to his teachers, asking them to comment. Of course they all wrote that he was no damn good. So the counselors called his parents and they had to come in, and there they were with the principal and the vice-principal and the counselors and the teachers and there was Greg, faced with all those adults come to deal with the fact that he was no good. There in the office, hearing all the teachers tell Greg's parents that he wouldn't do Spelling, wouldn't do Science, wouldn't do this and that (wouldn't even do Shop, for Christ's sake!), in the face of all those helpful, frowning adults, Frank and I suddenly saw that Greg was really O.K. We remembered that he always helped out collating the magazine; we remembered he'd gotten the ladder and fixed up the lights for the play I'd insisted on putting on; we remembered that he always knew how many kids were in each class when we needed to know in order to distribute *Infinity;* we remembered that he'd helped Piston carry the kite down to the field, and we just remembered that he was usually around when something really needed to be done—in short, we all of a sudden realized that he was a pretty helpful, alert, responsible kid, and we said so. Everyone was astonished. Could he spell? Did he do Egypt? Did he make book ends? We insisted. He was an O.K. kid. We convinced ourselves because we knew it was true. It was a big step for us. We left realizing that we had just realized that this fuck-up kid who drove us crazy was really O.K. and that, far from the class being better if he was gotten rid of, he was actually needed in CA. Therefore, we had to admit, in some way, somehow, our New World class was O.K. too. I mean, if the most fucked-up kid in the class was O.K., as we quite clearly *felt* he was O.K., (although our Old World logic told us he wasn't), and if we were willing to say out loud that he was O.K., if we were going to tell his parents that their kid was O.K. . . . well, it means that even if we had to admit we weren't going to find gold, that anyway discovering the New World was something in itself, and was probably enough for us to do that year. Frank and I came out of the meeting looking at each other strangely, wondering what had happened to us.

Chapter IV

Creative Arts

I'm sure it was during that very year, sometime in the spring, that certain shocking photographs began to come to the attention of the staff. These pictures all were alike in one respect—they showed a naked youthful male figure from about bellybutton to mid-thigh. Beyond that general likeness, each was different, of course. Lots of pubic hair, or scanty pubic hair, or in between—dark or medium or light (the photos were not in color). Very definite suntan lines, or medium, or none. Convoluted or spiral or just plain indented bellybuttons. Then the dicks—circumcised or uncircumcised to begin with, long and skinny, or short and fat, or long and fat, or short and skinny, or medium-sized "average" dicks.

What was it all about. Well, while Frank and I were trying to get the kids to do something creative, the kids invented a little art of their own. Boys cut out from school, during lunchtime or perhaps after school or even before school, down to the Tierra Firma Shopping Center where there was a photomat machine and booth. For a quarter you could get your picture taken. So instead of sitting there grinning into the lens with your hair all combed, you pulled down your pants and shorts, pulled up your shirt and stood up on the seat while a confederate shoved in a quarter and others stood outside making sure no one came around. It was all done in a split second and then you all had those photos. At school these could be given to others who would then be able to pass them around to the girls. The passing around had to be complicated enough so that no one knew who was who (often the kid himself didn't know any more whether that particular bellybutton, pubic hair and dick was himself or someone else) and then the girls could try to guess who was who, or what was who?

You can see the virtue—the creativeness, I ought to add —in this whole thing. I mean, once a girl even looked like she might try to guess, she was involved in a terrible admission. If she disdained the gambit, it was an admission of another sort too. Besides, who can resist guessing? The best thing was that there was no danger involved, since no one knew any longer whose picture it was anyway.

Frank and I heard about it through Piston. *Some other kids,* he told us, were doing that, taking those pictures. He made us promise not to tell any other teachers, but in fact shortly afterwards they all knew about it. They knew about it because kids told them, or made sure the pictures were passed around in the room where the teacher would have to see them, try to ignore them as she might. Some arts cannot complete their virtue until they are exposed to the enemy.

The teachers were upset about this degeneracy, of course, but I think they were tickled too. It never became the subject of faculty meetings, for instance, like the dull sins of gum chewing and running in the halls. After a short time, some of the girls (no doubt those who had done the guessing) began to show up with their own pictures. These showed, at the top, two hands holding a pulled up sweater or blouse, below that two twelve- or thirteen-year-old breasts and below that an uncertain expanse of skin and occasionally a bellybutton. But at the same time the school went into action in a kind of underground way, i.e., not by faculty meetings or sending mimeographed letters home to alert the community or anything of that sort, but only by talking and laughing with itself until it finally talked and laughed to the vice-principal, who then had to go down at lunchtime and stand around in front of the photomat as the school knew he would have to do and would do and that was the end of the activity.

It had lasted long enough—two or three weeks, just about the same time as a school play or art festival or any other creative school endeavor. I doubt anyone was unhappy when it was over. Two or three days were profitably spent in talk about it, complaining happily about the Up-Tight vice-principal who wouldn't let anyone do anything they wanted to do and about the cowardice of the girls who were afraid to photograph their cunts, while the girls retorted that (1) it was just too bad the boys didn't have nothing up above to show and (2) the boys must be pretty ignorant of the location of cunts if they thought there was any way to take pictures of them in that photomat.

Occasionally during the rest of the year such pictures as hadn't been confiscated or lost or hidden secretly away at home showed up in class. Then there would be a bit of an uproar, some grabbing, the same innuendo about guessing, and then someone would say *Remember that?* and everyone would remember it and all about it as a bit of history and good old times that year in the seventh or eighth grade at Spanish Main Intermediate School.

CHAPTER V

Return of ⎫ Son of ⎰ The Hawk

One Sunday afternoon towards the end of the year Frank and I went one step further. At the time we didn't know or care that we were going One Step Further—that is only how I see it now. We were up in the country having a picnic and talking along the way about movies and it occurred to us that you could make a movie very well at a school and we began to make it up. We made up an entire movie then and there and since Frank knew about cameras and film and since he had a Sears and Roebuck movie camera we made up our minds to do it. We figured out a great script about a mad kid who murders everyone in a school.

The only thing I had to offer was a marvelous Hawk mask which a painter had made for Jay one Halloween. We decided to use that mask as the main image of the movie— the costume the murderous kid would put on when he felt murderous. See, he would be a respectable kid, Student-Body President perhaps, whose daddy or older brother or something (I forget) would have been The Hawk a while back and killed a lot of people and then disappeared, but the kid remembered. No one else knew about it or knew that the kid's father or brother had been The Hawk.

Frank and I showed up at school on Monday feeling great. Were we planning to suggest to the kids in CA *How About Making A Film?* and hear them say No We Don't

43

Want To, or There's Nothing To Do Around Here, and then we'd try to persuade them into it and they'd say Have You Seen Mike Hunt? Hell no. It never occurred to us to wonder whether they wanted to make a film at all. We wanted to make a film ourselves and spend the rest of the year doing it. We didn't want to find out what the kids' notions of films were. We didn't want to see what they would do with the film. We didn't want to inspect their creativity.

Had we wanted to See What The Kids Would Do With Film, we'd have no doubt come up with something more constructive—a film about Attitudes And Relationships or The Question Of Authority and/or Democracy In The Classroom . . . as it was, we really wanted to make a Tarzan film but couldn't quite see how it could be done and settled for The Hawk.

Let me make the point, before I forget it and breeze on, remembering the movie. If, in the New World, the role of the teacher as giver of orders didn't work out (no one had to follow them orders) it was also true that the other role (the one Frank and I had imagined)—the teacher as Provider Of Things To Do, the teacher as Entertainer—didn't work out either. For wasn't that just what the kids had been telling us all year in their oblique, exasperating way? What did all that Nothing To Do In Here mean, if not that the kids didn't want entertainers, wouldn't accept them if they didn't have to, wanted the teachers to be something else entirely?

Wanted them to be what? What was the difference between all the grand things we'd thought up for the kids to do and The Hawk? Why, merely that we didn't want to do any of the former ourselves and we did want to do the latter. Why should we have assumed that the kids would want to do a lot of stuff that we didn't want to do, wouldn't ever do of our own free will? It sounds nonsensical, put that way. Yet that is the assumption under which I operated, Frank operated, for many a year, under which almost all teachers operate, and it is idiotic. (Does the math teacher go home at night and do a few magic squares? Does the English teacher go home and analyze sentences? Does the reading teacher turn off the TV and drill herself on syllables and Reading Comprehension? Or do any of us do any of those things, even in the classroom?)

Wanted them to be human. Men. Wanted them to define themselves. (Do I define myself as a person who writes fake Peace Corps journals?) Wanted them to stick by Harry Sullivan's rule: Human beings are more alike than not. What you don't do, we probably don't want to do. What you learn from, we probably learn from.

We fired right off on Monday afternoon with the movie. Our main location was the tennis courts next to the field below the school. It was a huge field of grass which was never used by anyone except for girls' PE for softball, two or three weeks out of the year, although the school was overcrowded. Everyone complained about the fact that the other field—the one the kids were allowed to use—was too crowded to play on; at the same time everyone decided not to allow the kids to use the field in question because they would have to be supervised and that would double the duty for teachers and that was out of the question. No one used the tennis courts either, except for the girls' PE about three weeks out of the year and some teachers who played once in a while after school. We went down, Frank and I, seventh period to those tennis courts; a bunch of kids and I watched while Frank filmed the lines running up and down the court very artistically and then I chalked the title *Son of The Hawk* or *Return of The Hawk* (I really don't remember which it was) on the green cement and Frank filmed that and also the legend *A C-Arts Production.* Part of Frank's seventh period class watched too (it was either Social Studies or English) and the rest were—where? It was the same with my own eighth period class who were told by me to either come watch or get into the film or just stay in the room . . . The Hawk made us irresponsible.

By then a lot of kids wanted to be in the film and a lot didn't. We picked who was to be who and divulged the plot. A lot of kids wanted to know why we wanted to call it *Return of The Hawk* (or *Son of*) but we didn't really care to explain. We knew they hadn't seen all them old movies so how were they to know? We were pleased to be authoritarian. Everyone picked a tall, handsome, vain kid named Jon to be the hero and we agreed, mainly because the name was right. We picked Jane to be the heroine; we picked Harvey to be The Hawk, since he was the only one who was brave enough to say he wanted to be The Hawk. We picked Jane, by the way, because she had done all that work all year long and we liked her and because she admitted she wanted to be the heroine. We would have picked Meg and Lily too, except that they said they didn't want to be in the movie. They had other things to do and would be satisfied with bit parts when they weren't busy.

The movie opened. Julie (Jane) and Jon came down the steps holding hands, carrying tennis rackets. They paused for a kiss. Then they went down and started playing tennis. They played a bit. Cut to the fence; a terrible claw (which Jane had spent some time making out of an old rubber glove and cardboard fingernails and green and red paint) was seen shoving a green tennis ball through the fence and rolling it towards the players. The camera followed it rolling along so everyone would know it was important. Show Julie picking up ball and talking. Cut to title which I chalked on the green cement: Oh look, Jon, a green tennis ball! Show Julie holding ball. Then show Julie's hand turning green. Some kid paints Julie's hand a little bit with

46

green paint, Frank films it, the kid paints a little more, he films that—pretty soon Julie's whole arm is green! It is a poison ball! Oh Jon! calls out Julie, and falls over dead. Over by the fence, for a brief instant, the shadow of the hawk mask, then legs running up the stairs. The legs have red tennis shoes on, painted up beforehand. Jon runs over and sees Julie is dead, grinning into the camera all the time.

About that time Frank decided to wait for the "rushes" before shooting any more. When the film was developed and we showed ourselves those rushes, the film became a movie and became real. Everyone saw where the movie was headed, several kids wanted to make suggestions about what to do next, two kids wanted to be cameramen, and everyone wanted to be in it. So that the next day when we started again, there was Jon grinning and saying Poor Julie's dead! and suddenly hundreds (it seemed) of cops rushed from everywhere. There were three authentic cops' jackets and a number of detectives in long raincoats and dark glasses (one leading a dachshund on a leash)—there were also two new cameramen. They filmed Jon, suddenly afraid the cops would think he did it, running to hide in a garbage can, from which half of him stuck out. They filmed the cops and detectives combing the school, climbing over the fences, investigating the office (the principal might have done it!) and Piston as detective snooping around the girls' bathrooms. They took off and filmed The Hawk making an obscure phone call from a booth at the gas station down by the shopping center—the purpose of the call not clear, except for the fact that everyone concerned got to leave the school grounds, and all the kids who watched the movie (they realized that it was a real movie and people would be coming to see it) would know they'd left the school grounds.

Next The Hawk was shown in the darkened science

room, mask on, preparing his deadly green poison. Everyone volunteered to smoke cigarettes to produce clouds of smoke and an air of mystery. The Hawk was shown pulling out a lot of junk from an old closet, including an old newspaper, mocked-up by Jane (now, as Julie, dead, and reverting to make-up and prop manager) which told about the old Hawk; the present Hawk swore revenge.

Well, anyway, the plot changed entirely from our original Sunday afternoon conception. It turned out The Hawk's motivation was that he loved the girl Julie, who didn't love him, in spite of the fact he was Student-Body President, but instead that damn conceited Jon. The Hawk had sworn to get her, psychologically twisted as he was, it was implied, by memory of his criminal relative. So there was a lot of panic in the school. Shots showing girls screaming, kids whispering in class (Who is The Hawk?), teachers trying to calm things down, and a splendid burst of paper airplanes flying around and landing to show the legend Watch Out For The Hawk! or The Hawk Is Coming! Hordes of girl reporters besieged the principal (Lou, in dark glasses, was persuaded to look outraged) and he was quoted as saying If we catch The Hawk, he'll be Suspended! Vern the counselor looked serious and allowed as how The Hawk wasn't very well adjusted, or something like that. Julie's mother and father (two kids with Jane-produced gray hair and a mustache) tearfully and cheerfully said We told her not to play with boys! All the time there were shots of those giveaway red tennis shoes walking around here and there, unsuspected.

Frank and I had been edged out as director and cameraman and organizer without any fuss. While everyone had talked about what ought to happen, during the rushes a boy named Phil had written it down and produced a "shooting schedule." He directed from then on because he wanted to direct and knew how to say "shooting schedule." The two

48

cameramen took over as cameramen for the same reasons
—they wanted to be, could do it, and did it. The director
consulted with Frank, and the cameramen recognized my
lust to become a cameraman (never having taken so much
as a Brownie photo in my life and afraid of doing so now,
while actually dying to) and showed me this and that and
let me film a few scenes. Certain kids took over the chalk-
ing up of speeches on the tennis court. Other kids took over
the organization of crowds when we needed them, bursting
into classes and saying We need a crowd! (No one ever
suggested filming crowd scenes during lunch, when no
classes would have to be interrupted.) Seventh and eighth
periods became the time when *The Hawk* was being filmed;
the other school considerations—passes, grades, authority,
work or not-work, There's Nothing To Do, narcs, complaints—were forgotten. Frank and I, talking things over,
found ourselves pleased—not that the Class was going
well, but that the Film was going well. When it rained, we
all just sat around the classroom content and relaxed,
doing nothing without anxiety about doing nothing or
should we be doing Nothing or Something or how to tell our
parents we weren't doing nothing? and was it educationally
sound to do nothing? . . . for we weren't doing nothing,
but instead we were sitting around waiting for the rain to
stop. It is a big difference.

Well, there were a few shots of Jon, who'd been hiding
out from the cops, sneaking around the school trying to find
out who The Hawk was. Finally he got into the science
room one (simulated) night, and discovered the mask and
claws and poison and the old newspapers, hidden away in a
cardboard box in a cabinet. Then he knew (reading the
name of The Hawk's old man or brother) and there was a
dramatic smoke-filled shot of him smearing the Hawk
mask with the green poison, grinning into the camera all
the time. Phil was upset by now with all that grinning and

49

vanity, but couldn't stop it and there was nothing to be done about it. The next scene showed a poster announcing a Memorial Assembly For Julie and a lot of kids standing around it, girls crying . . . all of this working up to the grand finale.

We filled the multi-use room with kids. Up on the stage came Harvey, the Student-Body President. He began to lead the salute to the flag. All the kids stood up. Cut to his feet. He's wearing red tennis shoes! ". . . with liberty and justice for all," says the title on the green cement. Everyone sits down. Jon gets up in the audience. He comes up to the stage, carrying a cardboard box wrapped with a big ribbon. He presents it to the President. The President is astonished. "For me?" he says. He opens it, unsuspecting. Out of the box he pulls the Hawk mask! His look turns to anger and hatred. Driven mad, he puts on the mask and shakes his fist at the audience. *The Hawk! Our President's The Hawk!* yell some kids. Shots of girls screaming. Then, *Get him!* shout the kids, and the Hawk leaps off the stage. Shots of The Hawk running out of the multi-use room, shots of the crowd chasing him, the last movement of Brahms' Fourth blasting away (later—on tape I mean, at the premiere—I finally got to do something). We had to retake that scene many times because the crowd kept catching The Hawk before he got out the door. They caught him and tackled him and mobbed him over and over again. Fuck this! yelled The Hawk finally, shoving kids off him, these dumb assholes are trying to really kill me! Finally he gets out and flees around the school and then down the steps to the field and the tennis courts, the crowd hot after him. A lot of tricky stuff with speeding up the camera and slow motion. Close-ups of the mask, showing it turning green. Harvey is marvelous; we are all amazed. Staggering, jerking, almost falling (the poison is getting to him), shaking his fist, running in circles, on and on the scene goes, piling up like

Brahms . . . he finally collapses in slow motion. The crowd comes up, also in slow motion. Jon reaches down and pulls off the mask. The Hawk's face is green. He is dead. The crowd's fury is over. All look sad. The tape changes to Miles Davis playing "My Funny Valentine." Girls cry. Miles sounds regretful. Everyone starts to go. Jon is all alone with the dead Hawk. The cameramen have learned not to focus on his face, but now it can't be helped. He looks into the camera, grins, and says, "My best friend!" Then he sits down, takes off his shoes and puts on the red tennis shoes. Long shot from above the field, the tennis courts empty except for the dead Hawk, the sitting Jon. Miles plays out the tape to the end.

We put on a grand premiere. We had posters all over, giving the stars' names, the credits; we dittoed off cards for audience reaction, set up chairs in the music room, a white elephant of a building, round without windows, which had been built by some smart architect and which looked modern and which was useless for everything. It was just right for a movie. We showed *The Hawk* over and over, to a hundred kids at a time, watched every showing ourselves, and felt superior to everyone. We spent the rest of the year doing that, and talking about the movie among ourselves when we weren't showing it. We'd spent about two months making it; it was exactly twenty-two and a half minutes long; it had cost just slightly over twenty-five dollars. We asked ourselves just why it was that the hero put on the red tennis shoes at the end? Was he going to turn into another Hawk? Was it just some kind of sentimental gesture? We didn't know. All we remembered was that there at the end someone had called out Put on his shoes! and everyone had felt that was right and so Jon had done it. It was pointed out that no one in the audience had ever asked about it, and so it must be just right, even if we didn't know why.

51

Chapter VI

A Dog at School

Dogs often wander into the classrooms at schools, and always cause an uproar. Kids cannot contain themselves when dogs appear in the midst of Egypt lesson, for what reason no one seems to know. Why couldn't they, the kids, just let the dog be in the class, wandering around, sniffing here and licking a few hands there, quietly, moseying about in the style of dogs while the class continued with the most important part of the lesson about Egypt? But no, they can't. They got to rush the dog, they got to pick him up and drop him, they got to offer the dog candy and pieces of sandwich, they got to yell and scream and act like they never saw any dog before in their whole lives. So the teacher then got to say Get that dog out of here! (saying later in the teachers' room, *I* don't mind the dog, I even *got* a dog at home and *like* dogs, and if those kids could just have the dog in there without all that fussing during the crucial lesson about Egypt when I just *got* to get it over to them, what's the problem? haven't they ever seen a dog before?) and nine kids got to chase the dog around until the teacher got to grab the dog herself and throw the dog out and shut the door and then argue with the kids about having the dog in the room (if you could just *have* the dog and not have to make such a commotion, she says to them, trying to explain, not wanting to be some kind of monster, hating dogs, while all they want is that *dog*).

52

What's it all about? Well, of course, that dog is alive, and old Egypt is dead. That's not crucial to all kids, you know. Some kids like Egypt a lot and eat up all the Egypt books the library has got, which is plenty. I can easily imagine Piston right now (it is several years since I have seen Piston) reading The Book of the Dead with great concentration (stubbornness) while every dog in the world licks his feet and tries to play and eat his sandwich. Piston doesn't even know them dogs are around, for he has got other things to do, namely make his way through the underworld.

Outside Smiley's Bar and Bait Shop in Bolinas there lives and operates a fabulous, obsessed dog. Bolinas, by the way, is probably the dog capital of the world. There are dogs everywhere—lying in the streets, cluttering up the gas station, sniffing the baits of fishermen, roaming the beaches, trying to get in the grocery store, waiting for people at the post office—everywhere you go there are plenty of dogs. They are all big dogs, all are friendly, all wag their tails, all hope for handouts—they are, in short, good dogs and everyone in Bolinas digs them, I think.

The dog outside Smiley's is a German shepherd of uncertain age. Not young, anyway. A bit scraggly, thin of hair on the back, long in the tooth as they say. Someone owns him; I'm not sure who. It wasn't until about the middle of August that I noticed him. Of course, as I emerge from Smiley's I am a bit foggy in the mind and not apt to notice much; I am heading for the pier to see what's happening with Jay and Jack and the pink or rose-tailed perch or the once-in-a-lifetime rubber-lip. I noticed him because one day he came into Smiley's. There he dropped an old gray tattered tennis ball between his paws and waited, looking intently at the ball. As no one made a move, he backed off from it a bit, six inches at the most. By then everyone at the bar was looking at him. Jerry came out from behind the bar and made a grab for the ball. Quick as a wink, the dog snatched it up; immediately, he let it down again, right between his paws. Jerry moved slightly, a feint. The dog didn't move. Then he grabbed for it, and the dog snatched it with his jaws. He let it down again. No one seemed disposed to try to get it. He moved back, moved back again, edged just a bit farther back. Jerry was back behind the bar. I inquired. That's all he does, all day, and maybe all night, ever'day, said Jerry. That's his thing, and he does it. I drank some beer and got down off the bar stool to try him out. Edged toward the ball. Moved. The dog's jaws had it before I got close. He dropped it again. I moved for it. He had it. Dropped it. Moved. Snap. Drop. Moved . . . me, a new man, playing ball, everyone watching a minor event in the beginning of the day. I went back to my beer. About the time I was ready to leave, an old lady, drunk as a coot at ten in the morning, got off her stool and said so long to Jerry. She ambled down the bar, heading for the door. As she got alongside the dog she suddenly launched out with a tremendous kick at the grimy tennis ball on the floor. It was beautiful. Her shoe touched the ball just as the dog's jaw fastened on it. She fell on her ass with a tremendous roar of laughter and the dog stood up with the ball just barely clasped in his jaws at the very edge —a close thing, a tie, a standoff between equals. The old lady got up and gave the dog a big salute as she went out. The dog, satisfied perhaps, went out too.

Every day after that I looked for the dog. I introduced Jay and Jack to him. He played with them indulgently like an old hero hitting fungoes to the rookies. I saw him every day, at all hours of the day, and he always had the tennis ball, and he always had it there between his paws, or had backed off a foot or so from it, giving the whole world a chance if it thought it was good enough, staring down with the utmost concentration (stubbornness) at that ball, not questioning the fact that the world was as interested in it as he was.

54

One morning I came out of Smiley's and there he was in the middle of the street. There was nothing extraordinary about the day. No omens, signs or portents. I was just heading for the pier, having drunk a couple of beers and read the sports page. The dog had left the ball a good foot and a half from his jaws, recognizing in me an inept player, hoping to entice me into a grab. Well, I was game, and approached. As I poised foggily for a snatch, a tremendous uproar of barking came from behind the dog. A great gang of other dogs had apparently discovered something intolerable about the state of affairs of the world and begun an outcry. The old obsessed dog, startled, re-entered the real world of dogs for the first time in years, just long enough to turn his head one split second—the splittest of split seconds—and did so just as I grabbed, by luck, and when he turned back to The Book of the Dead I had it in the back pocket of my Levi's and was standing there innocently looking up at the the sky to see if it might rain. Lord have mercy! That dog's head turned nine ways at once, and then he jumped straight up in the air, came down, looked everywhere, up, down, sideways, in back, rushed into the bar, came out, searched one side of the street and then the other, turned around on his axis, examined the sky, scratched the ground, implored heaven, yelped piteously, barked, snarled . . . Terrified, I took out the tennis ball and (not having received any Gold Medal, which I deserved) gave it a toss down the road so he'd have to chase it. He did. Got it, brought it back, let it down between his paws, backed off, staring at it intently. Nothing was going to change, whether heaven willed it or not. I see it, said Jerry from the door of Smiley's, but I don't believe it! Of course I knew it was only luck, and the dog knew it was only some inexplicable jest of the gods, so neither of us was much affected; in fact we just went on with our lives as if nothing had happened at all.

55

But it goes to show that you have got to be obsessed to drag your real life into Egypt and The Book of the Dead (in fact I have never heard of any junior high school Egypt teachers bringing in The Book of the Dead to their classes, dog-ridden or not), and even then, even for the obsessed, anything real and alive coming into your classroom like a dog or a bee or a monstrous kite is bound to claim your attention if only for a split second. And if you are not obsessed (and there are still many of us who are not, believe it if you can) then you have simply got to throw books at the real, feed the real sandwiches, murder the real, at least glance for that split second at the real, no matter what the subsequent cost—be it loss of tennis ball or note home for unsatisfactory attention and work habits.

CHAPTER VII

An Environment for Lizards

Last year we never had a lizard in the room. This year, right now, we have thirteen. Last year Tizzo and Junior and Karl occasionally wanted to go out and *hunt for lizards* but they never brought any back, which was because what they really wanted to do was get off the school grounds, smoke and be free. It was only some errant folk memory which made them think of lizards as an excuse in the first place. Occasionally they brought back a sow bug or a worm, to show they were serious. They ain't got lizards around here like they used to, they told me.

This year seven boys showed up the second day with lizards. Give you curriculum planners cause to reflect.

They have these lizards arranged in an aquarium full of dirt, rocks, some dried-up ice plant, an old abalone shell and a tin with water in it. From day to day there are also different pieces of clay, sculptured into tunnels and caves for the lizards to hide in. Alas, there is no hiding, for also in the aquarium at all times are five or six pairs of hands, busily rearranging and resculpturing the lizards' Heimat, taking out the lizards, making more devious and restful tunnels and caves, rebuilding the rock grottoes, putting the lizards back in, digging up, smoothing out the dirt, taking out the lizards again, pouring in a load of sand from the jumping pit . . . no harm is meant to the lizards, in fact everyone is quite solicitous, buying meal worms for them, hoping to see them lose their skin, yelling at each other to be careful . . .

Well, it is bugging me, all right. I approach for a subtle talk. Careful to compliment the lizards, for which Richard has made signs stuck in the dirt, saying Blue-belly and Alligator, I try out the idea that maybe the lizards would like to be left in peace. The hands are busy in the dirt as I speak. Everyone agrees. They are trying to make the lizards happier by making tunnels and caves to rest in and to hide in, I'm told. Of course. I bring up the notion that in the lizards' natural environment (I say) it is an odd but true fact that hands are not digging them new holes every day, not making interesting new rock formations, not unloading tons of sand making it nine different levels like Troy but that in fact they have quite a while to get used to and make use of whatever ground they (for whatever reason) end up in. Everyone agrees. For instance, I add, you guys found them lizards under the ice plant, and if everyone didn't keep digging up the ice plant, maybe it would grow and—everyone agrees. They tell each other to quit digging up the place. All hands are busy inside the aquarium. In short, I say, why not leave them awhile to the present highly adequate ararangment? Them lizards (I say) won't ever have time to grow a new skin at this rate. They'll be too busy exploring. Right? Right. The lizards are jerked out so they'll be out of the way of a new freeway; they lie stunned on the counter next to the sink. Back in they go. Everyone advises everyone else to leave them alone and not keep on messing with them. One lizard's tail is painted blue. Everyone watches to see if they will crawl into the new holes, but no one can wait and fingers prod them along. Lots of advice about leaving them alone. Mr. Herndon is right, you guys!

Leave them alone then, I want to say. Out come the lizards. In go some more rocks.

Then leave them alone for a while, goddamnit! I do say, loudly. Everyone looks at me in astonishment.

58

My wife Fran goes to visit Tierra Firma Elementary School, where our kids go, one morning and ends up staying the day. She is appalled at the playground scene. It appears that the kids (kindergarten to sixth grade) are all running around yelling about *kill* and *murder* and *beat up* and about *stupid* and *MR* and *dumb-ass* and two kids are holding another kid while a third socks him in the belly (it happens to be Jay, our oldest, who is getting socked) and two little white kids are refusing to let a bigger black kid play football with them and so the black kid starts to beat them up and when the playground woman comes over they all three give her a lot of shit and run away and she can't catch them . . . another large group of kids are playing dodge ball and throwing the ball hard and viciously at one another's heads, and some of them are crying, and other kids wander around crying, and there is a whole other population of kids who stand fearfully on the outskirts of the grounds just trying to keep out of the way . . .

Back in the classroom after lunch she observes the concerned teachers trying to have some discussion with the kids about how to treat other people, about violence, about calling names—suddenly, says Fran, they are all these goddamn nice neat marvelous white middle-class children, even if occasionally black, talking about equal rights and observing the rights of others and not giving way to vagrant impulse and how war is bad and everyone is smart (even them fucking MR's) and how in a democracy everyone must be responsible for his or her own actions. They all know what to say! hollers Fran to me. They have all the words! They discuss superbly. They are a veritable UN of kids, schooled in the right phrase, diplomatic, unctuous, tolerant, fair . . . the hypocritical little bastards! Sucking up, that's what they are! And believing it at the same time! Talk is cheap!

59

No doubt. It is the original prerogative of the white American middle class to be sucking up while at the same time actually believing everything it says. Lizards can tell you all about it.

CHAPTER VIII

The Stream of Life

Frank and I promptly abandoned the New World. Or the school abandoned it. In fact, both parties agreed. One of the factors was that Lou quit as principal and farmed himself out to pasture at San Francisco State. Well, he had been there two years, and that was par. But the new principal happened to be the very same man who had pulled his son out of CA within three or four weeks after school began, telling Frank that he didn't intend to have his kid in a class where you didn't learn nothing. There was the fact that Frank and the new principal had some long-standing grudge against each other, and Frank didn't intend to be working some class where the kids would be running around the place and that principal would get to complain to him about his students. There was the fact that Frank had been teaching about ten years in junior high school (as I have now) and he was just plain weary of it. He wanted to spend his days by himself, for a change, to think and write and go to the track.

There was also the astonishing fact that the school as a whole showed no signs of wanting to enter the New World, or even to recognize it. The most positive response to CA among the faculty was from people who figured Frank and I had figured out a way to goof off and not-teach—the more general opinion was that CA encouraged other kids to wonder why they couldn't do nothing too, couldn't have permanent hall passes, and thus that it was an undesirable element of sabotage. CA, of course, continued to exist. Once something is started in a school, it is not easily given up, no matter if anyone likes it or not. It became the province of the drama teacher. The justification for keeping it was that it gave the students a wider choice of electives, which naturally meant that if they didn't like Drama they could take CA, which turned out to be just like Drama. I had really decided that you couldn't have the New World for one class a day. It would have to be all or nothing; I planned to agitate for the all.

Summer came. We went up camping on the Trinity River. Mainly we went there because I was certain I would catch a steelhead in that river. We traveled the length of the river from the coast to Weaverville, passing up camping places because they were too gravelly or had trailers or looked like state parks or because we wanted to go on and see what the next one looked like, and finally ended up at a place called Big Bar where there was a forest service camp with room enough for only three camps and there we called it a day. It was a wonderful place with huge yellow pines on the edge of a creek overgrown with brush and those bright leafy small trees through which sunlight filters and glitters. The powerful Trinity rushed past at the foot of the hill. Jay roamed the place in his Levi jacket and black cowboy boots. Jack, six weeks old or so, lay on his back on a blanket. When we arrived a guy and his family were just leaving, having just spent one day. Plenty of trout in the creek, he told me. You can't help catch them. Down at the store, a mile or two away, the owner, George, told me, Plenty of steelhead in the river. We went out to the high bridge there and looked over, and sure enough there were the steelhead lying back of the boulders and in the pools. Actually I might have thought those steelhead were sunken logs or just shadows, but George knew all about it. Well, I put in several eight-hour days working on that river without ever catching a steelhead. I worked overtime on the creek, catching about one small trout an hour. On the other hand, if I went down to the great river with Jay and if we stood out in the river (chest high for Jay who had to stand in front of me to avoid being swept off his feet), we caught all the trout in the world, although George assured us you couldn't catch no trout in the river at this time of year. We kept going over to the store, where every day I would see these two big steelhead in the ice-chest. No matter how often I asked when and by whom those steelhead were caught I couldn't ever get a straight answer from George, and in fact I came to the conclusion that these two big steelhead were mummies, but just the same I'd talk with George about catching steelhead and buy a Mepps Spinner of a different size or color or a couple of salmon flies or some night crawlers or whatever George said you could be sure to catch steelhead on today. Then Jay and I would get a beer and a 7-Up and go sit outside on the bench and George would blow up a balloon inside and bring it out and secretly rub it against his chest and then stick it on Jay's head. Well the balloon would stick there; Jay was astonished every time. Old Glue-head! George would cry. He was as astonished as Jay, it seemed. You must have got glue on yore head, he'd tell Jay. Jay knew he didn't have no glue on his head, because we didn't have any glue. Still, how did that balloon stick there? Maybe you got some of that pine pitch, George would suggest. Jay always felt that might be it, since he had that ole pine pitch all over every other part of him. He'd feel his head and try to discover pine pitch, and sometimes he thought yeah, he did feel a little pine pitch up there and sometimes he thought no, he didn't feel any.

When I got back the school had a new program. The junior high school assumes that it was invented in order to bridge the gap between elementary and high school, but it is always uncertain which way it ought to lean. In our case, Spanish Main had started out leaning toward the elementary side, but by the time I got there it was definitely taking a hard line toward high school, telling the kids stuff like you have to grow up, take responsibility, get along with more than one teacher. But over that summer someone had had second thoughts, it seemed, and recognized that in the school there were a number of kids who didn't take to the hard-line high school approach. It was decided to call these kids "immature" and deal with them in a self-contained classroom, for one year, "to make their transition easier." There were only a couple such classes. Apparently the one thousand or so other kids weren't immature.

It seems to me now that that was the beginning (at SM) of two tactics used by public schools to win their battle for existence; first, to establish special groups of kids in various categories ranging from "immature" through neurologically or emotionally or educationally "handicapped" to "deprived" to the marvelous, blatant "non-achiever," and second, to take teachers who wish to teach in some odd way and let them teach those odd kids. For all the terms for special kids really just mean kids who can't or won't or don't do things the way the school thinks they ought to be done; once labeled as special, the school can pretend that there is a *normal* group which is well served by the custom of the school. The school's obvious inability to satisfy many children can then become natural, since the kids are "special" and *shouldn't* be satisfied by any normal procedures and the school does not need to change its ways at all, has only to create some arrangements on the outskirts of the school to keep them special kids and special teachers out of the way.

I wasn't thinking of that at the time. Frankly, the first few days I was besieged by parents who wanted to know if their kids were in some sort of dumb class. What the parents instinctively knew was that any special arrangement probably meant the school considered their kids to be dumb or goofy, and in any case, didn't think they would be going to Harvard. They wanted to know how their kids happened to get in this class and they wanted it understood that their kids weren't dumb, and if it *was* a dumb class they wanted their kids out of it and promised to cooperate by making them do homework, forbidding TV, and so on. Well, I ended up telling the parents what the school told me, which was that the kids were supposed to be "immature" rather than dumb, that in fact they were probably a brighter group than most, that the school was not selling them out of Harvard, and in any case I wasn't. That satisfied almost everyone. Immaturity was O.K. with them.

I tried to think then why it was that these kids were supposed by the school to be immature. Now, I decide to isolate the quality of stubbornness. I know that it is only in terms of the book that I say so. It is simply that the kids as I remember them demonstrated no other particular quality which they might be said to hold in common. Some were very smart, some were not smart; some did lots of school work, some did very little. Some had broken homes, some didn't. Some were minorities, some weren't. Some couldn't get along with other kids, couldn't accept criticism or conform; some could. Hal Smith was a stout blond kid who got all A's, did the work, and had his life planned; he was going to enter the Coast Guard like his father and pilot those boats across the bar. He had a notebook full of *Life* magazine pictures of tremendous waves roaring up at the mouths of Oregon rivers, of small Coast Guard boats battling them. Charles Ford was a witty child of stern Lutheran parents, who did nothing right except school work, who would only catch baseballs one-handed with a right-handed glove on his left hand and who wrote cynical and satiric papers about fairytales á la *Mad* magazine. Rosie was a girl who spent all day reading books, crouched down in her desk, which she moved to a corner, and her afternoons out of school with fruit flies, upon which she made endless experiments. Ray had already given up on school work because he couldn't do none of it, add, read, or write, and wanted to spend his days cleaning up, taking roll, investigating what other kids were doing and putting up good stuff on the board. Howard was a science-mad kid from Canada whose cum folder remarked that he, while an excellent student, wouldn't participate in sports; he was the only kid in the class who played hockey in some junior league—of course the school had no hockey league to play in. Lucy and Sally were beautiful giggly girls who wanted to interact (as we say) with me all day long. After school they sat on my car, defying me to go home. Susan was an Italian girl of great social consciousness, full of clear and accurate notions about the injustice of the world. Eileen and Rosa were Catholic girls whose main concern was their mothers' wish that they attend Catholic high school, who didn't want to do it, who kept trying to keep out of trouble in order that their mothers wouldn't have some objective reason to send them there, who knew they were going there anyway (and they did) but who wanted to make sure that there could be no reason like bad grades or bad citizenship which their mothers could call upon as justification for their actions—that their mothers would just have to say in the end, I just am going to send you there because I want to, and then they, Eileen and Rosa, would win the battle. There was Robert Chow, a fat lump of a Chinese kid who wouldn't do anything at all in school, but who was later discovered by Rosie to have been raising (or growing) fresh-water clams in various tanks in his house since he was seven or eight, a feat which, so said Rosie, was thought almost impossible by the experts she was always reading.

Well, there were obviously some twenty-five or so others, too—I imagine I remember more kids from that class than from any other I've had—none of them alike, all different people as to desire, need, aspiration, even though the school had decided to classify them as being all the same, i.e., immature. Perhaps the school had hoped I would figure out some lessons aimed specifically at immaturity, that I would either cure them of immaturity or, if incurable, figure some way to teach them in spite of it; or perhaps the school only hoped I'd keep them out of everyone's hair for a year. Obviously that wasn't my concern. I hadn't invented immaturity nor been consulted about it by the school and so I could ignore it except to wonder occasionally why it was that these particular kids (and by implication, I myself) were chosen to be immature. Considering my recent past, the New World and all that, I could have brooded about the gulf between something called *learning* and something called *achieving in school,* about the teacher as authority or entertainer or provider of work—about the razor's edge you must walk, between the expectation of the kids (one to which they cling firmly, even though they may despise it) about what school *is* and your own conviction that most of that is worthless at best. In fact, though, I slipped into the year, the class, as easily as a fish into water without (as I feel) much thought about it, without trying to reform the school and the world, following the kids' leads and offering mine for them to follow, feeling good about coming to work and living easily in the classroom. Everything followed *naturally,* is what I want to say; only now, in retrospect, do I want to write down something about the way we lived in and out of school with the purpose of taking a look at that razor's edge and how you may walk it if it appears during your journey that you must.

For if we are talking about what the school wants kids to do, we are talking about seventh grade spelling books with twenty words to spell and define each week for thirty-six weeks, talking about math books with per cent problems to do and interest and decimals and review of add-subtract-etc., talking about social studies with Egypt and the Renaissance and talking about science with water cycle and gravity and health-vitamin-germs-Pasteur-don't-smoke. (The school changes textbooks; in math besides the above now it is commutative and associative to define; in science DNA and ecology and don't-take-drugs; in language it is watered-down and crude linguistics. Egypt remains.) If you feel that what the school calls learning is bullshit shall you inform your students of that and forbid them to do the school work? If you feel that what the school calls learning is bull-shit shall you inform the kids of that and still make them do it? If you feel that what the school calls learning is bull-shit ought you to pretend that you don't feel that? Pointless questions. Arrogant questions, besides; you forget that the kids really know the score, know that no matter what you, some nutty individual teacher with whom they've been saddled for no reason of their own, think about it, they've their parents and future teachers and their cum folders and the high school counselors and achievement tests and four years of high school and college and grad school and the Coast Guard to satisfy. They have lives to lead, something which is often forgotten (I had, too, a fact which became rather obtrusive around this time), and for many kids the school was only a gambit to be achieved in some way within those lives—part of them, important perhaps, but not a point of philosophy, nothing relevant, crucial only in that it shouldn't get messed up and be allowed or forced to intrude. Still, I was affected by the New World. I couldn't say that the school work was learning. I couldn't judge the students on the basis of whether they did it or not, did it well or O.K. or lousy. Still the students were waiting for me to give out the course of study in all those academic disci-

68

plines—language, social studies, science and math—so that they could deliver another year's performance according to their own lights. So that Hal could establish another leg on the way to the Coast Guard, so that Charles could satisfy his notion of what he ought to do before doing what he liked, so that Eileen and Rosa could have something to use against their mothers, so that Rosie could have something to not-do, so that Ray could have something going on to observe and approve and disapprove (he was of course the greatest judge and moralist of school work, as are most kids who get F's in school). What—should I refuse the kids this staple of their existence? Refuse them an item they had good use for? Not likely. On the other hand, was I going to indicate a serious attachment to this bullshit? Not likely either. I got in all the textbooks the school had, in all the subjects, got the supplementary books, the high, average and low readers, math puzzles, Lifes in Syrias (tangential to Egypt), Negro histories, Clouds and Bugs, Flax and Other Products, Atlases, and so on. I put up on the board segments of each to be done (read and questions answered about) each week or (in the end) each month, according to a simple schedule which would allow for the completion of this work in these books by the end of the year, supposing some kid wanted to complete this work in these books by the end of the year. I made ditto sheets of my own about form classes in the new grammar, about why Egyptians showed both feet pointing the same way, about "The Rocking Horse Winner," about why ice is lighter than water.

Only I refused to pretend that I had to "teach" any of that stuff. We all knew it was stuff to do, rather than anything which had to be learned or even could be learned. I knew that most of the kids could already do it if they wanted or needed to do it, and that some of the kids couldn't do it because they really couldn't read or figure it, which was because it was against the principles of their lives to do it. It is the old German notion of apprenticeship; this year you get a nail, the next year you get a hammer, the next you get to hit the nail with the hammer. I know that is crazy and the kids know it is crazy and the Germans know it is crazy but we also know that is how things are, even if we don't know how they got that way or who decided it. If we want to be carpenters or enter the Coast Guard we'll hold still for this craziness, knowing that it has nothing at all to do with whether or not we become good carpenters or with how we will finally encounter the breakers off the Oregon coast, for that is entirely up to us at that point in the river where everything narrows, the game narrows, and it is up to our individual courage as men, women, girls, and boys.

But look what happens when you do that. You don't have to stand up in front of the class and make everyone shut up and listen to you as you explain the assignment, demonstrate how to work equations, point out what metaphors are . . . you don't have to pretend that order and silence have to do with learning (or even with doing school work!) and you don't have to pretend that no one can produce work without your lecture, and in short you don't have to be a contemptible ass and that is good. What you can do then is to say loudly every Monday morning that You (you students) *already know* this, *already know* what the school intends to teach you this year and any other year, that the means to produce this and satisfy the school and the Coast Guard is *already in your heads*—you get to say Quit asking me if this or that is right or if this or that ought to be capitalized or if such and such is a noun or class I word—you get to repeat (as teacher) all that kind of information is already in your heads, you only have to reach in there and get it out—you get to say I'm not playing that particular school game with you, where I start explaining and you start not-paying attention (since you don't need or can't use the explanation) and talking or fucking around and then I'm

70

supposed to say Pay Attention and you're supposed to say I am (while you're not, since it's not necessary and therefore obligatory that you don't, while obligatory to me as teacher that you pretend you are)—you get to say: "And then went down to the ship, / Set keel to breakers, forth on the godly sea, and / We set up mast and sail on that swart ship, / Bore sheep aboard her and our bodies also . . ." and so get going with the day, the week, the journey. . . .

You get to arrive at school in your car and go drink coffee and smoke and talk (if you've someone to talk to) until the bell rings and then begin another smoke and go to the bathroom and get another cup of coffee to take to class and when you arrive late the kids are settling into the day and the room, someone is taking roll and the lunch count with some shouts about who is really here even if they aren't really *here* yet, and when you come in several kids rush you with urgent requests about going to the library or to their lockers or to phone their moms or get some other kid's homework out of a third kid's locker and you can agree or forbid or stall them, saying Wait until I have a little coffee, a number of other kids are sitting around drinking their Cokes and eating doughnuts which they've just bought on their ways to school . . .

But you don't have to stand in front of the class and give out some lesson and explain things which no one needs explained to a restless group who have a lot of other things on their minds and who (as soon as you finish explaining) will ask you questions about what you just clearly explained. There's time, you can say to yourself; and when the first urgent group is dealt with and given passes and gone you can talk to the next group of kids who just want to talk, about what's going on today or what their moms said or their brother did or what outrage is being served for lunch or do you want some gum? You can have all the roll slips and lunch-count slips and hall passes and library passes and the slips for ordering movies and prints and film strips and supply-order forms available in your desk for the students to fill out and order and go get and (since they understand the bureaucracy of the school at least as well as you do) you can be assured that they will keep your desk straight and order stuff on time and keep the room well supplied with three-hole lined paper and ditto paper and paper clips and staples and take inventory of the books from time to time (faking reports for losses or stolen just as well as you will) and getting the couple of kids who have spent some diligent time learning to forge your initials do all the signing on all these slips and notify the class of assemblies and dances and games and threats from the administration and clean up the room on occasion and put up the assignments on the board and check off the papers according to who has done what of the regular work and get the mop from the custodian when paint is spilled. . . .

And then sometime during the day if it looks like the time is right or you just feel like it or indeed anxiety tells you you must do it, you can get around to getting up and standing there and telling everyone to shut up and then sum up what's going on in science or remind everyone that today we decided to read everyone's stories or say I want everyone to be careful with the goddamn paint and sometimes that is just the right thing and everyone wants to be drawn together and be a group (and sometimes it's not and you can either forget it or get tough and make everyone, if that's what you really feel like, which it sometimes is) . . . but quite possibly it will be Janet instead who has dreamed up the idea of *Culture Hour,* what this class needs is some *Culture!* (I teach her the word *Kultur,* which she likes very much) standing up there, a little blond chick yelling Shut up for Culture Hour! and an uproar of laughing and griping and sitting down because everyone really knows Janet is going to *have* Culture Hour no matter what and they might as well get it over with and besides everyone really likes the grand bullshit of the idea, and Janet then reads Robert Browning or "Hiawatha" or *The Nonsense Book* or something of her own or some other kids' stories so long as they are cultured and everyone scoffs and makes uncultured remarks and has a grand time. . . .

And while teachers are complaining they haven't any *time* you see that you have all the time in the world, time to spend with Lucy and Sally telling them they got glue on their heads and threatening them about what you're going to do if they get on the hood of your car again until they are satisfied, time with Eileen and Rosa, who have discovered that if they get caught a couple of times smoking in the bathroom their mothers will react most satisfactorily, time to talk with Howard, who has discovered simultaneously a real woods out in back of the drive-in and The Byrds and is trying to make sense out of both (the woods have foxes and a skunk and a red-tailed hawk flying overhead and some kind of marvelous purple moss which the Museum of Science don't know about and who would have thought that right here in this prototype [his word] of suburban developments there would be a real woods, and here too that is just what The Byrds are singing about)—every day there are going to be kids who want to spend some time talking to you, as adult, as teacher, as whatever you are, wanting to relate their adventures and troubles and excitements and miseries and aspirations and confusions or hoping perhaps to get some clear idea of the world they live in through you. At the same time there are going to be a lot of kids in the room who don't want to talk to you at all, that day, just want to be left alone with their school work (it may happen) or eats or books or drawings or models or to talk to each other or get mad and begin fights or arguments, they can get along very well without you, it seems, and you can let them. Then you will even have time to go round to Ray

73

or whoever else it is and teach them something that they really need to know, not only in order to get along in the school but in order to be *equal* in America—get Ray some book to read and sit down with him awhile and read it together and *teach* him, get Robert to pull himself together enough to attempt the mystery of dividing and teach *him*, go around later on to Ray and say you *can* read, now read me some. You can teach some kids something that they need and want to know, so long as you have the time, including of course showing some kids how to do the week's or month's official work if they want to do it and are having trouble with it (if they want to be official achieving seventh graders, which oddly enough many kids want to be) or talking with kids about what they might do otherwise if they don't want to be those same official seventh graders but are interested in writing or drawing or painting or making empty gallon cans of ditto fluid cave in for Science. You have time to protect some kids and get mad at others, you have time to answer over and over again questions about what kind of cigarettes you smoke and when did you start to smoke, are you married, how many kids do you have, would you let your kids smoke, let them grow long hair, do you think Robert is really smart? what would you do if your kids cut school, got an F, smoked in the bathroom, what kid of car, what was the war like, did you get in any fights, can you dance, did you like girls when you were thirteen, don't you think the PE teacher is unfair about giving out checks, Mrs. so-and-so said this yesterday, do you agree with that? Time to talk about all that, without worry, since the official part of the school work is going on, or not going on, without your total involvement in it. Time to read your book in there too, look at the want ads in the paper if you feel like it, telling everyone to leave you alone, time to cut out of the class and go visit the shop or the art room or some other class to see what's going on, knowing everyone will get along while you're gone. . . .

74

Time to live there in your classroom like a human being instead of playing some idiot role which everyone knows is an idiot role, time to see that teaching (if that is your job in America) is connected with your life and with you as a human being, citizen, person, that you don't have to become something different like a Martian or an idiot for eight hours a day. Time to deal with serious concerns of the kids and time to deal with put-on concerns and time to fuck around and time to get mad either seriously or not seriously . . . but you can only live that kind of life in there if you are willing to realize that the dicta of the school are crazy but that at the same time the kid's life is connected to the school in complicated ways and you'd better offer him the chance to take any part of it he wants or has to. These dicta do not exist in themselves. *One is not Duchess one hundred yards from a carriage.* They too are part of what Dewey would call the continuum of existence. I prefer Wittgenstein's words—the stream of life.

Perhaps now I can bring up a few other things which bear upon the stream of life. Before we left Big Bar, George told us that no one had camped there since the Depression, when, he said, as many as thirty families had lived there for months at a time. He also brought over a fresh-caught three-pound steelhead as a gift. He was taking pity on me, he said. I saw you a-fishing away like that and not gittin' any so one day I just thought to go stand out on the bluff beyond my place there for a few minutes and of course I got this one right away so I brought it over so you could at least have one to eat.

A summer later, Jay and I were driving back from the desert where we'd gone to see his grandma. He was sleeping in the back, and then all of a sudden I realized he wasn't sleeping any more but in a coma and I found the hospital in Modesto at about three in the morning. A young doctor there did about a thousand things at once and very likely saved his life. The doctor thought he might have gotten some agricultural poison or eaten deadly nightshade, but then he thought that he had encephalitis, and he was taken the next day in an ambulance to San Francisco and he stayed in the hospital there for a few weeks. Tests didn't show anything and no one could figure out what kind of encephalitis or how he'd gotten it or if and in any case there wasn't much to do except see if he lived or not, while maintaining a lot of life support at the hospital. A specialist from Oakland saw him and offered my wife the opinion that if he lived, it could only be as a kind of vegetable. I made up my mind on the spot to kill the specialist later on, as soon as things got over with.

After it became clear he would live, we took him home. We spent an odd year. Jay was simply turned off, like a radio with its tubes burnt out, or one just unplugged. All he could do was breathe and swallow. Fran spent hours every day for a year, moving joints. Bending his legs, moving feet, turning neck, wrists, ankles, shoulders, moving the joints of every finger and toe up and down, all of it done with the knowledge that it hurt. We spent hours talking to Jay, telling him stories as he lay in the bath, his head supported since he couldn't hold it up, had no voluntary control of any part of his body. The thing is, it was absolutely clear to us that he heard us, in some way understood what was happening. We could see a glint in his eye, perhaps. So that when one day he could hold up his own head, when he could sit up, when he could move his own finger, when he could crawl . . . then we could be elated just like when Jack began to crawl as a baby and believe even more in that glint or ghost in his eyes. Yet when Jay began to try to talk again it was the opposite of Jack learning to talk. For in Jay's head it was clear he knew what he wanted to say, but that he just didn't know how to get his mouth and tongue in shape to say it, whereas Jack could produce any sound he wanted, he just didn't have anything much to say, being only about a year old.

Well, this was going on during the time of the classes I've written about. I'm sure I have a couple of years put together in there, and I know the exact chronology is wrong in some way. Let me just add that you get an entirely different idea of societies like Easter Seal and such if you really need help from them and if you get it in the form of help with physical therapy and occupational therapy; you get a different idea of doctors if your own is a man who really concerns himself with your child and if, knowing that no miracles of modern medicine are going to do the trick, tells you that what you have there is not some different kid, but the same kid who needs you to help him and work with him, and who is going to be O.K.

After about a year, Jay was in shape to want, above all things, to play and be with other kids. He was then just able to totter around a little, holding on to walls and furniture. So we used to carry him down to the alley outside our flat where all the kids played and he'd sit in the sun and set up soldiers or play with cars with other kids and then they'd perhaps play ball and we'd watch Jay go crawling lickety-split after the ball when it got away from other kids, planning to get into the game on whatever terms, not knowing ourselves whether to laugh, cry or what. He also wanted to go back to school, since none of the other kids were around during the day, being in school themselves. The principal at the school he'd been to for kindergarten hemmed and hawed and did we think it was the best thing and he might get hurt and in the end she really refused, and we settled on Excelsior! School in the city, a special public school for orthopedically handicapped kids plus a scattering of severely retarded kids. A bus came every morning and picked Jay up with his football helmet on, which the school required in case he fell on his head, and at the school he got loaded

77

onto a wheelchair until he was walking better and got out of the wheelchair, and he got therapy there and got on the bus to come home, and it was good that Excelsior! School existed. But then, after the first jubilant relief about this long, dusty road back, we began to see the evil of such a school, and, if I may say so, it is the very evil of all public schools. It is only that in the harsh light of a place where all the kids have some real handicap—i.e., they can't walk or talk or see or hear or hold things in their hands, as opposed to fake culture-invented handicaps like being poor or rich or black—the evil becomes clearer, more blatant. I began to hear from Jay that he was being kept in from recess in order that he finish his writing or math or something. He wasn't being allowed to paint because he didn't finish his workbook in time. When I heard that I felt like I was going to go crazy. I'd worked in school for many years, yet I couldn't believe it. I went down, Fran went down, we both went down, and talked to the teacher, talked to the principal. We wanted to tell them that Jay just couldn't write any faster—we tried to make it clear clinically to them that none of his movements were automatic but all relearned and had to be thought about, that he could not move quickly, couldn't think faster, that just picking up his pencil meant he had to think about which fingers, how to curve them, how to flex the muscles to grasp it, how to move his hand so that certain shapes came out, A's, B's, and C's, 2's and 4's, plusses and minuses. We tried to convince them that what Jay needed above all was to play, to start getting back that sixth year he'd entirely missed, to relocate all those seemingly random movements of play and fooling around and moving about and manipulating things on his own hook, to talk to other kids and horse around with them . . . we tried to tell them about how the Easter Seal therapists and the doctor wanted him to be doing large motor movements like specifically painting, spreading those big

splashes of color onto paper . . . and we'd come home together or separately from these visits thinking it wasn't going to do any good at all or thinking we were crazy, me
cursing and wanting to kill someone and crying and Fran
cursing and wanting to kill someone and crying and in
the end accusing each other of either not being tough
enough or of being too tough and antagonizing the school
(what if they were right? what if they take it out on Jay?)
and fighting among ourselves and being insane enough to
get hold of Jay when he came home and tell him for God's
sake to try and work faster. . . . I shake right now with
absolute rage when I remember the calm teacher and the
firm principal telling us that perhaps Jay was a little lazy,
after all, kids, you know . . . (and in my mind he is crawling along the alley on banged-up and scraped knees after a
baseball in order to be playing) and affording us the school
philosophy that handicapped kids, being handicapped,
ought to be just a little bit better in everything than regular
kids, having their handicaps to get over, which was just
about what the black teachers used to say (perhaps still
do) at the black school I taught at, you black kids got to be
nicer and more disciplined and more conformist, since,
having that initial handicap, you got to have an MA to get
that janitor's job . . . yet that was the only school he
could go to, yet they were giving him quite excellent physical therapy, yet he was going to have to get along with the
school, still how can such a kid possibly be called in the
name of reason anything like lazy, still he needs to play,
still how can it be important about nine minus what when
he had still got to stand there and figure out deliberately
and consciously how to move hand and arm and doorknob
so that the door opens when he wants it to?

Just so. Just so the public school practices alienation on
the land, and it is a practice which affects its teachers, its
kids and the parents of its kids alike, some obviously more

harshly than others. You may be sure you know everything about your kid, or about how you want to teach, or about yourself as a kid, but if the school tells you different you'll find that wedge driven in there between you and your child, between you and your class, between yourself as you know yourself and yourself as the school tells you about yourself.

In the end, I was able to decide to take Jay out of Excelsior! School and take him out to Tierra Firma School in my own district where I knew and admired the principal and the teachers, a small public school with big grass fields and no stairs (it always interested me that a school for orthopedically handicapped children should have three floors of stairs to climb)—but that was after Jay was walking pretty good and even able to run a little, and because being a teacher I had the opportunity to make the change. But before that I visited Excelsior! one day when Jay was in the third grade, still being kept in from recess quite a bit, and his group of kids was facing the teacher who was holding up flash cards about math, while the kids gave the answers. I sat in back of Jay. From where he sat the light came in through the window at just the right angle so that when the teacher held up the card to him the card was made semi-transparent and he could see the answer. So could I. The teacher kept holding up the cards and Jay kept reading the answer off the back, 17, 22, 11, 4, working his tongue and lips around to make sure the sound came out right. When I left, the pleased teacher told me Jay's math was really improving and I said I was happy to see it and when Jay got home he looked sidewise at me and asked if I happened by any chance to notice that you could see the answers on the backs of the cards, and I said yeah, I did just happen to notice that and then he grinned and said I sit right there every day at math time—and we have math the same time every day!

And I laughed and told Jay he was a no-good tricky wart

and felt the weight of Excelsior! School fall off me and I was rid of it forever. Jay had figured out the school and gotten a break with the sun at eleven in the morning and knew how to use it and that was when I knew unquestionably that he was going to be O.K., and I could stop wanting to kill someone because that evil was just a fake too, for you might have to be there where it was going on but you didn't have to fall for it, you didn't have to practice it or abet it or even battle it on its own terms, you could just tell it to go take a flying fuck at the moon and it would be displayed as a shadow, *powerless*, unless you—you parents, teachers and kids—give it power.

The kids in my class were all stubborn, I said. Perhaps that was why they were called immature. Not only was Ray stubborn in refusing to do school work and also refusing to do nothing, not only were the girls stubborn in refusing to stop using the school to force their mothers out into the open, not only was Rosie stubborn in refusing to stop reading her books during math lesson, but Hal and Charles and Howard were stubborn too, in refusing to submit to the school's intention that they just do the work and get A's. They had what they thought of as their futures to consider and wanted to *learn* something from that work, doing the work better than was wanted and spending too much time on it, demanding fuller explanations for which teachers had *no time*, messing up the schedule of work. Still that is only my reasoning now. At the time I occasionally wondered, Why were these kids called immature?

It happened somewhere along all the above, in time, that what we all were interested in was the intramural sports program. We entered football and basketball and got regularly smeared. But in baseball season, we developed a big hit-and-run Chicago White Sox-type team (I was reading Bill Veeck's biography at the time). The girls came down and led cheers, we held practice sessions and got lucky, and near the end of the year we entered the finals, the World Series of Spanish Main School. Winning junior high softball teams are usually composed of two or three big guys who hit the ball a mile, perhaps two actual good ballplayers who field well and can make the right play, and the rest bums like everyone else. The effort of the team is to talk the big guys into showing up for the game at noon, instead of going off with the girls or for a smoke, and then the good ballplayers get on with well-placed singles and perhaps a bum or two gets on base off an error, and then the big guy gets up and hits the ball three miles and the team wins. We had Sam, who supposedly could hit the ball a mile but who in fact almost always struck out. For the rest we had medium-sized fair ballplayers—no one really great, but also no one really horrible. Even Charles with his wrong-handed glove usually caught the ball out in right field. We got into the finals by actually throwing out guys who hit grounders, by catching fly balls, by hitting grounders to the bums on the other team and taking second after their bums threw it over the first baseman's head, by playing what we called "heads-up" ball, by not arguing too much among ourselves, and mainly by showing up for every game so that we won quite a number by default. Well, at that time there was usually quite a crowd showing up for the Series, four out of seven games on consecutive noontimes, and while we got respect for even being there at all, no one gave us a chance. The other team had three big well-known Monsters, a couple of belligerent All Star good ballplayers, and they murdered us the first game, making no errors (therefore we didn't score) and the Monsters cleaning up for about ten runs. Two of the Monsters didn't show for the second game, and we won. We won the third too, since their two All Stars got into a fist fight about who should have handled a grounder between third and short and got thrown out of the game. After that they were afflicted with internal dissension, as the sports pages call it, and sent down their teacher to ask for a postponement the next day. We stood on our rights and refused, winning therefore by default.

The next morning Hal discussed with me a plan which, he said, he'd had in mind all year. It concerned the rules for junior high intramural softball—in this case, the particular rule against stealing bases, a rule made because the catchers were always bums and couldn't catch or throw. The rule said that the runner must keep his foot on the bag until the ball leaves the pitcher's hand. Hal thought that rule somewhat ambiguous. What if, he said, their runner is on base, and I start to pitch the ball, only instead of letting it go at the end of the swing I just hold onto it? Well, I said, that'll be a balk. Sure he said, a balk. The runner could take second base. But when the ball is supposed to leave my hand, the guy running is going to take his foot off the base to get going. When I hold on to it, there he'll be off the bag. He's gotta be out!

We talked about it. The other kids gathered around offering opinions. The issue came to be whether the guy would be out before he took second base, whether the balk or the foot off the bag took precedence. No one knew, but Hal reasoned that the kid umpire wouldn't know either. He figured either way we couldn't lose, if he pulled it at the right time, namely when they had a guy on base and their Monster up to bat. Either the guy on base would be out, leaving the Monster with nothing to clean up even if he hit a homer, or else their team would get mad during the argument over the rules and they might even have another fight, and default, or just be so mad they couldn't play well. It was worth a try.

We went out the next noontime, leading in games 3–1. About the fourth inning it was 0–0, their Monsters having only hit fly balls a mile up into the air. Then, with one out, they got a belligerent All Star on base and a Monster up to bat. Hal threw a couple way outside to the Monster. Each time he let it go, the All Star dashed halfway to second. Then Hal wound up, flung the ball viciously—and held on to it! He just stood there, holding out the ball at arm's length. The All Star stood frozen in his tracks halfway to second. The Monster stood there, bat cocked to hit the ball downtown. You could have put the whole tableau in a museum, like Raising The Flag At Iwo Jima.

Then hell broke loose. The other team rushed the poor kid umpire, led by the furious All Star. Our team rushed the umpire. The rest of the school, our girl cheerleaders, watching teachers . . . yelling, pulling, shoving, God almighty, a perfect or awful scene, depending upon how you looked at it. In the end, the umpires didn't know what to do about it, of course, and finally the PE coach in charge of the games got the idea of what all the argument was about and said Balk! Balk! Play ball! Then Hal rushed him, the coach, and tried to talk about the ambiguity of the rule and how could it be just a balk since it had to be an out too? and by that time I'd rushed the coach too, remembering that was what we managers were supposed to do, but he just told me and Hal to get the hell out of there. Hal, however, couldn't let it go at that. He had to explain to the coach how he'd figured out about the rule and that the coach couldn't just say Balk! not logically anyway, and that was when the coach got the idea for the first time that it was a deliberate thing, that Hal had planned it all, just to fuck up the game and cause trouble, just to get any kind of advantage, and so he told us to shut up and start playing ball or forfeit the game.

He was really angry, and after the game (which we lost about 10–0 again, losing the next two by similar scores also) he came over and said What you guys pulled today was the most *immature* thing I ever saw! He was a guy I liked and respected at the school, by the way, and he meant that if you find some chink in the armor of the school or the game you ought to let it alone and just take your lumps. Still, Hal and all of us didn't figure to take our lumps if we didn't have to, and we also thought along with Bill Veeck that if we did, someone was going to have to take theirs too. So despite my present speculations, it was right then that I learned why it was that the school had pegged us all as immature, and I know it was something worth learning.

PART TWO

Explanatory Notes

FIND A GOOD SCHOOL AND SEND
YOUR KID THERE

If Excelsior! School deals with really disadvantaged kids then Tierra Firma Elementary deals with advantage. Its kids come from Tierra Firma itself, the first suburb of San Francisco, discovered or invented for the reason all suburbs are discovered or invented—its people hope to drop out of the problems of America and enjoy its promise.

The people of Tierra Firma are the advantaged of America. They make enough money to afford cheap developer-built houses, cars, boats, bowling balls and plenty of Sta-Prest pants, but, since that is true of many other groups of people in America, including the rich, that is not the source of their advantage. They are advantaged because they believe in the promise of America and are actually satisfied by it when they get it and by the striving which they must constantly do to keep getting and believing in it. They believe, for instance, that as long as you are free to buy things on credit then you can keep going to work in order to pay those payments and that the one justifies the other and makes it meaningful. They know what you are supposed to do and by and large make an effort to do it and see the results and they are not cynical about the results. They have perhaps moved from big old Mission Street or North Beach wooden carpenter-Gothic houses and flats, where the plumbing is always going out of whack and streetcars run past the door, to three-bedroom tract houses with a back

88

yard and a palm tree in the front and a garage and streets where the kids can ride bikes, and they are glad they did so. Middle-class and rich people disdain Tierra Firma and move into those same old wooden houses and pay $40,000 and another $20,000 to fix them up good because they are not satisfied with America, just like the poor who have to stay in them without fixing them up. The advantaged move to Tierra Firma. They are advantaged because, I repeat, America still holds promise for them; if you do right, you can really get all this that Tierra Firma affords, and since that is exactly what they do want, and since they can get it, they are satisfied. No doubt many of them understand the political and economic manipulations necessary in order for Tierra Firma to exist; no doubt they have gripes about property tax and this and that; no doubt they know the poor exist and something perhaps ought to be done about it; no doubt many are against the war; no doubt they are not all racists; and no doubt they know the TV ads are phony . . . but they are cast in the present right image of the country and know that they can and will make it in America *because they are really satisfied* with what they have got out of it. I know that if you hang around with liberal intellectuals or with militant Third World people or with poor people or with radical college students or, simply, if you hang around with people who are dissatisfied with the state of affairs, you will get the idea, and hope it is true, that most people in America are dissatisfied and then you will predict major changes in the country. To correct that mistaken state of mind, I hope you will go to work in Tierra Firma someday.

The fact remains that Tierra Firma Elementary School is one of the best public schools I have ever seen, and that is why I took Jay out there to school, and why, when Jack decided he'd like to go out there too, I took both my boys. It is a good school because of the principal, and because of the teachers whom he collected together over the rather long period of time that he has been principal there. It is a good school because for a few years there was a district superintendent who tried to get intelligent, serious people to come to work in the district and, once they did, allowed them to work. I have a good deal of respect for all the people involved in Tierra Firma School; they are, by and large, exactly the kinds of people that educational writers are always saying ought to be working with kids in schools. They are bright, serious, hardworking, confident, innovative, humorous, well-read, creative, with-it. They are not repressive, narrow, grade-oriented, vain, afraid, hung-up on testing, conventional, or chickenshit. They have guts; they like and respect the kids. The school itself is O.K. In modern one-story motel style, all the rooms open directly to the outdoors. There is plenty of space—a large asphalt play area for basketball, bikes and four-square, a big grass area, a little-kids' playground with swings and slides and monkey bars and tanbark, and a huge upper field of grass which is what convinced Jay to go there. He could see himself running free on that big grass field, looking like a whooping crane about to take off.

All right. But see, this is the same school that Fran visited and all the kids were running around on that really pleasant playground yelling about murder and MR and fuck you. That is what the kids are supposed to be doing in them no-good schools, in them ghetto schools, in them big-city pore schools, in them rich hippie dope-smoking schools, in them terrible repressive tracked grade-mad bureaucratic lesson-planned honky colonialist Fascist pig Cossack San Francisco schools with Irish or Italian old ladies who ought to have been nuns or ex-Navy disappointed commanders for principals. That is not what, in theory and on principle, kids are supposed to be doing in what few good schools there are in existence, for in fact the very reason for making the effort to have any good schools is so that the kids won't be in this bad shape. So why, if it's really a good school ain't it doing any good? Why is it that in this good school with these good people that Jack, in the first grade, who is really what everyone agrees is an excellent student—he can read, as far as I can see, anything, he can write, and not only that but he likes to draw and write and read a good deal of the time, he can in short do everything that the school, any school, wants him to be able to do and not only that but he is wise enough to be reasonably well behaved and polite when it counts . . . why is it that if one day on the way to this good school he realizes that in his urgency to get up to Mr. Ling's corner store and buy some fake wax teeth to show off and later chew, he has forgotten to bring along his homework in writing or math . . . why is it that then he bursts into tears? Why is it that then no effort of mine will console him? Why is he frightened? He, of all kids going to that good school, has the least reason to be frightened.

There is one reason, and only one, and it is crucial. That is that an American public school must have winners and losers. It does not matter in this respect what kind of school it is. In Berkeley, now that Mr. Sullivan has integrated the schools, it is the black kids who sit in Remedial Reading and the white kids who sit in Enriched this or that. When they are together in some general course the well-dressed sharp clean-and-pressed shoe-shined poor black kid sits in class next to the Salvation-army-surplus-store-ugly-dressed white rich kid and the beautiful pore black kid doesn't know what the teacher is talking about and the white ugly rich kid knows everything and can read or even has read everything the teacher can, even if that surplus-store white kid disdains the whole thing and won't answer or discuss or even attend class, even if he goes and smokes shit across the street or heads for the communal hills . . . try as he may to become an outcast the school knows that he is a winner even if he rejects winning. The intelligent hip young teacher will be copying his ugly clothes while pretending to try and straighten him out, get him off drugs, interest him in Egypt, which the teacher probably don't know nothing about. Or the intelligent old conservative teacher will be talking in the teachers' room about how bright the long-haired ugly-clothes kid is even if a pain in the ass and that the school must find a way to motivate him, or force him, the country needs him, and so on. After class the black kid finds eight other black kids who have just had the same classroom experience and they link arms and walk jiving down the hall, covering the passageway wall to wall, forcing every one of them ugly know-it-all white play-poor winning motherfuckers with professor-fathers to change direction, go around the other way, shrink up against the wall. This phenomenon is then called racial unrest.

But over in Oakland there will be an all-black school, Mr. Sullivan not having passed through that town yet. It may be that the school would prefer to have some ugly white kids to be winners, but they in fact ain't got any. Does that mean a school full of losers? Not at all. That school has got to have winners too, and so some sharp poor beautiful black kids wind up in the A group and some others in the H group. It may be that if the kids in the Oakland A winner's group transferred over to Berkeley they would end up being losing kids, or it may be not. It doesn't make any difference. In Oakland they are winners. The H kids find the A kids in line at the cafeteria and hit them in they mouths.

In Tierra Firma, up until recently, all the kids have been these same advantaged lower-middle-class kids (white, black and brown) I've already mentioned. They ain't by and large ugly rich Army-Navy-store whites nor lime-green-creased pore beautiful blacks. So therefore the school only

92

has winners? Certainly not. What kind of school would that be? Some of them advantaged kids have got to lose. It may be that if the losers of Tierra Firma transferred to Berkeley or Oakland then they would be winners. Or it may not be. The students who end up in a place like M.I.T. are certainly the winners of the Western world, the smartest, most with-it, craftiest Western technological human beings ever produced but even then all of them cannot be winners. Some of them must flunk out, because M.I.T. being a school in America has also got to have losers. Would those M.I.T. losers be winners at S.F. State? Maybe so and maybe not.

That is why Jack, my beloved son of seven years, bursts into tears and cannot be consoled. That is why some students of M.I.T. are throwing dodge balls at each other's heads, and a large group of physicists stands around the outskirts of the school grounds crying, and why nothing can console them even if someone hits them or doesn't hit them in they mouths.

They cry because the losers are going to get some revenge some way. But they also cry because the winning is never permanent. You may be a winner in the first grade, but by the fourth you may be losing. The rites of passage of the school go on and on. Each year it is circumcision time all over again; obviously you may weep for what has been hacked off by the time you are thirty-five and have a PhD.

How does the school make certain that it will have winners and losers? Well, obviously by giving grades. If you give A's, you must also give F's. Without the rest of the grades, the A is meaningless. Even a B is less good than an A—in short, every kid who does not get an A is failing and losing to some extent. The median on the bell curve is not a median, it is not an average, it is not a norm, not to the school and not to the kids in the school. It is a losing sign, a failure, and a hex. You must be way out there on the right-hand edge where the curve approaches the base line. But it is the nature of bell curves that most everyone cannot be there.

But even if the school abandons grades and IQ and achievement testing it will still produce losers aplenty and winners. The fundamental act of the American public school is to deal with children in groups. Once it has a group of children of any age, it decides what those children will be expected to do, and then the teacher, as representative of the school, tells the children all at once. The children hear it, and when they hear it they know whether they can do it or not. Some of the children will already know how to do it. They will win. The teacher comes into the teachers' room the first day and says I already know who the good students are. I can predict the grades of almost every kid. Sure enough, the prediction works with minimum variation.

You deal with the children in groups. You teach first graders to read. You write *ch* on the board, and ask Who knows how this sounds? Some kids already know and raise their hands with tremendous relief. They are going to make it this year. Others think they know, but aren't sure. (Maybe *ch* has changed since their mamas told them.) Others never heard of it. They might be happy to know what it sounds like (why not?) but at the same time they see that a lot of other smart kids already know.

Whatever class, age group, grade, section it is, in a public school, the subject matter is carefully arranged so that some of the kids will already know it before they get there. Then, for a little while in the primary grades, the school will try to teach those who didn't know it already. But it doesn't really work. It doesn't work because the winners keep intruding, raising their hands in advance of the question, or because while the teacher works with the losers on what the winners already know the winners are free to read or draw or talk to one another and therefore learn other stuff and when the loser gets into the second grade, having learned what the school demanded that he knew before he entered the first grade, the second grade will have assessed what the winners know and the losers don't and produce that as the subject matter for the year. Later on, of course, the school will refuse to teach the losers at all. *In all public schools in the United States* the percentage of kids who cannot really read the social studies textbook or the science textbook or the directions in the New Math book or the explanations in the transformational grammar book is extraordinarily high. Half the kids. The school tells everyone that reading is the key to success in school, and no doubt it is, a certain kind of reading anyway. Does the school then spend time and effort teaching those kids who can't read the texts how to read the texts? Shit no, man. Why mess up a situation made to order for failure? At Spanish Main Intermediate School there are some eleven hundred students, at least half of whom can't read the books they lose and have to pay money for at the end of the year. The school hires one remedial reading teacher, who will only deal with about forty students per year. Even then, this teacher will not really teach the kids to read, but of course will review some complicated and nutty system which (again) some of the remedial reading students already know (although they can't read) and the others don't, for the remedial reading class is part of the school too. Well of course the school says it ain't got money enough for all them remedial reading teachers, otherwise it would love to teach everyone to read. But it does have money enough for a million social studies teachers to teach Egypt to groups of kids, a small percentage of whom already know everything about it, a larger percentage of whom know enough to copy the encyclopedia, the text, or other kids' homework, and another large percentage of whom can't do anything but sit

95

there, get in trouble, provide jobs for counselors and disciplinary vice-principals and consultants and psychologists (all of whom get paid to deal with problems the school causes every day) and become an unending supply of failure for the school.

So Jack does not misinterpret the school. Were you thinking that the homework was given to see if he could do it? To see if he had learned what was taught? You haven't learned your lesson. The homework was given to the winners to see if they would do it that night and bring it the next day. (It was given to the losers to show them they couldn't do it.) If they forget or refuse, they may have to stop being winners. For the fate of winners in a school is that they must do, over and over again, exercises and reviews and practices and assignments that they already know how to do, over and over again for twelve years, then four more, then four more . . . just as Jack has got to stop reading his books every morning in order to get ready to go to school in order to spend time doing workbooks and exercises so that he'll learn to read his books.

The school's purpose is not teaching. The school's purpose is to separate sheep from goats. You can find a very good school with lots of grass where the teachers don't yell at you. It separates. By all means send your kid there.

JAIL

Of course I have forgotten to tell you again, what you already know. That is that the fundament of the school, even before winners and losers, is that everyone has got to go there.

Even if you are rich or have eccentric or far-out parents and go to private schools or invent free schools for yourself, you still deal with the public school. But in any case most of you are not or have not any of the above. You must go to school.

If kids in America do not go to school, they can be put in jail. If they are tardy a certain number of times, they may go to jail. If they cut enough, they go to jail. If their parents do not see that they go to school, the parents may be judged unfit and the kids go to jail.

You go to jail. All of the talk about *motivation* or *inspiring* kids to learn or *innovative* courses which are *relevant* is horseshit. It is horseshit because there is no way to know if students really are interested or not. No matter how bad the school is, it is better than jail. Everyone knows that, and the school knows it especially. A teacher comes into the teachers' room and says happily, I had the greatest lesson today! and goes on to tell the other envious teachers what it was that they hadn't thought of themselves and says, The kids were all so excited! It is horseshit. The teacher has forgotten (as I forget) that the kids have to be there or they will

97

go to jail. Perhaps the grand lesson was merely more tolerable than the usual lesson. Perhaps the kids would have rejected both lessons if they could.

That is why the school cannot ever learn anything about its students. Why famous psychologists can successfully threaten pigeons into batting ping-pong balls with their wings, but can never learn anything about pigeons.

As long as you can threaten people, you can't tell whether or not they really want to do what you are proposing that they do. You can't tell if they are inspired by it, you can't tell if they learn anything from it, you can't tell if they would keep on doing it if you weren't threatening them.

You cannot tell. You cannot tell if the kids want to come to your class or not. You can't tell if they are motivated or not. You can't tell if they learn anything or not. All you can tell is, they'd rather come to your class than go to jail.

No Man

I have heard a teacher come into the teachers' room at report-card time and, after making out grades on those slips of paper, lean back and sigh and then say, for everyone to hear, Just look! Three-fourths of the students in my class have gotten D's!

The teacher received a gratifying murmur of sympathy from the rest of the room. We've all had them classes, they seemed to say. What a job this is! No one offered to mention how it was that those kids all got those D's. The teacher showed no sign at all of remembering that the kids in her class got those D's precisely because she had just taken her pen and written the letter D on three-fourths of the report cards.

That is the only reason they got D's. That is the only reason they became a group of D-getting kids whose teacher ought to be given sympathy. If she had written down A's instead, they would have been a group whose teacher deserved congratulations and envy. Either way, it would still be the teacher who took a pen and wrote down the D or the A on the card. The card then magically became the kid. The cards then magically became the group. I repeat, the teacher took a pen and wrote down D. Someone, a person, did it. Took the pen and wrote down D and . . .

The teacher genuinely does not realize that the class has D's only because the teacher herself just wrote down D's with her own hand, her own pen, in her free period, on slips of paper which are prepared to receive any mark at all. All she remembers is that *this class got D's,* the dumb, recalcitrant sons of bitches.

A study was done once on teacher dreams. These dreams were full of anxiety, and things kept happening which no one could account for. The teacher couldn't find her room, or he couldn't find his roll book, or the kids wouldn't sit down, and the principal and the consultant and the superintendent came in and all of a sudden the teacher had forgotten to wear any pants or she was naked and the administrators were frowning . . . what the study didn't mention was that those are the same dreams students have. I've had dreams in which I was trying to find my high school biology class and I wandered through unfamiliar halls which ought to have been familiar, trying to figure out what I had been doing the whole year and wondering what I was going to say to the biology teacher who was giving (I knew) the final test today and I didn't know anything about it and somewhere along the way of that dream I would change into being the teacher and the students were the ones who knew all about it and I didn't know what questions to ask in this final test and my pants had been stolen and how in the world could I have a hard-on right now sticking up above the desk even if I tried to stoop down, and there was the goddamn principal, all dressed up, waiting.

Well, these are classic dreams. They occur to people who do not imagine that it is they themselves who determine what happens wherever it is they work. Teachers imagine that they determine nothing. After all, who built the school? Not the teachers. Who decided that there would be thirty-eight desks in each room? Not the teachers. Who decided that thirty-eight kids in Room 3 ought to learn about Egypt in the seventh grade from 10:05 to 10:50? Not the

100

teachers. Who decided that there ought to be forty-five minutes for lunch and that there ought to be stewed tomatoes in those plastic containers? Not the teachers. Who decided about the curriculum and who decided about the textbooks? Not us. Not us! All we know is that we have this room and thirty-eight kids come in and if there are thirty-eight desks it's perfectly clear that the thirty-eight kids belong in the thirty-eight desks and therefore ought to sit down in them, and if we have thirty-eight books of one sort or another it's obvious that each of the thirty-eight kids ought to get one, and now that they have one it's also logical that we ought to assign something to read and do in them, and in order to do that we have to talk and if some kids talk while we talk we get to explain the logic of the situation to them at length just as I have done here, and then having assigned something it's apparent that we ought to collect the assignments and it's reasonable to give some kids A and some F . . . but in the end it ain't our fault. We had nothing to do with it. It ain't our fault!

We feel we have nothing to do with it, beyond the process of managing what is presented to us. Presented to us by whom? The principal? But the principal tells us at faculty meetings that this is the situation, he didn't invent it, we all must only live with it. The superintendent? He gives us an inspiring speech on opening day, but beyond that he makes it clear that our problems are not his invention. We are all in the same boat, he wants to tell us. The board of education? The state board? The superintendent of public instruction? No, man, they didn't do it. Who decided that Egypt is just right for seventh graders? Who decided that DNA must be something which all kids answer questions about? Who decided that California Indians must enter the world of fourth grade kids, or that South America must be "learned" by sixth graders?

Nobody, it seems, made any of these decisions. Noman

did it. Noman is responsible for them. The people responsible for the decisions about how schools ought to go are dead. Very few people are able to ask questions of dead men. So we treat those decisions precisely as if dead men made them, as if none of them are up to us live people to make, and therefore we determine that we are not responsible for any of them. It ain't our fault! It ain't our fault!

That is exactly what the kids say. Accepting that, it follows that we must also accept classic dreams.

THE DUMB CLASS

One afternoon during our free seventh period some-one looked around and said This faculty is the Dumb Class.

It was so. Given the community or the entire country as a school—reversing the usual image of the school as mirror of society to make society the mirror of the school—and given that community as one which is tracked or ability-grouped into high, high-average, average, low-average, high-low, low and low-low, the faculty or faculties, teachers, *educators,* are the dumb class.

We are the dumb class because we cannot learn. Cannot achieve. Why not? Cannot concentrate, have a low atten-tion span, are culturally deprived, brain-damaged, non-verbal, unmotivated, lack skills, are anxiety-ridden, have broken homes, can't risk failure, no study habits, won't try, are lazy . . . ? Those are the reasons *kids* are in the dumb class, supposing we don't say it's because they are just dumb. But the characteristic of the dumb class is that it cannot learn how to do what it is there to do. Try as one may, one cannot make the dumb class learn to do these things, at least not as long as it is operating together as a dumb class. Even if those things are completely obvious, the dumb class cannot learn them or achieve them.

Is it so that what the dumb class is supposed to achieve is so difficult that only superior individuals can achieve it, and then only with hard work, endless practice? Is it so mysterious and opaque that only those with intelligence and energy enough to research and ferret out the mysteries of the universe can gain insight into it? Eighth period I was involved with this dumb class which was supposed to achieve adding and subtracting before it got out of the eighth grade and went to high school. Could the class achieve it? No sir. Given an adding problem to add, most of the dumb class couldn't add it. Those who did add it hadn't any notion of whether or not they'd added it correctly, even if they had. They asked me Is this right? Is this right? This ain't right, is it? What's the answer? If you don't know whether it's right or not, I'd say, then you aren't adding it. Is this right? screamed four kids, rushing me waving papers. Boy, this dumb class can't learn, I'd say to myself. Not a very sophisticated remark, perhaps.

For a while I would drop in on the Tierra Firma bowling alley, since Jay and Jack were always dying to go there. One day I ran into the dumbest kid in the dumb class. Rather, he came up to us as we were playing this baseball slot machine. Jay and Jack were not defeating the machine, to say the least, and as a result had to put in another dime each time they wanted to play again. Well the dumb kid showed us how to lift the front legs of the machine in just the right way so that the machine would run up a big score without tilting, enough for ten or so free games, all by itself. After it did that, he told us, you could go ahead and really play it for fun. Jay and Jack were pretty impressed; they thought this dumb kid was a genius. Those big kids in your school sure are smart, was how Jack put it.

Well, as Jay and Jack happily set out to strike out and pop-up to the infield on the machine for those free games, the dumb kid and I walked around and watched the bowlers and had a smoke and talked. In the end, of course, I asked him what he was doing around there. He was getting ready to go to work, he told me. Fooling around until five, when he started. What did he do? I keep score, he told me. For the leagues. He kept score for two teams at once. He made fifteen bucks for a couple of hours. He thought it was a great job, making fifteen bucks for something he liked to do anyway, perhaps would have done for nothing, just to be able to do it.

He was keeping score. Two teams, four people on each, eight bowling scores at once. Adding quickly, not making any mistakes (for no one was going to put up with errors), following the rather complicated process of scoring in the game of bowling. Get a spare, score ten plus whatever you get on the next ball, score a strike, then ten plus whatever you get on the next two balls; imagine the man gets three strikes in a row and two spares and you are the scorer, plus you are dealing with seven other guys all striking or sparing or neither one . . . The bowling league is not a welfare organization nor part of Headstart or anything like that and wasn't interested in giving some dumb kid a chance to improve himself by fucking up their bowling scores. No, they were giving this smart kid who had proved to be fast and accurate fifteen dollars because they could use a good scorer.

I figured I had this particular dumb kid now. Back in eighth period I lectured him on how smart he was to be a league scorer in bowling. I pried admissions from the other boys, about how they had paper routes and made change. I made the girls confess that when they went to buy stuff they didn't have any difficulty deciding if those shoes cost $10.95 or whether it meant $109.50 or whether it meant $1.09 or how much change they'd get back from a twenty. Naturally I then handed out bowling-score problems and paper-route change-making problems and buying-shoes problems, and naturally everyone could choose which ones they wanted to solve, and naturally the result was that all the dumb kids immediately rushed me yelling Is this right?

I don't know how to do it! What's the answer? This ain't right, is it? and What's my grade? The girls who bought shoes for $10.95 with a $20 bill came up with $400.15 for change and wanted to know if that was right? The brilliant league scorer couldn't decide whether two strikes and a third frame of eight amounted to eighteen or twenty-eight or whether it was one hundred eight and one half.

The reason they can't learn is because they are the dumb class. No other reason. Is adding difficult? No. It is the dumb class which is difficult. Are the teachers a dumb class? Well, we are supposed to teach kids to "read, write, cipher and sing," according to an old phrase. Can we do it? Mostly not. Is it difficult? Not at all. We can't do it because we are a dumb class, which by definition can't do it, whatever it is.

Yet what we are supposed to do is something which, like adding, everyone knows how to do. It isn't mysterious, nor dependent on a vast and intricate knowledge of pedagogy or technology or psychological tests or rats. Is there any man or woman on earth who knows how to read who doesn't feel quite capable of teaching his own child or children to read? Doesn't every father feel confident that his boy will come into the bathroom every morning to stand around and watch while the father shaves and play number games with the father and learn about numbers and shaving at the same time? Every person not in the dumb class feels that these things are simple. Want to know about Egypt? Mother or father or older brother or uncle or someone and the kid go down to the public library and get out a book on Egypt and the kid reads it and perhaps the uncle reads it too, and while they are shaving they may talk about Egypt. But the dumb class of teachers and public educators feel that these things are very difficult, and they must keep hiring experts and devising strategies in order that they can rush these experts and strategies with their papers asking Is this right? and What's my grade?

Yet, released from the dumb class to their private lives, teachers are marvelous gardeners, they work on ocean liners as engineers, they act in plays, win bets, go to art movies, build their own houses, they are opera fans, expert fishermen, champion skeet shooters, grand golfers, organ players, oratorio singers, hunters, mechanics . . . all just as if they were smart people. Of course it is more difficult to build a house or sing Bach than it is to teach kids to read. Of course if they operated in their lives outside of the dumb class the same way they do in it, their houses would fall down, their ships would sink, their flowers die, their cars blow up.

This very morning in the San Francisco *Chronicle* I read a scandalous report. The reporter reports the revelations of a member of the board of education, namely that 45 per cent of the *Spanish-surname children* (that is how we put it in the paper these days) who are in mentally retarded classes have been found, when retested in Spanish, to be of average or above-average intelligence. The board member thought that "the Spanish-speaking kids were shunted into classes for the mentally retarded because they did not understand English well enough to pass the examinations they were given." He figured that, just like if he was told that a bowler had a spare on the first frame and got eight on his next ball, he'd figure that the bowler's score in the first frame ought to be eighteen. Well, in this matter assume that the board member is the teacher in a dumb class. He's trying to tell the school administrators something obvious. Does the administrator learn, now he's been told it, that ten and eight are eighteen? No, the assistant superintendent for special services says that "the assumption was that they understood English well enough to be tested by the English versions of the Stanford-Binet and the WISC intelligence tests." He thought that "it wasn't so much the fault of the test as it was the cultural deprivation of the child at the time of testing" which caused these smart kids to be retarded. Asked if these smart retarded Spanish-surname kids were now going to be moved into the regular program, he *revealed* that no, that wasn't the case, for they were *"still working* with the elementary division to seek a proper *transitional* program, since these children were still *functional retardates"* no matter what their IQ.

The reporter, acting in his role as critical parent, found out that the tests *were* available in Spanish but that Spanish-speaking kids *weren't* tested, therefore, in Spanish (because of the above assumption). The tests *weren't* available in "Oriental," and the "Oriental" kids *weren't* tested, therefore, in "Oriental." Well, that made sense, so the reporter pried out the information that the school district got $550 extra a year for each kid in mentally retarded classes. The reporter implied cynically that they were doing it for the money and that if they let all these bright retarded Spanish kids out there might be a shortage of $550 kids to be retarded.

But it is the dumb class we are concerned with. Here this administrator is told something obvious, told to learn it, told to achieve this difficult knowledge that them Spanish-speaking kids are only dumb if they are tested in a language they don't understand. But being in the dumb class, he don't learn it. He may be the smartest man in the world, able to keep score for league bowling, read The Book of the Dead, go water skiing, make bell curves. But in the dumb class he can't learn anything, and there is no reason to expect that he ever will as long as he is in there.

Four- or Five-Minute Speech for a Symposium on <u>American Institutions And Do They Need Changing Or What?</u>

It's perfectly possible (I'll begin) to make remarks about institutions, for everyone is certain to believe in the real existence of something this word stands for—i.e., a something which exists in order to make certain that some kind of human activity, chosen just on account of the naturalness and inevitability of that activity, remains natural and inevitable.

If a school is an institution, then the prerequisite inevitable activity is the natural desire of human adults to instruct their children. They desire to instruct them in what their world knows of magic or skill and they instruct them in the everyday ways of their world—what to eat and how to eat it, whom you can marry, when you may grow up, whom to obey, how to become President.

One ought then (I'll go on) to point out that institutions have characteristics, of which two seem crucial, at least to this speech.

The first characteristic of any institution is that no matter what the inevitable purpose for which it was invented, it must devote all its energy to doing the exact opposite. Thus, a Savings Bank must encourage the people to borrow money at Interest, and a School must inspire its students toward Stupidity.

The second characteristic is that an institution must continue to exist. Every action must be undertaken with respect to eternity. This second characteristic is the reason for the first. For unless a Savings Bank can persuade the the people not to Save, the Savings Bank will go broke. But the Savings Bank must continue to exist, since otherwise the people would have No Place To Save. Just so, the School must encourage its students not to learn. For if the students learned quickly, most of them could soon leave the school, having Learned. But if the students left the school it would cease to exist as an institution and then the students would have No Place In Which To Learn.

Following that argument, we can arrive at a description of an institution: An Institution Is A Place To Do Things Where Those Things Will Not Be Done.

If the institutions are reproached forcefully enough, they will admit it. Thus the Savings Bank will say, You want to Save? So hide your bread under the mattress! Bury it in the back yard, you bastard!

And the School: You want to Learn? Hire a tutor! Watch TV! Get your parents to teach you! Fuck you!

An institution and its arguments are both circular. Change it? Better change the music of the spheres instead!

Change! An institution is like an English middle-class audience going to see a play by George Bernard Shaw.

Change! An institution loves change and criticism. It adapts. It endures. It is hip to the warp and woof of the nation. It perns in the gyres, if necessary. For example, if the parents of America, realizing that their child has already learned all he needs from the school, namely how to write his name, read C-A-T and recite the Preamble, wish to send him out to be apprenticed or to a job in the garment district where the child can learn about the ways of the world and at the same time make a little bread for the family, the school incites the Institution of Congress to respond with a law about Universal Education, to wit, every parent must send his child to the School until age x. (Fuck you, says the school.) A hundred years later when things have changed—the kids want to work, the Union don't want them children, the nation would rather the kid went to Junior College—the school pretends that the Law was made to *make the children* go to school until age x.

Change! An old conservative general once rose to complain that the Youth had lost all respect for its Elders, that it had lost interest in the Games, that it had no Character. He did not think it would do well at another Thermopylae. He thought it had to do with the Schools. The Schools, he said, rob Youth of its Imagination, which is the only important Quality it has! In saying that, he implied that imagination and character were somehow associated, an idea which we find ludicrous.

Change! An institution can only be changed in the same way that a mountain is changed by highway engineers into a pile of dust. No institution, once invented, has ever ceased to exist. Nor has any institution ever changed, except according to the exigencies of time as above. Not changed, only adapted. Its fundamental purpose remains, namely to provide a place to do things where these things won't be done.

The School is not going to change. Criticism feeds its existence by giving it something to do, namely adapt. The school can eagerly join in criticism of its textbooks, for example, knowing that textbook publishers are preparing a billion Standard Anti-Textbooks which will show up in every class or Anti-Class some fall morning along with a neat mountain of justifying Anti-Pedagogy. The Anti-Texts will prevent learning just as well as the texts did, since they are to be used in the School. A large organized group of Anti-Parents will demand the texts back. Black Anti-Texts will have to appear. On the basis of the Anti-Texts, School administrators will get to spend their time making policy statements, getting hired, transferred and fired, and answering the telephone, proving that they still exist. . . .

So it is that institutions don't change, but people do. There is no law any more that people must go to church or pay attention to the church, and so many people don't, while others do. That is the best you can expect, and good enough. You can apparently get one institution to combat another, and it would be most useful to get rid of the law that all kids have to go to some school or other until age x or any other age. The public school is the closest thing we have in America to a national established church, Getting-An-Education the closest thing to God, and it should be possible to treat it and deal with it as the church has been treated and dealt with. This treatment has not really changed the existence of the one institution and will not harm the other, but it has allowed the growth of alternatives to it and that is what is wanted, even if some of those alternatives have become, and will become, institutions themselves.

One day I had to talk with the father of a kid in my class. The boy had been in constant trouble in school since the beginning. He would not do school work, and he refused the only alternative offered by the school, namely to do nothing. He was a bright, busy, active boy, and none of his actions fit what his teachers and the school wanted him to do, even though many of them (not all, by any means) were perfectly reasonable and even constructive in themselves. The father opened up very fiercely by informing me that he knew the boy needed discipline, that he was willing to do his part, followed with a list of punishments he was prepared to inflict and said I had his permission to be tough, to belt the kid around when he needed it, and so on. He was accepting a role which is pretty familiar to teachers —it is what they mean when they write *Parents Coopera-*

tive on cumulative folders—that of the parent who accepts the verdict of the school about his own child.

I told him that those punishments and that insight about needing discipline weren't anything new, were they? Hadn't he and the boy's teachers agreed every year, and hadn't they belted him and restricted him and kept him after school and isolated him in the classroom and forbade TV and made him sit two hours in his room each night to study and sent him to the office and paddled him and suspended him for seven years of schooldays and wasn't it clear that however wonderful and cooperative those plans were, that they hadn't worked?

Yes. He recalled that in kindergarten the boy spent an entire half year just sitting in the office, never being allowed to go to class or out to recess, because he was so bad. Then he said harshly, How can a kid that young be that bad? and (sitting there in a windbreaker and Levi's, having taken off from work to come up to cooperate with the school) burst into tears. It was a great relief to both of us. After a bit we were able to talk about our own schooldays and how we didn't always dig them nor the school us, and that we guessed we were both making it O.K. as adults no matter what the school might have thought of us, and then he said that he really thought the kid was a pretty good kid if a little wild and stubborn maybe, and how he even thought him a pretty smart kid and how good they got along together working or going out somewhere whenever he wasn't busy cooperating by not letting themselves go out or work together and by believing his boy to be stupid and bad.

He had believed that it was his duty as a parent to treat his own boy as if he didn't like him, even though he knew he did like him, because the Institution of the School knew what you were supposed to like and what you weren't, and didn't mind saying so.

That is what is meant by alternatives—namely, that

none is offered the ordinary parent or the kid in America who wants to remain somehow connected to the mainstream of American life, be responsible, be a citizen, not drop or bug out of it, but doesn't want to do so or can't do so at the expense of denying what he knows of himself. There was no way I could give one to either the boy or the father, but after our talk he began to accept a kind of alternative of the mind. If the boy got in minor trouble and had to stay after school or got bad grades, the father began to ignore it, and if he was called in by teachers to cooperate he didn't come and if the boy was suspended so that the father had to come to school in order to get the boy back in it (and if he didn't the boy could be sent to Juvi for truancy, remember), he began to tell them that the teachers didn't give the boy respect, they treated him badly, the vice-principal had it in for him. He always got around to asking them the same question—Why was it that a kindergarten kid ought to be kept in the office by himself all day long for half a year and how could a kid that little be so bad? It was a question that even the school was unable to answer and so the father was able to escape.

AT RANDOM

Some Indians, way up North, depended a lot on hunting elk for their livelihood. As long as they pursued elk along their regular hunting trails and found and killed elk, everything was O.K. But it happened every once in a while that the regular hunting trails failed to produce any elk at all. Instead of keeping on with their regular paths and starving, the Indians used magic to find the elk. The magic always worked. So some anthropologists went up to the Indians to find out what was what with that magic. Did magic work, they planned to discover, or was there some rational explanation, or was it just luck? The anthropologists sat around and watched the hunting and saw that there came a time when the elk ran out. When that happened the Indians took some elk bones out of a bag and cast them on the ground, and whichever way those bones pointed, they took off in that direction to hunt elk, and when they did that they came back with elk which they had found and killed. The magic worked. The bones were right. The anthropologists thought about it and finally realized that what was happening was that the elk, after being hunted along regular elk paths for some time, began to avoid those regular paths. The elk weren't a dumb class, and so they browsed along somewhere else because they were tired of getting interrupted and killed. When the bones were thrown, they pointed in random directions, and many of those directions were not going to be the same as the direction of the regular elk paths. So the elk were avoiding the regular paths and the bones were avoiding the regular paths and the Indians were avoiding the regular paths and so Indians and elk discovered each other on those random paths.

In order to convince themselves to avoid their normal habits, the Indians resorted to magic.

A famous rat psychologist has been trying for some years to conduct experiments which would show him how to raise the IQ of rats. One might wonder why he wanted to do that, considering that them rats would still be functional retardates no matter how smart they got. Nevertheless he persevered and set up lab situation after lab situation and educational environment after educational environment and the rats never seemed to get any smarter. Finally, and quite recently, he issued the statement that the only thing he could discover in ten years which made rats any smarter was "to allow them to roam at random in a spacious and variegated environment."

FLAX

Smiley's Bar and Bait Shop School was the only school I've ever seen in which the word *flax* was never mentioned. It was at Smiley's, by the way, that I had enrolled myself in a course called How to Survive in Your Native Land, a course invented by my friend Stan Persky in Vancouver. If it was true that I had little hope of finding out the answer, it was also true that I hoped that as long as I was enrolled I might continue to survive.

Flax is what school is all about. In my own old-fashioned geography books I went to various countries in the company of Bedouin and Greek and Turkish kids and the thing that most remains in my mind now about those imaginary kids is that they always grew flax. I myself put flax on my maps alongside corn and wheat and coal; I wrote down flax to answer questions about the products of countries. I never knew what flax was, but I knew that if I kept it in mind and wrote it down a lot and raised my hand and said it a lot, I would be making it.

Flax is actually a slender erect plant with a blue flower, the seeds of which are used to make linseed oil. Linen is made from the fiber of the stalk. I know this now because I've just looked it up in the dictionary. It is quite possible that it does grow in all those countries like the book and my test papers said. But beyond that, a thing like flax has an important place in a school. Unlike corn, say, which in L.A.

we could drive out and see in fields and buy from roadside stands and take home and eat, unlike wheat or cotton or potatoes, I think you could live your entire life in America and never see or even hear of flax, never know about it or need to know about it. Only in the school, only from the geography book, only from the teacher, could you learn about flax.

It showed you how smart the school was, for one thing. For another, it showed you what Learning was; corn, for example, wasn't Learning precisely because you *could* go out and see it in the fields and buy it from roadside stands and take it home and shuck it and eat it and your mother and father could tell you about how they used to grow corn and how to tell fresh corn and about names of corn like Country Gentleman, which my father preferred. You could do all that without ever going to school and so it didn't count. Finally, it showed the school who among the students was willing and able to keep flax in mind, to raise his hand and say it aloud, to write it down, and put its name on maps. So that in the cumulative records of each child the teacher could write down for the next teacher the information that

Child reads flax, writes down flax and says flax.	*Leader.*
Child sometimes remembers flax.	*Nice kid.*
Child can't remember flax.	*Child is black and/or deprived.*
Child digs flax, but inadvertently says "chili-dog" instead.	*Brain-damaged?*
Child don't dig flax a-tall.	*Reluctant learner.*

I think you could make up an entirely new Achievement Test, doing away with expensive and tedious vocabulary and graphs and reading comprehension, doing away with special pencils for IBM scoring and doing away with filling in all those rows. Just pass out a sheet with the word *flax* printed on it in big letters and count the seconds it took for a kid to raise his hand. That would tell you everything that an Achievement Test is designed to tell you.

Even in the Victory Gardens of 1942 America (where such an outlandish name as *Swiss Chard* became part of my experience, growing non-stop in the back yard), no one was ever known to grow flax, no one saw flax sprouting under the eucalyptus trees, no newspaper articles were written about anyone raising flax in the vacant lots, no war hero mentioned flax as contributing to the war effort. It remained, like Learning, a monopoly of the schools.

PART THREE

Richard sits under a tree to my left, eating his lunch. On a newspaper spread out in front of him lie small roots and grasses. Look, he says, I've got twelve varieties of edible plants! I taste one. It's rather bitter, something like parsley. He names a few of them for me, but doesn't remember the rest. How does he know they are edible then? They might be poison, Rich, I tell him. You might have poisoned me just now, letting me eat that unknown plant. That tickles him and he grins, but adds seriously that there is no danger. He just forgot the names. But they aren't poison. You can eat them all. That's why they are called edible plants, he lets me know.

CHAPTER IX

Rabbit Mountain

A while back at Spanish Main School, it came to pass that *Immature* was out of style, and *Non-Achiever* was in. That is what drives everyone mad at a school, even if no one is aware that they are being driven mad. Humans like history, like to know why things start and end, like to have reasons for it, and the school never has any reasons. It doesn't have any because, in fact, it doesn't have any. But at the same time the word Non-Achiever began to appear prominently on the course listings at S.F. State, the counselors referred to it all the time, the teachers began using it, you could see it on cum folders.

History *was* involved, of course. There had always been kids in schools who were smart—that is, the school said they were smart, they could be shown to have been smart at some time in their lives on the school's own tests—but who did not do well in school, who got bad grades and who were a pain in the ass. Naturally they annoyed the school. Smart kids who got good grades were O.K., and dumb kids who got bad grades were O.K., but smart kids who got bad grades weren't O.K., since the implication was that they were deliberately rejecting advantage, the whole notion of winning, the very virtue of the school. If they would only try! the school would tell the parents who came in to cooperate, and then the school and the parents would sit down together to try and figure out how to make the non-triers try. So non-achievers weren't anything new; why were they all of a sudden so fashionable? It was simply because now History had brought about the circumstance that there were just too damn many of them. If you have one healthy non-achiever in your class who bugs you while you try to explain stuff, you can deal with him—invite his parents in, isolate him or humiliate him or send him to the office or the counselors and you get the bonus of pointing out a good lesson to your class of slaves which is worth the trouble. But get three hard-line non-achievers in there and you ain't going to be able to teach Egypt the way you had in mind because they are going to see to it that you spend all your time dealing only with them personally until you end up just throwing them out—and when you throw them out (and if you throw out three kids at once you don't look good) then the counselors have to see them and their parents and spend all their time with them and the vice-principal has to see them and spend all his time and then the principal has to and if forty teachers begin to throw out three students each then the whole school is spending all its time with them cats and so they are winning—and even then it remains the school's unshakable conviction that all kids have to be in some *room* or another all the time, even after it is clear to the school that a lot of kids ain't going to make it in rooms, since there is no other place to be in schools except in rooms. So the teacher who just threw out three intolerables gets back three more from some other teacher who also just threw out three. The school has no other ideas, and the non-achievers go from room to room, teacher to teacher, stopping by in between at the counselors or the V.P. or at Juvi, getting suspended, having parents in, coming back and ending up back in them rooms where they have proven themselves to be intolerable.

So the notion came up to have a special group of non-achievers, to be treated differently, to be dealt with outside regular school. I think the idea came from the counselors; it was supported by a new vice-principal and even by the principal, who was the same man who had taken his kid out of CA back then because it was crazy. Everyone had plenty of good motives and we spent some time together going over them. But the real reason was that the school had defined another Special Group and wanted to get it away from the regular group so that the regular group could go on doing what was right without interference. The Administrative Group tried to get Spanish Main teachers to volunteer for the job. They offered inducements; the normal school rules would be suspended for the group, the teachers would get money to spend as they liked on materials, there would be consultants for in-service, they could design their own curriculum, and, most important, they would get two Free Periods during the day instead of just one. No one volunteered. Despite the inducements, no one wanted to work with the *Achievement Block*, which was what the group got called. It was a special group; special groups in a school are wrong and everyone knew it. But the school persevered. Its mind was made up, and so it just hired the next two teachers who applied to work the Achievement Block; another man, who had worked for years in the elementary school district and who now wanted some junior high experience so he could be an administrator, was hired too. So there we were, going to have some eighty kids in the fall, do whatever we thought was Right.

We would have four teachers, five rooms in a line together. We decided that two of the rooms would be called Resource Rooms, and the other three classrooms. We envisioned paradise; the teachers would announce that they were holding classes in the classrooms and the kids would be free to come if they wished. If not, they could stay in the resource rooms, where we teachers would trade off, where nothing would be obligatory. We spent most of our three grand for resource-room materials—paints and clay and plaster and phonos and tape recorders and TVs and Bell telephone kits and science kits and games and puzzles— toys, so that while the kids were doing nothing they'd have something to do. Our main notion was that the kids didn't have to come to class unless they wanted to, so therefore when they did they would be quiet, listen, pay attention, read and work and we would have these great classes. My own vanity was that we would demonstrate how to use the school (them instruments), and give the school a lesson in change. Since we would have the kids for almost all their school day—they would take only PE and one elective, usu- ally art or shop, in the regular school—we could really break away from its evil influence, really have school, really learn. I thought of it as a new beginning.

But in fact, the year proved to be the end of a road. The end of the road where people imagine (I imagined) that if you abdicate your total authority as an adult, then the kids will be free to choose what they want. The end of the road which says that if the adults do not make decisions about what to do, then the kids will be able to make them. The end of the road where we hoped that the students would tell us what to teach, how to teach. . . .

But the students were living in the same world as we were and lacked the same answers we lacked. They couldn't show us how to teach. Perhaps they hoped we would show them. Our classes went the same route as regu- lar classes. Kids appeared and smarted off and disrupted things and broke the science equipment and wouldn't work. When we said, If you don't like this class why don't you cut out? You don't have to be here you know! the kids answered with familiar refrains: There's Nothing To Do Back There, or Have You Seen Mike Hunt? It was the old lesson of CA which I (being a member of the dumb class) hadn't been able to learn.

What we were doing was offering the kids an intolerable

burden. We offered to make them decide what they would do. But they couldn't decide, because they had been in school for seven years and besides that knew from their lives-long all about the expectations of their parents and of the country of America. They were not free, no matter how often we said they were. No more were we. So that they *knew* they ought to go to Writing or Science or Social Studies when it was offered, because that was what you were supposed to do at school, not just goof around scattering the parts of the Bell telephone kit around the resource room while the teacher in charge pretended he thought it was a fine thing to do. But when they got there, to the classrooms, they knew too that the class had nothing to do with them, or they were afraid of it, or they would be involved in failure—that anyway it was alien to them and that therefore they were going to wreck it before it wrecked them.

I think the matter of grades is the best example. Now we were perfectly ready to abolish the whole idea of grades. No grades, we said loudly, and with perfect conviction, to the assembled group. We'd be free of them instruments of oppression. What? screamed the students, no grades? What kind of bullshit is that? They didn't want to go home first, second, third and fourth quarters without no report cards, trying to explain why they didn't have none and being called MR's. They wanted a grade in every subject, so as to prove that they were too taking them subjects, just like everyone else. Even an F was better than nothing. So we said How about we give everyone all A's? That was no good either; *if someone does work, and someone else don't, he ought to get a better grade!* Well then, we said, we'll let you guys make out your own grades; you can give yourself what you think you ought to get, what you want, what you need for whatever reason. We thought that would be satisfactory, but in fact it wasn't, because there we were, placing the burden back on the kids. So, determined that everyone would be free, we failed to solve anything that first year. We encouraged everyone to live a fantasy life, and paid the price for it in terms of a failure of solidarity. At the end of the year only Bill and I stayed on to try again; the other two quit—one to teach regular science and the other to take a job as vice-principal in another district.

The school was not done with the Achievement Block though, perhaps because there were still plenty of non-achievers around, perhaps just because it existed. It persisted, and hired the next two people who applied at the end of the year to work with AB. There we were—myself, Bill, and two women, Eileen and Arpine. No four people could have been less alike. Still, in the few days we had to talk together before school started we managed to talk about our school-within-a-school on entirely different terms. It still seems to me like some sort of miracle—just like when I was a kid fishing up on Hat Creek and my father would have a limit of trout and I wouldn't be catching a one and he'd come up and say, You ain't holding your mouth right! and fish with me for a while (having nothing else to do) and I'd start catching fish without ever knowing why. We began to talk about the kids we'd have, the kids we were supposed to teach, and try to figure out what they really needed to learn. What we typically had were kids whom the school tested in the first grade and found to be very bright, leaders, reading at fourth grade level, and so on, and whom the school tested again in the fourth grade and found they couldn't read or write, their IQ's were supposed to be about 85, their parents uncooperative. What had happened in the meantime? Had they been hit by a truck? Nothing appeared to have happened, except that they had been in school four years.

We considered these questions: How come some kids couldn't learn in school? How come some other kids could?

What was it that everyone in America could agree on that kids needed to learn? Why did they need to learn it, or did they? We came to no conclusion about the first questions; even though we all felt we knew all about it, all we could say was that some kids were defeated by school, diminished by it. On the latter questions we had no such problem. We had all lived in America, in the West, South, Middlewest and East. No one could doubt that the parents and uncles and big brothers of every class and of every conviction in America expected kids to learn to read and write. We thought that good enough for us, and why not? Were we in America or not? Why had public schools been started at all if not to see that kids learned to read and write who otherwise—if their parents couldn't read, or if their parents were too poor to hire a tutor or couldn't teach them themselves— might not be able to do it? As for why—they needed to learn it in order to become *equal* in the country. (What else were black parents talking about when they stormed school board meetings all over the place demanding that the schools *teach* their kids and throwing out white radical educators who, in their great disappointment with America, invaded the black community hoping the black kids would teach *them* something?)

Well. In conferences and meetings and panels these past couple of years I used to talk about our school-within-a-school a lot, and what I always wanted to explain and describe was the grand feeling of solidarity we had there, teachers and students alike, for two years. I never could do it, and I can't do it now. That I can't is a defeat, and a defeat I'm now swallowing without pleasure. You readers will have to do the best you can with it as I have.

The problem is that everything we decided was a platitude and therefore hardly sounds like revelation. Our decisions, our principles (and I've no idea any more which of them got stated openly, which we just found ourselves assuming tacitly) were these:

The school exists, and most everyone is going to go to it. It ain't going to change either, hardly. It is *absolutely irrelevant* to the lives of children, who don't need school at all, who want to have real work to do, who want revelation, adventure, who want to learn what the school is designed to prevent them from learning, who need to go up on mountains, dream, and invent their names. There is no way to make it relevant, because it simply ain't. Public schools are irrelevant; free schools (whether invented by parents or children) are irrelevant; in-between private progressive schools are irrelevant. All irrelevant and harmful, like much else in this country, to the lives of people. You cannot sit around waiting for the revolution and doing all kinds of contemptible shit in the meantime. You can't cop out by inventing anti-schools, since you are still just dealing with the fact of school, public school, in this country. You have to decide what you are going to do now, wherever you are.

Human beings are more alike than not. What we, as adult teachers, think is important, the children probably think too.

It is O.K. for the adults to decide what's going to go on. To be authoritarian. Decide, simply because no one else can do so. What other use is there for adults, if not to decide things for kids? But you have to decide in terms of what is really necessary, not just in terms of your own convenience. You can't just acquiesce to habit, you can't just accept the decisions of dead men, and call that deciding. Your decision has got to be in terms of what everyone in the community already knows—what The People know.

We decided that we would teach reading because the kids couldn't read well, and because you had to be able to read in America in order to be equal. We decided to teach only that, in order not to diffuse things, in order not to pretend that things were important that weren't. We knew that we, The People, didn't give a damn about Social Studies or DNA or the rest of the whole kit and caboodle of junior high academics. (If a particular kid really did, he could learn about it, now or anytime.) We decided that the whole purpose of the time the kids spent with us would be to teach them to read well, and that the morning would be spent in keeping or getting their minds in shape to do it. We decided. Our risk. Our responsibility. Our duty, then, to figure out, now that we'd decided, how to do it.

It was then, and not before, that I began to call our school, in my own head, *Rabbit Mountain*. Rabbit Mountain was a term invented by some poets in North Beach once upon a time. Sitting in the bar, they invented a college which they were going to have. The Rabbit and the Mountain make reference to important events in their lives, and tangentially even to my own, and of course the name was thought just right for a place which would have neither rabbits nor mountains. None of those details are important here. Rabbit Mountain never existed except in the minds of all of us, and the poets have argued since, or died. But the point, the *business* of Rabbit Mountain, was solidarity. So it endures.

Me, Arpine, Bill, Eileen, Students. The counselors— Vern, Dick and Suzanne. Bruce, the vice-principal; the principal, who disliked everything we did, but supported us on every side. Judy the field-trip expert. Student teachers. David came to work at Spanish Main after it was officially all over, yet he was immediately a member of Rabbit Mountain (The People's) School. We worked, man, worked in America, in full knowledge that them instruments of repression wasn't going to be turned into instruments of love. We were members of Rabbit Mountain and we had solidarity.

With this chapter I feel like John. Now John was a kid at Rabbit Mountain and agreed to work his ass off about reading, agreed to reject his fears and desire for perfection and just try to learn to read. In the end, he really learned. That is, he ended up in the eighth grade and by pure stubbornness he could read at what the school called sixth grade level. He started off at what the school called the first grade level. So he didn't make it to what the school would call a hero of education and the school wouldn't recommend him for Harvard, very likely. It was a defeat, in a way. It was a victory too. It depends on how you look at it. I know that with this chapter I'm in the eighth grade, and only able to operate at the sixth grade level. I can't explain how it happens that you can enter Rabbit Mountain School, even though I once thought that was what the whole book would be about. You have to hold your mouth right, that's all I can say.

CHAPTER X

Lesson Plan

Rabbit Mountain was a morning school. The kids stuck with us for the first four (academic) periods. Then they had lunch and afterwards followed (or didn't follow) the ordinary regimen of Spanish Main School—PE, electives, and so on. We supplied obligatory Reading and more or less obligatory Math; that is, you were supposed to go to Math, but on the other hand Bill would let you out on quite flimsy excuses. Arpine and Eileen wouldn't let you out of Reading unless you were dead. So any given period would find some fifteen to twenty kids in Math, six or seven each in the two Reading classes, and the rest with me. That rest varied in number as kids visited with fake passes from regular classes, as they transferred in and out of Rabbit Mountain or as their parents did it for them, or as they tried out regular classes in science or social studies or whatnot, or as they came back from trying them. We were, to say the least, rather fluid. For a student it meant that he came to school and went to Reading and then Math (or the reverse) and then to my room for two periods. Or he came to my room and then went to Reading and Math.

For people who want to talk about structure, this is a structure. I mention it because it is a way to deal with working in public schools which any group of teachers, working together, can manage. It left us free to do what we thought important. It left us free to make our own small reading classes, for instance, if we wanted to. It left us free to act on our other principle, namely to get out of Spanish Main —any one of us could get in our car with five or six kids and go somewhere any day without "permission" from Spanish Main, without filling out forms, *on impulse*. It freed us from the kind of self-indulgence where you blame the board or the administration or the country of America for your own lack of decision. In short, it freed us from the regular school structure of Noman while also liberating us from Mike Hunt and We Ain't Learning Nothing In Here. For kids are affected by structures too; I think it was clear to them at a glance that what we had in mind was necessary, reasonable and possible.

At Rabbit Mountain we offered to deal with what the school called a "problem," one which it had simultaneously invented, produced, and refused to face. From that offer we gained our liberty. When we decided to stop having an official Rabbit Mountain, it was we who decided it. We decided because we were tired of shoring up the system while it tried to sabotage us by referring openly to MR's and freaks and the dumb class. (What? We ain't going to have our experimental class no more? said the school. Our lives are not experimental, we answered coldly.) We were tired of laying the burden of being a special group onto the kids. We looked forward, with some malice, to turning loose our liberated non-achievers into eighth grade classrooms. We demanded regular classes and knew we would be able to work, to work together, in the same way. We did. We worked together, we had solidarity, we did what we had to for Noman, we did what we thought was important, we did what we thought was important to the community, and for the rest we did as we damn pleased.

CHAPTER XI

The Pony Express of the Silver Screen

When Red Silver came into the room you knew about it, in the same way you would know about it if a whirlwind came in. Everything was suddenly rearranged, as whirlwinds put cars on top of telephone poles or chicken coops in the basement. The desks were moved, windows opened if they were closed (or closed if they had been open), the radio turned either on or off, the back of the TV unscrewed and the image either improved or destroyed . . . he rushed through the room ringing all the changes, touching everything, and everything he touched got changed. Two minutes after he came in another kid might go over to a cabinet to get some paint and the cabinet door would fall off, perhaps mashing the kid's toe, for Red had just removed the pegs which held the hinges. Or he might suddenly be there with long nails from the shop, slipping them into those hinges on those doors from which he had slipped the pegs some other day. If you went to get a drink, the water fountain spurted out a stream six feet high and got everyone wet—or it barely squeezed out a tiny miserable trickle. Red Silver was there in either case with a mop or a wrench, doing the right thing and also doing the wrong thing, but mainly *doing*. Change! was his motto. However things were, do something to them, make them different, allow nothing to be the way it was. Red Silver was the same kid whose old man came in to see me before; the same kid

134

who had spent the second half of his kindergarten year sitting alone in the office, not being allowed to go to class or to recess because he was so bad.

I was always trying to figure out things for Red to do besides take my room apart and put it back together again. It shouldn't have been so difficult. Red was willing and eager to do anything that "helped the school" (although the school was less than eager to do things which "helped" him), that is, anything that was real work, that accomplished something, that you could tell the difference in things when the work was done. He would help the janitor move chairs, swab floors, paint, fix broken tables. He would fix projectors, mess with TV's, help with addressing mail-out letters to parents, he would have cut the grass, fixed faucets, unclogged sinks (he clogged ours often with paste or clay in order to be able to take it apart and unclog it)—but it's surprising how little of that kind of stuff there is for kids to do in a school. He didn't do "work"—that is, school work—precisely because it didn't make any difference to anything if the school work was done or not. For after it was done, either the teacher or the kid or the kid's parents (if the work got an A and thus ever got to the parents) threw it away in the wastebasket, and nothing was changed at all by it. Whether it was done or not made no difference to the world at large, except to the wastebasket and, of course, to your grade, the latter being an item long past concern to Red.

Red could have spent his time fixing up all the things there were to fix in all the rooms of the school—all the things the teachers were always complaining about—faucets, windows, desks (raised or lowered to fit kids), blackout curtains (he was an accomplished sewer), pencil sharpeners, and so on, but there was no way for a kid to roam around the school checking all the rooms for fixable items. The teachers would object to his presence, and after all their kids would be saying, Why can't we fix it? Besides, there were Maintenance Engineers who came down in trucks two months after they were called and there was a man to cut the grass who always ran the power mower past your window during the most important part of Egypt lesson and there were official Pore Kids already hired to swab the lunchroom floor for their "free" lunches.

But once, during a teachers' meeting, in a lull after some urgent talk about how to combat gum and tardiness and running-in-the-halls, came the notion that there ought to be a group of kids who could be counted on to run the projectors when teachers wanted to show movies in their rooms. Now when I was a kid, there was always a Silver Screen Club. The kids in the Silver Screen set up projectors and ran off classroom movies whenever teachers wanted them run off. They had time off from class one period a day to be free to take the projectors and the films wherever they ought to be taken, set up and show the film, rewind and take everything back where it came from. If there was no film to be shown on a certain period, they could spend their time fixing the projectors or splicing broken films or just goofing off in the Silver Screen room, a storage room where all that stuff was kept. Naturally they were all officially dumb kids and everyone knew it; who else could be allowed to miss Egypt once or twice or more each week except kids who were too dumb to learn about Egypt anyway?

Nevertheless, this idea had never come up in our school. The teachers all individualistically showed their own films, counted on themselves to run them off, signed up for and got their own projectors. The result was almost always the same; the film broke, the projectors didn't work, the teachers didn't know how to rewind the film, the kids assigned by the teachers to show the film didn't know how and wound up with *The Red-Winged Blackbird* or the *Aswan Dam* all over the floor or upside down and backwards, the sound wouldn't go or the kids fucked around with it, making it scream out one moment, whisper the next—the teachers, all of whom had, by California law, taken Audio-Visual in teachers colleges so they would know all about projectors and tape recorders and film strips and tachistoscopes, and so on, standing there helpless with the film spewing out of some odd hole in the projector while the kids yelled and laughed, finally calling the principal, who did know all about projectors and who would fix the trouble—except that then it was too late and there wasn't time to show the film and the teacher would be left with fifteen minutes of the class period with Nothing To Do, having scheduled the movie for that day's lesson plan—and then at the next teachers' meeting the principal could be counted on to deliver a lecture about projectors and offer to give a course (after school) to teachers and kids, which no one wanted to take because it was after school.

Well, this notion was brought up as if it were revolutionary, discussed pro and con (them kids would have to miss Egypt) and not decided like most everything else and dropped in favor of sticking to regulations about gum, which were also not decided. But I thought of Red and the very next day approached him with this idea—how about he got together three or four other kids and showed them all about projectors and set up a sign-up sheet for teachers, when they wanted what movie shown in what room, and delivered film and operator at the right time and right place for a guaranteed showing?

Before I'd even finished explaining all about it, Red had picked three other kids and hustled them out the door and off they went. He was, as I said, quick. I heard about this first phase later on that day from the librarian, whose job it was to keep and issue audio-visual equipment. What's going on? she started off by saying, and then went on to tell me that Red and three other kids had burst into the library, demanded the keys to the storage room, said I authorized it, confiscated the A-V sign-up book—it seemed like he already knew all about it, she said, he just hopped into my back room and took it out of a drawer, now how did he know that?—and took off. She wasn't upset. Quite the contrary: if Red wanted to take care of the A-V stuff, or if anyone wanted to take care of it, she was happy to let it go. It was a pain in the neck, she said. She knew Red anyway, having forbidden him the library quite a number of times because of the fact that after he left, somehow, the first kid to take a book from some particular shelf found that whole shelf falling down on his toe because Red had removed the pegs which held it in place. Naturally, she said, I don't know he did it because I never saw him do it, but it occurred to me that he might have after he kept showing up each time the shelf fell down, saying I hear you got a bad shelf, I'll fix it for you—and by some miracle of coincidence just happened to have some of those pegs in his pocket. Well, she said, maybe he just always carried those pegs around in case some shelf happened to fall down . . . you could see she liked Red (and so I liked her) and appreciated his spirit, say, even if she didn't propose to have that spirit around in her library all the time.

The second phase was that I began to hear from other teachers about Red bringing around the sign-up sheet and *browbeating* (that was one teacher's term) them into signing up in advance for the projectors and the films. It meant that they had to decide, on occasion, two or three days in advance, when they wanted to show a certain film that they had ordered. That was what they were supposed to do anyway, and of course what they wrote the obligatory weekly lesson plans for, so they would know what they were going to do for the week, each day, period and so on, and so Red was really only forcing them into obeying regulations. But since most of their lesson plans were fantasy anyway, and since many of them wanted to show the films at the last moment when it appeared they had nothing else to do, some objected. They weren't having some kid tell them when they could show a film. They were, though, as it turned out, for Red already knew that all the films came in from the county office at about ten o'clock Wednesday, and confiscated them all, scheduled them (according to teachers' wishes if they signed up, according to his own if they didn't) and planned to show them then, in that room, regardless. I think Red saw the rooms and periods and courses and films as parts in the inside of a TV set that didn't work right, figured these parts out logically (and quickly) according to their relationships to each other and how they ought therefore to work, and made plans to fix them.

On Monday the plan started out. I wasn't present. Red and the other kids had been holed up in the closetlike room where the equipment was kept for the last two days. Red was figuring out the schedules (and rearranging the room) and the other kids were smoking, that was how I figured it. Occasionally one of them would show up in my room to say they were here—i.e., not cutting—and rush back with every show of important affairs going on. All the other kids asked Where are they going? What are they doing? Why can't we be doing that?

The three other boys were only flunkies during the planning phase. They didn't get to figure out the schedule. They got to smoke. Their virtue was that they knew very well how to run the projectors and how to fix them if minor things went wrong. Red had a supply of extra bulbs—those little bulbs which light up when the sound is working, and if they go out the sound don't work, those bulbs, costing about five dollars apiece—and they got to keep those in their pockets.

But they were the Riders. If you can imagine Red sitting

there in his closet in St. Joseph, Missouri (not far from Abilene, not far from Fort Kearney and Massacre Canyon), on a Monday morning at eight-fifteen giving the signal, and the Riders fire off on their fresh ponies heading for North Platte, Julesburg, Ogallala, Fort Laramie, or Rooms 4, 25, 32, shoving those projectors already loaded with twenty-minute films about *The Nile* or *The Industrial Revolution* or *A Medieval Village*, running at full tilt down the halls, the casters clattering, arriving at the rooms (forts) and issuing orders to pull the curtains, pull down the wall maps turned backwards to serve as screens, out with the lights and Ta-Ta! there goes the film. It goes. The Riders observe it with critical eyes. They adjust sound and focus constantly. It's over. They rush out, not rewinding, clamp on fresh film, leap to horse and down the corridors again to another room, the next film, to the cheering of crowds. They have copies of their schedules in hand, prepared by Red, who has been accused of not being able to write. They follow the charts along the Platte, past the junction of the Rio Grande, heading for South Pass and Ogden, and by noon they have each shown eight films, two twenty-minute films in each forty-five-minute period, allowing the teachers almost no time for taking roll, admonishing tardy kids, motivating the class to take note of the film, making threats about future grades, laying down rules for film watching or note taking. Teachers, Red imagines, can do that after they leave or before they come, but when they get there, Manuel and Mike and Danny, the Riders, have them fresh horses ready, saddled and bridled, sling on the mail pouches, fire up the film, thirty seconds only for the sound to warm up and away! At noon it is time for lunch, and sixth period, after lunch, it is time for the important work of rewinding the films and setting out tomorrow's schedule, time for a smoke, time to miss seventh period too, but not time to miss eighth, which is PE, which everyone hates worst of all and which no one dares miss.

Monday in the teachers' room, everyone is ecstatic. Imagine mail from New York in only fifteen days! Civilization and Progress wherever you look. How pleased they all are that Your Kids (meaning mine) can Organize Themselves for Useful Service! Manifest Destiny and All Is Not Lost. It is an argument for Technical High Schools—These Kids can Work with their Hands, give them some Responsibility, and so on.

By Tuesday afternoon things slowed down. There were few films to show that morning. Nevertheless those that were shown followed the same wild rush; Red's schedule abhorred wasted time. Wednesday new films came in, were scheduled and took off early Thursday morning for Salt Lake City, racing down the halls, bursting into rooms, cutting short opening formalities, rushing out with the projectors and films, running down the trails again . . . that afternoon the opening glow was over and I began to hear complaints. These complaints took on an odd, negative, indirect flavor.

No, they weren't rude. Polite in fact. Just . . . what? *Firm*, seemed to be it. Everything had to stop in the room when the Riders arrived to show film. I know they have a schedule to meet, but . . . No, nothing went wrong, in fact it ran beautifully and there was none of that horrible delay while we have to fix the machine or adjust the film and the kids get out of hand, and yes, it's really nice having someone competent to show it and nice that it arrives right on time. But . . . But what? Well, my kids keep asking why they can't run the film themselves (even though they've been running it for some time and still goof it up each time, I wonder if they do that on purpose?) and after they leave I have to explain why they are doing it and getting out of class and all and why my kids can't and it takes up almost as much time as when we ran it ourselves and . . . well, all of a sudden in comes this damn Danny who I had last year and almost drove me crazy and never would do any work at all even though I called his parents about every day —they never would come in to cooperate neither—and tells me it's time to show the film and I didn't expect it and told him we weren't ready and he tells me that it's time to show the film, look at the schedule . . . why didn't you sign up when you wanted the film? well, I wasn't sure when it would fit in, it depended on how much we got done, it's necessary to create the background for the movie, otherwise . . . then too, all that running in the halls just when we were trying to get the kids to Stop Running In The Halls. . . .

Thursday afternoon some kid in some class came up and *messed with the projector* just before Mike got ready to switch it on and he told the kid to beat it and the kid refused and Mike told that teacher to get her kid away from the projector and the teacher blew it and said it was her class and perhaps he ought to let someone else help with the projector, *after all it didn't belong to him,* and all the other kids in the class yelled *Yeah it don't belong to you, you know!* and after that got settled and the film was over the same kid wanted to rewind it and Mike refused of course but the teacher said Let him do it! adding, You can show him how, he needs to learn how, which was exactly what Red had forbidden Mike and Danny and Manuel to do since if everyone really learned, their monopoly would be finished, but the teacher made him do it anyway, and he reported to Red and Red called all the Riders back, took all the films back to the office, stored the machines (not sabotaging any, he told me), took the key back to the librarian, threw away the schedule, and said they quit.

Halfway to Sacramento Red Silver just reined in, got off his horse, and took a taxi home.

He wasn't depressed. It had been fun, he said, starting it off, but he wasn't all that eager to just sit there in St. Joe doing the same schedule over and over again. Mike and

Danny and Manuel were bugged though, because they had to return to classes and didn't get to do all that smoking or all that running down the halls lickety-split nor have those responsible executive positions. They made a stab at organizing it themselves, but argued so much about who ought to start doing what that they very soon gave it up. The school just went along as if nothing had happened, the principal was soon heard again on the subject of the A-V equipment, its use and misuse . . . but no teachers ever said anything to me about it, one way or the other.

CHAPTER XII

Reading in Your Native Land

A while back I got a letter from Corporal Ron Schmidt. Schmidt had discovered that there were grown men around who really couldn't read and that in fact some were in the Army and some even in his own unit right there in Vietnam. It bugged him—how could a man not be able to read? He made up his mind to teach this guy named Roy Washington. There didn't seem to be any primers around, so he and Washington started learning to read from an old paperback copy of *Cool Hand Luke*. Later on Schmidt got some grade-school reading material from his mother, who was a teacher back home.

So after a bit, Schmidt wrote, Washington was reading some and he went around telling everybody about how he could *read,* and Schmidt used to see him reading away at the notices on the unit bulletin boards, reading training manuals, shipping labels and signs. It reminded me of old Harvey, and like Harvey and me, Schmidt and Washington were pretty pleased with themselves and planning ahead.

The only trouble was that shortly after that Washington got killed in Vietnam. *Zapped* the letter put it. "I got over Roy getting it [Schmidt wrote me], but not the fact that he could not read. That's a real kick in the head; here a man dies and all that I worry about is he couldn't read before I met him."

Chapter XIII

How Teachers Learn

So in the beginning of the school year, 1968, we agreed to really teach reading. In the days before school started we—Eileen, Arpine and I—pooled our combined vast knowledge on that subject. We figured it would be considerable, and indeed it ought to have been considerable. Arpine had never taught before, but she'd just come from courses in reading and children's lit with at least one first-class person at S.F. State; Eileen had already taught reading at a number of different places; I was (since my book came out) a big-shot educator who appeared on TV and was asked to give talks on what was wrong with the schools.

In fact, it soon became clear to us that we didn't know a damn thing for sure. I mean, Eileen knew how to go in there and Teach Reading; she'd done it before and hadn't got killed or anything and she could do it again. Arpine knew a lot of books kids were supposed to like, had heard a lot about motivation, and had read Sylvia Ashton Warner. All I really had in my head, as it turned out, was that if you got a lot of books around and didn't do anything else, the kids would end up reading them. I also knew that that wasn't true. It might be true in some other situation (like in my head or in someone's else's head) but it wasn't true in this particular seventh and eighth grade school which happened to be where we were. One or two kids would read them, one or two kids would write Fuck in them, one or two kids would throw them, and the rest of the kids would ignore them; that was what would happen right here.

After a couple of days and after a hundred coffees and a thousand cigarettes and a million words and quite a few lunchtime beers we were able to agree that we didn't know nothing. With that we all (I think) quite happily knocked it off, went home for the weekend and were ready to start.

Long after that I was at a conference with Herb Kohl, among others, and there, amidst young black and chicano kids denouncing the assembled teachers as rascists and amidst calls of motherfucker and chickenshit and amidst guitars and grass and wine and people sleeping together in the grass in their sleeping bags . . . amidst all this and other cheerful bullshit (most of it arranged by Herb) down by Santa Cruz I heard Herb calmly telling a large group of teachers that they ought to be serious about their work. That if they taught reading they ought to go out and get and read everything written on the subject of reading and teaching reading; everything—good, bad, and indifferent, read it, talk about it to each other, that they ought to interiorize all these methods and theories and practicums and notions, paying no attention to the fact that, say, Max Rafferty or John Holt liked or denounced this or that, that they ought to get all the materials possible of all possible sorts, all of this while they were teaching reading classes, and that then as they taught they would have all this in their heads and at the same time be developing their own styles of how to teach, so that all this stuff would be ready to hand, to fit in whenever it in fact did fit in. That arguing about generalities about "look-say" or "phonics" was silly; that the details of either general method were useful or not depending on what shape the kid or kids were in and what they needed. That, in short, what they needed to do was get serious, by which he meant learn everything they could

146

about what they were supposed to be doing, and then decide for themselves how they themselves were going to go about it, and decide it again every day according to what they could see was going on in their classes.

What that meant was something I understood very well, I think, but somehow to hear it in the midst of all those groovy goings-on was marvelous. It was like the calm, philosophic eye of the hurricane. I think it was the last thing anyone expected to hear that day, myself included. The teachers were prepared to hear themselves denounced by the kids in familiar terms—racist, fascist, pig, lackey, co-conspirator of capitalist, totalitarian, colonialist, imperialist, and so on; and to either protest indignantly, denying the indictment, or cry to themselves, accepting it. They were prepared to hear about freedom and creativity; they were prepared to hear about openness and alternatives. They also hoped, on occasion, to get some "guidelines" (for which read lesson plans) on *how to be* open and creative and free and understanding and non-fascist, non-pig and so on.

It put me back right into the first year of the Achievement Block, before it became Rabbit Mountain. Then I'd figured to be open and creative and anti-imperialist, etc., of course. But what it all really amounted to was this: I had hoped the kids would show me how to teach. After they did so, I would tell everyone else. But by the end of that year, it was clear the kids didn't know either. Perhaps they'd been hoping all along that I would tell them. We were both waiting around. Together, we amounted to zero. So there, the next year, Arpine and Eileen and I were embarking upon the revolutionary idea that teachers ought to know something about what they were doing. And there was Herb, yet another year and a half later, allowing as how that was so. It amounted to this: *no eye, no hurricane.*

147

We opened up with testing the kids, determined to try everything once and for all. We had a perfect situation for doing so, for grouping them on the basis of the tests, and for seeing what difference it made, since we were able to test them all individually and handle them in small groups afterwards. We gave an Oral Reading Test, determining from it not only something called Grade Level in reading, but also fitting them into categories according to what kinds of reading difficulties they might be having—i.e., they read well but didn't comprehend, or the reverse; they misread simple words, or inserted words which weren't there, according to context; they had troubles with certain sounds, diphthongs, consonants . . . we had a checklist of this kind of stuff and followed it through. After a couple of weeks of this we had our eight groups of seven to eight kids apiece, both Arpine and Eileen teaching four periods of reading each, each group about as rightly and rationally and scientifically placed according to grade level and kind of reading problem as you could imagine, short of only having one kid in each group. At the same time we were getting these books out of the library, and consulting with the Special Reading teacher about what she'd done with many of the same kids last year and getting the district language consultant down with her advice and help with materials and methods, and interviewing salesmen who called on us with this and that workbook, machine, book, classroom magazine or newspaper, drill system, skill developer . . . we read those pamphlets and books that no one ever looks at, things like *Guidelines to Reading, Reading Development in the Elementary Child, Motivating Reading for the Underachieving Student, The Case for Reading,* the kinds of books held in state college and district education libraries with three authors (the titles of the above are all made up, since who can ever remember them?) and we read Holt and Warner again and we read Tolstoi and I hauled out Bloomfield's marvelous neglected book and we would have read *Reading, Existence and the Absurd, The Zen Method of Reading Improvement,* or *Up Against the Wall Reading Teacher!* if we could have found them. We had a bit of money for ordering stuff, and the librarian helped us go through catalogues and the principal expedited our orders and books came in and newspapers and *Scope* magazine and *Mad* magazine and *Popular Mechanics* came in and *Teen-Age Tales* came in . . . and after six or seven weeks, or maybe more or maybe less—none of us would know that now, I'm certain—we had to admit that everyone had been extremely cooperative and helpful and that we ourselves had been the same and that we had done about all we could think of to do. So in our two prep periods together, we began to try and think about everything we'd done and gotten and how it was working and what it was all about, as far as we were concerned, right now.

First of all we noticed a number of peculiar things about the testing. We noticed first of all that on the individual oral test the kids came out much lower than they did on the school-wide group test they'd been given, part of the Iowa Achievement thing. Well, that was no doubt because guessing didn't help and being test-wise didn't help, and cheating was almost impossible. But we also noticed that quite a few kids in our reading classes who the test said were reading at third or fourth grade level were in fact reading very complicated books, carried these books around in their pockets, talked about them—books like *Black Like Me,* or an abridged version of Trevor-Roper's books about the Nazis, or a history of World War II battles. It was clear they could read those books. We also remembered the results of giving each other the Oral Reading Test. That test consists of a sheet with paragraphs printed on it, beginning very easy and going up to rather difficult. Each paragraph has a few questions to be asked orally of the student after he reads it. You listen to the kid read and mark down notations of the kinds of errors he makes, then you ask him the questions about what he reads and see if he understood it. When he makes more than five errors (I think it is) on any one paragraph he is to stop, and you figure out from that his reading grade level, look at his kinds of errors and presto! he's placed.

Well, we remembered that we'd all made mistakes on the comprehension part. I made a mistake answering a question at the third grade level and two more further on. The third grade paragraph was something about a family in the park having a picnic; the mother and the father were watching the kids play and laying out the food. What are the parents doing? asked the Test. Watching the kids play, I told the Test. Wrong! said the Test, they are laying out the food! I came out to be reading at the seventh grade level.

We also felt that the test was extremely vulnerable to the conscious or unconscious influence of the test giver upon the results; that if the test giver's job or reputation depended on the kids' improvement, or if she just really wanted them to improve, it was pretty damn likely that they would improve on the test. It was also open to standard objections to testing; it told the kid, via the tester's voice, that it didn't care about speed, that the kid wasn't to worry about that and should take his time. At the same time the kid could see that the tester was timing him. It told the kid not to worry about mistakes but just do the best he could, but naturally the kid could see the tester making little marks as he was reading. Finally Arpine and Eileen knew by this time that the careful grouping, which had in fact caused us all a lot of trouble and time arranging schedules, was a complete failure in terms of its goal, leaving aside whether or not the goal was a good idea in the first place. With all, it was now clear that among say eight kids all supposed to be reading at 4.5–4.8 reading level, making errors A, B and D (but not C), there were in fact eight kids some of whom were reading all kinds of stuff, some who would only read the newspaper, some who would only read *Mad* magazine (or look at it anyway) and some who wouldn't read anything at all. Thus the test could only mean something if you never looked at the kids themselves. Once you did, you had to abandon it. It was a good lesson and I recommend it.

I suppose the point has been made—try to get hold of everything at all relevant to what you are going to do and see what's there. It sounds obvious, but in my experience few teachers do it, or even consider it. In fact, almost none of these books and ideas and materials contained anything useful at all and we speedily threw them away and forgot almost all of it. What remained of this investigation were odd bits of knowledge (clues to reading problems, occasional things to try with a kid who didn't seem to be getting anywhere) which could be usefully pulled out anytime, most of which we could have remembered ourselves from our own childhood, I think . . . but it was the investigation that was important to us all, for two reasons. First, we knew we had *done* all that bullshit—we *knew* that the standard methodologies of "teaching reading" were pitifully irrelevant at best to that goal. Second, the investigation itself was a basis for our own solidarity. *We* were deciding to read all that stuff, *we* were deciding to figure out (if we could) what we were doing, *we* decided to abandon most of what we came across and that was important in a place where the people most directly concerned with children decide almost nothing about what they are going to do with them.

In the end—but that's wrong; there was never any end to it, for in our new situations now we still seek each other out to talk about kids and what's happening with so-and-so and who liked this book and . . . so, as the year went on we came to our own simple conclusions which were not anything strikingly original, to say the least, which we came to imagine everyone knew, which had been stated in many ways by people a long time ago and were being said by people right now, but which were ours, and we could state them (and more important feel right with them) and put them to use and *do* them, and that not in a free school or anything else but in a goddamn public American junior high right here and now.

Briefly, we just knew it was absurd that a normal O.K. American kid of any class or kind of twelve years old shouldn't be able to read. Why was it? Because reading is not difficult. Anyone can do it. It is an activity which no one seems to be able to explain but which everyone can do if given a chance. It is simple for people to do. If you know enough to tie your shoe and come in out of the rain, you can do it.

If you can't do it, you must have been prevented from doing it. Most likely what prevented you was teaching. For one thing, if you have to get taught the same "skills" for seven years over and over again, you probably get the notion that it is very difficult indeed. But more important, the "skill" involved in reading is at once very simple and quite mysterious. Once you can look at C-A-T and get the notion that it is a clue to a certain sound, and moreover that very sound which you already know means that particular animal, then you can read, and that is certainly quite simple, even if the ability of humans to do this is opaque. What you probably need to do then is to read a lot and thereby get better at it, and very likely that's what you will do, again, if no one stops you. What stops you is people teaching you skills and calling those skills "reading," which they are not, and giving you no time to actually read in the school without interruption.

That, basically, seemed what was wrong with everything we had investigated. With the tests, with the "methods," with the class structures, with the teacher's determination to teach . . . that no one had ever had much time in school to just read the damn books. They were always practicing up to read, and the practice itself was so unnecessary, or so difficult, or so boring you were likely to figure that the task you were practicing for must combine those qualities and so reject it or be afraid of it.

I think of a normal reading class, as it was when I was in school, as it is in my own school, as it is in most schools. What goes on? The bell rings. Roll taking, admin tasks, demands for order. Speeches from the teacher, motivating the kids to read. Perhaps fifteen minutes' worth of that. Then an assignment or a few assignments, figuring that the teacher has "grouped" the kids. The kids get out the reading textbooks. Five minutes more to find the book, find the page, complain about the dumb story and ask about do we have to read this? About the time the kids are looking at the title or reading the first paragraph (or not-doing either) out comes the ditto sheet containing the real assignment—questions on the reading. Who has red hair? Why didn't the man stop after he ran over the puppy? Why did the kid ride the rocking horse? Give your opinion. Summarize the action. Who are your favorite characters? What would you have done? Or the teacher writes the questions on the board (if she has read the story herself) or tells the kids which questions to do out of the back of the book. Either way, there are twenty minutes left in the reading period and all the kids immediately stop reading the story because they know that what is important to the teacher is that they answer them questions. Naturally the teacher gives out the questions so she can check up on who read the story and who didn't; everyone then forgets that it is these same questions which have just prevented everyone from reading the story. You watch the kids stop reading and start flipping through the pages looking for the answers to the questions. Find the word *red* and near it the word *Johnny* and there you have the answer to question I; *Johnny* has red hair.

Take a look at the Oral Reading Test. Take a look at the textbook methods for Teaching Reading. Look at the books themselves. None of it is about people reading books or newspapers or magazines, but instead about Reading Comprehension. So you have short paragraphs, beginning out of nowhere and ending in the middle of nowhere, and the only reason you would ever look at the paragraph is if you have to answer the questions. The Reading Test resembles nothing else called a book; no one would look at it and think it something to read. It is full of short bursts of print, surrounded by arrows and staccato headlines adjuring you Read! Think About! Widen Your Interest! A New You! and full of red-outlined boxes with print inside them and color photos and questions about every bloody thing. Does that look like a book which you might find on a shelf or in the drugstore and look through or decide to take or read? So that even if this piece of shit does contain "The Rocking Horse Winner" or a thousand stories you might actually like, you ain't going to read it. Or if you are just reading everything in sight like quite a few kids, then in your determination to actually read the story just as if you were *reading* something, you won't have time for the questions, which will by the way seem even more stupefying if you've read the story and liked it, and you find yourself getting a bad grade in Reading, precisely because you've been reading.

There you are. All this has been, and is being said—I say it again, not because I think no one will know it if I don't, but because it belongs to the business of this chapter, which is really not about reading, but about the anthropology and politics of a school.

Somewhere along the way we knew that what we knew about how to teach reading was what our memories could have told us, what we always knew, and that was that reading is best taught by somebody who can already read and who knows and likes the kid—the kid's mother or father or uncle or tutor or teacher—sitting down with the kid with a book and reading to the kid and listening to the kid read and pointing out things about sounds and words as they go along. That in the past everyone had known how to do that as part of being a parent or an uncle or an older brother and so everyone still knew, if they just wanted to remember it. That the "problem" of reading was simultaneously caused and invented by schools and their insistence on teaching "classes" and "groups"—and by the resulting quest of teachers to find ways to "teach," i.e., ways to standardize and to measure. That there simply is no way to measure what is crucial about reading a book—namely whether or not the kid liked the book, whether he imagined himself involved in the adventures of Jim Hawkins, whether or not he was changed by it. "This should change your life," says Rilke. Who can measure that? And yet it is all that counts.

So we were caught curiously in the middle. We were in a school which hoped to measure and standardize everything, and in which the kids themselves knew that everything important got grades, could be measured and was standardized. No one was getting A's for being moved to tears when John Silver took off for the last time in the longboat. What we had to do was recreate the way of teaching reading which existed before schools were invented, and use it in the school itself. Reading not as a skill (to be measured), but as an art (that which changes). Nothing could have been simpler. Get a lot of books in the room, tell the kids to bring their own, go around during the period and sit with each kid for a couple of minutes and let him read a bit to you, read some to him perhaps, talk to him about the book and what's going on in it, point out (perhaps) this and that word, sound, and then let him go on and read it while you go over to the next one. Say over and over again—in the classroom, in the teachers' room, in your sleep perhaps—A good reading class is when the kids come in with their books, sit down and read them, and don't stop until the bell rings. Resist the urge to talk and discuss, resist the urge to watch the kids all happily working in the workbooks and programmed materials, resist the urge to motivate and to teach something to everyone at the same time, resist the urge to measure one person against another or everyone against any standard; resist every day all the apparatus of the school which was created in order to enable you to *manage* and *evaluate* a group, since it is just that management which destroyed the kids you have in your class.

You must examine your authority for what it is, and abandon that part of it which is official, board-appointed, credentialed and dead. Then you must accept the natural authority you have as an adult, belonging to a community of adults which includes the kid's parents and relatives, all of whom expect the kid to get a "good education"—by which they mean he becomes literate and equal, not that he becomes a non-reading intellectual. Your assumption must be that being literate is a human facility, and everyone can do it, and that you teach *one person at a time* how to do it if he needs to know. Then you are a teacher, instead of a manager; not before.

So it was simple, and tough. Everyone always wonders if such a way really can work (as if management does). I propose telling you flat that it does. It works if you have eight hard-line non-achievers, as our reading classes at Rabbit Mountain had; it works if you have thirty-five "regulars," as I have now. It works in the school terms—i.e., according to the standardized tests—if anyone gives a damn. It works in my terms. It works not by method but by virtue of the measure of trust between you and the student, who is very likely someone who has learned in school to avoid trust and must learn through you to accept it, as you have to learn it through him. Naturally that is tough and may indeed take most of the year. Learning to read is not tough; accepting the possibility of learning may be so for both of you. I remember students of Rabbit Mountain who were rather disappointed when they finally got it through their heads what all the fuss was about—having battled themselves for so long about reading, they wanted it, when they came to face it, to be a more heroic task.

It worked. I knew it worked because by the end of the first year I stopped hearing all those complaints about reading class. I stopped hearing kids ask me for passes to get out of Reading, to go here and there on some important errand which had to be done during reading period. I stopped hearing about how awful Eileen was and how mean Arpine was. I even heard the dreadful admission that someone was looking forward to going to Reading, looking forward to reading their book, looking forward to a little peace and quiet where they could be left alone and *do what they wanted*.

School began that next fall as if it had never stopped. We just kept on going. We were pleased with ourselves. The new kids came in and took to reading right away; they knew they had troubles in reading, they admitted it and they knew we were going to show them how to get over those problems and they wanted to and we could do it—ah, it was all clear and right. We tested no one. We arranged groups just by taking the first eight on our list and so on down the line. We laid off the workbooks and skill books and all that and invited the kids to pick up on the books and papers and magazines in the room, to take any part of them, like a crap game. Off we went.

I say we. Naturally I wasn't doing any of this. No more was Bill. I was seeing the kids in my two groups of thirty or so two hours a day. Bill had them all for math in four groups. I'd gotten together a lot of new math stuff and had some idea about Bill using it; I gave it to him, but he wasn't excited. He thought the kids needed to just do the regular school math, which most of them found simple enough. To just do it in a regular school way without fuss and without making a big deal of it. He was probably right; it was reading which was our main thing, the purpose of the whole program. One high-powered purpose at a time was enough. But we all four sat around and talked in the afternoon, waiting for our last class—our link with the school at large —and in between doing crossword puzzles and talking about Eileen's car, which was always being stolen away piece by piece from her garage, and laughing and commenting about the kids, we always managed to get in a few words about what was going on with reading. It was, after all, a real question: Could you really teach anyone, or help anyone to learn something, in a public school in the seventh or eighth grade?

Now the main school had made a change this year. It had decided to start teaching reading to all seventh graders again, after a long layoff. Why it had done so wasn't too clear. Perhaps it had to do with the district-wide achievement scores which Sam, the principal, read off to us at a teachers' meeting. The kids of this advantaged district were way down below the national average in everything. They were down in math and language and social studies and in reading. Sam used to drop into the teachers' room during those afternoons and talk to us a bit as we sat there, a solid unit facing the scattered individualist teachers at the long tables. He told us that it was odd: the only subject area in which the kids did well, as a districtful, was in science, and the funny thing was that science was the only subject not specifically taught in the elementary schools. What about that? he asked. We had no trouble drawing an inference there and began to yell and laugh, in our usual keyed-up way (remember our solidarity, and how little you get of that in America, let alone American schools, and you'll understand being keyed up) about how the more teaching the less learned and so on. We probably made a few un-called-for remarks to the other teachers about how to not-teach their classes if they wanted them to learn something. Sam chuckled too, and it was the beginning of fairly regular meetings in the afternoons, Sam coming in talking about what admin job he was trying to avoid, and we telling about reading and the kids and incidentally giving a lot of advice on how to run the school. We began to feel he was on our side.

Well anyway, the school was doing what schools typically do. Seeing that they had spent the most of their money on the elementary grades on reading, and spent the most time in school on reading, seeing as how they had hired the best reading consultants and the consultants had gone to the most reading conferences and reading courses and seeing as how they had bought the best texts and supplementary texts and enrichment texts and remedial texts and spent the most time with in-service for reading teachers . . . and seeing as how all of a sudden the achievement scores told them that all of this time and money and effort weren't working at all, that the kids who were subjected to this expertise and outlay were in fact sinking lower and lower every year . . . seeing all this, they made a decision to keep on doing just what they had been doing but to do it one more year, i.e., in the seventh grade.

In the face of that, Rabbit Mountain School rather lost

its head. The whole thing, we began to orate excitedly at every moment, was just what we'd been saying. We'd rehearsed our remarks for a year and now they came out easily. We became zealots. We saw that it was our historical duty to change the school. When reading teachers began to be heard about that time, telling each other about how bad their reading classes were, how the kids didn't want to read, and wouldn't read and how difficult discipline was in them, and how you keep teaching the "skills" and yet it didn't seem to do any good, they still couldn't read or both, we thought we saw the system falling apart, the barricades being prepared. We exulted. Everyone was admitting failure, no one was proposing solutions. We were not failing. The way was clear for us to step in, grasp the historical moment.

Before this, we had made deliberate decisions not to be evangelical, not to bug the other teachers by proving over and over again how smart we were, not to tell them their classes and methods were humiliating and useless, not, in short, to try to convert them, and not to make them angry. Arpine in particular had argued for us to improve our "image"—we ought not always sit together, we ought not curse in loud voices, Bill ought not read aloud about Portnoy shooting blasts of semen into his catcher's mitt at the top of his voice to us in the teachers' room, we ought not laugh and yell and play games (making it clear we had plenty of free time to waste) while other teachers labored over their lesson plans and lists and grades and papers to correct—that all that was vanity of vanities, harmed Rabbit Mountain School and wasn't our point, which was to find a sensible way to work at our jobs. We'd all agreed many times, without changing our ways, but up until then we hadn't, in fact, tried to convert the school.

We had a bright moment of enthusiasm when our fervor was abetted by teachers coming up to ask our advice. They did so for the right reason, we thought; if we were able to convince our bad guys to read, they ought to be able to get their bright, achieving, average, normal, regular kids to do so. That moment was dulled shortly afterwards when it became clear that there were fundamental objections to everything we had to say.

Why are they asking us, Arpine wanted to know, if they have all these objections in advance? All their objections mean that they really want to go on doing just what they are doing. So why ask? I had no trouble giving a cynical answer. They ask in order to object. Having asked and objected, their honor is saved. They can say, It ain't my fault, there is no reasonable other way (if there was I'd surely do it), thus their way is O.K. and it is the kids who are at fault. Let *them* change! They were like Brecht's government which, in answer to public dissatisfaction with itself, cries out, Get a New People! Get kids in my room who dig my way of running the class, and then all will be O.K. Get them other kids (they implied) out of here.

Faced with that (and not believing my interpretation), Arpine took a big step. She went home and wrote out, on paper, an analysis of the process of learning to read, of the manner in which schoolteaching prevented kids from reading, and of the way to run an individual reading class, its goal and the role of the teacher in it. She took it to school and dittoed it off. She talked to Sam about it. She got him to agree to a meeting of reading teachers at which he would preside, citing the decline of reading achievement in the district and the school, at which the paper would be passed out, and at which she, Arpine, would try again to convince the teachers to change their ways, backed up by Sam in his role as principal. Sam was supposed, that is, to give tacit approval to this way of running a class; his informal comments to us had indicated his personal feeling that it was the right way to do things.

That meeting never came off. Two or three weeks went by and all that happened was that we began to realize that the meeting hadn't come off. We speculated about why not, but see, we were working all day, or anyway part of the day, and when we weren't we were talking together about the work and the kids or about Eileen's car, now completely stolen . . . we had plenty to do, I mean to say; we didn't have to depend on the politics of Spanish Main School in order to have something to occupy our minds. Arpine put the ditto sheet into the other reading teachers' boxes in the teachers' room one day, but that was about all we did. Something would turn up, we figured.

Toward the middle of the year (it must have been) we picked up rumors that the reading teachers had decided to try to solve their problem together. They were holding regular meetings with the principal, we heard. What did they have in mind? Well, Arpine's solution apparently not meeting their needs, it seemed they considered tracking—dividing the kids up into ability groups. That was what they were having meetings about. We began to get a little outraged, the inevitable product of unrecognized zeal. How come reading meetings were going on without inviting Arpine and Eileen? Were they reading teachers or weren't they? What was this tracking bullshit? I went into the principal's office and asked Sam politely to make sure we were notified of future reading meetings. He agreed; his attitude was one of mild surprise that such a request even had to be made. It was obvious, he seemed to say, that we'd be included, and how was Arpine's Crusade going?

I reported back about Arpine's Crusade. We all got angry. We suspected the term Crusade; it gave us the notion that Sam wasn't serious. Arpine invented the name Slippery Sam right then and there. We swore and lectured and maddened one another that afternoon out loud, for everyone to hear. In the end, we concentrated on the tracking notion.

We'd put a stop to it, that was that. After all, we'd done homework. We had plenty of references to studies proving that tracking was no good. We could cite; it harmed the "high" group; it harmed the "low" group; it didn't make any difference with the "average" group. The only reason for doing it was the convenience of the adult teachers, i.e., they could then fantasy that all the kids in their class were exactly the same, give them all the same "lesson" and thus (since they were all the same) evaluate them according to a "standard" (low, average, high) which they (Noman) had invented. We decided to challenge the reading teachers to present evidence that tracking was a useful notion. We would ask them to refer to actual studies which presented any evidence that tracking was beneficial to the students. It was a setup. We knew they couldn't do it. First of all, we knew they hadn't done any research and wouldn't do any. Second, we knew that even if they did, they couldn't come up with any research which supported their point. Third, we were elated to use their own bullshit against them . . . that is, we could use the achievement tests, the marvelous bell curves, the aptitude tests, the grades, the standards, the measurements, all those things in which they all believed but had never looked at, against them. There was no way we could lose. It was a grand feeling.

The important thing to see about this is that we were crazy. For while Rabbit Mountain was employed as described above, Spanish Main School had failed to notice our attack, hadn't shown up for battle, had in fact ignored that war and begun a different campaign. At a teachers' meeting shortly afterwards, Slippery announced casually, along with news about the PTA and some changes in bus duty, that counselors would be sending out forms to some teachers requesting the teacher to place the kid for next year's reading—i.e., high, average or low. It was simpler than the math grouping, pointed out someone, which had high, high-average, average, low-average, low and low-low. Slippery went on to say that the grouping was in preparation for the New State Reading Texts. That was the first we heard of New State Texts. (Oh! Ah! Hmmm! chorused the faculty. New texts—the state was on the job, solving problems.) Since the state had grouped the texts in about a hundred different ways, the least we could do, he implied, was to group ourselves. (That was the first we heard the texts were tracked.) He didn't seem to remember that there was any war about tracking, nor did he really need to. His tone was that Of course it was all a bother, having to fill out yet more forms, but that was part of the job and let's do it in the best spirit possible. We of Rabbit Mountain were like some Japanese infantrymen unaccountably left behind on an obscure South Pacific island, hiding out daily, foraging by night, cleaning our weapons in a cave, imagining terrific and decisive battles any moment, seeing landing craft in our dreams—only it is 1969, the war has been over a long time, and no one on either side remembers what it was about. No one knows those warlike preparations are going on out there.

For while we were working out our two learning years with the kids, the State of California had been making arrangements with some publisher or other to print millions of books. Even before that, the publisher was gambling on the predictions of his own hired experts, whose notions were based on the observations by other hired experts of some limited behavior of small animals placed against their will in unfamiliar surroundings. None of this was public knowledge. During that two years the school noticed that test scores in reading were going down, and reading teachers were able to see that they just couldn't hack it any more. Those particular small animals had all probably died by this time. The reading meetings were being held, not to talk about how to teach but to arrange details about how to track the kids and perhaps to start jockeying around to get the high groups. It wasn't even a conspiracy; none was needed. The reading teachers just wanted to track the kids because that was what junior high schools did, and because by spending all their time planning how to do it, they could avoid thinking about what they really ought to be doing. They wanted to avoid that at all cost. The reading meetings were never public. In the middle of the reading meetings the state let everyone know, all of a sudden, that it was going to give out New Texts, that them New Texts would be all arranged into high, low and in-between, three or four different kinds of each, with workbooks, skill books and everything.

Along with that, the state had no difficulty figuring out what percentage of California school kids were bright, dumb and average (although the state didn't know any of them) and published the books in numbers to fit those imaginary percentages. It was like a miraculous intervention for everyone. The reading teachers could see that they had been doing right, since what they wanted to do fitted right in, glory hallelujah, with the state, with the experts, with the small animals who had been trial-and-errored into oblivion. The state knew that it was doing right because its experts said it was making things easier for all them reading teachers who were tracked already or were planning to track, or would now start planning to track kids. Slippery knew he was doing right because he had gotten out of having to take any stand himself. The experts gathered up more small animals, purchased from people who raise small animals in order to sell them to experts who need to get results to predict things to publishers who need to advise states that wish to provide reading textbooks to teachers who are contractually hired to measure the ability of rats to weep over Long John Silver for nine months out of every year, and they were making money and assuring themselves of continuing jobs, so they were doing right. The animals are not public knowledge, the experts are not public, the bureaucrats of the state are not public, the publishers are not public, the way of arriving at any of these decisions is not public, the authors or editors are not public (their names appear on the books but since no one reads them they are not public) and there is no one to whom you can look for an explanation of why they are doing it, no one to whom you can go up and take him by the lapels and shake him and say What the fuck are you doing? The entire thing had been done by dead men. Who done it? Noman done it.

It was no one's fault. The next time Sam came in, we tried to tell him that it was *his* fault. We told him we knew that he understood what we were talking about, that he understood the stupidity of tracking, specifically that none of his or the school's problems were going to be solved that way. We reminded him that he had said many times, right there in the teachers' room with everyone listening, that most of the things most reading teachers were doing were an utter waste of time and a hindrance to anyone learning anything. We wanted to know why he let them just keep on doing it? Why allow them to track the kids? Why let them keep the kids from reading? We told him that if he didn't *allow* them to use the texts, to track, to give out ditto sheets, to do all that stuff which prevented the kids from reading, that they would have to enter a new world since the old one was forbidden. That he didn't have to even tell them what to do but only what not to do. That would give them a chance to learn how to teach, lead to public discussion among the teachers about how to teach in the public schools in America, and (incidentally) to some solidarity among the staff. The kind of solidarity which arises among people who are seriously trying to figure out how to do their jobs. The principal, we told him, ought to provide educational leadership.

He abdicated. He said public education is a game you

can't whip. You just have to play it the best you can and drink plenty of martinis. He told us the schools were too big, too centralized, run by cynical PR men, thick-headed bureaucrats, used-car salesmen, and neurotic ladies . . . it was always going to be a mess, but that if anyone got hung for that mess, it wasn't going to be him. He talked a bit more, intelligently and affably, but in the end that was all he had to say. He knew it was horseshit and he allowed that he was going to do it anyway, because that was how it was being played and because it was easier and he knew he could make it.

Right. If you don't play it smart, you might end up like Schmidt, teaching zapped Roy to read. Of course, if you do play it that way, you have to end up a zombie. You have to end up a person whom no one will take seriously. If you don't do something, I told Slippery Sam, then you have to face the fact that no one will be able to take you seriously again. Well, I regretted making that pompous remark then, and I rather regret it now. Nevertheless, that was that. You cannot use them instruments of war, repression and death to promote work, knowledge and love. Fakery is fakery. Work is work. Love is love. Small animals are small animals. Dead men are dead men. None of them can be turned into anything else. I agree that it is hard lines.

Chapter XIV

The Price of Amphibians

An expression only has meaning within the stream of life.

—Wittgenstein

This chapter is about the fact that it is so, that an expression only has meaning within the stream of life. It is also about the logical notion that in order, roughly, to know what something is (within the stream of life) you ought to be able to know what would be the case if it were not.

Alienation is such an expression. Within that particular tributary which is a school, it has the meaning that an individual gives up his Self (denying what he knows to be so in favor of what the school says is so) in order to achieve success and avoid failure. Of course, success and failure are expressions too and only have meaning within the stream in question, but by the time anyone remembers that, he is usually forty and reduced to writing about it.

For my students, and for myself, this alienation from ourselves means in practice that they (we) do or don't do things as a matter of reaction—as if we came in to school each day as so many blanks, having wiped ourselves clean of desire between breakfast and getting off the bus or out of our car. We turn ourselves off as I turn off the car radio just when the front wheels hit the curb at the teachers' parking lot. Once officially in the school we dispose of our cans of Coke and our smokes and await the presentation of our daily (streams of) lives by the school, and it is to that presentation that we respond. Re-act. We don't act first ourselves, and let the school respond (while we watch it), for the reason that we are alienated (as presupposed) and because we are sane.

What would we be like (what would be the case) if we were not? Not alienated. From ourSelves.

In September of 1967 I looked through the cumulative folders of the kids we were going to have at Rabbit Mountain for the coming year, that is to say, the next Monday. I read what I already knew—the first grader with testable high IQ, the remarked bright student, leader, reads-at-third-grade-level, headed for the big time; and the fourth grader with low-average capability, IQ 89, lazy kid, must-be-pushed-to-achieve, reads-at-second-grade-level, discipline-problem, parents cooperative. The first grader and the fourth grader are the same kid.

I was not prepared for the phrase *identifies with amphibians*. The rest of the remarks on this kid's folder were indefinite. It was as if the folder was composed entirely of question marks. *Lazy, bright, success, leader, follower, reading level, achievement, cooperation,* apparently didn't come into it, so the teachers wrote what amounted to nothing. Only the one teacher, having written out (I imagined) some thirty such folders before, bored and maddened by the effort, had torn this one remark out of the systematic abstraction of the school's nature. It was as if, in the middle of the seventh grade social studies book about the amount of flax cultivated by Palestinian Arabs in their refugee camps, I could come across a page from *The Golden Bough* or an engraving of a priapus.

Monday mornings on the first day of school all kids come in and sit down to await announcement by the teacher of their daily lives in that class, that period. It is surprising how beautiful they are, even as blanks—or as they wait, filling in the blanks with future re-actions as you talk—and all the teachers every first day are full of enthusiasm and even hope, as if they finally had gotten a Good Class and now, they seem to say, Watch me teach! Richard didn't come in and sit down and await anything. He came in the door and straight up to me, smiling and holding an eight-inch brown-backed yellow-bellied water dog out to me in his right hand, saying Did you ever see a water dog before?

A water dog is a kind of newt or salamander common to all warm-water California coastal streams. I used to catch them all the time. Its skin is sandpapery. Perhaps it gets its name from the fact that its visage seems not to be reptilian but gives an odd impression of warm-bloodedness—you get the notion, if you hold a water dog, that it likes you. If you go underwater in streams like the Navarro you'll see them in deep holes, legs outspread, sinking slowly towards the bottom from which, when they reach it, they will push off and swim upwards, orange-bellied, towards the surface. They are amphibians.

Richard was a medium-sized twelve-year-old boy with a pleasant face, a wide smile, a blue jacket zipped up all the way. After showing me the water dog and telling me where he got it, he went back to the cabinets and began looking around for something to put the water dog in. While I called the roll and mispronounced names he found one of the aquariums and ran some water in it and put the water dog in it and while I talked about the school and its formalities he went outside and came back in with some rocks and some dirt for the aquarium and then he watched the water dog swim and crawl around. He took it out a couple of times and held it, but he didn't do any landscaping on the dirt and rocks because he knew the water dog didn't give a damn about that, and he didn't give a damn about that. He didn't make any noise and didn't disturb anyone, but all of us felt how utterly wrong his entire behavior was, since I was there in front of the class talking and they were sitting down pretending to listen and he was wandering around inside and outside with dirt and rocks and fooling with the water dog and all of us wanted to do it too and so we knew it was wrong. He didn't seem to be listening to what I was saying but when I got to the part where I explained that if you were absent you had to bring a note the next day, or if you were leaving school to go to the dentist or something you had to bring a note and give it to the health office, Richard raised his hand. What about, he asked, if you were going to your psychiatrist? Well. That told us all we wanted to know. The water dog, roaming around, that dirt, wandering in and out, not sitting down—things all the kids would be doing or wanting to do all the time, but which no one would do on the first day. We were dealing with a nut. That made it easy to understand.

I've always wondered what made Richard ask that. He never again referred to any psychiatrist or to therapy or anything of the sort. Perhaps he really wanted to know if the procedure was the same. I don't know.

For the first weeks of that year, Richard got along very badly. Everything he did seemed to be odd and not with it—everything he did got to be the focus of everyone's resentment and terror in the first few weeks of What To Do? In a very direct way he was ruining me as the teacher, or in the way I was trying to work with the kids as their teacher. That is, the kids attacked him precisely where I couldn't stand it, as if they (the other kids and Richard) had conspired to involve my personal terrors from the start. The kids attacked the water dog, they attacked Richard, and they revenged themselves on the thin black blind worm-salamanders which he brought into the aquarium, dive-bombing them with rocks, putting them on the heater, throwing them against the wall.

They attacked things he made. We had a big box of wood scraps from the shop and of beautiful odds and ends from a picture-framing shop and everyone was gluing them together with white glue and making constructions. But whereas everyone else made abstract architectual monuments (having already been to school art classes where any image of the real had been forbidden for some years) Richard preferred to make little toy trains and streetcars and tracks for them and then he played with them. He didn't play with them for long though, for the kids smashed them almost as quickly as he made them, threw them, stomped them, broke them, laughing and with anger.

Richard reacted to these acts with squeals of rage, with tears, with demands to me. He made placards from construction paper on which he wrote appeals to public opinion and to authority in the form of the vice-principal:

> Some kids in the eighth grade, like [followed by a list of names] are wrecking trains made by Richard S. All people in the school must get together and beat them up so they can never do it again.

> To the V.P.! Cruelty to animals is against nature. These kids are killing salamanders by heat and by bombing with rocks. They are [list of names]. Call them into the office and suspend them for ten days.

He taped these placards up on the walls of the room, he put them up in the halls outside, he hung them in the office, he even took them into the V.P.'s office and put them on his desk. The placards drove the other kids wild. They couldn't stand to see their names up there in public association with cruel acts, and they were really afraid that the V.P. *would* call them in, *would* suspend them, *would* call their mothers (it was the beginning, I can see now, of Richard's magical power) and so they tore the placards down, they threatened Richard, they hit him, killed the water dog, approached me with demands.

In the middle of all that, Richard displayed another eccentricity which provided excuse for revenge—namely, he had a great love for a kind of small-time obscenity. It mainly revolved around the word *dick*. (He never said any of the other common kid swear words; he said fucking, but never fuck, and he only used it to mean actual intercourse, never as just another vulgarity.)

So anyway, my memory has an image of Richard in an ebullient mood, having forgotten for the moment about cruelty, going around to kids talking about their dicks, and inevitably being persuaded by boys to go up to the girls and say something dirty. What Richard usually said was *Take out your dick!* The girls, the very same girls who were saying all the words Richard didn't say all the time and writing Fuck and Fuck you and Let's fuck in lipstick on the walls of the girls' bathroom, reacted with indignation and slapped Richard and made demands of me. When I foolishly told them to forget it, they counterattacked by going to see the V.P. and telling him (with what mixture of sexuality and prudishness can be imagined) about Richard told them to take out their dicks, and so he called in Richard and talked to him warily about dicks and girls and forbade Richard to say dick . . . and of course this counterattack enabled him to totally ignore Richard's own public complaints about kids who tortured amphibians to death and broke things you made, for somehow that didn't count alongside some nut or freak kid who told girls to take out their dicks!

That was something you could get involved with! That you could take seriously! But dead salamanders, well . . .

(See man, this is what an American public school *is*. Let's cut out talking that shit about curriculum and learning about flax and all. The above is a School. Get it through your heads.)

All of this put me in the middle. I had to get mad at the kids who bombed the salamanders. I had to get mad at the kids who broke Richard's stuff. I had to discuss the phony outrage about dicks. I had to hear from the V.P. about should Richard be in EH classes. The worst thing was that my anger was real. I felt capable of killing a kid who stood there laughing while a moist salamander fried on the heater. I did hate the chickenshit girls. And I also began to hate Richard for his utter childishness, his ignorance of what the other kids were up to, his failure to respond as a twelve-year-old ought, his total remoteness from group custom and behavior. For, instead of staying neutral (which was my plan) while the kids sweated out the crucial problem of Who Are We In This Room and What Shall We Do, I was being forced into the position of forbidding stuff all the time, of threatening, of being angry, or moralizing. It didn't matter, somehow, that it was real—that is, I really did think the killing and breaking was wrong. It didn't matter that I really thought everyone should be able to tolerate Richard. And it especially didn't matter that what I was really furious about was true—that they were attacking Richard as a substitute, as an excuse for not attacking those things which were at the root of their anxiety and frenzy, but which involved some risk in attacking, namely their parents and teachers and their lives at school eight hours a day.

So it was really quite nutty. On the one hand, I kept wishing Richard would start building abstract junk, call people assholes when he thought I wasn't listening (or deny it if I heard it), pitch pennies against the wall, smoke in the bathroom, break other kids' stuff or throw chalk, torture the water dog, make hip teen-age sexual innuendo to the girls, complain about mean teachers and grades and that he wasn't learning anything, and speak sagely of marijuana, using the words *pot* and *lid* a lot . . . in fact, become just like the other kids. Then I could *work with him, straighten him out,* get him to face his *real situation*—in short, do what I was ready to do, what the class was for, what I figured to do with the group. What was that? Why, merely to force them, through my existence in the room as *person* rather than giver of daily streams of life against which to react, rather than as successful or unsuccessful entertainer, to decide the course of their own lives.

On the other hand, that goddamn Richard was already at the point I hoped the other kids would reach. He already knew what he wanted to do, every moment of the day, he was prepared to do it, and could do it, did do it, liked to do it, it harmed no one, it wasn't isolated from his total life (he continued at school the things he did at home), he used the school's resources (science books, films, maps, geographics, aquarium, dirt and rocks)—he knew what he wanted, learned from it, required no instruction, shared his knowledge and experience, asked advice . . . he was there! It was great! It was also intolerable, because he was nuts. No one planned to put up with a nut who was also content. He wasn't alienated. No one could stand it. He was fair game.

Then changes began to happen. Richard made some of them. He stopped building trains and stuff. He didn't bring any more salamanders or water dogs. He began to concentrate on drawing cartoons and drawing maps. He made the cartoons on ordinary school paper, and the maps on huge pieces of butcher paper which he got from the office. They had a weird kind of association. The maps covered eight-foot-long pieces of paper with streets, freeways, alleys, telephone poles, street signs, street lights, bridges, under-passes, streetcar lines, depots, bus stations, bus stops, train stations and airports. The main characters in the cartoons were automobiles—generally old, famous makes like Due-senberg and Rolls ("Hey, Duse," a Rolls would ask, "What happened to you?")—and talking fireplugs and talking telephone poles and talking buildings, plus an occasional human who was usually identified as one of the members of the class or as myself and who had a bit part. Events in the classroom always played a role—someone who had attacked Richard found himself being run over by a Duesenberg somewhere in the cartoon, for instance, and when a lot of kids began to play chess later on, talking chesspieces began to enter into the action.

In itself, this changed nothing. The cartoons and maps only emphasized what everyone knew—that Richard was a nut and a babyish nut to boot. He kept wanting to show them to everyone and everyone kept being disgusted and upset. His writing, for one thing, was quite illegible; it was too large, too crowded, didn't go in a straight line. (The school nurse, confronted with some of it, wanted to talk about brain damage.) He writes like a baby! everyone wanted to say. That didn't matter to Richard, since he wanted to read it out loud to everyone anyway. (Looked at from this standpoint, it was rather literate, involved some-what sophisticated puns and was at least as interesting as the average comic book.)

The change had more to do with Tizzo and Junior and Karl, who were the Big Three of the class, and who had a certain identity in the school as a Big Three. It's odd how these combinations occur among kids. The three were in no way alike and there seemed no objective reason for either their association or their identification as a unit. Perhaps it was a question of superlatives. Tizzo, for instance, was the toughest kid in school, with the possible exception of one other boy. (All year long kids tried to instigate a fight between the two, but it never happened.) Karl was the hippest kid in school, in the superficial sense of hipness which prevails among twelve- and thirteen-year-olds. He had the longest hair, knew all the music, associated with musicians (but did not play) and was one of the few kids (at that time) who actually smoked, rather than just talked about, grass. Junior could only be called the charming-est, or perhaps the carefree-est. He was beautiful, for one thing— dark curly hair, an open, friendly face, smiling, unworried, not angry, expressive of some term like happy-go-lucky.

In their relations to the school, they were equally diverse. Tizzo was a kid from an earlier age and another place. He didn't criticize the existence of the school, didn't question the rightness of its principles, didn't object to his place in it, which was to get (as he saw it) average grades (not too many D's and F's) and stay out of trouble. His trouble was his great anger at injustices within the system, as they affected him. He took it for granted that teachers were mean (else how would they control guys like him?) but there were limits. If a teacher didn't let him out of class every day to go to the bathroom (and have a smoke) that was reasonable; if the teacher never let him out, or gave him moral lectures when he asked, that was unreasonable. If he didn't try in a class and got an F or a D, that was O.K. if he *tried* (at least sometimes) and still got an F or D, that was unreasonable. When it was unreasonable, he got angry, slammed books, cursed the teacher, hit other kids, and got in trouble.

Karl was a critic. His aim was to get out of school as soon as possible. He wasn't concerned about degrees of things. He resented being made to go to class and was uninterested in whether the teacher was good or bad, nice or mean. His

177

goal was the Continuation School, where his older brother had gone and where all the hip kids went (according to Karl), where they let you smoke in class, and where you could learn what's happening. He constantly criticized the structure of the school and the curriculum. His grounds for discontent were that it was useless and irrelevant. His philosophy was direct and simple, and also typical; he did nothing to hurt anyone else, therefore he should be allowed to do as he pleased. It was his business; he had nothing to learn from anyone.

Tizzo and Karl, however, both attended regularly, Tizzo in order to keep out of trouble and stick to his Roman sense of order, and Karl because only at school could you get a sizable audience for existential criticism of it. Junior, by contrast, came when he felt like it, almost always late, sometimes not at all. My image of Junior is of him coming in the room at eleven and saying that he thought he'd drop by for lunch. When he dropped in, he was immediately the center of attention. What did you do all morning? everyone would ask. Well, Junior hadn't done anything. I just watched Captain Kangaroo, he'd say smiling, and then I went back to sleep and got up and ate some stuff and got dressed and thought I'd come on over here for lunch. Hey, Mr. Herndon, he'd say, can I go out to the bathroom? And then Junior and five or six other lucky kids would go over to the bathroom and smoke and talk until lunchtime. I always felt good when Junior wandered in, and so I knew the kids felt it also. It was good to have him around (that's all you can say), you missed him when he wasn't there, and that was his superlative quality.

I want to remark here about fathers, or upon the absence of them. Unlike black inner-city ghetto pore deprived (choose your term) schools, most kids officially had fathers in our district, but in fact fathers were rarely mentioned. Kids talked about mothers. It was mothers they tried to satisfy, mothers who got mad if you got in trouble, mothers who came (with few exceptions) to the school, mothers who wanted you to get good grades and go to college, mothers who wrote you fake excuses (like Junior) or who you didn't want to feel ashamed of you (like Karl). I think I can tell a kid who has a real relationship with his father within a week of having him in class, it is that unusual. The point, for the present story, is that Tizzo was such a kid. He had an Italian father. His father was (according to Tizzo) rough and tough and would beat the hell out of him if he got in trouble. He wanted to avoid it. His father thought he ought to go to school, be clean and neat, get there on time, not smart off to the teachers, and not flunk. Period. Tizzo had a lot of tales about how strong his father was, even though he was smaller than Tizzo, who was at thirteen already a man physically, being about five feet ten and weighing perhaps a hundred and seventy. He also had a lot of tales about working with his father, going around with his father, fixing up the house with his father—in short, of manly relations with his father. In fact, he was learning how to be a father himself. He knew what his father did at work, what he did at home, what he thought, and how to please him. His concern was uncritical. His father was right, his demands not impossible; he Tizzo was imperfect and couldn't always control his temper and when he couldn't, deserved to be punished, deserved his father's anger, deserved to have to stay home instead of spending the day fishing for striped bass off the beaches of San Francisco. He didn't like the punishments, he thought the school could let up on him a bit and didn't have to be quite so tight, and he hoped continually for a break, a little luck in getting through, but he didn't criticize its general right to exist.

So the Three approached me one day. All of a sudden they were concerned about Richard. All these other little punks keep picking on him, they told me, and they had decided to do something about it. Richard has a right to exist even if he is nuts. He isn't hurting anyone else, said Karl, and so he has a right to do his thing. And everyone picks on him just because they are chickenshit, said Junior. They pick on him because he can't take up for himself, and because Richard is so nutty that the vice-principal won't do anything to them when they bug Richard, cause he thinks it's all Richard's fault because he is so crazy and tells the girls to take out their dicks. Tizzo said, They do it because they can get away with it!

So their analysis was that all kids would torment anyone and anything if they could get away with it. The only reason kids would act decently towards other creatures was if they were afraid of punishment for acting otherwise. That was what their lives, in and out of school, had taught them. They didn't treat Tizzo badly, because they were afraid he'd beat the shit out of them. They didn't treat Karl badly, because he'd put them down for being wimps and had the reputation to make it stick. They didn't treat Junior badly, because then he wouldn't smile at them and ask them to come along to the bathroom. Richard, having no saving graces of that kind, and having no protection from adults because he was nuts, had to take it.

Tizzo et al planned to turn things around. They proposed to supply the punishment to any kids who *bothered* Richard. Well, I said O.K. Why shouldn't I? It was a step in another, if not the right, direction. It also meant that Tizzo and Karl, who had been (to be honest) among Richard's chief persecutors, wouldn't be doing it any more, and that would be a break for Richard.

It became, immediately, an instrument of terror. All the kids became fair game themselves; they were in the same relationship to Tizzo and Karl and Junior as Richard had been to them. As soon as they had conferred with me, the

Three foraged out firing on kids. They belted them for what they'd done a week ago to Richard, for what they'd told the V.P. a couple of days ago, for what they were planning on doing to Richard tomorrow. The three were full of anger. They hit half the kids and threatened the rest. If kids who were physically (if not morally) tougher than Karl or Junior protested, they were confronted with Tizzo. Girls, who were not to be hit according to Tizzo, were made to sit down in desks and not move. (If they moved, they were hit anyway. It was their own fault; they were told to stay put.)

We spent perhaps a week under the Terror, a week of outcry and protest and attempted discussion. Why was I allowing goon squad rule?

Why are you tormenting Richard?

How come Tizzo et al, who had been tormenting Richard, were all of a sudden allowed to hit kids for tormenting Richard?

How come you are all tormenting Richard?

How come we have to have some nutty kid in our room?

How come you bomb water dogs?

How come Richard get to tell us to take out our dicks?

How come you want to write Let's fuck! on the bathroom walls?

How come Richard has to make all that nutty stuff?

How come you care what he does?

How come Tizzo and Karl and Junior, who are part of us, i.e., our leaders to whom we look up, turn against us when all we are doing is exercising our normal white sane American middle-class, or almost middle-class, prerogative of tormenting anyone and anything that isn't clearly us and tormenting it *without any fear of retribution*? What other good reason could there be for remaining this normal white, etc., with all its load of fear, guilt and alienation, than daily assurance of this reward? Why, considering our own agreement that everything we want to do—everything from writing Fuck you to talking to each other in class—is wrong and deserves punishment, ought some kid to be doing whatever he wants and think it is O.K.?

After about a week, the Terror began to peter out. Junior, having come to school regularly and early in order to keep Ordnung, began to arrive at noon. Tizzo and Karl found their interest beginning to flag. Perhaps they had only wanted to re-establish their Big Threeness in concrete terms; having done so, they didn't figure to keep up this eternal slugging. They weren't cruel, only angry. Still, it worked, in a way. Prevented by the goon squad from pinning the sins of the world on Richard, the class began to look elsewhere for something to do.

In the meantime, Richard, left relatively alone, had not been idle. He began to exploit his three major aptitudes— natural history, maps and magic. Indeed, he began to gain grudging admirers. He scoured the library and came up with fantastic photos of snakes devouring other beasts, or magnified tarantulas' jaws, or piranhas, cobras, moccasins and other death-dealing reptiles. No one could resist them. Since Richard was the only kid willing, at that time, to do the work necessary to produce this fascinating material, everyone had to gather around him in order to look, everyone had to hear his stock of snake lore and no one could just snatch the book and run and look at it by himself because of the Terror.

It was the same with his maps. He had begun to make huge maps on fifteen-foot lengths of butcher paper. To his great pleasure and astonishment he discovered that the school could afford butcher paper, as much as you wanted, in whatever lengths you wanted, as often as you wanted. Life was good. He spread the paper out on our long table, the ends drooping over, and covered it with freeways, overpasses, bridges, streets, alleys, stop signs, turn offs, thoroughfares, bus stops, streetcar tracks, depots, and the rest.

Up until this time, we had all figured it was fantasy; our judgment was variously that it was interesting or nutty or disgusting but, either way, predicated on the fact of fantasy. When it was discovered that it was not fantasy, it was like revelation. How that happened I'm not sure, but, in any case, I recall kids coming up to me and saying that goddamn Richard says his maps are real and what did I think of that? So for a while we all stood around interrogating Richard about maps. Sometimes he was eager to answer— to trace the beginnings of a freeway in South San Francisco and show where it went, where bus connections could be made, where turnoffs to Tierra Firma could be expected— but at other times he displayed irritation, an irritation directed at dilettantes who were (1) not serious and (2) *bothering* him by getting in the way of his work. Still, he was convincing. If a kid asked, Rich (all of a sudden it was Rich, not Richard-you-nut), how would you get from here to Haight-Ashbury (mentioning one of the few places in the city that all the kids had heard of), what bus would you take? then Richard would stop working and get serious and answer the question in detail; what jitney to take, where to get off, what number bus to get on then, what street to transfer at, where to get off and then walk two blocks north . . . or kids who had once lived in San Francisco would say, Look, Rich, I used to live at such and such a street, number so and so, tell me what bus goes by there and where it came from and where it goes. Richard would think a bit and then say, Well, it would be Muni bus Number 48 (or whatever) coming from . . . and then go ahead and trace the entire route of the bus, street by street, finally allowing the bus to go right past the kid's former house on its journey into the mysteries of the city.

Then Richard's maps, having the decisive quality of the real, began to attract co-workers. It turned out that Richard was not against having houses drawn in on streets, or

183

Doggie Diners or movie theaters. So that one morning I was treated to the sight of a bunch of kids sitting by the table over Richard's map, eagerly drawing in Marin's Travel Agency, Holt's Conservatory, Kohl's Burlesque (20 —girls—20), Grand's Nursery (Exotic Plants), Stroud's Orpheum and Foundation, Spino's Health Farm, Perry's Gym, and so on. Other kids rushed me with demands for pencils, pens, marking pens and crayons and I got in a little sarcasm about *students* being *prepared* for work but in the end, not being prepared with any such items myself, had to send to the office for them. For I too had plans for Richard's map, and spent some time later elbow to elbow with kids (Move over! I can't move over, I'm drawing right here! Well I got to have room to draw! Well, I have to have room too!) drawing in Herndon's French Restaurant, a medieval affair with towers and moat and an immense menu featuring Sole Margeury with Petits Pois, which (I admit) was much admired.

Thus did Richard triumph momentarily over us all, a triumph in which we were happy to acquiesce. Richard's (now our) map was completed in perhaps a week and was hung up on the wall and admired, not only by us but by counselors and administrators and art consultants and visiting firemen from San Francisco State. It had a Fillmore district with soul food and dance halls and it had a Chinatown with opium dens and curio shops and it had museums and movies and Aquatic Park with bongo drummers and naked-lady sunbathers and it had a Haight-Ashbury with poster shops and drug emporiums and it had suburbs with shopping centers and houses with the kid's names on them and police stations and a gigantic Juvenile Hall with guard towers and machine guns and a big sign out front which said Junior's Juvi.

All in all it was pleasant to come in and watch fifteen or so kids sitting along the table opposite space on the map, drawing and coloring and looking at one another's stuff. Naturally we had incidents. There were bad guys who wanted to write Fuck on the map, and there were objections to the tyranny and unfairness of Richard, who, acting as Planning Board, allotted drawing space according to some design in his mind not readily apparent to the rest of us. There was also some outcry about Richard's naming of the streets (a job he allowed no one else to do) wherein inevitably some kids had major freeways named after them (Tizzo Memorial Parkway) and others were only allotted minor streets or even alleys. Still, the map was finished, with an awful decrepit falling-down tenement named after the vice-principal, located on a tiny alley of the same name which was carefully decorated with garbage cans, old whiskey bottles and refuse. Two days later Tizzo got mad at Richard because of the Memorial Parkway. Some brave kid had pointed out to him that *Memorial* meant that he, Tizzo, was dead. What the hell, Rich, I thought I was your friend, said Tizzo. Sure, Tizzo, said Richard, you are. But that map's in the future! It's all in the future.

I doubt that Tizzo was satisfied by that answer, but all he could do about it was to remember some kid who had written a passing Fuck on the end of the Parkway and threaten him a bit.

Richard was probably the only kid who was not completely satisfied by the map. I could see he liked the attention and the unaccustomed feeling of working with other kids on a project of his invention. At the same time, he made it clear that they *bothered* him. He had to keep watch over them so that they didn't encroach on space he had allotted for something else. He had to argue with them about details. He had to take them into account, and that was a *bother*. More important, I think, he had to compromise his idea of reality—the map was now clearly a fantasy, could only be a fantasy, at best something of the future. It *might* come true; that was as close to the real as Richard could make it.

I said magic. Free of persecution and momentarily full of power as Director of Map Activities, Richard indulged himself. Kids began to rush me with complaints in a new key. Tell that fucking Rich to stop turning me into a frog! Richard said I was turned into a fart! He said I am immobile!

It's true, ain't it? I remembered to answer slyly. It's true, you *are* a frog, a fart, you can't move! No it ain't, they said, of course it isn't. What are you worried about then? I would say. But they *were* worried. Richard had them in the old grip of the Logos, and they genuinely didn't want him to do it.

The ritual was simple, Richard would come up to kids, walking on his toes and grinning with secret delight as usual, and ask them Say Om. (Or Say X or antidisestablishmentarianism or Shazam.) The kids couldn't ever resist and so they'd say it. Then Richard would say, You are now a frog, or Now you don't exist. Then the kids would disprove it (they hoped) by running hollering to me. They were prevented from solving it more simply by the memory of the Terror.

I enjoyed this action quite a bit, but in the end I could see everyone was really quite bugged and I began to tell Richard to lay off. I expected it to be difficult. All of a sudden we were some nomadic tribe caught between Attila-the-Big-Three and Richard-the-shaman. We alienated folk were in danger. I called Richard over and began to explain why he had to stop turning everyone into frogs. But Richard just said, innocently and quite reasonably, After all, Mr. Herndon, it's only a joke!

It was as if that remark, turning us almost against our will away from our urge towards supernatural explanations of all our difficulties, loaning us sanity and the real, just as mothers soothe their children at bedtime by telling them that TV program, that Monster, Vampire, The Glob, Murderer, they aren't real, they are just stories, they are made up, just pretend . . . the kids still have nightmares, of course, since nightmares can't be done away with by applications of reason like wet compresses, but they can be recognized and talked about as nightmares, given a name apart from breakfast or play or sunshine . . . as if that remark turned us off of Richard, diffused our focus on him, and let us back into our own lives in the classroom. Most likely, of course, it wasn't that at all, there was no actual moment of turning away but only some gradual release, unclear as to its moments, from our obsession. But memory wants to pinpoint its feeling of history, so as to make art. (The Muses are the daughters of Memory.) We began to go our own ways, ways which only occasionally touched Richard's or his ours. Kids occasionally did some drawing on Richard's maps. I occasionally stapled his cartoons up on the board alongside other stuff. Richard occasionally gave informal lectures on the habits of amphibians. When a group of kids developed a flourishing business making ceramic chesspieces he joined them, but not as a co-businessman. He made his own clay chesspieces alongside them, using the same clay at the same time, but that was all. His knights looked like sea horses, his pawns like tiny fireplugs.

The year went on. Richard wasn't the only kid in the class. Maps were not the only projects. Salamander torturing wasn't the only barbarism. Richard's mother came to see us a couple of times. She reminded us all of Richard; she gave the impression of being too placid, perhaps a bit vague, not worried enough. Naturally we had to see her in contrast to the mothers we usually saw who were mad for success, were outraged or wept, wanted to settle and fix everything in their kids' lives in half-hour conferences on their way to afternoon league play at the bowling alley. She mainly hoped that he would make some friends. She was happy with our program without knowing or caring to know much about it since Richard told her the school didn't bother him. I got a few calls from Richard's therapist, who wanted to know how he was getting along. It became clear that the therapist saw Rich as a pretty hopeless case, i.e., that he was never going to be a "normal" kid, that the best that could be hoped for with all the therapy in the world was that he could keep out of an institution and perhaps hold some kind of job like the ones social workers invent for severely retarded adults. Later in the year I worked up courage enough (and believed it enough) to tell the therapist about Richard's real ability and, more important to him (for Richard's intelligence didn't seem to him to be the issue so much as what he could *do* with it), about his actual acquired knowledge of the real world in concrete terms of geography and science. I told him I thought that if Richard could get through the age of being a kid and a teen-ager without being physically or spiritually murdered, that he might emerge (to a startled society composed of the therapist and ex-classmates and aging teachers) as a perfectly reasonable thirty-year-old citizen, albeit a bit eccentric like many another citizen, working at some fairly unusual job, one which very few other people could do. The therapist seemed to like the idea and in fact we both got a little excited about it then and there. He seemed to have visions of museums and classifying salamanders. I thought about the post office, where I used to work, and the difficulty of memorizing mail-routing schemes, the contests in the coffee rooms among supervisors and old hands about where certain streets were, what they used to be called, what routes served them, and so on, and I conjured up Richard, the Grey Eminence of the P.O. in a dusty back office drawing charts and schemes, settling disputes and reading the archives. In fact, when I thought of the future of America in terms of science-fiction (the predictions of which I always believe), I rather thought that Richard was one of the few kids in the class who had any real chance of having a job, of having work to do that a machine couldn't do and wouldn't be doing. Richard and Junior, by the way, whose uncle was a bail-bondsman.

P.S. Because the rest I write about Richard appears here like a postscript. Of course it ain't a postscript to Richard, or to Tizzo or to Richard's dad, or in fact at all to anyone, really. Readers ought to beware of the trouble with books. Still later in the year Richard's mother came to see us again, and she was quite upset for the first time. Richard's dad was upset, that was the thing. There was this report which Richard was supposed to write for his music class (a kind of music appreciation which all kids in the seventh grade take at our school, twelve weeks) and which he was in fact writing. Well, I'd seen him writing it in class and heard about it from him. Naturally he was writing about all sorts of old instruments and drawing pictures of talking Sackbuts and Serpents and Viols d'Amore and coming up to me with his sly and expectant grin and wanting to know if I knew what this and that was? But he was also writing it at home, and one evening his father took a look at Richard's report and apparently it was just the last straw for the father —there it was all scribbly and you couldn't read lots of it and there were maps and streets interspersed with accounts of Theobald Boehm inventing the flute—so the father got really angry and decided to show Richard how reports ought to be written and they sat down and talked about headings and footnotes and theses and paragraphs and documentation and clarity and so when that was all done and Richard indicated yes he understood what the issue was, the father told Richard to get going and rewrite that report and he did. I felt the father understood about Richard's real ability and intelligence and knowledge and curiosity and couldn't stand it, as we all can't, that Richard wouldn't put this all to use in normal bright-kid fashion, earning normal bright-kid success and evaluation. Along with that, I could imagine the father hoping Richard would get busy and play a little ball, get in a little normal trouble for smoking in the bathroom or cutting class.

So Richard did, but in the end wasn't able to hold to it and finally produced his big music report, name up in the right-hand corner and a title and skip a space and start in with a paragraph about sackbuts and a drawing centered nicely on the page and some more writing and then *Misericordia!* sprawled across the page, as Richard's mind made some irresistible connections in Xanadu, marched a procession of talking fireplugs, of cartoon frames enclosing Duesenbergs lecturing a crowd of applauding sea horses or chesspieces about musical instruments— Oh man, give a thought to fathers at this moment!

What is a teacher's part in this whole thing? It is only to pay attention and give protection. The rest I was able to leave to Tizzo. Tizzo maintained his relationship to Richard; he insisted on remaining Richard's friend. He kept an eye out for him, instructed him on what to do or what not to do, and he played with him. They played a game in the room where Richard was a bad ill-tempered car, speeding and going through red lights and being a road hog, and Tizzo was a police car and afterwards a judge who sentenced Richard-the-car to jail and locked him up in the closet. Then he would extract promises from the bad car about being good and reforming and let him out, at which the bad car would immediately start speeding around the room and have to get arrested all over again. Richard thought he'd like to play this game every day, but Tizzo saw that was no good. He restricted Richard to one day a week, usually Friday, and only one period. Often other kids would get into the game too. Although most kids complained about Richard's childishness all week long, many of them in fact found such childishness very attractive. Since Tizzo was doing it, they could often permit themselves to play.

Tizzo, who had a father, was practicing up to be a father. He had a good use for Richard. Richard had a good use for Tizzo too, since he was learning to be a kid. Unlike the therapist and myself and Richard's own father, Tizzo didn't want Richard to turn into some other person, but only to accept the human condition. I can still hear him telling Richard forthrightly that he wasn't really a car (I know it, Tizzo, Richard would say, it's only a game) and that he could only pretend to be a car on Fridays. *That's the only day you can be a car!* Or, *Rich, I thought you were going to stop telling people to take out their dicks!* Oh, yeah, Richard would say, *I was, but I forgot. Bullshit, Rich, you didn't forget,* Tizzo would say, *you just wanted to and went ahead and did it.* Sometimes Tizzo would try to explain to Richard why it was that he could call people assholes and it would be O.K., and once in a while he'd try to get Richard to call someone an asshole, just to try it out and see if he got any satisfaction out of it, but Richard didn't want to call anyone an asshole, couldn't see any reason for it, and couldn't understand what Tizzo was getting at. In the end, all Tizzo was trying to get Richard to see was that human beings had to accept the idea of being *bothered* once in a while—that was what it was about. That if you accepted that, then you also could revolt against being bothered *all* the time, and that was as free as you could be.

Occasionally Richard would get mad at the tyranny of Tizzo and produce a placard:

> Some person in the eighth grade who thinks he is tough is trying to be Julius Caesar and tell other people what to do. The whole eighth grade should get together and make him stop doing this.

Then Tizzo would get mad and say he didn't care what Richard did and if the vice-principal got him it was just tough shit and Richard would indulge himself and be a car on Monday or Tuesday. Then suddenly it would be over and I could tell when it was. The bell would ring and it would be time for Tizzo to go to Reading, which he was mad at because Eileen wouldn't let him go to the bathroom—the bell would ring and Tizzo would just stand there in the room and I'd say Get going, Tizzo, and he'd say Sorry, Mr. Herndon, I can't go to Reading, Rich just turned me into a frog! And whenever that happened, Tizzo and Richard and I and many another kid standing around would laugh like hell and I would bang Tizzo on the back as he went out and he would hit me in the ribs and Richard would skip out grinning with his arms raised up like a cheering section and we would all recognize for an instant the foolishness and absurdity of our ways through the world and feel the impact of the great, occasional and accidental joy which would be our only reward along those paths.